Great Economists and the Evolution of Economic Liberalism

"In these times of political disorder and confusion, this book offers a fascinating interpretation of liberalism's influence on the thinking of great economists, who's lives and times changed the way economics can be perceived."

"Peter de Haan traces the legacy of liberal thought as embodied in the intellectual achievements of economists who bridged the gap between ethical considerations and economic theory. This book is a very welcome and instructive to policy makers, as well as an addition to the literature on economics and philosophy, which will not just enlighten students of economics and philosophy, but also the interested reader in general."

—**Ronald MacLean-Abaroa**, *former Mayor of La Paz, former Bolivia's Minister of Finance, and retired senior lecturer at Harvard's Kennedy School of Government*

Peter de Haan

Great Economists and the Evolution of Economic Liberalism

How Philosophy Has Helped Shape Economics

palgrave
macmillan

Peter de Haan
Den Haag, The Netherlands

ISBN 978-3-031-93830-6 ISBN 978-3-031-93831-3 (eBook)
https://doi.org/10.1007/978-3-031-93831-3

This Palgrave Macmillan imprint is published by the registered company Springer Nature Switzerland AG.
The registered company address is: Gewerbestrasse 11, 6330 Cham, Switzerland

For Babette, Floris, and Edward

Preface

There is very little I remember from the lectures of my professors way back in the early 1970s. But one memory does stand out. During a lecture about public finance, the professor mentioned John Maynard Keynes whose macroeconomic theory was very popular at the time. After having mentioned Keynes, he strayed from his lecture notes and enthusiastically told us about Keynes's interest in ballet. He mentioned that Keynes had married a Russian ballerina and that he was a protector of the arts. Intending to continue his story about Keynes's very interesting personal life, the professor all of a sudden realized that he should return to his, much less entertaining, lecture notes. One more memory: Keynes's *General Theory* was taught along the lines of Alvin Hansen's famous explanatory book *A Guide to Keynes.* The book was littered with equations—many more than in Keynes's masterpiece. Hansen devoted very few words on the evolution of the economic science, let alone on Keynes's life and work.

Why is it that, after all these years, I still remember both? It probably is because all lectures I attended were only about technical and complex subjects; indeed, the economics curriculum went straight to the heart of the matter: Models, graphs, equilibrium or—when analysing the business cycle—the lack of it. Nothing about the history of the economic science; let alone the deeper philosophical inspiration of great economists' theories.

Unhappy with the limited nature of the curriculum, I took an interest in the history of economics. This gave me a better understanding of the origin of successive economic theories. This was not all. The next step was to find out to what extent economists would have been inspired by philosophers. After all, economics has, unlike the natural sciences, political, philosophical and—not least important—moral content. To my delight, nowadays the economics curriculum pays more attention to the history of economics and to economists' philosophical inspiration.

Which philosophical inspiration received the economists presented in this book? A famous economist was invited by Michael Szenberg to contribute a paper about his life's philosophy which would be included in Szenberg's book on the subject. The invited economist, however, declined the invitation as he could not mention a single philosopher who would have inspired him. Perhaps this economist was too involved in his or her economic analysis to be distracted by philosophy. But great economists did not just get inspiration from liberalism, they also contributed to philosophy, as this book explains.

The Book's Outline

Chapter 1, Introduction, deals with the question what economics is; is it a science or not? The relationship between philosophy and economics and how it evolved is also presented. Liberalism had a large influence on economists from Adam Smith onwards. Not all great economists took positive inspiration from liberalism; indeed, some of them were not so positive about it.

The economists presented in this book are all game-changers, as they did not just change the way economics can be perceived, they also presented proposals to achieve a more prosperous, just, and equitable world.

To give a proper political and economic context in which the presented economists developed their ideas, Chap. 2, Economic and Political Developments, briefly describes this changing context starting with the end of the *Belle Epoque* and beginning of the Great War up to the present. As liberalism is this book's philosophical common denominator, Chap. 3, Liberalism, presents a thumbnail history of liberalism and its interaction with political and economic developments. Special attention is given to liberalism's economic dimension, including neoliberalism, and how it fared in practice. Chapter 3 ends with an analysis of the relationship between liberalism and democracy, and the challenges involved.

The following chapters are presented in a historical order. Part I of each chapter describes the economist's brief biography, the relevant political environment, and his or her academic work. Part II deals with the economist's philosophical inspiration, including short biographies of the philosophers concerned.

Chapter 4, Karl Polanyi's Critique of Market Liberalism, is about Polanyi's rejection of, what he called, market liberalism. While rejecting most aspects of liberalism, Polanyi nevertheless passionately defended freedom—a major notion of liberalism.

The title of Chap. 5 is Keynes and Hayek—Both Liberals but Economic Adversaries. They differed fundamentally in the way each analysed economics: Friedrich Hayek praised the free market, the price system, and small government, while Keynes strongly argued in favour of government's role in overcoming depressions and unemployment. Keynes and Hayek are together presented in this chapter as they represent two mainstream schools of thought: Keynesianism and neoclassical economics. Their spirited debate did not end with them; on the contrary, it was continued by younger generations of economists, notably Friedman and Samuelson. In their correspondence Keynes and Hayek exchanged unprecedented fireworks. Despite their deep differences, both found their philosophical inspiration in liberalism. However, their respective understanding of liberalism, described in this chapter's Part II, differed substantially.

Chapter 6 is entitled Friedman and Samuelson at Odds on Keynes. Apart from a description of their respective life and work, Part I also includes the debate between them; indeed, the debate Keynes and Hayek had started. Milton Friedman and Paul Samuelson did not just continue the debate, they also deepened and extended it. Both Samuelson and Friedman were initially inspired by the Keynesian Revolution. Friedman, however, distanced himself from Keynes. During the 1970s, Keynesianism was eclipsed by neoclassical economics. Friedman played a prominent part in this transformation. Part II explains why Samuelson remained, in philosophical terms, a liberal, while Friedman gradually flirted with libertarianism, without becoming one. Given Friedman's flirtations with libertarianism, Robert Nozick's philosophy of libertarianism is presented as well.

Chapter 7 is entitled Amartya Sen—Economist-Philosopher. Apart from his summarized entertaining autobiography, Sen's wide command of economics and philosophy shines through in Part I. The focus is on Sen's critique of John Rawls's *Theory of Justice* and Kenneth Arrow's Impossibility Theorem. Part II describes in more detail Rawls's theory, followed by Sen's critical analysis and his alternative capability theory. The same applies to Arrow's social choice theory, including his Impossibility Theorem. As

Rawls revived contractarian theory, the *Annexe* about social contract theories, ranging from Thomas Hobbes to Jean-Jacques Rousseau, concludes Part II.

Chapter 8, Mariana Mazzucato Attacks the Philosophy of Neoclassical Economics, zooms in on Mazzucato's passionate and thoroughly argued plea for a radical overhaul of neoclassical economics' philosophy. She argues that the notion of value had been lost; neoclassicals had replaced value by utility. Along the way, economics had lost its moral dimension. This influenced the way financial institutions are appreciated, i.e., as value creators, while government is understood as not creating value. This led to unbalanced developments in the economy, such as the growing gap between rich and poor, hollowing out government's capacity, and environmental degradation. Mazzucato pays special attention to the value-creating role of government, and suggests directions in which economies could move. Part II deals with Mazzucato's inspirators, ranging from Hannah Arendt to 'worldly philosophers' Keynes, Polanyi and Joseph Schumpeter.

Chapter 9 is about Piketty. The title is Thomas Piketty's Crusade Against Inequality. Part I includes a brief summary of Piketty's bestseller *Capital in the Twenty-First Century*—a passionate, impressive, and wide-ranging historical analysis of the growing gap between the wealthy and the rest. Unchecked, the gap will further widen, argues Piketty. Reviews of Piketty's bestseller by fellow-economists conclude this part. Part II describes Piketty's ideological inspiration, elaborated in his *Capital and Ideology*. His inspirators are, apart from Rawls and Sen, comparable to Mazzucato's. Piketty's comments on them conclude Part II.

The book ends with an Epilogue (Chap. 10) in which liberalism's prospects are summarized. These prospects are not favourable, as liberalism is under threat. Yet the Epilogue ends with a ray of hope: 'Time will tell whether or not liberal democracy, including liberal economic policies, will overcome the threats and, once again, prevail.'

The Hague, El Perelló
March, 2025

Peter de Haan

Acknowledgements

Having one's drafts reviewed by others is key. After all, authors are to some extent blind for their mistakes and shortcomings. Reviewers, not afraid to expose these mistakes and shortcomings, greatly help to improve the final result. The author, receiving their comments, may, now and again, be hurt in his or her pride, but so be it. With this philosophy in mind, I approached reviewers to have a look at the chapters I had finished in draft. I received critical—yet constructive—comments, which I gladly included in the final text.

Dick de Beus, economist and retired Director General of one of the Netherlands' largest pension funds, gave me very valuable suggestions. In addition, he did not fail in pointing out flaws. I gratefully accepted them, and they helped to strengthen this book's contents.

Dr. Auke Leen, economic historian, who recently retired as senior lecturer in the history of economics at Leiden University, gave me very valuable suggestions, in particular about Friedrich Hayek, whose life and work are described in Chap. 5. Needless to say, I eagerly took Leen's comments on board.

Economist and Philosopher Alfonso Garcia Salaues, with whom I collaborated at the Netherlands Embassy in La Paz, Bolivia, was particularly helpful in correcting some of my interpretations of the thinking of philosophers presented in this book. I trust they have now been put right.

Retired Ambassador Kees Beemsterboer honoured my request to review one of the chapters I had drafted. He did so with critical attention, which certainly greatly helped to improve the text and, at the same time, its accessibility, for which I heartily thank him.

Former President of the Republic of Bolivia Dr. Eduardo Rodrigues Veltzé was kind enough to share his comments and suggestions with me. He drew my attention to relevant literature I was not yet aware of. I have included his suggestions in the final text, with heartfelt thanks.

Retired top lawyer Peter Kardoes, while bringing to my attention that he is neither an economist nor a philosopher, accepted my request to review a draft chapter. His comments were every bit helpful as those you would expect from a professional economist-philosopher. So, thanks, Peter!

Philosopher, Dr. Melissa Vergara Fernández lectured at the Erasmus Institute of Philosophy of Economics when I asked her to help me broaden my knowledge of the philosophy of economics. She did so with dedication. She also gave me literature references from which I benefitted greatly.

My son, Edward de Haan, helped me in designing three graphs presented in Chap. 2. Edward studied history and international relations at Leiden University, which did not prevent him from being much more diligent in dealing with data and graphic design than his father. Therefore: Thank you, Edward!

My wife, Dr. Marisales Ramón Chordá, reviewed quite a few draft texts. As she has the gift to unearth the heart of the matter of any text, she helped me in better arguing what the intended heart of the matter at hand was. I accepted her suggestions with gratitude.

Finally, I heartily thank my editor, Wyndham Hacket Pain, for his unwavering support. Without his commitment, this book would not have seen the light. I also thank Paul Smith and other Palgrave staff who greatly helped me getting the manuscript ready for printing.

Competing Interests The author has no competing interests to declare that are relevant to the content of this manuscript.

Contents

List of Figures

List of Tables

CHAPTER 1

Introduction

The other day I heard a philosopher criticizing colleagues for making questionable statements that, he felt, crossed the boundaries of philosophy. When asked what philosophy exactly is, he said that this was a difficult question; it would be better to ask what philosophy is *not*—it is not an empirical science applying measurable objective norms he said.

Economics Nobel Laureate Edmund Phelps remembers that in Harold Pinter's play *The Homecoming*, Pinter presented people bewildered over how little they know. In the play, Lenny asked his visiting brother Teddy, a British philosophy professor in America, how to live. The professor replied: 'It's not my field'.[1] Pinter suggested that specialization in many branches of science, including philosophy, might have gone too far.

Returning to the philosopher who suggested to ask what philosophy is not, this intriguing statement made me wonder what exactly economics is and whether economics would indeed be a science. Thomas Carlyle (1795–1881), who characterized economics as 'the dismal science' had this to say about economists: 'Teach a parrot the terms supply and demand

[1] Phelps, E. (2023) *My Journeys in Economic Theory*. New York: Columbia University Press, 41.

P. de Haan, *Great Economists and the Evolution of Economic Liberalism*, https://doi.org/10.1007/978-3-031-93831-3_1

and you've got an economist.'[2] John Maynard Keynes (1883–1946) once quipped: If economists could manage to get themselves thought of as humbler, competent people, on a level with dentists, that would be splendid! Economists as competent technicians! I sensed that this was a bit too simple.

In *Economic Philosophy*, Cambridge professor of economics Joan Robinson (1903–1983) observed that economics has always been partly a vehicle for the ruling ideology of each period as well as partly a method of scientific investigation.[3] She argued that without ideology we would not know what we want to know. Or, in other words, without ideology we would never have thought of the question what we want to know in the first place. A society cannot exist unless its members have common feelings about what the proper way is of conducting its affairs. These common feelings are expressed in ideology, argued Robinson.

Does economics make progress? This question was dealt with by Robert Solow (1924–2023) in a talk he gave for the American Academy of Arts and Sciences. Solow echoed Robinson's observation about economics. He said that it was important to note that many of the questions economics deals with carry a lot of ideological content. After all, the outcome of economic analysis bears on some enduring and divisive issues of political and social choice. Solow added, however, that besides their deepest political beliefs, and our attitudes toward the nature of social life, positive economics is intensely relevant too. For example, one wants to know how the market system works before one decides if one would like the government to make it work differently. More is at stake in these issues, Solow said, and he added that one of the important differences between ornithology and economics is that political and business empires are not much interested by the findings of ornithologists. Economics, however, is not for the birds.[4]

[2] Leigh, A. (2024) *How Economics Explains the World; A Short History of Humanity*. New York: Mariner Books, 4. Leigh wrote on p. 5: 'The secret of our discipline is that the most powerful insights come from a handful of big ideas that anyone can comprehend.'

[3] Robinson. J. (1974) *Economic Philosophy*. Harmondsworth: Penguin Books, 7.

[4] Solow, R. Does Economics Make Progress? In: *Bulletin of the American Academy of Arts and Sciences*, Dec., 1982, Vol. 36, No. 3, pp. 13–31.

Robinson also dealt with the classics, from the perspective of value, and the neo-classicals who focused not on value but on utility. The whole point of utility, argued Robinson, was to justify *laissez faire*. Everyone must be free to spend their income as they like. As such, neoclassical economics abolished the *moral* problem. In an effort to become more rigorous, neoclassical economists stripped from their analysis difficult moral questions. With utility came mathematics and this seemed to promise a new dawn for economics as a truly scientific subject.

As regards Robinson's scientific investigation aspect, J.J. Klant (1915–1994), a Dutch methodological economist, warned: 'Economists who have not yet been able to corroborate their theory according to the rules of the game should be more modest. Those who are sure of their ground because they are strong believers, should not be ashamed to call themselves what they are, philosophers.'[5] Indeed, it is the scientific investigation dimension of economics that makes economics a science.

Unlike the natural sciences, economics includes political and philosophical content. Keynes added a *dynamic* aspect to this understanding of economics. He observed that an economist should have a profound economic intuition and an unusual combination of keeping an open mind to the shifting picture of experience and of constantly applying to its interpretation the principles of formal thought.[6]

Austrian economist Carl Menger (1840–1921) proposed that the aim of economists was to *explain* past events and regularities; they further aim to *predict* future events, and, thirdly, economists *control* through the design of appropriate policy and planning. This is one opinion, but there are more. According to London School of Economics professor Lionel Robbins (1898–1984), economics is the science which studies human behaviour as a relationship between ends and scarce means which have alternative uses.[7] Simply put, economics is the science of how people maximize their well-being in the face of scarcity. Indeed, what lies at the heart of economics is well-being, not income.[8]

[5] Klant, J.J. (1972) *Spelregels voor Economen (Rules of the Game for Economists)*. Leiden: Stenfert Kroese, 200.

[6] Skidelsky, R. (2010) *Keynes; A Very Short Introduction*. Oxford: Oxford University Press, 10. Skidelsky argues that Keynes's observation expressed his own philosophy of economics in a nutshell.

[7] Robbins, L. (1932) *An Essay on the Nature and Significance of Economic Science*. London: Macmillan, 15.

[8] 'As Australian-born economist Justin Wolfers notes, economics is no more about money than architecture is about inches.' Source: Leigh, A. (2024) *How Economics Explains the World; A Short History of Humanity*. New York: Mariner Books, 146.

Alex Rosenberg, professor of philosophy at Duke University, casts his net much wider: '[t]hat anyone tempted to define economics in Lionel Robbins' terms… without essential reference to human species (and perhaps a limited number of other species on this planet) is, in effect, committed to treating economics as the abstract and purely mathematical enterprise of pure linear (and non-linear) programming.'[9] Rosenberg argues that economics is also a biological science. In fact, he maintains that all social sciences are biological sciences, as they are devoted to the study of the causes and effects of the behaviour of members of a particular species, *Homo Sapiens.*[10]

Economic research is about economic phenomena created not by nature, but by human beings. Strict regularities are few and far between. Klant observed that economics is a social, cultural, and also a historical science.[11] Economic theories are to a large extent intellectual answers to changing societal questions. Changes in the political and economic domain sometimes result from changes in economic theory, but it could also happen the other way round. Regarding this latter aspect, the development of modern economics coincided with the Industrial Revolution, and it was not until the Great Depression that economists developed a deep understanding of the business cycle.

Robinson said that economics is partly ideological; she did not use the term philosophical. In this book, both terms are being used, depending on the context. Thomas Piketty and Amartya Sen, two economists presented in this book, provide some clarity on both terms.

Thomas Piketty, regularly uses the term ideology; after all, one of his books is entitled *Capital and Ideology*. In it, he describes his

[9] Rosenberg, A. If Economics is a Science, What Kind of Science Is It? In: Kincaid, H. & Ross, D. (2009) *The Oxford Handbook of Economics*. Oxford: Oxford University Press, 60.

[10] *If Economics is a Science, What Kind of Science is it?*, 60. On p. 62, Rosenberg explains his opinion as follows: 'In the human sphere the moves and countermoves characteristic of strategic interaction alternate so rapidly that few trends last long enough even to tempt the social scientist into thinking they are laws. Indeed, the few trends persistent enough to tempt social scientists into thinking of them as laws will almost always turn out to be solutions to design problems in competition with infrahuman species.'

[11] Klant, J.J. (1987) *Filosofie van de Economische Wetenschappen (Philosophy of the Economic Sciences)*. Leiden: Martinus Nijhoff, 10. On p. 11, Klant defined economics as follows: Economics deals with economic problems in a society, including the ones resulting from economic activities of the state. And on p. 28, he observed that economics does not offer knowledge of the world; it is a means to get to know her better. (My translation from Dutch).

understanding of ideology. They include a set of a priori plausible ideas and discourses describing how society should be structured, in an attempt to respond to a broad set of questions concerning the desirable or ideal organization of society.

Perhaps philosophy is more difficult to define. In general terms, philosophy is the study of the fundamental nature of knowledge, reality, and existence. However, remember the philosopher, when asked what philosophy was all about? He said that it was better to ask what philosophy was *not*. In *One Hundred Philosophers*,[12] Peter King observes that philosophy is *not* a system of opinions. Instead, philosophy (just like natural sciences) is a process, not a product; a method to think and reason about any subject.

The second economist, Amartya Sen, explains the role philosophy plays in his work. He says that philosophy can—and does—produce extraordinarily interesting and important work on a variety of subjects that have nothing to do with e.g., the deprivations and inequities and unfreedoms of human lives. This is as it should be, and there is much to rejoice in the expansion and consolidation of the horizon of our understanding in every field of human curiosity. However, warns Sen, philosophy can only play a part in bringing more discipline and greater reach to reflections on values and priorities as well as on the denials, subjugation and humiliations from which human beings suffer across the world.[13]

The Ebbs and Flows Between Economics and Philosophy

In the past, great economists were also philosophers, such as Adam Smith, David Hume, John Stuart Mill, and Karl Marx. They included moral convictions in their philosophical and economic work. Once the Industrial Revolution took off, economics, like other sciences, evolved into a science on its own, and branched out into a dazzling number of specializations, as Pinter cynically observed.

One result was that economics became separated from philosophy. This separation deepened after World War II (WWII), when the general opinion among economists was that economics should stay away from philosophical reflections; their conviction was to concentrate on the facts. Much

[12] King, P. (2004) *One Hundred Philosophers; A Guide to the World's Greatest Thinkers*. Palm Bay: Apple Press.

[13] Sen, A. (2009) *The Idea of Justice*. London: Allen Lane, 413–414.

of economics became 'neat and elegant', as Amartya Sen observes.[14] Jokingly, Sen adds that some of modern economics seems indeed to be based on the corset-maker's old advice: 'If madam is entirely comfortable in it, then madam most certainly needs a smaller size.' In other words, economists' principal question became: *what is*; i.e., what can be observed and measured. While philosophers, in particular philosophers of science, moved their attention to the natural sciences, and started thinking about theory assessment and scientific methodology.

But could economists indeed stick to facts only? Given the way economies function (just think of recurring recessions, market failures, financial crises, unemployment, inflation, the gap between the haves and have-nots, etc.), there was every ground to doubt the solid *moral* foundation of economics. Before WWII, economists such as Robinson, Keynes, Polanyi, Hayek, and after the war Sen, Noreena Hertz, Mazzucato, and Piketty, among many others, integrated philosophical notions and moral judgments into their work.

Philosophy, observes professor of philosophy Julian Reiss, has changed too. As I just mentioned, philosophers increasingly combine research on ethical questions (i.e., *what ought to be*)[15] with empirical information (i.e., *what is*), mathematical models and—now and again—experimental methods.

This mutual interest, which began roughly four decades ago, led to the establishment of academic institutions in which the intersection of economics and philosophy is the main focus. A concrete example is the Erasmus Institute for Philosophy of Economics of Rotterdam's Erasmus University. The institute's work focuses on the theoretical, methodological, and ethical foundations of economics.

In sum, the time that debates on important normative issues were exclusively left to philosophers is over; economists also address them. A cross-fertilization process is unfolding. Reiss summarizes this development well: 'In other words, economics and philosophy have drawn closer to each other by economists having started to ask questions that were once considered philosophical in the pejorative sense of 'non-scientific', and philosophers

[14] Sen, A. (1984) *Resources, Values and Development*. Cambridge: Harvard University Press, 1.

[15] Reiss, J. (2013) *Philosophy of Economics; A Contemporary Introduction*. London: Routledge, 3. Philosopher Daniel Hausman also argues: '…to ask what the goals of economics are is to ask not only what they have been, but also what they ought to be. Source: *The Inexact and Separate Science of Economics*, 5.

having started to address their questions in a way that resemble science more closely than traditional philosophy.'[16] Daniel Hausman et al. agree; they argue that understanding moral philosophy can help economists to do economics better, and how greater knowledge of economics and ethics can help policy analysts to improve their evaluations of alternative policies.[17]

Liberalism's Influence on Game-Changing Economists

To this day, liberalism's philosophy, more than any other, shines through in economics. That is why this book tells the story of how great economists were influenced by liberal philosophers. Some of them were positively inspired by liberalism, while others were critical—at times very critical—of liberalism's main elements.

Since the Industrial Revolution economics evolved into a science on its own, I present economists who, since then, developed new insights in how economies function and evolve, thereby also expanding liberal philosophy. To what extent these economists were inspired, positively or negatively, by liberalism is also described. The economists presented in this book are all game-changers, as they did not just propose new insights in the way economics can be perceived, but they also put forward proposals to achieving a more prosperous, just, and equitable world.

References

Hausman, D., McPherson, M., & Satz, D. (2017). *Economic Analysis, Moral Philosophy, and Public Policy*. Cambridge University Press.

King, P. (2004). *One Hundred Philosophers; A Guide to the World's Greatest Thinkers*. Apple Press.

Klant, J. J. (1972). *Spelregels voor Economen (Rules of the Game for Economists)*. Stenfert Kroese.

Klant, J. J. (1987). *Filosofie van de Economische Wetenschappen (Philosophy of the Economic Sciences)*. Martinus Nijhoff.

[16] *Philosophy of Economics*, 4. It is gratifying to note that Reiss dedicated his book to the Erasmus Institute of Philosophy and Economics (EIPE).

[17] Hausman, D., McPherson, M., and Satz, D. (2017) *Economic Analysis, Moral Philosophy, and Public Policy*. Cambridge: Cambridge University Press, 1.

Leigh, A. (2024). *How Economics Explains the World; A Short History of Humanity.* Mariner Books.

Phelps, E. (2023). *My Journeys in Economic Theory.* Columbia University Press.

Reiss, J. (2013). *Philosophy of Economics; A Contemporary Introduction.* Routledge.

Robbins, L. (1932). *An Essay on the Nature and Significance of Economic Science.* Macmillan.

Robinson, J. (1974). *Economic Philosophy.* Penguin Books.

Rosenberg, A. (2009). If Economics Is a Science, What Kind of Science Is It? In H. Kincaid & D. Ross (Eds.), *The Oxford Handbook of Economics.* Oxford University Press.

Sen, A. (1984). *Resources, Values and Development.* Harvard University Press.

Sen, A. (2009). *The Idea of Justice.* Allen Lane.

Skidelsky, R. (2010). *Keynes; A Very Short Introduction.* Oxford University Press.

Solow, R. (1982). Does Economics Make Progress? *Bulletin of the American Academy of Arts and Sciences, 36*(3), 13–31.

CHAPTER 2

Economic and Political Developments

Introduction

Where to begin when telling the story of economic and political developments? Some economists, such as the *doyen* of historical world economic statistics, Angus Maddison (1926–2010), said that it all started in year 1; others maintained that both started around the year 1500, after the New World had been discovered and when Europe began making economic progress. There are yet others who begin their story as of 1820 when the Industrial Revolution had made its impact.

The popular opinion was that economic growth was much slower before the nineteenth century. It was believed that the roots of modern growth lay in a sudden take-off (i.e., the Industrial Revolution) in the late eighteenth century. Maddison observed that, over the past two centuries, we have a clearer notion of the change of growth experience, process of catch-up, convergence and divergence, and their underlying causes, not least since 'research has concentrated on the past two centuries.'[1] He added that much less [statistical analysis; PdH] had been done on earlier centuries. Having taken Maddison's observations at heart, what follows is

[1] Maddison, A. (2003) *The World Economy: Historical Statistics*. Paris: OECD Development Centre of the Organisation for Economic Development and Development, 13. Maddison mentioned on p. 242 that even before the Second World War, only 10 countries had official estimates of national income, assembled without international guidelines to provide comparability.

P. de Haan, *Great Economists and the Evolution of Economic Liberalism*, https://doi.org/10.1007/978-3-031-93831-3_2

not going back to antique times, or even the time preceding the eighteenth century. My story starts at a 'watershed-moment', i.e., the abrupt end of the *Belle Epoque* and the start of the Great War.

Until 1914, Europe—in particular the United Kingdom (UK) and runner-up Germany—called the shots. Since then, the United States (US) eclipsed the UK as the world's new economic hegemon. Other fundamental shifts in the world economy took place. The October Revolution of 1917 in Russia ushered in an entirely new central planning model under autocratic rule. The Soviet Union evolved into a formidable political opponent of the 'free world' until the Soviet empire imploded in 1991. Meanwhile, the free world, in particular high-income countries, had become affluent. In the far East, Japan had started its stunning economic ascent after the 1867 *Meiji Restoration*. The Four Asian Tigers (South Korea, Taiwan, Singapore, and Hong Kong) experienced rapid economic growth after WWII, followed by China, India, and other emerging economies towards the end of the past century. Extreme poverty was halved by 2015.

After a period of relative economic stability, the Great Recession broke out in 2008. It took the biblical seven years before solid signs of recuperation emerged. Five years later, the Covid-pandemic and ensuing lockdowns brought the world economy to a temporary standstill. The world economy is no longer playing by shared global rules; trade wars, protectionism and subsidized national industrial policies undermine these rules, including the institutions, such as the World Trade Organization (WTO) supporting them (Table 2.1).

Table 2.1 Per capita GDP 1820–1950 (1990 international Geary-Khamis dollars)

Country				
Year	*US*	*UK*	*Germany*	*Former USSR*
1820	1257	1706	1077	688
1870	2445	3190	1839	943
1913	5301	4921	3648	1488
1950	9561	6939	3881	2841

Source: Maddison, A. (2003) *The World Economy: Historical Statistics*. Paris: OECD Development Centre Studies

The Great War

When the Great War (1914–1918) broke out, the gold standard was suspended. The *Belle Epoque,* a long period of free international trade and prosperity, came to an abrupt end and Europe's economic decline began. WWI also marked the breakdown of nineteenth-century western civilization.

The *Treaty of Versailles,* which was concluded on 28 July 1919, did not particularly reverse Europe's political and economic fate; on the contrary. John Maynard Keynes, who participated in the Treaty's negotiations as a member of the British delegation, had warned that what the victorious Allies demanded from defeated Germany in terms war reparations, loss of coal and iron ore-rich territory, and overseas possessions, would lead to political instability and economic collapse.

Keynes was right, and ill-conceived monetary policies, such as the return to the gold standard after the end of the war, combined with protectionist trade policies, contributed to a dramatic drop in international trade which eventually led to the Great Depression.

The Roaring Twenties

After a brief post-WWI recession, a period of progress followed, particularly in America—*the Roaring Twenties.* Pent-up demand triggered a spectacular increase in the production of consumer goods. Cars, radios, and sophisticated household appliances found their way to millions of consumers. Charlie Chaplin's movie *Modern Times* was a humorous critique of *business progressivism*, emphasizing production efficiency, as practiced by Henry Ford's assembly lines pouring out millions of T-Fords. The mood was optimistic. More and more Americans speculated on the soaring stock market. Credit was cheap, thanks to the Federal Reserve System's (Fed) expanding credit policy.

The Gross Domestic Products (GDP) of, for example, the US, Australia, Canada, the Netherlands, Sweden, and the UK, registered robust economic growth as Table 2.2 shows.

Table 2.2 GDP levels 1921–1927 (million 1990 international Geary-Khamis dollars)

Year/Country	*USA*	*UK*	*Australia*	*Canada*	*Netherlands*	*Sweden*
1921	579,986	195,642	26,818	30,307	30,670	15,854
1922	612,064	205,750	28,225	34,741	32,342	17,351
1923	692,776	212,264	29,579	36,801	33,140	18,273
1924	713,989	221,024	31,524	37,360	35,561	18,847
1925	730,545	231,806	33,002	41,445	37,058	19,544
1926	778,144	223,270	33,792	43,680	40,028	20,640
1927	785,905	241,240	34,305	48,010	41,700	21,284

Source: Maddison, A. (2003) *The World Economy; Historical Statistics*. Paris: OECD Development Centre Studies

The Great Depression

The booming 1920s—a period of innovation, creativity, and prosperity—abruptly ended with the Wall Street crash on 29 October 1929, when the stocks at the New York Stock Exchange took a nose dive. *Black Tuesday* came as a shock; $14 billion in share prices were lost. Few pundits had expected the collapse.

In 1931, the Great Depression hit Britain and continental Europe in full force. In the autumn of 1931 one of Austria's largest banks, *Kreditanstalt*, collapsed, triggering a financial crisis. European investors, who had their money deposited in London-based banks, withdrew their sterling deposits in a frantic attempt to cash them. The pound devalued, and Britain—which in 1925 had returned to the gold standard[2]—ended the pound–gold convertibility in September 1931.

At the time, mainstream neoclassical economics had no adequate response to the crisis; in fact, its economic recipes only deepened the crisis. Bank runs and a scramble for gold led to declines in national money supplies. Many Marxists viewed the depression as the final crisis of capitalism. After all, had not Marx written in the *Communist Manifesto* that commercial crises, by their periodical return, put the existence of the entire

[2] Winston Churchill was the Chancellor of the Exchequer at the time. He proposed Parliament to reinstate the gold standard. This prompted John Maynard Keynes to write Churchill the following note: 'Dear Chancellor of the Exchequer, what an imbecile Currency Bill you have introduced!' Source: Frank, B. (2023) *In the Long Run We're All Dead; The Lives and Deaths of Great Economists*. London: Haus Publishing, 82.

bourgeois society on trial? Great Depression expert and former Fed chairman Ben Bernanke quoted in his *Essays on the Great Depression* (2000) Barry Eichengreen's analysis of the depression's causes:

> Monetary contractions in turn were strongly associated with falling prices, output and employment. Effective international cooperation could in principle have permitted a worldwide monetary expansion despite gold standard constraints, but disputes over World War I reparations and war debts, and the insularity and inexperience of the Federal Reserve, among other factors, prevented this outcome. As a result, individual countries were able to escape the deflationary vortex only by unilaterally abandoning the gold standard and re-establishing domestic monetary stability, a process that dragged on in a halting and uncoordinated manner until France and other gold bloc countries finally left gold in 1936.[3]

Germany had to pay back their citizens who had invested in German war bonds, as well as large amounts of war reparations to the Allies. The German *Reichsbank* printed more and more money. The result was hyperinflation. Frederick Taylor's *The Downfall of Money,* presented the spectacular plunge of the mark-dollar exchange rate from 4.19 marks to the dollar (August 1914) to approximately 2.5 trillion marks to the dollar (December 1923).[4] Germany's hyperinflation was preceded by inflation in Austria immediately after the end of the Great War. Austria had lost its empire status, the country was broke, and there was a shortage of almost everything.

There was one economist who shook up economic conventional wisdom. He demonstrated that the economy's self-correcting mechanism, as prescribed by neoclassical theory, did not work. He argued that government had to actively intervene to pull the economy out of the depression and restore full employment. He analysed the economy in aggregate terms, such as aggregate demand, aggregate savings and investment; thereby inventing *macroeconomics.* His name was John Maynard Keynes. He published *The General Theory of Employment, Interest, and Money* in 1936, triggering the *Keynesian Revolution.* Neoclassical economics held that the market would naturally establish full employment. However, as a result of 'price stickiness' (a Keynesian invention), workers would refuse to

[3] Bernanke, B. (2000) *Essays on the Great Depression*. Princeton: Princeton University Press, 276–277.

[4] Taylor, F. (2013) *The Downfall of Money*. New York: Bloomsbury Press, 361–370.

lower their wage demands, even in a depression. In *The General Theory*, Keynes demonstrated that an economic equilibrium could go together with permanent unemployment. He argued that to counter this, traditional deflation policies made matters worse. Instead, aggregate demand had to be boosted by fiscal measures; i.e., tax cuts and government spending. The Keynesian revolution eclipsed neoclassical economics, but not forever as future economic and political developments would demonstrate (Figs. 2.1 and 2.2).

Even before Keynes's *General Theory* came out, some governments already applied a Keynesian approach to the depression. The best-known is president Roosevelt's *New Deal*, launched immediately after Roosevelt's inauguration in March 1933. Roosevelt was at heart a balanced budget supporter. However, the newly elected president instinctively understood that his government must 'spend money when no one else had money left to spend'.[5] The New Deal intended to prevent financial collapse, stimulate demand, and provide work and relief for millions of unemployed people through increased government spending, financial reforms, and job creation programs.

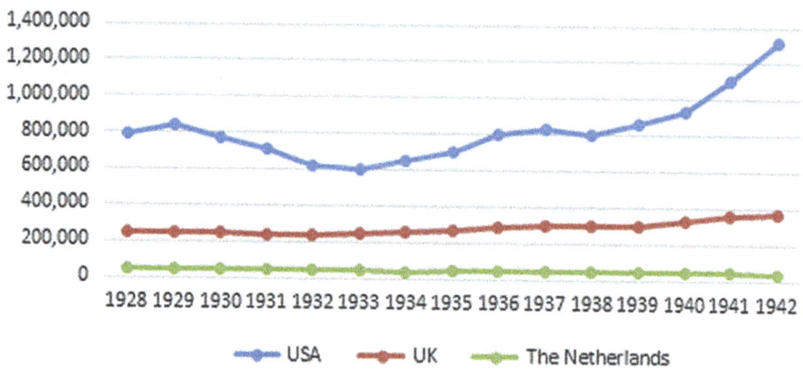

Fig. 2.1 GDP levels, 1928–1942 (million 1990 international Geary-Khamis dollars). (Source: Maddison A. (2003). *The World Economy: Historical Statistics*. Paris: OECD Development Centre Studies)

[5] Eichengreen, B. (2015) *Hall of Mirrors; The Great Depression, the Great Recession, and the Uses—and Misuses—of History*. New York: Oxford University Press, 352.

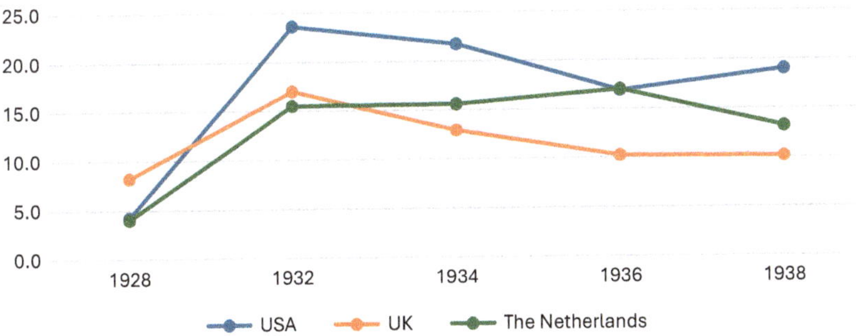

Fig. 2.2 Unemployment development, 1928–1938. (Sources: US Department of Labor, Industrial Bureau of Labor Statistics. UK: Social Democracy for the 21st Century: A Post Keynesian Perspective and Centraal Bureau voor de Statistiek)

Indeed, Roosevelt took a variety of measures, such as the establishment of the Tennessee Valley Authority (a regional economic development agency and electricity provider), the enactment of social security, and the Works Progress Administration, which managed the Civilian Conservation Corps (a temporary facility providing jobs to 2.5 million young unemployed Americans). The *Glass-Steagall Act* of 1933 separated investment from commercial banking.

Roosevelt's stimulus initiatives—and his personal resolve—had a positive effect on the nation's *confidence*, boosted by his fireside radio chats. For example, he stressed during his chat on 22 October 1933: 'If we cannot do this one way, we will do it another. Do it, we will'. In his 1936 speech accepting the Democratic nomination, looking back at the depression, Roosevelt declared 'We have always known that heedless self-interest was bad morals; we know now that it is bad economics.'[6] Both Keynes and Roosevelt became known as prominent representatives of new liberalism.

Another Keynesian *avant la lettre* was Adolf Hitler. The more powerless the Weimar Republic was in quelling Germany's hyperinflation, and in creating jobs, the more popular Hitler's National-Socialist party became. In January 1933, Hitler was elected German Chancellor. He put the unemployed back to work through massive public works (such as Germany's *Autobahnen*), and started to prepare for war. In 1938, Germany's unemployment rate was down to only 2%.

[6] Krugman, P. (2009) *The Conscience of a Liberal*. New York: W.W. Norton & Company, xiv.

World War II

Nazi-Germany wanted to create a Greater Germany (more *Lebensraum*—space to grow) and access to raw materials. Germany remilitarized coal-rich Rhineland which had been administered by France, as stipulated in the Treaty of Versailles. Hitler also wanted to reunite all German speaking peoples, by taking back the territories that Germany had lost after the Great War. Germany invaded Czechoslovakia in early 1939. The UK and France did not interfere, in a vain attempt to preserve their policy of *appeasement*. But when Germany invaded Poland in September 1939, France and Britain declared war. Germany violated the 1939 Molotov-Ribbentrop Pact, by invading the Soviet Union in June 1941, whereupon Stalin declared war. Meanwhile, Germany's Axis ally, Italy, had occupied Ethiopia in 1935, and Mediterranean countries such as Albania and Greece in 1939.

In the East, the third Axis partner, Japan, had occupied Manchuria on mainland China. Manchuria was rich in natural resources, which Japan lacked. In its further search of raw materials, Japan occupied French, British, and Dutch colonies, thereby underscoring its ambition to drive the colonial powers from Asia: *Asia for the Asians,* was the slogan. The Japanese air-raid of 7 December 1941 on America's Pearl Harbor naval base, prompted President Roosevelt to declare war.

Capitalism or Socialism: That's the Question

The Great Depression shattered the belief in the capitalist system. The sense during the 1940s was that something was fundamentally wrong with it. Apart from fascism, which had gained wide popularity in Germany and Italy, an alternative political and economic system was drawing attention: Central planning applied by the Soviet Union, where all property belonged to the state. After all, the Soviet Union's economy was not plagued by depressions and unemployment. Was central planning under autocratic rule perhaps a better way to run an economy than a capitalist system as applied by Western democracies? This question occupied the minds of politicians and scholars alike.

Karl Polanyi's (1886–1964) *The Great Transformation* (1944) criticized market liberalism in its annihilating influence on societies. Friedrich Hayek's (1899–1992) bestseller *The Road to Serfdom,* which also came out in 1944, warned against government intervention, as this would put a society on the slippery slope down to despotic rule; people would not be free to make their own choices any longer.

The Soviet Union gradually caught up with America in technological achievements, symbolized by putting her first *Sputnik* as well as the first cosmonaut Yuri Gagarin into space, before the United States was able to do so. This triggered concern and a competitive spirit in 'the land of unbound possibilities'. John Kenneth Galbraith (1908–2006) observed in *The New Industrial State*:

> The competition in space exploration is largely.... devoid of military implication....It is held to be of the utmost importance to the international prestige of the United States that its vehicles be first to the moon, the other parts of the solar system and the less convenient reaches of the universe.[7]

The concern was not limited to technological progress. Paul Samuelson (1915–2009), for example, predicted in his famous textbook *Economics* that the Soviet Union's GDP might outstrip America's between 1990 and 2000.[8]

After the Soviet Union had drawn its *Iron Curtain* after WWII, the Cold War began. The Soviets spread their political and ideological influence throughout the world. In particular, newly independent developing countries were sensitive to Soviet ideology. The 'free world' under America's leadership, did the same. The stand-off between the two superpowers came to an end when, on 26 December 1991, the Soviet Union imploded—the Cold War had ended. John Cassidy explained its collapse from an economic vantage point:

> Economics...is largely about incentives. Communism collapsed because it failed to encourage innovation, enterprise, and hard work; capitalism has thrived, broadly speaking, because it rewarded these things, while punishing conservatism and dawdling. The market system is heartless and unforgiving, but, as even Marx and Engels pointed out, it is uniquely productive.[9]

[7] Galbraith, J. K. (1967) *The New Industrial State*. Boston: Houghton Mifflin Company, 340–341.

[8] Samuelson, P. (1970) *Economic; An Introductory Analysis*. New York: McGraw-Hill, 831.

[9] Cassidy, J. (2009) *How Markets Fail; The Logic of Economic Calamities*. London: Allen Lane, 285.

The free world was jubilant! In 1992, Francis Fukuyama published *The End of History and The Last Man* in which he suggested that the liberal order did not have any competitors left.[10]

But let us take a step back in time.

Preparing for the Postwar Period

After two world wars and the Great Depression, the time was more than ripe to put order in the world's political and economic affairs. This was done: Post-war physical and financial reconstruction was undertaken and trade *rules of the game* were established. The United Nations Organization was created as well.

Bretton Woods

Even before WWII ended, measures had been taken to prevent the mistakes of the Treaty of Versailles. International monetary stability was ensured through the Bretton Woods agreements, negotiated by all 44 allied nations in July 1944 in Bretton Woods, New Hampshire. The disruptive volatility in the value of international currencies before WWII was replaced by a system of fixed exchange rates. 'Bretton Woods' included the establishment of the International Monetary Fund (IMF) and the World Bank (WB); the latter tasked with funding reconstruction and development. Another Bretton Woods objective was free trade. The General Agreement on Tariffs and Trade was established in 1956. In 1995 the Uruguay Round of the GATT was concluded which resulted in the creation of the World Trade Organization (WTO).

Marshall Plan

This was not all. A combination of American magnanimity and strategic interests came together in the *Marshall Plan*, whose $13 billion financial support greatly helped put Western Europe on its feet again after the war. The aid also made the beneficiaries less vulnerable to Soviet influence.[11]

[10] Fukuyama, F. (1992) *The End of History and The Last Man*. London: Penguin Books. In Chap. 4, Fukuyama's projections are presented in more detail.

[11] Marshall aid had initially also been offered to the Soviet Union and her allies. However, Stalin declined and forced Czechoslovakia and Poland to decline as well.

The Marshall Plan laid the basis for Europe's economic integration. Thanks to the Plan's emphasis on productivity improvement, Europe caught up with America over the next two decades. Europe's economic recovery was spectacular: Between 1947 and 1951 Western Europe's GDP rose by 30%.

The Allies did not economically bleed Germany like the *war reparations* did after WWI. West Germany received US$1.4 billion Marshall aid. The Americans realized that without Germany's recovery, the recovery of other European countries would be problematic. In 1952, West Germany joined the European Coal and Steel Community (ECSC). The ECSC was the predecessor of the European Economic Community, established in Rome, Italy, in 1957, by France, Germany, Italy, Belgium, the Netherlands, and Luxemburg.

In early September 1945, Japan was defeated by the Allies. Douglas MacArthur, Supreme Commander for the Allied Powers, was tasked with overseeing Japan's recovery. Like Germany, also Japan received American reconstruction support of $2.4 billion with the aim of establishing democratic self-government, economic stability, and Japan's peaceful co-existence with the world. Japan's economy recovered very rapidly; in 1953 it was back on its feet when it had reached its pre-WWII level.

United Nations

After the establishment in 1943 of the United Nations Relief and Rehabilitation Administration, the following year the United Nations Organization was created, which—unlike the short-lived League of Nations, established after WWI—still plays an important role in diplomatic and military peace keeping, in emergency and development aid, as well as attending to global concerns such as poverty, human rights, refugees, food, health, the environment, and climate change.

The Welfare State

Another preparatory measure for a post-war era was the Beveridge report. Already in 1941, the British government requested William Beveridge (1879–1963) to develop proposals to alleviate poverty in the country, as a first step on the way to the establishment of a welfare state.

A golden age was beckoning; the three decades after the end of WWII, were a period not just of reconstruction but also one of very rapid economic growth and, indeed, the gradual development of the welfare state.

Affluence

The postwar period up to the first oil shock of 1973, is known as the *Golden Age*. America, Canada, Western Europe, Australia, New Zealand, and Japan all registered robust economic growth. The economies of the four Asian Tigers (Hong Kong, Singapore, South Korea, and Taiwan) were taking-off. This was not the case for the former colonies of the European imperial powers that had gained independence. They were not successful in promoting economic growth or in eradicating poverty. These newly independent developing countries were grouped together under the term *Third World*.

During the Golden Age, scarcity made way for affluence. Incomes converged to some extent; people even felt that pure capitalism was something of the past; investment in social services became the rule rather than the exception. In 1958, Galbraith wrote a bestseller about this new phenomenon in America: *The Affluent Society*.[12]

Towards the end of the 1960s and beginning of the 1970s, economists and liberal philosophers took a renewed interest in the issue of income and wealth distribution. This is not surprising as, over the past three decades, incomes had risen considerably. Questions as to how income growth had been distributed between different income earners, triggered many publications. For example, the first Nobel Laureate in Economics, Jan Tinbergen (1903–1994), together with economics professor Jan Pen (1921–2010) published *Income Distribution*.[13] They approached the issue from an egalitarian perspective. They asked questions like: Was it *fair and just* that there were large differences between income earners? Could the term 'just' be objectively established? In 1971, John Rawls (1921–2002) had published his classic *A Theory of Justice*, which dealt with the central issue of *justice as fairness*, which Tinbergen and Pen also had addressed.[14]

[12] Galbraith, J.K. (1999) *The Affluent Society. Fortieth Anniversary Edition*. London: Penguin Group.

[13] Pen, J., Tinbergen, J. (1977) *Naar een Rechtvaardiger Inkomensverdeling (Towards a More Just Income Distribution)*. Amsterdam: Elsevier.

[14] Rawls, J. (1971) *A Theory of Justice*. Cambridge: Harvard University Press.

Amartya Sen, and many other scholars, analysed Rawls's theory as well. Sen—while deeply impressed with Rawls's thinking and his theory's elegant construction—rejected Rawls's theory. Inspired by Rawls, Sen developed his *capability approach*.[15]

The Return of Neoclassical Economics

Stagflation

During the early 1970s, the economic growth engine started to sputter due to stagflation—a combination of slow economic growth, rising inflation and unemployment. There are various explanations for this phenomenon: inflation reached double digits in the early 1970s as monetary authorities paid insufficient attention to inflation in their zeal to boost employment. The rapid growth in welfare state benefits had contributed to soaring budget deficits. Working conditions had improved and labour costs had risen, resulting in inflexible labour markets. Many firms lost their competitive edge and had to lay off personnel. The result was that unemployment started to rise. In 1973, and again in 1979, OPEC, the cartel of oil exporting countries, decided, to raise the price of oil. These factors—put together—triggered stagflation.

Keynesians could not explain *stagflation*.[16] They had an unshakable belief in the so-called *Phillips Curve*, which said that there was an inverse relation between inflation and unemployment: When inflation went up, unemployment would go down. But not just inflation shot up, also unemployment rose; how come?

[15] Sen, A. (1983) *Commodities and Capabilities.* Hennipman Lecture. Amsterdam: North Holland.

[16] This is what Galbraith had to say about the issue in *Economics in Perspective:* 'Wage and price determination was a microeconomic phenomenon, and microeconomics had been separated off by Keynes and left to the classical market orthodoxy. In orthodox microeconomics the wage-price spiral could not occur; producers of goods and the wages they paid their workers were still subject to market forces that the producers did not control. And if, as with monopoly or oligopoly, they did control them, it was in order to maximize profits, not to retrieve increases in wage costs forced by the unions. The separation of microeconomics from the purview of Keynesian economics and policy thus prevented a microeconomic model that could not be accorded an inflationary role. This separation was important; it was at the very heart of the great compromise of Keynes with the classical tradition, the compromise that preserved the market nexus', 268.

Milton Friedman (1912–2006) could explain this unexpected phenomenon. He argued that if government brought unemployment down to below the *natural rate of unemployment*, workers would claim higher wages and businesses would increase prices, triggering a wage-price spiral.

In addition, he (and his co-researcher Anna Schwartz) had also observed that too much money in circulation triggered too much demand for goods, leading to inflation. Hence, to do something about inflation one had to limit the supply of money; this was Friedman's *monetarist policy* in a nutshell. Hayek, who had earlier on unsuccessfully attempted to counter Keynes's insights about the causes of a depression, joined Friedman in promoting conservative neoclassical economic policies.[17] Both were instrumental in paving the ideological way for neoliberalism, as further elaborated in Chap. 3.

Friedman and Hayek left Keynesians behind in embarrassment, while taking the opportunity to promote their conservative neoclassical convictions. Their timing was perfect as Ronald Reagan had won the American presidential elections and Margaret Thatcher became Britain's Prime Minister. Both translated Friedman and Hayek in neoliberal political terms. Chile's leader Augusto Pinochet did the same, and quite a few other leaders after them.

Slaying the Inflation Dragon

The approach taken by America provides a good example of anti-stagflation drives. As regards the US, Friedman's advice was not wasted on Fed chairman Paul Volcker (1927–2019), who had been appointed to 'slay the inflationary dragon', in Volcker's own words.

The US Congress had passed a law in 1977 establishing the Fed's dual mandate of promoting stable prices *and* full employment. During Volcker's tenure, the Fed's objective of full employment understandably made way for its other objective: Keeping inflation in check. In the period 1980–1982, Volcker slowed the money supply. But he eventually also had to increase

[17] In this overview of economic developments over the past century, I use the term neoclassical economics. Once Hayek's and Friedman's conservative interpretation of neoclassical economics was translated into economic policy terms, neoliberalism appeared. This is what Joseph Stiglitz observes: 'Neoliberal economists constructed a theory to support their views, not surprisingly called neoclassical economics.' Source: Stiglitz, J. (2024) *The Road to Freedom: Economics and the Global Society*. London: Allen Lane, 29.

the interest rate. Initially, the American economy went into recession. But by 1983, the inflation rate began to fall. Growth resumed, and in 1987, unemployment dropped to 6.2%. Volcker's successor at the Fed, Alan Greenspan, wrote about this episode in his memoir:

The consequences of his policy were even more severe than Volcker had expected. In April 1980, interest rates on Main Street USA climbed to more than 20 percent. Cars went unsold, houses went unbuilt, and millions of people lost their jobs—unemployment rose to near 9 percent in mid-1980, on its way to near 11 percent by late 1982 .... But by the middle of the year, after peaking at nearly 15 percent, inflation began gradually to decline. Long-term interest rates inched down too. Still, it would take three years before inflation was fully in check.[18]

Neoclassical Economics Takes Centre Stage

Friedman's book *Capitalism and Freedom* was inspired by Friedrich Hayek's philosophy, as contained in *The Constitution of Liberty*.[19] Friedman confessed, however, that he was even more impressed with Hayek's philosophical and political convictions than with his neoclassical proposals.

Friedman and Hayek became the new *masters of the universe*, as one author quipped.[20] Their conservative neoclassical philosophy was widely communicated by a transatlantic network of think tanks, journalists, and politicians. Ha-Joon Chang summarized the essence of their neoclassical thinking in one sentence: Individuals know what they are doing, so leave them alone—except when markets malfunction.[21]

Neoclassical economics studies the optimizing economic behaviour of rational and perfectly informed individuals. It focuses on the efficient allocation of resources through the unfettered functioning of the market; i.e., with little or hardly any government interference. It assumes that markets, including the effects of transaction costs, always reach a point at which supply equals demand. Unemployment will disappear once the labour

[18] Greenspan, A. (2007) *The Age of Turbulence*. London: Allen Lane, 85–86.

[19] Hayek, F. (2006) *The Constitution of Liberty* London: Routledge, Classics Edition.

Friedman, M. (2002) *Capitalism and Freedom*. Chicago: Chicago University Press, Fortieth Anniversary Edition.

[20] Stedman Jones, D. (2012) *Masters of the Universe; Hayek, Friedman, and the Birth of Neoliberal Politics*. Princeton: Princeton University Press.

[21] Ha-Joon Chang. (2014) *Economics: The User's Guide*. London: Pelican Books, 120.

market will have adjusted through the upward or downward movement of wages. In the end, the economy will always reach a situation of general equilibrium. In short, neoclassical economics is an elegant, comprehensive, and appealing theoretical structure. Moreover, the functioning of markets allows individuals, firms, and countries to specialize in what they are best at and so contributing to an economy's productivity, which—in turn—improves living standards.

However, the neoclassicals' *Achilles heel* is their assumptions, as stripped bare by Keynes and by later events. Economics Nobel laureate Joseph Stiglitz questioned the neoclassical assumption of the functioning of markets, in that not all participants involved in the exchange of goods or services are equally informed, resulting in market failures. He also observes that Friedman and Hayek assumed completely rational behaviour of economic actors (i.e., *homo economicus*) while behavioural economists had discovered that these actors are far less rational, but also less selfish.[22]

Just as Keynes succeeded because unemployment was the problem in the 1930s, Friedman and Hayek succeeded because inflation and big government were the main problems of the 1970s. In short, neoclassical economics prevailed, like it did before Keynesianism became mainstream thinking.

The Great Moderation

The 1970s and early 1980s were, as we saw, turbulent times: stagflation had to be controlled at the cost of rising unemployment; firms were filing for bankruptcy. The costs of the Vietnam War resulted in ever larger US budget deficits. France, wanted to change their US dollar reserves into gold. The pressure on the dollar became so high that the fixed dollar-gold exchange rate, as stipulated in the Bretton Woods agreements, could no longer be maintained. On 15 August 1971, President Nixon ended the fixed dollar-gold exchange rate.

As of the mid-1980s, the economic climate was changing for the better. A long period of steady growth ensued in the Western world, also known as the period of the Great Moderation. Top-ranking economists believed that they had found the way to fine-tune economies so that recessions were phenomena of the past. In his 2003 Presidential Address to the prestigious American Economic Association (AEA), Robert Lucas (1937–2023) emphasized:

[22] *The Road to Freedom*, 14.

> Macroeconomics was born as a distinct field in the 1940s, as a part of the intellectual response to the Great Depression. The term then referred to the body of knowledge and expertise that we hoped would prevent the recurrence of that economic disaster. My thesis in this lecture is that macroeconomics in this original sense has succeeded: its central problem of depression-prevention has been solved, for all practical purposes, and has in fact been solved for many decades.[23]

However, Lucas apparently overlooked Nordic countries' banking crisis of 1991–1992, Mexico's financial crisis in 1995, the Asian crisis two years later when the exchange rates of some South-East Asian countries took a nose dive in 1997. In 1998, Russia was near-bankrupt and had to be supported by a joint American-IMF financial injection. Brazil (1999) and Argentina (2001–2002) also had their financial crises. During the Great Moderation period there were other hiccups like the bursting of three speculative bubbles: In technology stocks, real estate, and in oil. An IMF Working Paper of June 2012 estimated that there were 147 banking crises between 1970 and 2011.

Yet, the economies of high-income countries and emerging economies were humming along, boosted by cheap credit and by the rise of globalized trade, resulting from a sharp fall in tariffs and scrapping of capital controls. After a long period of converging incomes and wealth, the gap started to widen again. Japan was the odd man out; its economy was in a deflationary deadlock which the political leadership seemed unable to address. However, anybody with a bit of common sense could know that the Great Moderation could not last forever. After all, economic ups and downs are reflective of human nature. And sure enough, a massive recession was in the making.

The Great Recession

Fed chairman Greenspan retired in 2006. He published his memoir *The Age of Turbulence* in 2007; one year before the American financial crisis broke out.[24] He must have sensed that something was boiling over in the American economy, as he wrote:

[23] Krugman, P. (2013) *End this Depression Now*. New York: W.W. Norton & Company, 91.

[24] In fact, the subprime financial crisis began to unfold in 2007. Events took a massive turn for the worse in the fall of 2008, when Lehman Brothers collapsed.

> Economists cannot avoid being students of human nature, particularly of exuberance and fear. Exuberance is a celebration of life.…Regrettably, a surge of exuberance sometimes also causes people to reach beyond the possible; when reality strikes home, exuberance turns to fear … It is also the basis of many of our economic responses, the risk aversion that limits our willingness to invest and to trade, especially far from home, and that, in the extreme, induces us to disengage from markets, precipitating a severe falloff of economic activity.[25]

It was not surprising that Greenspan saw trouble looming. In 2007, BNP Paribas, a French bank, suspended withdrawals from three of its funds, and in the US the housing bubble burst. The subprime mortgage market collapsed in the middle of that year; the recession started at the end of 2007. Wall Street's financial crisis followed in September 2008, immediately after the failure of Lehman Brothers, an investment bank, quickly deepening Europe's banking troubles, ushering in the *Great Recession* of 2008.

Lucas was wrong after all, when he declared during his AEA speech that economists had found the way to fine-tune economies. He apparently had not paid attention to the work of behavioural economists, who—as mentioned—undertook studies to find out whether neoclassical's *homo economicus,* acted in an economically rational manner. Psychologists Amos Tversky (1937–1996) and Daniel Kahneman (1934–2024), for example, found that the neoclassical assumption of rational behaviour did not always apply to human beings faced with complicated choices.

Lucas should also have listened to Hyman Minsky (1919–1996), a Keynesian, who quite accurately predicted in *Stabilizing an Unstable Economy* (1986) what eventually happened. He argued that periods of economic stability (such as the Great Moderation) lead to an expansion of debt financing, triggered by new financial assets. An investment boom is the result. During the boom, competition between lenders increases, while their sense of caution diminishes. Many lenders make loans to borrowers who barely can pay the principal and interest. These types of loans have to be rolled over regularly. In time, banks start extending credit to people and firms not able to pay even the interest, and the credit system becomes unstable. This is precisely what happened 22 years after Minsky formulated his *financial instability hypothesis.* Unfortunately, his warning was ignored because Keynesians were not listened to at the time.

[25] *The Age of Turbulence*, 17.

When the financial crisis broke out in 2007, neoclassical economists were at a loss. They had not predicted what really happened; their assumptions were apparently not universally applicable.[26] They had closed their eyes about the negative effects of the ongoing deregulation process. The US Congressional Oversight Committee summoned Greenspan (aka *The Maestro*), then 82 years old, to the Hill to share his thoughts on the financial crisis. British newspaper, *The Guardian*, reported this on 24 October 2008:

> The Committee's chairman, the Democrat Henry Waxman, asked Greenspan: 'You found that your view of the world, your ideology, was not right, it was not working?'. Greenspan's response was: 'That's precisely the reason I was shocked because I'd been going for forty years or so with considerable evidence that it was working exceptionally well'. Waxman then pressed on: 'My question is simple. Were you wrong?' Greenspan: 'Partially…I made a mistake in presuming that the self-interest of organisations, specifically banks, is such that they were best capable of protecting shareholders and equity in firms…I discovered a flaw in the model that I perceived is the critical functioning structure that defines how the world works. I had been going for 40 years with considerable evidence that it was working exceptionally well.'

The process of deregulation in America had already begun under President Ford, and was continued in the late 1970s by the Carter Administration, when the airlines were deregulated. In 1999, President Clinton signed into law the Financial Services Modernization Act, which allowed commercial and investment banks to merge and create vast financial institutions.[27] Since 1992, Clinton's Democratic Party moved into a business-friendly direction, regaining the political middle ground. President Clinton's *Third Way* policies consisted of balanced budgets, private-public partnerships and finance for growth, including, as we saw, financial deregulation.[28] Chapter 3 describes Clinton's policies in more detail.

[26] As for predicting, Galbraith once quipped that the only function of economic forecasting is to make astrology respectable.

[27] Carmen Reinhart and Kenneth Rogoff noted in *This Time is Different*: 'In eighteen of the twenty-six banking crises they [Obstfeld and Taylor; PdH] studied, the financial sector had been liberalized within the preceding five years, usually less', 155.

[28] British Prime Minister Tony Blair had adopted comparable economic policies.

Why was it that, apart from Minsky and a handful others, economists had not predicted the financial crisis and subsequent Great Recession? One answer is that the neoclassical *assumption* of self-regulating markets, did not apply. Another one is that economics had evolved into a variety of specialized, compartmentalized fields which did not see eye-to-eye. Neither macroeconomics nor financial economics—unlike Minsky—had paid much attention to the workings of financial institutions such as banks. This was obviously a serious omission, the reason being that the dominant theories had been developed at the time of the Great Moderation, when there were no major economic shocks in high-income countries. And—let's face it—economics is not a science like chemistry and physics. Ha-Joon Chang formulated it accurately: '…there are no objective truths in economics that can be established independently of political, and frequently moral, judgments.'[29]

Behavioural economists are, as we saw, sceptical about markets' rationality. Their argument is that human beings tend to be too confident of their abilities, and they tend to extrapolate recent trends into the future. These two characteristics explain bubbles. Furthermore, losses can make investors irrationally risk-averse, which would explain dramatic price falls once a bubble bursts. Their insights led to a new branch of specialized economics: *neuro-economics*.[30]

How the Recession Was Countered

The US authorities took a Keynesian approach. Apart from fiscal measures, also monetary stimuli were applied. Bear Stearns, an investment bank, was taken over by JP Morgan Chase for a fire-sale price. This happened six months before Lehman Brothers collapsed on 15 September 2008. Lehman was not a commercial bank; so, it did not have depositors. Money market mutual funds held Lehman's short-term notes. When Lehman failed, the mutual funds' shareholders panicked and these funds suffered runs. This triggered runs by large investors on the money funds' investment-bank parents. Finally this then led to the collapse of the securitization market.

[29] *Economics: The User's Guide*, 451.

[30] McFadden, D.L. (2013) The New Science of Pleasure. *NBER Working Paper 18687*. Cambridge: National Bureau of Economic Research.

The federal government did not rescue Lehman. This is what Eichengreen concludes: 'The failure to endow Treasury and the Fed with the authority to deal with insolvency of a nonbank financial institution was the single most important policy failure of the crisis.'[31] There were rumours that Goldman Sachs and Morgan Stanley were also in trouble. Their stock prices plunged and clients started to withdraw their deposits.

Fed chairman Bernanke and Secretary of the Treasury Henry Paulson requested Congress to approve a huge rescue plan of $700 billion, to recapitalize the banks through the purchase of preference shares. Acts were adopted as well, such as the Dodd-Frank Act of 2010. This act included measures ranging from limiting speculative trading by financial institutions, raising capital and liquidity requirements, creating a regulatory entity responsible for systemic stability, to the creation of a Consumer Financial Protection Bureau. What the act did *not* do, however, was to limit the size of banks; they could still grow 'too big to fail'.

The Fed—while keeping its interest rate close to zero—pumped $3 trillion into the American economy through buying government and mortgage bonds. In addition, the Fed widened its *Quantitative Easing* (QE) measures by monthly injections $60 billion into the economy. Bernanke declared that this would be continued as long as the economy needed it.[32] In March 2014, Janet Yellen, Bernanke's successor at the Fed, announced tapering of the monthly *monetary morphine*; a term coined by *The Economist*, by the way. Yellen's announcement led to unrest in the financial markets of Brazil, Russia, India, China, and South Africa (the BRICS countries). Other economies, such as Argentina's and Turkey's, had also gotten used to low international interest rates.

The Obama Administration bailed out General Motors (GM) and Chrysler, two of the *Big Three* American carmakers; both were practically bankrupt. Within one month from taking office, President Obama—á-la Roosevelt—launched a fiscal stimulus program, embodied in the *Recovery and Reinvestment Act.*

[31] *Hall of Mirrors*, 5.

[32] *The Economist* of 21 December 2013 reported the following: 'Not everybody is happy with this. Many fret that the Fed's bond-buying has done more to inflate asset bubbles than boost employment. Mr. Volcker worries that the Fed has 'got so much authority, used so much authority, made up some authority…To exaggerate, everything that happens in the economy is because of the Federal Reserve. I think it's a little dangerous and too much of a burden', 98.

The Recovery Act included tax cuts, social safety net expenditures, financial support to states, investments in renewable energy, health care, education, infrastructure and transportation. Its two years' budget was $787 billion, the equivalent of 5% of GDP. In comparison, Roosevelt's New Deal investments were equivalent to 1.5% of GDP.

Economists agree that the Great Recession ended in America in June 2009. However, Stiglitz and Paul Krugman, both New Keynesians, argued that the Recovery Act's budget was inadequate. Krugman felt that Obama should have proposed much higher funding for fiscal stimulus, since the instrument of monetary policy (i.e., cutting interest rates) was impossible as the rate was already close to zero. Needless to say, the Recovery Act met with fierce resistance from Republican law makers. They argued in favour of austerity, saying that 'the immediate pain would produce long-term gain'.

European Union member countries, and Euro-zone members in particular, reacted to the Great Recession as follows. After an initial period of fiscal stimulus, the Euro-zone countries, and other EU members such as the UK, introduced structural reform measures. A combination of insufficient fiscal stimulus and structural reform, led in 2100 to a double dip recession, deepening the euro crisis. One reason why the Euro-zone was in particular trouble is that economies as diverse as Germany and Greece were brought under one monetary set of rules.

From a fiscal point of view, the focus was on bringing budget deficits down. On the monetary front, the ECB injected two shots of emergency credit, together €156 billion, into European economies. The ECB, like the Fed, kept its interest rate low. In 2010, a European Financial Stability Mechanism (EFSM) was established to help member-countries in financial difficulties with loans, often together with IMF credits, in exchange for tough structural reforms by borrowing countries to bring their finances under control.

ECB President Draghi introduced two Long-Term Refinancing Operations (LTROs). On 26 July 2012, Draghi delivered a remarkable speech in London in which he stated: 'Within our mandate, the ECB is ready to do whatever it takes to preserve the euro. And believe me, it will be enough.' Draghi's speech had a positive impact; European stock exchanges registered a sudden increase in share prices, and the interest on bonds of Southern European governments dropped. The ECB was prepared to buy the bonds of vulnerable states. This facility became known as the Outright Monetary Transactions. In October 2012, the Permanent European Stability Mechanism (ESM) was adopted with a lending capacity of €500 billion. In the run-up to the creation of a banking union, the ECB conducted stress tests of major European banks in 2014. This *Asset Quality Review* involved 130 Euro-zone banks. Twenty-five of them failed the test.

Yet, unemployment in the Euro-zone area still ran high: 11.1% in May 2015. But in Greece (25.4%) and in Spain (22.7%) the unemployment rate, especially under youngsters, was much higher.

Although the Fed and ECB's inflation target is an *average* of 2%, after 2015, the actual inflation rate was much lower. Was this a harbinger of *deflation*? Harvard economist Lawrence Summers is associated with the term *secular stagnation*, capturing not just what was happening; i.e., sluggish economic growth, low interest rates and relatively high persistent unemployment, but also that stagnation might continue for quite some time. At any event, this prompted the Fed, ECB and other central banks to introduce a large QE program to stimulate economic growth. Regarding ECB's measure, Germany and some other Northern Euro-zone countries were not particularly thrilled with injecting €1.1 trillion into the Euro-zone economies; they feared that this might create housing and stock 'bubbles'. Moreover, it would take away the pressure on governments to implement structural reforms. Most commentators argue that fiscal stimulus measures were necessary to help prevent deflation which would result in less aggregate demand, less investment, and even more unemployment. In addition, people would be inclined to save more, which would add to the global savings glut.[33]

China was not much affected by the Great Recession. True, its growth percentage dropped from 11.9% in 2007 to 6.2% in 2009. Thanks to a massive $586 billion local demand stimulus injection by the Chinese authorities, economic growth bounced back to 11.9% in 2010. As a percentage of GDP, the Chinese stimulus was more than double the size of President Obama's $787 billion package.

After the Great Recession was over, China was confronted with other challenges, and worse was to come. There was overcapacity in the housing sector and in some industrial sectors, such as steel, shipbuilding, and mining. On the other hand, China's service sector was growing; in 2013, it

[33] Martin Wolf refers to Keynes in *The Shifts and the Shocks*: 'Keynes introduced the second alternative to economic theory—adjustment via the level of output and incomes in a slump when short-term interest rates are zero and long-term rates are as low as they can go, because of 'liquidity preference'- the point at which people prefer to hold cash to bonds because the yield on the latter is too low to make holding them attractive.... The immediate impact of higher desired savings, he noted, is then to lower demand and so lower output and incomes.' Wolf, M. (2014) *The Shifts and the Shocks; What We've Learned—and Have Still to Learn—From the Financial Crisis*. London: Allen Lane, 152.

contributed 46% of China's GDP, having eclipsed the output of industry (44%). Income inequality constitutes a potential threat to political stability. Corruption and an underdeveloped legal system could prompt foreign investors to withdraw from China. This was worrying as China's economy was driven by investment.

After the Great Recession's dust had settled, the world economy was undergoing rapid changes. This is what Martin Wolf observed at the time:

> These three underlying drivers—liberalization, technology and ageing—proceeded to shift the world economy into a new shape, one that created huge gross and net capital flows across borders, growing inequality within countries, radical shifts in the location of investment and the rise of liberalized credit. These shifts led high-income economies into 'secular stagnation'.[34]

The globalized economy almost collapsed after the outbreak of the financial crisis, and subsequent Great Recession. Massive bank rescue operations (paid for by tax payers), unorthodox QE monetary policies, but also austerity measures and new competition from emerging economies (leading to massive job losses in the manufacturing sector of high-income countries) prompted quite a few economists to write about the shadier sides of the global liberal order.[35]

One book stood out; in fact it became a bestseller after it was published in English in 2014: Thomas Piketty's *Capitalism in the Twenty-First Century.*[36] Like Keynes, after publishing *The Economic Consequences of Peace* in 1919, Piketty became a superstar. He concludes that there is no such thing as the *Kuznets Curve*, which says that economic growth first leads to increasing inequality in income and wealth after which a converging process will take place. True, convergence did indeed happen between 1920 and 1973 in the developed world. This was possible thanks to a

[34] *The Shifts and the Shocks*, 184.

[35] Just a few examples: Ha-Joon Chang. (2010) *23 Things They Don't Tell You about Capitalism.* Sedlacek, T. (2011) *Economics of Good and Evil; The Quest for Economic Meaning from Gilgamesh to Wall Street.* Skidelsky, R. and E. (2012) *How Much is Enough?; Money and the Good Life.* Stiglitz, J. (2012) *The Price of Inequality; How Today's Divided Society Endangers Our Future.*

[36] Piketty, T. (2014) *Capitalism in the Twenty-First Century.* Cambridge: The Belknap Press of Harvard University Press.

combination of shrinking wealth, as a result of economic shocks caused by two World Wars, the Great Depression, progressive tax policies, and rising wages thanks to strong labour unions.

Piketty considers the period 1920–1973 as a historical exception. But the income and wealth gap is widening again. Unions have lost some of their negotiating power; in many high-income countries wages remained stagnant. The widening gap between the rich and the rest, says Piketty, is a politically, economically, and morally disturbing development. He suggests that more should be invested in education, as better educated people can get better-paid jobs. His main proposal is taxing high incomes very highly and the introduction of a global wealth tax. As this is not easy to achieve, he proposes a gradual approach towards limiting the gap between rich and the rest.

At the time, Piketty was not the first one to draw attention to the causes of income and wealth inequality.[37] These were also exposed by Mariana Mazzucato. But she did not stop there. In *The Value of Everything*, Mazzucato argues that neoclassical economics is to blame, as neoclassicals were abandoning the classicals' notion of value. Neoclassical economics replaced value with the term utility.[38] This has had wide-ranging negative consequences in the way modern economies function, and how the market and government are perceived to contribute to the productive capacity of an economy. Contrary to what neoclassical economists propose, she passionately argues that governments also *do* create value. In this vein, Mazzucato presents America's government-inspired DARPA,[39] which boosted innovation and productivity in many different fields, from which the private sector has greatly benefitted.

[37] Among quite a few others, Ha-Joon Chang also wrote about inequality in *23 Things They Don't Tell You about Capitalism*: 'Despite the usual dichotomy of 'growth enhancing pro-rich policy', pro-rich policies have failed to accelerate growth in the last three decades. So the first step in this argument—that is, the view that giving a bigger slice of pie to the rich will make the pie bigger—does not hold. The second part of the argument—the view that greater wealth created at the top will eventually trickle down to the poor—does not work either', 137–138.

[38] Mazzucato, M. (2018) *The Value of Everything; Making and Taking in The Global Economy*. London: Allen Lane.

[39] The US Defence Advanced Research Projects Agency (DARPA).

Mazzucato's example has recently been included in Mario Draghi's report *EU Competitiveness; Looking Ahead* (2024). The report is to promote Europe's welfare, the environment and, another liberal value, freedom. Impressed with DARPAs achievements, the Draghi report strongly suggests to create comparable European Advanced Research Projects Agencies (ARPAs), to give innovation and, subsequently, EU's productivity enhancement a shot in the arm.

What More Happened After the Great Recession?

The period that followed the Great Recession can roughly be divided in four episodes. First, as already briefly alluded to, the episode of secular stagnation, followed by, second, the start of the trade war between America and China. If this were not enough to undermine the global liberal order, the third episode covers the Covid-pandemic. The fourth episode is characterized not just by the fight against rapidly increasing inflation but also by the promotion of protection, the launching of national industrial policies, and the problems institutions such as the IMF, WTO, and the UN encounter to effectively implement their respective mandate. The gradual build-up of the liberal order, as we have seen it developing since the end of WWII, is being undermined.

Secular Stagnation

In 2013, as already touched upon, Harvard professor and former Secretary of the Treasury, Lawrence Summers re-introduced the term secular stagnation. This term was indeed not new; it was first used in the 1930s by Alvin Hansen (1887–1975), another Harvard professor. Now, what did Summers say? In essence, the term secular stagnation meant that the savings amassed already before the 2008 financial crisis, could not be fully invested in productive investment. The result: Sluggish growth, low interest rates, and high unemployment. And this was precisely not what economies having overcome the Great Recession needed.

Monetary policy, in a situation where interest rates are near-zero, may not work, observes Summers. One has to return to 'new old Keynesian economics', as he calls it, to address the stagnation. Demographic developments (i.e., people grow older, and fewer children are born) eliminate the demand for new capital. The savings required to purchase a given amount of capital also declined. Capital goods themselves had gone down in price as well over time, encouraging delays in investment. The conclusion: Investment demand had substantially been reduced, while savings had increased; so, a 'savings glut' ensued.

One consequence was a downward trend in interest rates. Difficulties in absorbing savings resulted in reduced growth and in not achieving targeted inflation rates; in fact, actual rates remained around, or even below, 2%. On the other hand, as was predicted, bubbles occurred in the stock and housing markets. What was to be done, according to Summers, was that central banks needed to raise inflation, and making sure full absorption of savings, rather than crowding out investment.

The Trade War

Meanwhile, another problem cropped up. In 2017, the Trump administration withdrew from the Trans-Pacific Partnership, which would have become the largest free trade bloc in the world. This was a harbinger of what more was to come. In January 2018, President Trump launched a protectionist policy against China through increasing tariffs on imported aluminium (10% extra), steel (25% extra), and other trade barriers, so as to force it to end—what Trump claimed—China's longstanding unfair trade practices.

As could be expected, China retaliated, despite the fact that the country depended on export for its economic growth. Other international trading partners, such as the European Union, also announced higher tariffs. However, after negotiations between the EU and the US, both sides scaled the intended tariffs down.

President Trump hoped that America's own aluminium and steel industry, including employment, would benefit from the tariff hike. It did not work out as anticipated. One example: America's automakers now had to pay more for imported sophisticated steel for the production of their automobiles. This prompted them to cut production costs. They did so by closing down plants in the US, costing 14,000 auto workers their job. This is not what Trump's tariff policy had intended. So, in December 2018, during the G-20 summit held in Buenos Aires, the US agreed with China a 90-days suspension of the trade war. But this was not the beginning of the end of the trade war. To quote Churchill: It was the end of the beginning, as President Biden kept his predecessor's protectionist trade policy largely intact; a host of other countries followed suit.

The trade war does not just involve tariffs, it also involves sanctions as, for example, the Chinese company Huawei experienced. At any event, the

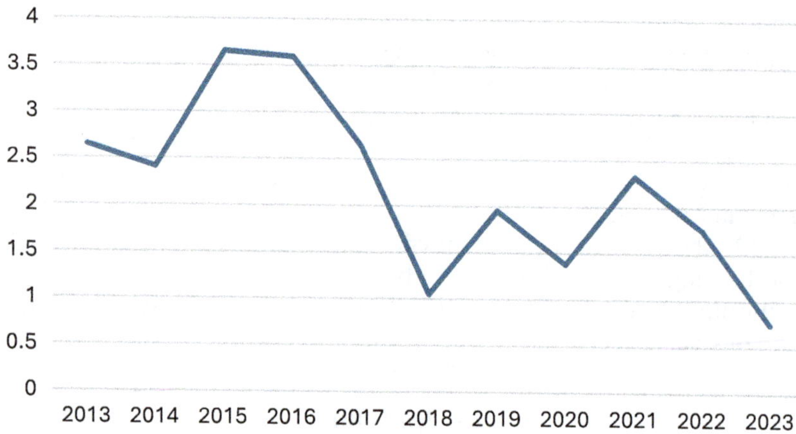

Fig. 2.3 Foreign direct investment, net inflows (% of GDP). (Source: Worldbank.org)

long period of gradually cutting import and export tariffs, and other international trade barriers, was over. WTO, tasked with overseeing international trade, is handicapped in implementing its role, not having a functioning Appellate Body. In short, protectionism is no longer an alien term. As a result, international trade and foreign direct investment (FDI) slowed down (Fig. 2.3).

Prices of consumer goods increased, and fewer poor people than in the past are leaving the ranks of the extremely poor. Tragically, extreme poverty has barely fallen since 2015. The poorest countries, that used to catch up, have stopped growing faster than richer ones, or are falling further behind. This is bad news for more than 700 million still extremely poor people and the 3 billion who are not extremely but merely poor.

The Covid-Pandemic

In early 2020, the Covid-pandemic broke out. Global income in the second quarter of 2020 fell by 5%. Every advanced economy was facing a recession. Around the world, around 400 million jobs were lost. The global economy came to a standstill after the first wave of lockdowns was implemented. World trade took a nose dive. Roberto Azevedo, then outgoing WTO's Director General, projected that over the entire year 2020,

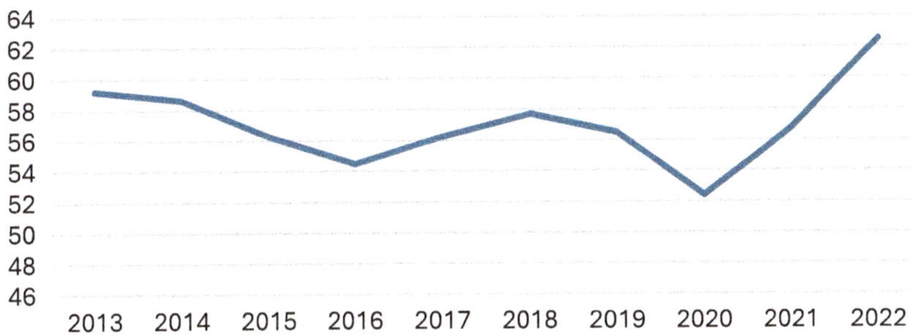

Fig. 2.4 World trade (% of GDP). (Source: Worldbank.org)

international trade could drop between 13% and 32%—an alarming prospect (Fig. 2.4).

The above graph shows that Azevedo was too pessimistic: Global trade volumes decreased by 10% rather than the higher percentages Azevedo had mentioned.

Keynesian policies made a comeback, as governments, that could afford it, acted quickly in pumping large sums of money into their economies to assist business and their employees, and deserving poor families. For example, the ECB bought up a whopping €2.5 trillion in government bonds to assist member countries in compensating financial damages caused by Covid.

In 2020, President Trump had already approved the so-called $2.2 trillion CARES Act to support affected businesses, employees and families. After Trump, the Biden Administration introduced another enormous $1.9 trillion rescue plan, which included a cheque of $1400 for most Americans (in addition to the $600 they had already received). The American Treasury and the Fed poured around $2.5 trillion into the banking system. These unprecedented financial doses triggered a debate among economists about steeply rising public debt, and a possible return of inflation, which at the time was still very low.

What were the expectations about Covid's global economic consequences? In 2020, the IMF, for example, was optimistic about the post-Covid period, although its projections carried a higher-than-usual uncertainty. Surely, the IMF anticipated a slower recovery as a result of damage to supply potential, and a hit to productivity as surviving businesses would ramp up necessary workplace safety and hygiene practices.

Nonetheless, IMF's *World Economic Outlook* projected that in 2021, world output would grow 5.4%. High-income economies, such as the US, the European Union, Japan, and Canada would grow 4.8%, while emerging markets and developing economies (including China, India, Asean-5, Russia, and Brazil) would grow a bit more: 5.9%. China's output alone was expected to grow 8.2% in 2021. Was IMF too optimistic in its forecasts? Perhaps slightly, but not far from what actually happened. As a share of global GDP, trade has bounced back from the Covid-pandemic.

The world-wide lockdowns exposed the interconnectedness of production and other economic activities. It appeared that countries had become too dependent on the delivery of strategically important goods (such as medicine and specialized vital equipment) from one or two countries. Just one example: Once the pandemic had broken out, Europe had become totally dependent on the delivery of mouth caps and protective equipment from China. This triggered the adoption of national, home-based, industrial policies, promoting the buildup of domestic supply chains and subsidizing production of e.g., clean energy, electric vehicles and computer chips.[40]

Inflation

After the lockdowns were over, it became clear that production and transportation costs had risen. Shortages of semiconductors disrupted the production of cars, computers, and smartphones. The price of oil had risen to $65 a barrel. Pent-up demand resulted in a spending spree. All these factors put together, contributed to the sudden rise of inflation.

America was running an unpredictable three-pronged economic *experiment*, featuring (i) historic levels of fiscal stimulus (mentioned above), (ii) a more tolerant attitude of the Fed towards temporary overshoots in inflation, and, (iii) indeed, large pent-up savings which consumers wanted to spend.

The Fed kept interest rates low for some time. The idea behind it was that the US government could spend as much as it liked including spending on President Biden's rescue plan. After all, borrowing money was still cheap. Obviously, the question was whether these dollar injections would not fuel inflation? America's Treasury Secretary, Janet Yellen, tried to

[40] The IMF found that a subsidy given in a big economy has a 74% probability is met within a year with a subsidy for the same product from another big economy.

assure the markets by saying that the US had the tools to deal with inflation. And Fed Chairman, Jerome Powell, said that even if the American economy overheated, it would be only temporary. But bond holders were not convinced. They feared that imminent inflation would lower the value of their bonds. Consequently, American and European bond markets registered an increase in bond yields. In February 2021, the benchmark ten-year American Treasury yield surpassed 1.6%. This was low by historical standards, but quite a bit higher than the percentage at the beginning of 2021.

Thanks to central banks buying-up government bonds, the worst fears about inflation receded again. But for how long? Should the Fed not be able to withstand the pressure of rising prices and decide to increase the interest rate to keep inflation in check, this would be bad news for markets. After all, what is happening in financial markets depended upon the expectation that central banks would keep interest rates low for a long time.

What was Europe's reaction? European developments were not much different from those of the US. The ECB, for example, pretty much followed the same careful monetary policy to bring inflation back to the 2% average—the same objective as the Fed's. The ECB had yet another concern; i.e., the difference between the economies of Euro-zone countries. Should the ECB rise its interest rate, this would be hard for indebted Southern European countries, such as Greece, Italy, and Spain—an ECB interest rise would be very costly for them.

Once inflation starts to rise, even moderately, it has the tendency to continue rising; and, indeed, it kept on rising. The figure below shows the development of inflation in the US, the EU, Britain, China, and Japan, demonstrating that in 2021, inflation indeed shot up quite dramatically (Fig. 2.5).

How Inflation Was Brought Under Control

Monetarists now know much more about the factors causing inflation than during the time stagflation occurred some 50 years ago. Policy makers have more instruments at their disposal to quell sustained price rises: Raising interest rates; limiting the money supply; and tapering bond purchases.

When, in the 1970s, inflation started to rise, unemployment also grew, contrary to what the Phillips Curve predicted, i.e., an inverse relation between inflation and unemployment. The peculiar situation now was that

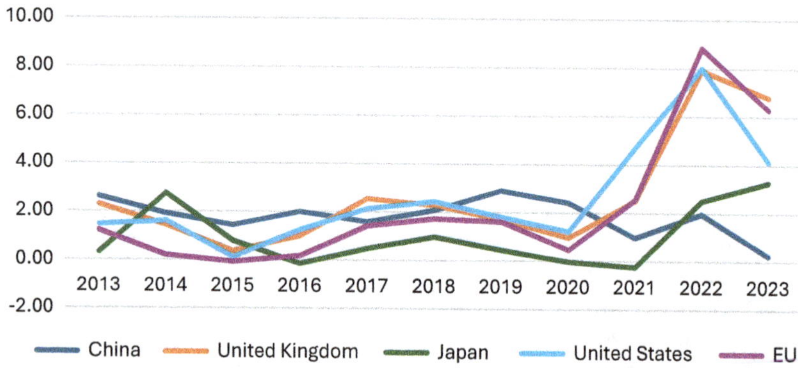

Fig. 2.5 Inflation, consumer prices (annual %). (Source: Worldbank.org)

although inflation sharply rose, unemployment remained low. Again, this was not in line with what the Phillips Curve said. After the Covid-pandemic ended, and inflation shot up, there were more vacancies than the labour market could provide—the labour market was pretty tight. Lawrence Summers now feared that in order to bring inflation down, unemployment would have to rise above 10%. Summers must have had the Phillips Curve in mind, and surely also the way in which Volcker had 'slain the inflation dragon' way back during the late 1970s.

The interaction between the tight labour market and the changing availability of raw materials and components help explain what happed. After the end of the Covid-pandemic, there was a shortage of these raw materials and components. This resulted in more pressure on the already tight labour market. If extra labour would have been available, this could have compensated the temporary shortage of input factors. Once more of these inputs became available, the pressure on the labour market subsided. The result: Inflation started to come down, while unemployment did *not* go up. Simultaneously, inflation expectations went also down.

This was good news for central banks. In a situation like this, including stable inflation expectations, the costs of countering inflation, are much lower than during Volcker's time when he brought stagflation under control at considerable costs. At this time of writing, the conclusion is justified that the Fed and the ECB, by applying step-by-step interest rate policies, brought inflation by and large under control.

Not Such Great Expectations

We saw that even before WWII had ended, the Bretton Woods institutions had been created. The same applies to the United Nations. GATT followed roughly a decade later. All of them—including the Marshall Plan—greatly helped to overcome the damage done by the war, and—even more impressive—these institutions, including the WTO, greatly contributed to creating order in international financial affairs, and cutting down international trade obstacles.

However, the erosion of the post-WWII global liberal order already began in the early 1970s. Ironically, it started in the US, when on 15 August 1971, President Nixon suspended the dollar convertibility into gold, after which, 19 months later, the Bretton Woods system of fixed-exchange rates collapsed.

The IMF, after having received criticisms of its harsh policy prescriptions in the past, now devotes growing attention to climate change and inequality at the detriment of its principal mission: Financial stability through sound macroeconomic management. In addition, with the rise of new international creditors, such as China and India, it is now more difficult for the IMF to broker deals with poor countries' debts not any longer on behalf of all creditors. In sum, IMF is in the midst of an identity crisis.

The trade war, initially between the US and China, further eroded the liberal principle of free trade, from which many trading countries (and their population) had benefitted. As *The Economist* concluded, the achievements of the 1990s and 2000s were unmatched in history.[41] Hundreds of millions escaped poverty in low-income countries; infant mortality worldwide is now less than half what it was in 1990. And, not to forget, China was admitted to the WTO.

Protectionism is on the rise, often combined with subsidized national industrial policies to ensure that strategically important industries (i.e., defence, health, battery production, semiconductors production, etc.) are either being *re-shored* or established (and subsidized) by governments. Who has not heard of slogans like 'Made in Europe', 'Made in India', or 'A Future Made in Australia'?

The WTO celebrates its 30th birthday in 2025, but it will probably not be a happy occasion as the organization has lost relevance, not least since America's repeated vetoes to fill vacancies of WTOs Appellate Body, which

[41] *The Economist*, 11 May 2024, 7.

is supposed to settle trade disputes. The freeing up of the global market, which had been built up step-by-step since GATT's days, is being undermined. The rising trend in protectionism is not helping either, let alone the proliferation of trade sanctions. As a result of wars, sanctions are imposed four times as often as they did during the 1990s' peace dividend era. But sanctions are not just imposed because of war. For example, the European Union imposed a provisional tariff of 37.6% on the importation of Chinese electric vehicles to protect European automakers from much cheaper imported Chinese cars. As for American sanctions against China, they intend to thwart the latter's technological ambitions, especially in semiconductors.

A process of de-globalization is ongoing. It will now be more difficult for aspiring emerging economies, such as Indonesia and India, to find customers for their export goods, as the global market is now being cut into several smaller ones; each applying their own rules. The global economy is atomizing rather than integrating. It will be harder for the still 700 million extremely poor people to get a slightly better life. The same applies to the almost 3 billion people living in regions that are getting no closer to rich world living standards.

Conclusion

This chapter started with the abrupt end of the *Belle Epoque* and the beginning of WWI. There are similarities between what happened then and what is happening now. The nineteenth-century globalized economy came to an end. Although the second term of Trump's presidency has just begun, the president already started a trade war with Canada, Mexico, and China. Very likely other countries will be victimized to, including the European Union. The least what can be concluded is that the liberal order, the world enjoyed over the past 80 years, is being undermined.

During the 1930s, tit-for-tat protectionism was widely applied. Also now, protectionism is on the rise, and so is subsidizing national industrial investments. The steep increase in the number of sanctions further undermines the liberal order.

The Great War ended a long period of economic bliss. From May 1945 to February 2022, there was no war on the European continent. The Russian invasion of Ukraine in 2022 was another harbinger of worse to come.

Economic history shows that, once the circumstances change, the dominant economic philosophy is being eclipsed by another one. We saw that happening after WWI, and again, after the end of WWII. The question is whether the world is entering a phase which will resemble what happened after the end of WWI? I do not have the answer. Marx once observed that history repeats itself, first as tragedy, then as farce. Let us hope that neither tragedy nor farce will be in the offing.

References

Bernanke, B. (2000). *Essays on the Great Depression*. Princeton University Press.

Cassidy, J. (2009). *How Markets Fail; The Logic of Economic Calamities*. Allen Lane.

Eichengreen, B. (2015). *Hall of Mirrors; The Great Depression, the Great Recession, and the Uses—and Misuses—of History*. Oxford University Press.

Frank, B. (2023). *In the Long Run We're All Dead; The Lives and Deaths of Great Economists*. Haus Publishing.

Friedman, M. (2002). *Capitalism and Freedom*. Chicago University Press, Fortieth Anniversary Edition.

Fukuyama, F. (1992). *The End of History and The Last Man*. Penguin Books.

Galbraith, J. K. (1967). *The New Industrial State*. Houghton Mifflin Company.

Greenspan, A. (2007). *The Age of Turbulence*. Allen Lane.

Ha-Joon Chang. (2014). *Economics: The User's Guide*. Pelican Books.

Hayek, F. (2006). *The Constitution of Liberty*. Routledge, Classics Edition.

Keynes, J. M. (1919). *The Economic Consequences of Peace*. Macmillan.

Keynes, J. M. (1964). *The General Theory of Employment, Interest and Money*. Harcourt Brace & Company.

Krugman, P. (2009). *The Conscience of a Liberal*. W.W. Norton & Company.

Krugman, P. (2013). *End this Depression Now*. W.W. Norton & Company.

Maddison, A. (2003). *The World Economy: Historical Statistics*. OECD Development Centre of the Organisation for Economic Development and Development.

Mazzucato, M. (2018). *The Value of Everything; Making and Taking in The Global Economy*. Allen Lane.

McFadden, D. L. (2013). *The New Science of Pleasure. NBER Working Paper 18687*. National Bureau of Economic Research.

Pen, J., & Tinbergen, J. (1977). *Naar een Rechtvaardiger Inkomensverdeling (Towards a More Just Income Distribution)*. Elsevier.

Piketty, T. (2014). *Capitalism in the Twenty-First Century*. The Belknap Press of Harvard University Press.

Rawls, J. (1971). *A Theory of Justice*. Harvard University Press.

Samuelson, P. (1970). *Economic; An Introductory Analysis.* McGraw-Hill.
Sen, A. (1983). *Commodities and Capabilities. Hennipman Lecture.* North Holland.
Stedman Jones, D. (2012). *Masters of the Universe; Hayek, Friedman, and the Birth of Neoliberal Politics.* Princeton University Press.
Stiglitz, J. (2024). *The Road to Freedom: Economics and the Global Society.* Allen Lane.
Taylor, F. (2013). *The Downfall of Money.* Bloomsbury Press.
Wolf, M. (2014). *The Shifts and the Shocks; What We've Learned—and Have Still to Learn—From the Financial Crisis.* Allen Lane.

CHAPTER 3

Liberalism

As liberalism is the book's philosophical common denominator, this chapter describes its evolution, and how liberalism influenced economics' game-changers, presented in this book. The economic dimension of liberalism will be presented in some detail. Democracy, yet another dimension of liberalism, will also be dealt with.

This chapter contains four parts. Part I includes a succinct overview of liberalism's history, with special attention for social contract theories, not least since contractual theory enjoyed a revival with John Rawls's *Theory of Justice*. Part I concludes with *On the Way to the Moderns*.

Part II, zooms in on the history of liberalism's economic dimension, beginning with Adan Smith and followed by John Stuart Mill. Part II also describes how new liberalism came about as developed by Thomas Green, Leonard Hobhouse, and John Hobson, and how it changed the political landscape in nineteenth-century Britain. Most scholars agree that the nineteenth century actually ended in 1914, when the *Belle Epoque* came to a sudden end as the Great War began.

Part III's title is *How Liberalism Fared After the Great War*. During this tumultuous period, in which the war was followed by the rise of Communism, the Great Depression and by another world war, new liberalism was translated into political and economic terms. Politically, President Roosevelt's New Deal, to counter the depression in America, was new liberalism in action. It was Keynes's *General Theory*, that not just revolutionized

P. de Haan, *Great Economists and the Evolution of Economic Liberalism*, https://doi.org/10.1007/978-3-031-93831-3_3

economics, but also provided the economic instruments to end the depression. Neoliberalism made its triumphant entry when stagflation broke out. Since neoliberalism dominated the political and economic domains during the past four decades, its reign—and decline—are described in detail.

Part IV deals with the close relationship between liberalism and democracy and concludes with concerns about liberal democracy.

Part I Liberalism: A Brief Historic Overview

Introduction

Liberalism, observes Francis Fukuyama, Senior Fellow at Stanford University, is a way of regulating violence, allowing diverse populations to live peacefully with one another. Liberalism protects basic human dignity, in particular human autonomy. Liberalism promotes democracy, individual freedoms, an independent judiciary, as well as gender and racial equality. And, very important, it promotes economic growth, including all the good things that come from growth, by protecting property rights, allowing the freedom to transact, and by creating employment.

John Gray, Emeritus School Professor of European Thought at the London School of Economics, also offers broad characteristics of liberalism. It is individualistic, in that it asserts the moral primacy of a person against the claim of any social collectivity. It is egalitarian, inasmuch it denies differences in *moral* worth among human beings. Liberalism is also universalist, underscoring the moral unity of the human species. Finally, liberalism is meliorist, in that successive generations can improve their sociopolitical arrangements, and the universalist element affirms the moral unity of humans and marginalizes local cultural differences. Gray concludes that 'It is this conception of man and society which gives liberalism a definite identity which transcends its vast internal variety and complexity.'[1]

Liberalism is a vibrant intellectual philosophy in which its basic insights are regularly challenged and rethought, resulting in new ideas, analyses, and proposals. It is, above all, a tolerant philosophy. In simple terms: You can believe what you want, but must do so in private life and not seek to impose your views on others. Let the free market, as much as possible, run its course. Keep government small, while not overlooking its role as

[1] Gray, J. (1986) *Liberalism*. Milton Keynes: Open University Press, x.

protector of private property and provider of social services. And uphold values such as pluralism, toleration, autonomy, bodily integrity and consent.

A Very Brief Historic Overview

Across the ages, liberalism had a variety of meanings. Liberalism is not just a tradition of thought, a value system, but also a frame of mind. Above all, liberalism shaped many economies and societies. True, during the nineteenth and twentieth century, Marxism also played an important part, not only as an alternative philosophy, but also as how it was practiced in e.g., the Soviet Union, China under Mao Zedong, Cuba, and North Korea. However, Marxism as applied by them was not successful, certainly not from an economic point of view.

Liberalism, as it is now understood, began in the eighteenth century in Northwestern Europe. This does not mean that ideas associated with liberalism had not been developed before that era. Marcus Tullius Cicero (106 BC–43 BC), for example, observed that friendship and the quest for knowledge would bring harmony and peace, protected property, and would produce a just society based on political service, affection, kindness, and liberty. Good *morals* would drive a healthy market, allowing ethical people to make exchanges in confidence. Trust, added Cicero, was a mechanism that freed up trade.

For centuries, scholastic philosophy had dominated European thought, even unto the Renaissance, when society was hierarchically led by absolute monarchs and the Church. Influenced by rapid economic, social, and political developments, this leadership model gradually lost political and philosophical credibility. What also played a part was weariness of wars of religion. This resulted in an era of intellectual curiosity and toleration. These were sources of a movement which eventually developed into eighteenth and nineteenth-century liberalism. This movement was certainly also inspired by what Enlightenment thinkers had proposed.

Social Contract

Before this movement emerged, philosophers such as Thomas Hobbes (1588–1679), John Locke (1632–1704) and Jean-Jacques Rousseau (1712–1778), introduced and further developed the notion of a voluntary *social contract*, stipulating social norms and political obligations. In short,

'....the idea of a social contract is meant to help us think about the moral legitimacy of collective action and the obligations and restraints it entails, a free exchange that might be voluntarily agreed on among the citizens of society.'[2]

Locke exemplified this new impulse of political philosophy. In his *Two Treatises of Government*, he proposed 'a state of nature' that directly complemented his conception of how political development occurred and, equally important, how it could be founded through contractual obligations. Locke is generally considered the founding father of liberalism, although he never used the term.

In his *social contract* theory, Locke argued that each individual had equal natural rights to *life, liberty, and property*, while governments should not violate these rights. Social contract theories all build on the idea that the state of nature is undesirable and that political institutions, such as the state, can help prevent or overcome anarchy. Humans living without such a central authority were facing uncertain conditions in a state of mutual competition.

Locke was not the first philosopher presenting a social contract theory. In *Leviathan* (1651), Hobbes had already introduced the term. However, Hobbes's and Locke's interpretation of social contract differed quite substantially. Hobbes favoured rule by an absolute sovereign, while Locke had a more restrained leadership in mind, being a party to the contract. Needless to say, their respective opinion about the character of human beings also differed substantially. In Hobbes's state of nature, each person would have a right to everything, and this would lead to, in his own words, 'a war of all against all'. Hence, to avoid civil war, Hobbes underscored the necessity of a strong central authority. Locke, on the other hand, depicted a rosier picture: Man seeks to be happy in a state of social harmony as a social animal.

Social contract theory was further developed by Rousseau. In *Le Contrat Social* (1762), he deviated from Hobbes and Locke. He argued that society and property constituted the real original sins. He observed that inequality was the product of self-love and pride. In the quest to satisfy people's pride, the wealthy and powerful created unnatural conventions and privileges to distinguish and celebrate themselves in a hierarchy.

[2] Stiglitz, J. (2024) *The Road to Freedom; Economics and the Good Society*. London: Allen Lane, 13–14.

Rousseau concluded that the chains of mankind were private property and elites: Property was a corrupting vice to be fought with empathy, but supported by a political push for economic equality.

The contractarian approach has been a dominant influence in contemporary liberal political philosophy. Particularly since the early 1970s, when John Rawls published *A Theory of Justice* (1971), and Robert Nozick (1938–2002) *Anarchy, State and Utopia* (1974). Both works are presented in Chap. 7, respectively Chap. 6.[3]

Let us take a step backwards, and briefly present what major events and developments took place in the eighteenth century in Europe and America.

The American and French Revolution

After 1765, political tension between England and its American colonies grew. The Seven Years' War over the issue of ***taxation without representation***, led to the American Revolution and, eventually, America's Declaration of Independence. In 1787, the Constitution of the United States was adopted by the federal government. The Constitution was not just a republican document, it was above all a liberal document.[4]

In 1787, the Marquis de Lafayette wrote to his friend George Washington that the spirit of liberty was now spreading in France. The French, having lived for centuries under an oppressive absolute monarchy, were ready for a liberal system of government similar to America's. We already saw that in *Le Contrat Social*, Rousseau attacked absolute monarchy and staggering inequality. His pamphlet provided intellectual ammunition for the French Revolution.

The revolution's causes consisted of a combination of social, political, and economic problems, which the government in power (the *Ancien Régime*) was unable to manage.[5] A financial crisis and widespread social

[3] Chapter 7's Annexe includes a more elaborate presentation of social contract theories.

[4] It is the oldest liberal governing document in the world. 'The freedom of modern European governments was, for the most part, obtained by the concessions or the liberality of monarchs or military leaders. In America alone, reason and liberty concurred in the formation of constitutions'. Source: Rosenblatt, H. (2018) *The Lost History of Liberalism; From Ancient Rome to the Twenty-First Century*. Princeton: Princeton University Press, 37.

[5] Maddison observed the following: 'In the case of France, the 1700–1820 growth rate is unchanged, but for the second half of the seventeenth century I assume stagnant per capita income because of hunger crises and the depressing influence of more or less continuous warfare…'. Source: *The World Economy*, 244.

distress ensued. In May 1789, a new National Assembly was established, which replaced the former Parliament. On 14 July 1789, the Bastille was stormed, which forced the Assembly to take radical measures, among them the abolition of feudalism, the State's control over the Church, and the Declaration of the Rights of Man. Nonetheless, the French Revolution ended in a reign of terror. It came to an end when in 1794 its most prominent representative, Maximilian Robespierre, was deposed and executed.

During the Napoleonic wars, France introduced in Western Europe a host of liberal notions, such as the liquidation of the feudal system, the liberalization of property laws, the abolition of guilds, legalization of divorce, and equality under the law for all men.

On the Way to the Moderns

Modern classical liberalism was not promoted by French thinkers but by a remarkable Swiss couple, who took a keen interest in what was happening during the French Revolution. Inspired by the revolution, Madame de Staël (1766–1817) and Benjamin Constant (1767–1830) formulated the ideas that became known as modern classical liberalism.

Madame de Staël had been exposed to Enlightenment ideas, while Constant had enjoyed learning about the philosophy of the Scottish Enlightenment at the University of Edinburgh. The couple supported the rule of law and civil equality, constitutional and representative government, as well as freedom of the press and freedom of religion, accompanied by moral and civic values, such as magnanimity, openness, and toleration.

But it was Constant who introduced the notion of the liberty of the Moderns. This notion included the possession of civil liberties, the rule of law, and freedom from excessive state interference. Indeed, Constant was a supporter of 'laissez-faire, *laissez-passer*'. He also believed that commerce was superior to war. He criticized Napoleon's martial appetite, on the grounds that it was illiberal and no longer suited to modern commercial social organization. He applauded the triumph of individuality through the growth of freedom of opinion and religion. As for religion, Constant proposed the separation of church and state.

Regarding his ideas about the economic affairs, he must have taken inspiration from his older contemporary Adam Smith (1723–1790) who had presented a popular liberal economic theory, praising the free market.

The Revolutions of 1848

Returning to Constant's thinking, he constructed a bridge between liberalism before, during, and after the French Revolution, and how liberalism evolved in France, Britain, and America. Regarding France, the revolution had not led to improvements, either politically or economically. In 1848, an agricultural and industrial depression broke out. Unemployment became rife accompanied by popular unrest. Early that year, a fresh revolution broke out in France, followed by uprisings in Germany, and Italy.

In France, the elections in 1848 brought to power a conservative majority, including monarchists. Louis Napoleon (Napoleon's nephew) was elected president. Some historians call the form of government he oversaw an early version of the modern police state.[6]

In Germany, early victories by liberals in 1848, triggered liberal fears, dissensions, and failures. These fears drove the fearful and opponents of liberal ideas in the arms of conservatives. In Prussia, Hohenzollern power was restored, and the authoritarian ruler Otto von Bismarck, also known as liberalism's gravedigger, called the shots.

As for Italy, revolts broke out which forced rulers to accede to liberal reform. Roman rebels overthrew the Pope. The leader of the Italian liberal movement, Giuseppe Garibaldi, entered the city and formed a government based on liberal principles, including religious liberty and the separation of church and state. Also in Italy this triggered a reaction of punishing repression.

In short, the revolutions of 1848 were a big setback for liberals. They had new powerful enemies. Not just from the Right; i.e., absolute monarchs, authoritarian leaders, and the Church, but now also from the Left; i.e., republicans and socialists. The latter had some successes in promoting social reforms by Napoleon III and by Pope Pius IX who signalled his willingness to institute social reforms, which he later withdrew.

Part II Economic Liberalism

Introduction

Since this book is about liberalism's influence on economic game-changers, let us look closer at the historical origins of liberalism's economic dimension. According to Bertrand Russell, early liberalism valued economic affairs:

[6] *The Lost History of Liberalism*, 134. For example, symbols of the French Revolution became illegal. Freedoms of the press and assembly were curtailed.

> Early liberalism was a product of England and Holland, and had certain well-marked characteristics. It stood for religious toleration; it was Protestant, but on a latitudinarian rather than of a fanatical kind; it regarded the wars of religion as silly. It valued commerce and industry, and favoured the rising middle class rather than the monarchy and the aristocracy; it had immense respect for the rights of property, especially when accumulated by the labours of the individual possessor.[7]

Surely, Russell also observed that liberalism encompassed more than just its economic dimension:

> The essence of liberalism is an attempt to secure a social order not based on irrational dogma, and insuring stability without involving more restraints than are necessary for the preservation of the community. Whether this attempt can succeed only the future can determine.[8]

Typical aspects of economic liberalism include property rights, free markets, and general equilibrium. Adam Smith, the first philosopher of classical economic liberalism, did not invent these terms. For example, Roman Consul-philosopher Marcus Tullius Cicero had designed a morally sound system of free commercial exchanges between members of the ruling class. Cicero included this moral dimension as he observed: 'For a man to take something from his neighbour and to profit by his neighbour's loss is more contrary to Nature than is death or poverty.' And he added: 'High morals—courtesy, justice and generosity in the act of exchange—were the principles that led to a harmonious and rich society.'[9] Cicero described his economic vision in *On Duties*, in which he observed that friendship and the quest for knowledge would bring harmony and peace, protect property, and produce a just society based on political service, affection, kindness, and liberty. And, as noted, good morals would drive a healthy market, allowing ethical people to make exchanges in confidence. Trust, added Cicero, was a mechanism that freed up trade. Historically, British liberal philosophers influenced the thinking of economists in particular. It is,

[7] Russell, B. (1979) *A History of Western Philosophy*. London: Unwin, 577–578.

[8] Ibid., 22.

[9] Soll, J. (2022) *Free Market; The History of An Idea*. New York: Basic Books, 17. Soll apparently could not resist the temptation of sharing with his readers that the meaning of cicero is chick pea.

therefore, no surprise that economic liberalism is closely associated with Adam Smith, and, somewhat later, John Stuart Mill (1806–1873). What Smith and Mill had to say about economic liberalism is presented below.

Adam Smith

Long before Smith, St. Augustine had observed that God had created the world with his ***invisible hand***: 'God's hand' is his power, and God achieves visible results by invisible means. Professor of philosophy and history, Jacob Soll, concludes: 'This was not yet Adam Smith's invisible hand, but it made clear that a higher power could regulate wealth.'[10]

Cicero's ideas about the market were different from Smith's, whose economic philosophy was inspired by Enlightenment philosophers, as elaborated in his famous *An Inquiry into the Nature and Causes of the Wealth of Nations* (1776). Smith argued that economic self-interest would not just serve market participants but also society at large. According to Helena Rosenblatt, Smith 'favoured allowing every man to pursue his own interest his own way ***upon the liberal plan of equality, liberty and justice***. Smith's 'liberal plan'... was about not only freedom but also generosity and reciprocity.'[11] Liberalism's economic dimension strongly drew on the thought of Adam Smith.

Now, who was this exceptional man Adam Smith? He was a lifelong bachelor who lived for quite some time with his mother in Kirkcaldy, Scotland. Smith was a popular and dedicated teacher, but at the same time notoriously absentminded.[12] He became a tutor to a young duke and accompanied him on a grand tour of France and Switzerland where he met the encyclopaedist d'Alembert, as well as Turgot, Voltaire, and Quesnay. After his return to Scotland, he settled in Kirkcaldy and wrote there *The Wealth of Nations*. Well before *The Wealth of Nations*, Smith had published *The Theory of Moral Sentiments* (1759), which he erroneously believed was his most influential work, although this work contributed to the inclusion of the moral dimension in classical liberalism.

[10] Ibid., 38.

[11] *The Lost History of Liberalism*, 34.

[12] 'On one occasion he descended into his garden clad only in a dressing gown and, falling into a reverie, walked fifteen miles before coming to.' Source: Heilbroner, R. (1995) *The Worldly Philosophers; The Lives, Times and Ideas of the Great Economic Thinkers*. London: Penguin Books, 45. 'On another occasion, he apparently fell into a tanning pit while anima-

Smith observed that economic actions of individuals, based on self-interest would produce the best results for society. Unhindered by government intervention, the market mechanism ensured that there was equilibrium between supply and demand. *The Wealth of Nations* presented a system of prefect liberty.[13] As mentioned, Smith introduced ***the invisible hand***, which to date remains central to the discussion of how markets operate.[14] Samuel Bowles, Professor Emeritus at the University of Massachusetts, provides a broader description of Smith's invisible hand:

> … his reasoning about the invisible hand led to something important: a mechanism (or more accurately, a set of them) albeit imperfect, for directing self-interest to public ends through a combination of competitive exchanges of privately held property and public policies aimed at getting the prices right where markets failed to do this.[15]

As for wealth creation, Smith argued that this would be brought about through the division of labour-specialization in other words.[16] Efficiency

tedly discussing free trade.' Source: Buchholz, T. (1999) *New Ideas from Dead Economists: An Introduction to Modern Economic Thought*. London: Penguin Books, 14.

[13] Smith felt that economics could be studied like physics and chemistry, by breaking down human behaviour into a small number of fundamental forces and modelling how individuals and organizations interact in such an environment.

[14] 'In Hayek's view, classical economists' greatest accomplishment was to recognize that a mechanism exists that coordinates economic activity. The mechanism did not have to be invented, and it was not the result of deliberate planning. Rather, it arose spontaneously as the unintended consequence of the actions of many individuals. The mechanism is what Adam Smith referred to with the famous metaphor the invisible hand.' Source: Caldwell, B. (2004) *Hayek's Challenge; An Intellectual Biography of F.A. Hayek*. Chicago: The University of Chicago Press, 197.

[15] Bowles, S. (2016) *The Moral Economy; Why Good Incentives Are No Substitute for Good Citizens*. New Haven: Yale University Press, 221.

[16] To show how powerful specialization really is, Thomas Thwaites's attempt to build a toaster himself from scratch underscores the point: 'Thwaites obtained iron ore from a disused mine in England, copper from a mine in Wales, and mica from a mountain in Scotland. When a home blast furnace failed to make steel, he resorted to smelting iron ore in his microwave. The plastic casing came from smelting down garbage. In the end, Thwaites's toaster experiment took nine months. ….Thwaites toaster was about 5000 times costlier than if he had bought one at his local retailer. …When Thwaites plugged his toaster in, it

would be the result of specialization, increasing the quantity of production while decreasing the price of each product, and so enhancing opportunities for market exchange. This specialization would also occur on a macro level between sectors of the economy, and also between nations, increasing domestic and international trade.

Regarding the role of government—in his words 'the duties of the sovereign'—Smith's universe includes government which had its proper function to fulfil. He maintained that, with a few exceptions, such as providing for national defence and making sure that laws are properly enforced, government should confine itself to clearing away outmoded conventions that prevent competitive markets from operating. Smith, perhaps ironically, observed that he had never known much good done by those who affected trade for the public good. He, however, added one more 'duty': Government-sponsored health and education, as they were 'in the highest degree advantageous to a great society'.[17]

Smith was concerned about the encroachment of government. But at the same time he was tolerant of government intervention in reducing poverty. He argued that when government regulation was in support of the workmen, it was always just and equitable. Smith had a soft spot for the poor. He wrote: 'No society can surely be flourishing and happy, of which the far greater part of the members are poor and miserable.'[18] Smith was, by and large, in favour of low tax rates, arguing that persons had to contribute, as nearly as possible, in proportion of their abilities. It was not unreasonable that the rich should contribute to the public expense, not just in proportion to their revenue, but something more.

In sum, Smith's economy is, above all, a self-regulating mechanism, in which the government plays a limited—yet important—part, stimulating a conducive business environment, providing universal education, reducing poverty, minimising wasteful activity, and erecting and maintaining public works and public institutions. Smith was driven by his *liberal plan* of social equality, economic liberty, and legal justice.

lasted five seconds before it began melting down.' Source: Leigh, A. (2024) *How Economics Explains the World; A Short History of Humanity*. New York: Mariner Books, 7.

[17] Smith, A. (2003) *The Wealth of Nations*. New York: Bantam Classics, 916.

[18] Ibid., 110–111. As for liberalism and the poor, Deirdre McCloskey once observed that the simplest case for liberalism is the very vulgar one of enrichment of the poor.

Economic Growth Taking Off

The Industrial Revolution turbocharged economic growth. Once economic growth took off, urbanization ensued and, gradually, a middle class emerged with commercial interests and property to protect.[19] The need to free markets from unnecessary control and other obstacles was more and more felt. Government's role became broader, as it was expected to ensure freedom of trade and, inspired by Locke, to protect property rights. The discipline of economics took shape, as Andrew Leigh observes.[20] Liberalism's economic philosophy promoted—in line with Smith—free markets, while enabling individuals to benefit from the exchange of goods. Its philosophy gradually evolved roughly between the sixteenth and seventeenth century, propelled by a remarkable number of technological inventions that spawned the Industrial Revolution. Economic liberalism of the eighteenth century, and especially the nineteenth century, 'produced a massive explosion of economic betterments for ordinary people.'[21] This was the case in the long run. It took the gains from the Industrial Revolution a surprising long time to reach British workers. For example, by 1830, half a century after its start, real wages had hardly grown.[22] During the nineteenth century, a modern global liberal order became firmly established.

Sustained economic growth also fed the wish to learn more to satisfy human curiosity. Universities were established throughout Europe, promoting study of the natural sciences and liberalism's philosophy, eclipsing traditional subjects such as theology, grammar and eloquence. Adam Smith, fellow-philosopher David Hume (1711–1776), and other like-minded scholars promoted liberal ideas of freedom and toleration.

[19] The best way of understanding the industrial revolution, argues economist Robert Allen, is as a set of interlocking revolutions: 'English agriculture was highly productive.....Because fewer people were required to produce food, England experienced an 'urban revolution', with one-quarter of the population living in cities in 1750. Urbanisation, in turn, fuelled a 'commercial revolution': a product of the dense social networks in London and other English cities.' Allen R. (2017) *The Industrial Revolution: A Very Short Introduction*. Oxford: Oxford University Press, 4–7.

[20] *How Economics Explains the World*, 8.

[21] McCloskey, D. (2019) Fukuyama was Correct: Liberalism Is the Telos of History. In: *Journal of Contextual Economics*, 288. On the same page McCloskey adds: 'Under liberalism it turned out that the common people contained a multitude of gifts for us all, from the mechanical harvester to the modern novel.'

[22] Leigh, A. (2024) *How Economics Explains the World*, 64–65.

Hume and Smith shared a number of economic principles. However, the difference between them is that Smith presented a comprehensive theory, while Hume's contribution to classical economics was limited. He argued that wealth does not consist of money but of commodities, and that the amount of money in circulation should be kept related to the amount of goods in the market. In addition, he observed that a low rate of interest was a symptom, not of superabundance of money, but of booming trade. In line with Ricardo's ideas about international trade, Hume felt that each nation had special advantages of raw materials, climate, and skill, so that a free interchange of products would be mutually beneficial. He also welcomed development beyond an agricultural to an industrial economy as a precondition of any but the barer forms of civilization.

The End of Liberalism?

Returning to the 1848 upheavals, the sentiment was that liberalism was done for. The question was: What had liberals done wrongly? In Europe, a general opinion gradually emerged that the underlying problem was *moral*—the population needed to acquire *character*! On the opposite coast of the Channel, the popular opinion among British thinkers was that if Britain had avoided revolution, it was in large part due to its national character—a journalist exclaimed: 'Thank God! We are Saxons.'[23]

Liberalism was not defeated. On the contrary, in Britain it made a comeback. Smith's economic liberalism caught on, and the Industrial Revolution triggered unprecedented economic growth. In 1859, the British Liberal party was created, in which the Whigs (to which Locke belonged) were influential. The party was in favour of dismantling aristocratic privileges, monopolies, and vested interests. Their proposed moderate political reforms invited entrepreneurs and manufacturers to join the party, as their interest was the promotion of free trade. Needless to say, large landowners, who would not have yet made up their minds, joined the ranks of the Conservative party. Radical reformers at the time, in particular Richard Cobden (1804–1865), were against government interference with trade, while defending free trade and internationalism. Cobden

[23] *The Lost History of Liberalism*, 143.

was a globalist *avant la lettre*.[24] However, complete free trade never really materialized as there was always a need for different sorts of government regulation.

John Stuart Mill

John Stuart Mill (1806–1873) was without doubt a champion of liberalism and, in particular, liberty. As a philosopher he is best known for his liberalism, his contributions to utilitarianism, and progressive ideas about women's rights. Mill also published a popular economics textbook. Later in life, he warmed to socialist ideas.

Feminist Liberalism

The British Liberal party influenced liberal political theory. But what about democracy? The development of genuine democracy in Britain started roughly around the middle of the nineteenth century. Women, however, remained excluded from voting. Mary Wollstonecraft (1759–1797) was the pioneer of liberal feminism, expanding liberalism to include women in the political domain of liberal society. Thanks to her and the actions of Mill and his wife Harriet Taylor, as well as British Suffragettes, women received full voting rights. As of 1918, women could be elected to Parliament. And a year later, women's voting rights were enacted.

In 1866, Mill was the first MP to call for women to be given the right to vote. Mill observed that what was called the nature of women was an eminently artificial thing—the result of forced repression in some directions, and unnatural stimulation in others. He argued that gender equality would be the best way to achieve, in utilitarian terms, 'the greatest good for the greatest number'.

Deirdre McCloskey argues that there still is a grave problem of subordination of women. She admits though that it would be strange

(*continued*)

[24] Cobden was above all an *enfant terrible*. He once set the landlords of England aghast with his discovery that farming was 'business' and that those who were broke must clear out. Source: Polanyi, K. (2001) *The Great Transformation; The Political and Economic Origins of Our Time*. Boston: Beacon Press, 192.

(continued)
to deny that there has been significant progress. Liberal feminists aim to eradicate all barriers to gender equality, as these barriers deprive the individual of rights and freedoms guaranteed by a liberal social order. Liberal feminists attack prejudice, such as the idea that women would be less intellectually and physically capable than men, resulting in discrimination against women in academia and the private sector.

According to feminist philosopher Rosemarie Tong, liberal feminists believe that 'female subordination is rooted in a set of customary and legal constraints that block women's entrance to, and success in, the so-called public world.'[25]

Since the 1980s, equity feminism emerged as a modern manifestation of liberal feminism, which can be characterized as a moral doctrine about equal treatment that makes no commitments regarding open empirical issues in psychology or biology.

His father, James Mill, was a Scottish philosopher, historian, and economist. John Stuart was a precocious child. At the age of three he was taught Greek. By the time he was ten, he could read Plato with ease, and two years later he started studying scholastic logic. At the age of 13, he was introduced to the works of Adam Smith and David Ricardo. No wonder he contemplated suicide when he was twenty years of age. However, the poems of William Wordsworth, and having met his spouse-to-be Harriet Taylor, helped him to enjoy beauty again and compassion for others. Mill worked more than twenty years for the East India Company. He was a Member of Parliament (MP) for the Liberal party. Before he died in 1873, he accepted to be Bertrand Russell's godfather.

In *On Liberty* (1859), Mill distinguished between self-regarding and other-regarding actions. The self-regarding actions were those with which no one had a right to interfere. Regarding other-regarding actions, Mill had this to say: The only purpose for which power can be rightfully exercised over any member of a society against his will is to prevent harm to

[25] Tong, R. (1989) *Feminist thought: A comprehensive Introduction*. London: Routledge, Chap. 1.

others. Intervention is justified only when other-regarding actions were detrimental to the interests of other members of a society. Mill also defended freedom of thought, speech and association, reflective of a decent open society.

He encouraged individual development of men and, quite exceptional at the time, women. Individuality was also the route to cultivating character. He proposed that a social, political, and cultural environment be created in which individual growth would flourish. Each person was unique, observed Mill. The diversity of individuals (including eccentrics) would not disrupt but rather enrich social life.[26]

In his *Principles of Political Economy, With Some of Their Applications to Social Philosophy* (1848), Mill argued that causal claims in economics seldom express universal regularities; he rather called them tendencies. As a result, laws in economics are at best tendency laws.[27] Mill believed that free markets could create economic equilibrium, provided measures were taken to improve the poor's living standards. Mill's early economic philosophy revolves around free markets. But he accepted interventions in the economy, such as taxation on alcohol, if there were sufficient grounds for them. Regarding taxation, young Mill defended equality of taxation, implying equality of sacrifice. He argued that progressive taxation was a mild form of robbery. Inheritance should, however, be taxed, said Mill, as a utilitarian society would agree that everyone should be equal one way or the other. Hence, receiving inheritance would put one ahead over the other unless taxed on the inheritance. Later in life, Mill adjusted his taxation proposals, so as to make a tax system helpful in alleviating poverty. He 'took for granted that state action would rectify durable inequalities.'[28] He maintained his idea of an inheritance tax, but added a fairly assessed income tax and taxes to restrict sumptuary consumption.

Mill was not a free trader *pur sang*; he was a *middle way* liberal in which laissez faire *and* socialist principles were combined. Influenced by Harriet

[26] Nowadays, Mill's opinion would, I believe, raise eyebrows, since the emergence of identity politics, and societies becoming more individualistic, have not necessarily contributed to social cohesion.

[27] 'Tendency laws are statements about regularities. However, they are not statements about regularities as they occur actually or empirically but rather about regularities that would occur if there were no interferences.' Source: Reiss, J. (2013) *Philosophy of Economics; A contemporary Introduction*. London: Routledge, 98.

[28] Snyder, T. (2024) *On Freedom*. London: The Bodley Head, 257.

Taylor, Mill developed a liking of socialist ideas and adjusted the contents of *Principles of Political Economy* accordingly. For example, capitalist businesses should be replaced by workers' cooperatives. The wage system, as he knew it, should be abolished in favour of a co-operative wage system. His change of philosophy was certainly also inspired by the prevalence of poverty in nineteenth-century industrial Britain. He observed that poverty was a failure of inadequate social arrangements.

But Mill was not an all-out socialist. He argued that socialism would destroy the competitive spirit of capitalism. Surely, Mill was an egalitarian, be it from the vantage point of equal opportunity. He said that it was the role of government to establish both social and economic policies that would promote equality of opportunity. He also valued the meritocracy principle.

Locke had argued that individual property should be respected. Mill underscored that individual property was the primary and fundamental institution. He believed that all individuals must start on equal terms, with a fairly even division of the instruments of production among all members of society. Once each member had an equal amount of individual property, each one must be left to his or her own exertion and not to be interfered with by the state. Education allowed people to develop into fully informed citizens, having the tools to improve their condition and, in addition, make fully informed electoral decisions. It was through education, Mill argued, that a person could become a full participant within representative democracy.

Mill the Utilitarian

Besides a liberal, Mill was also a utilitarian, which he transformed from a pleasure seeking doctrine into one based upon the permanent interest of people seeking improvement. Jeremy Bentham (1748–1832) and Henry Sidgwick (1838–1900) were other prominent utilitarians; together they were the so-called 'hedonists'. Betham was the most famous utilitarian, including his much-quoted happiness principle: Public policy should aim at providing 'the greatest aggregate happiness of the greatest number.' Betham argued that if one has a choice, one should prefer the outcome that produces that greatest good for the greatest number of people. Needless to say, utilitarianism's key term is utility. Utilitarianism maintains that the distribution of goods is just if it maximizes aggregate utility. But, again, what about the plight of the poor? If people's utility functions are decreasing, utilitarians favour a redistribution from the affluent to the poor.[29] It was the task of social reformers to change the legal framework and other crucial institutions (including prisons for example), to promote the well-being of all *individuals* in a society.

Summing up, Mill is the philosopher who best represents the internal contradictions of nineteenth-century free-market thought, in which belief in the productive capacities of free markets ought to be balanced by the government's role in promoting social reforms to create a more just economic system. Mill contributed to liberal thought by combining elements of classical liberalism with what later became known as new liberalism.

A Social New Dimension of Liberalism

During the nineteenth century, liberalism flourished in Britain. Urbanization and the rapid development of economic liberalism brought about positive and not so positive results. These not so positive results prompted Karl Marx (1818–1883) to develop his philosophy. The unacceptable result was the very poor material conditions of factory workers. Karl Polanyi observed that not until 1834 a competitive labour market was established in England. He concluded that industrial capitalism as a social system cannot have existed before that year.[30] Liberal thinkers found their inspiration from social reformers, such as the wealthy industrialist Robert Owen (1771–1858). He wrote about a new social system that, he hoped, would replace the current system that caused hardship for the poor.[31]

A new dimension of liberalism was in the making, advocating more government intervention on behalf of the poor. These liberal thinkers called for the state to take action to eliminate poverty and to limit

[29] The utilitarian approach, formalized in the theorems of neoclassical welfare economics, is to calculate social welfare on the basis of the aggregate utility of the composite individuals within a given population. Subsequently, policy proposals can then be judged on the basis of predicted net gains, or losses, in social welfare, following from different interventions.

[30] *The Great Transformation*, 87.

[31] More on Robert Owen is described in Chap. 4.

excessive inequality in the distribution of wealth—they developed new liberalism.

British philosopher Thomas Hill Green (1836–1882) introduced a new conception of liberty: *Positive* liberty. He rejected the idea that human beings were only driven by self-interest, emphasizing instead the complex circumstances involved in the evolution of human's moral character. Green argued that human beings were quite capable of re-assessing their life plans.[32]

But how could the poor possibly fulfil their duties to society given their miserable conditions? Green argued that appropriate measures ought to be taken, including sanitary laws, factory inspections and, as Mill and Smith before him had proposed, public education. The state, Green concluded, had to create the conditions to help bring all this about.

He paved the way for left-leaning liberals by stating that personal development and interdependence were complementary aspects of the *common good*. In other words, society is an organic whole in which all individuals had a duty to promote the common good. Russell commented about Green: 'T.H. Green, for example, was a Liberal but an idealist.'[33] Leonard Hobhouse (1864–1929), professor of sociology at the University of London, and John Hobson (1858–1940), economist and social scientist, were instrumental in further developing this new liberalism.

Regarding the central position of the individual in liberalism, had that idea been given up? By comparing society with the human body, Hobson argued that a living body (i.e., society) was only healthy when every individual part of it (i.e., the individual) was healthy as well. Hobson then returned the attention to the individual: It was therefore in the interest of the individual *and* society to cultivate personal well-being.

[32] Herbert Asquith, about to become the British Liberal prime minister, who attended Green's lectures, reacted sceptically to Green's last message by commenting: 'I believe in the right of every man face to face with the State to make the best of himself and subject to the limitation that he does not become a nuisance or a danger to the community to make less than the best of himself. Source: Freeden, M. (2015) *Liberalism; A Very Short Introduction*. Oxford: Oxford University Press, 97.

[33] *A History of Western Philosophy*. London: Unwin, 585.

Earlier than Keynes's under-consumption insight, Hobson argued that, as a result of unequal distribution of income, the poor had insufficient income to survive in dignity. Their consequent under-consumption created economic crises, and personal misery. Hobson blamed imperialism for this sorry situation, as the wealthy invested in overseas projects, exploiting the political control of British colonies. Keynes explained under-consumption as the consequence of (i) mass unemployment, resulting in a drop in aggregate demand, and (ii) the failure of the government to fill the demand gap.[34]

Hobhouse took inspiration from evolution. He observed that evolutionary development replaced competition with, as he called it, rational sociability. Human beings were the first product of the evolutionary process that could take charge of their own evolution. The end-result would not just free individuals but also create a harmonious community, overseen by a benevolent democratic state. Social reform would help to bring this utopian result about. He argued that socialism served to complete rather than to destroy liberal ideals.

Hobhouse viewed the community as a producer of social goods—the main good being the well-being of the people. He broadened J.S. Mill's emphasis on human development to include ethical awareness and a deliberate interdependence among people; in other words, he connected the individual with his or her social environment. He was also a supporter of

[34] Word has it that, initially, Keynes was not impressed by Hobson's insight in under-consumption. Later, he adjusted his opinion and appreciated Hobson's insight, although Hobson's had a different cause than Keynes's, as elaborated in Keynes, J. M. (1964) *The General Theory of Employment, Interest and Money*. Orlando: Harcourt Brace, on pp. 364–371. From this text, one learns that Hobson was a heterodox economist, shunned by his opponents who were all strong adherents of classical economics. It is in this light no wonder that Hobson wrote *The Physiology of Industry* together with A.F. Mummery, who was not an economist but an industrialist. Hobson explained how he came into contact with Mummery. Then Hobson made a funny observation: 'My intercourse with him [Mummery; PdH] I need hardly say, did not lie in the physical plane.' In their book, the authors presented under-consumption. Keynes observed on p. 365 of *The General Theory* that 'the publication of this book marks, in a sense, an epoch in economic thought.' Keynes then showed how significant and well-founded the authors' criticisms and intuitions about classical economics were.

the idea of the right to work and to a living wage, supported by unemployment and health insurance (which the Liberal government of Lloyd George introduced in 1911). The state was there to redistribute material goods to the disadvantaged members of society.

In short, new liberalism brought moral considerations back into liberalism. Hobhouse and Hobson contributed to the transformation of the Liberal party's politics. New liberals saw individual liberty as something achievable, however, under favourable social and economic conditions. They argued that poverty and ignorance could only successfully be addressed through a welfare-oriented interventionist state.

Liberal economic policies had produced a dramatic improvement of the economic condition of ordinary people. Meanwhile, in the course of the nineteenth century, socialism and trade unions became established actors in the political arena. The more the labour market contorted the lives of the workers, the more they demanded for the vote. Gradual granting of political rights to the working class ensued, giving them a voice. The British Labour party entered Westminster in 1906. In other European countries, comparable developments took place. In 1897, for example, the Dutch labour party became represented in parliament.

Social reform proposals became visible in new liberalism. They boiled down to government improving the social conditions of the working class. New liberals saw social emancipation as the extension of liberty. Hence, a new notion, not just of individual utility but also of *social* utility became the norm. By the turn of the nineteenth century, the working class was an influential factor in the state, The trading classes, on the other hand, whose sway over the legislature went no longer unchallenged, became quite conscious of the political power involved in their leadership in industry.

The gradually created global liberal order became firmly established during the second half of the nineteenth century when the first wave of globalization emerged, also known as the *Belle Epoque*. However, this prosperous period abruptly ended when, in 1914, the Great War broke out. The success of liberal economic policies apparently could not prevent it.

In sum, free markets enabled people to exchange their goods, and doing so contributed to public benefit. Liberal economic policies promoted economic growth a great deal. Once sustained economic growth ensued, its positive, but also its negative effects became visible. Regarding the latter, liberal thinkers proposed new ideas underscoring interdependence and government providing welfare.—new liberalism emerged.

Part III How Liberalism Fared After the Great War

Russell said that the stages in the evolution of ideas have not been solely due to the inherent movement of ideas; they have been governed by external circumstances and the reflection of these circumstances in human emotions.[35] Political and economic circumstances in the world influenced ideas of liberal thinkers; but also the other way round. These developments sometimes undermined the popularity of liberalism, while during other times, as we shall see, they inspired thinkers to broaden liberalism's philosophy, offering ideas and policies to address the challenges involved.

The Great War created the dividing line between the nineteenth century and the twentieth century. Communism in practice emerged, first in Russia in 1917. Former empires collapsed; the liberal order of the past century required urgent rethinking and, above all, addressing political and economic instability.

Once the *Belle Epoque*, and the subsequent Great War were over, liberalism became under threat, strengthening calls for more state control and for alternative political systems. Authoritarian philosophies inspired fascist political parties and Marxism-inspired communist parties. They replaced traditional liberal-minded parties in various European countries, such as Russia, Austria, Germany, Italy, and Spain.

Marxism

Adam Smith established the basis of classical economics, consisting of liberal notions, such as a fair and free allocation of resources through the efficient functioning of the market mechanism. Smith called it the ***natural order*** of freedom and justice. Karl Marx rejected Smith's natural order, criticizing the vey principles of classical liberalism and its consequences at the time, ranging from poverty, unemployment, and pure misery.

Marx's theory is, as we know, elaborated in *Das Kapital* (*Capital*); the first scientific analysis of capitalism and its collapse. *Capital's* contents can be summarized in two propositions:

(*continued*)

[35] *A History of Western Philosophy*, 618.

(continued)

(i) The conditions of production are the fundamental determinants of social structures, and
(ii) The forms of production themselves have a logic of their own; i.e., they change according to necessities inherent in them so as to produce their successors by their own working.

Marx argued that economic activity resulted in the *verelendung* (immiseration) of the workers. Economic relations were being dictated by who had the political and economic power. Competition would not result in a just and fair distribution of profits. Instead, capitalists needed to invest more and more to survive. Workers' wages stagnated at best—In the end workers would end up in misery.

Marx wondered: What was the good of industrial development, what was the good of all technological innovations, toil, and population movements if, after half a century of industrial growth, the condition of the masses was still just as miserable as before? But there was hope, professed Marx. He presented a just and egalitarian alternative to exploitative capitalism. In short, Marxism projects a *utopian* society.

Despite some positive analyses of Marx's comprehensive theory,[36] his projections proved to be wrong.[37] in addition, Marx neglected

(continued)

[36] For example, Part I of Joseph Schumpeter's *Capitalism, Socialism and Democracy* (1942) deals with the Marxian doctrine. Schumpeter admired Marx because he was able to give hope to millions of people: Marx promised them utopia. No wonder Marxism evolved into a near-religious cult. Moreover, what distinguished Marx from other economists was that he recognized the importance of the role of social classes. Sen also appreciates some aspects of Marx's thinking: 'I would argue that some of the most fruitful uses of Marx's ideas in our world today—the reach of coherent description, the relevance of objective illusion, the plurality of distributive goals, the dual role of ideas and material conditions—have to draw on his general reflections, sometimes even passing observations, that he aired and very briefly illustrated, often without pursuing them further.' Source: Sen, A. (2021) *Home in the World; A Memoir*. London: Penguin Random House, 222.

[37] Just one example. Marx predicted that wages would go down. However, in the last third of the nineteenth century, wages began to increase: The improvement in the purchasing power of workers spread everywhere, and this changed the situation radically.

(continued)

the possibility of durable technological progress and steadily increasing productivity, which is a force that serves as a counterweight to the process of accumulation and concentration of private capital as presented in *Capital.*[38]

Marxist *praxis* (as Marxists would say) as applied in e.g., the Soviet Union was far more radical and more logically consistent.[39] Private returns on capital were eliminated and private ownership of the means of production was abolished, including land and buildings as well as industrial, financial, and business capital. Some historians characterized what the soviets did as the most remarkable political experiment in modern times, which impressed quite a number of newly independent developing countries at the time.

What was forgotten, however, is that private property and the market economy do not only serve to ensure the domination of capital over those who have nothing to sell but their labour power. Both private property and the market also play a useful role in coordinating economic activities of millions of individuals. In the end, it proved to be not so easy to do without them. Re-adjusting is something that liberal democracies do much better than totalitarian systems. Timothy Snyder observes that 'after 1968 [when the Soviet Union invaded Czechoslovakia; PdH] no one in power cared about Marxism. The dream of a communist future gave way to endorsement of the status quo, which soviet leader Leonid Brezhnev called 'really existing socialism''[40]

(*continued*)

[38] Thomas Piketty observes that Marx's accumulation principle of infinite accumulation 'contains a key insight, as valid for the study of the twenty-first century as it was for the nineteenth.' Source: Piketty, T. (2014) *Capital in the Twenty-First Century*. Cambridge: The Belknap Press of Harvard University Press, 10.

[39] 'Convinced that history could take only one course, they [the Bolsheviks; PdH] believed that they had to drive the USSR through an imitation of capitalism before they could create socialism.' Source: *On Freedom*, 123.

[40] Ibid., 72.

(continued)

In sum, Marxism in practice demonstrated that it simply does not work; it created massively unproductive economies, private initiative was not tolerated, the majority of the population remained poor, and Marxist-inspired societies were led by brutal autocrats.[41]

The Great Depression of the 1930s, forced British and American liberal philosophers and economists alike, to come up with responses. This they did; they responded twice. The first response came from new liberalism, which—as noted—emerged in the nineteenth century as social liberalism, when social reformers started campaigning for the improvement of economic and social conditions of the working class. They asked: If individuals could maximize their well-being, why could this laudable principle also not apply to societies as well? We already saw that Hobhouse viewed the community as a producer of social goods—the main good being the well-being of the people. Hobson analysed the individual as an integral part of the body of society. It was therefore in the interest of the individual *and* society to cultivate personal well-being.

During the 1930s, the time was more than ripe for the conception—and introduction—of social welfare policies! In the Democratic and Republican parties in America, new liberalism's proposals were building up. Their intellectual leader included Herbert Croly (1869–1930), who took inspiration of what Hobhouse had proposed at the time. Croly was one of the creators of the Progressive Party, making Theodore Roosevelt their tribune.[42]

[41] In Vasily Grossman's monumental novel *Life and Fate* (1960), written during Stalin's brutal rule, the following text is not just moving, it also reflects Stalin's iron grip: 'I wanted since childhood to open a shop, so that any folk could come in and buy. Along with it would be a snack-bar, so that the customers could have a bit of roast meat, if they like, or a drink. I would serve them cheap, too. I'd let them have real village food. Baked potato! Bacon fat with garlic! Sauerkraut! .... Leather chairs, so that the lice don't breed. The Customer would sit and rest and be served. If I were to say this out loud, I'd have been sent straight to Siberia. And yet, say I, what harm would I do to people?' Quoted from Reiss, J. (2013) *Philosophy of Economics; A Contemporary Introduction*. London: Routledge, 262–263.

[42] Gerstle, G. (2022) *The Rise and Fall of the Neoliberal Order; America and the world in the Free Market Era*. Oxford: Oxford University Press, 81.

The second liberal response came from Keynes and President Franklin Delano Roosevelt. With the publication of *The General Theory* in 1936, Keynes revolutionized economics. He proposed a *mix* of liberal economic policies and government intervention that helped policy makers to end the Great Depression; this became one of the central notions of new liberalism (more on Keynes's new liberal ideas, see Chap. 5). Keynes remained all his life a (new egalitarian) liberal, while his major opponent Hayek had a conservative opinion about what liberalism meant in political and economic terms, also elaborated in Chap. 5.

President Roosevelt's New Deal, a wide-ranging economic *and* social stimulus package, was new liberalism in action, in which the state played a far larger part than conservative liberals would have liked. American philosopher John Dewey confirmed at the time that American liberalism had nothing whatsoever to do with laissez-faire, and never had.[43] It was a radical project, which was so effective that it became mainstream. Mellon Professor of American History at the University of Cambridge, Gary Gerstle, summarized well what the New Deal meant for labour and capital:

> A compromise between capital and labor had been foundational to the New Deal order. Labor had gained progressive taxation, social security, unemployment insurance, the right to organize, a national commitment to full employment, government backing for collective bargaining, and limits on the inequality between rich and poor. Capital had gained assurances that government would act to smooth out the business cycle, maintain a fiscal and monetary environment that would assure reasonable profits, and contain labor's power.[44]

Roosevelt remained though a staunch defender of the classical liberal principles of individual freedom and property rights.

Also in Britain measures were taken. In 1941, the government requested William Beveridge to develop proposals to alleviate poverty.[45] *The Beveridge Report* (1942) became the basis on which the British welfare state would be built. Inspired by new liberalism's philosophy, the welfare state was a liberal creation. Liberalism now also included an active and expanded role of the state.

[43] *The Lost History of Liberalism*, 261.

[44] *The Rise and Fall of the Neoliberal Order*, 146.

[45] Often his spouse Janet, an economist, is not mentioned as one of the report's authors.

Post-World War II

After the end of WWII, Keynesianism, in combination with post-war reconstruction and the introduction of Beveridge-inspired welfare policies, resulted in a *Golden Age* of rapid economic growth, the emergence of the welfare state, and allowing workers in the Global North to enter into the middle class. This golden age of controlled capitalism lasted roughly thirty years.

> 'It was the Keynesian advocacy of an interventionist state and regulated markets that gave liberalism its modern economic meaning: a doctrine of favouring a large, active government, regulation of industry, high taxes for the rich, and extensive social welfare programmes for all.'[46]

However, it was not sustainable. Stagflation, a toxic mix of sluggish growth, rapidly rising inflation and unemployed put an end to the *Trente Glorieuses*, as the French called this period.

John Rawls contributed greatly to liberal political philosophy when, in 1971, he published *A Theory of Justice*, which became a milestone, in furthering social contract theory. In his book, principles of justice are being applied in structuring a just and fair society. In 1974, Robert Nozick published *Anarchy, State and Utopia*, gaining academic respectability for his libertarian viewpoints. Inspired by Rawls's *Theory of Justice*, Sen developed the capability approach. Sen's main point is that it is not enough to be legally able to do something, but to have the real possibilities of doing it.

After stagflation had broken out in the early 1970s, a new breed of economists, in particular Hayek and Friedman(both known as *Masters of the Universe*[47]), grabbed the opportunity to bury Keynesianism. Instead, they promoted their neoliberal ideas of the free market, securing the efficient allocation of resources, and limiting government's role to a bare minimum. Their message was widely communicated by influential think tanks and news media, greatly influencing politics, initially in America and Great Britain.

[46] Steger, M, & Roy, R (2021) *Neoliberalism; A Very Sort Introduction*. Oxford: Oxford University Press, 10.

[47] Stedman Jones, D. (2012) *Masters of the Universe: Hayek, Friedman, and the British Neoliberal Politics*. Princeton: Princeton University Press.

Neoliberalism

Introduction

Neoliberalism is a particular form of free-market capitalism. It emerged after Keynesianism proved incapable of addressing stagflation. Neoliberals argued that crippling government regulation, excessive public spending, and high tariffs had been responsible for sharply rising inflation and unemployment, resulting in poor economic growth.

Neoliberalism's pejorative's meaning aside, the term includes a deregulated economy in which the national and global market function freely; government is limited; state enterprises are privatized; and personal advancement is promoted. Neoliberalism can be perceived as an economistic ideology. However, this does not capture all its aspects. For example, Michel Foucault's 'governmentality'[48] includes entrepreneurial values such as competitiveness, and self-interest. The term also encompasses individual empowerment and the devolution of central state power to smaller localized units. Neoliberal modes of governance encourage the transformation of bureaucratic mentalities into entrepreneurial identities where government workers see themselves as self-interested actors responsible to the market and contributing to the monetary success of slimmed-down state enterprise.[49]

Neoliberals are not a solid group sharing the same ideology. Neoliberalism appears in different varieties, reflective of its flexibility to adapt to the particular political and economic environment within which it is being implemented.

Despite its impressive achievements, such as lifting millions of the world's poor out of misery, neoliberalism not just created winners but also losers.

Its Origins

Neoliberalism's origins are European; Vienna was its birthplace. After the Great War had ended, Von Mises and Hayek developed much of what later became known as neoliberalism. They concluded that classical liberalism, and in particular laissez faire, had not been able to successfully relaunch Europe's economies after the Great War. 'The failure of liberalism is what

[48] Burchell, G., Gordon, C., & Miller, P. (1991). *The Foucault effect: Studies in Governmentality*. Chicago: The University of Chicago Press, 1–51.

[49] *Neoliberalism*, 13–14.

would make socialism, and later communism, one of the most prominent creeds of the twentieth century.'[50] As a counterforce, Mises and Hayek were looking for a sharper liberal doctrine, providing European economies a better future. They called this pronounced version of liberalism: neoliberalism.

Neoliberalismis quite different from new liberalism. The former emphasizes the advantages of competitive markets and personal advancement, much more than nourishing of citizens' well-being. As Freeden observes: 'Neoliberals subordinate social, political, and cultural spheres to a professed self-regulating economic market and their principles are supposed to inspire the ways all social activities are run.'[51] Government is only facilitator of national and global trade, rather than also deliverer of welfare or social justice. In other words, neoliberalism lacks new liberalism's social aspects. Freeden concludes that neoliberalism does not really belong to what broadly is understood by liberalism.

Greatly concerned about developments in the Soviet Union, the Colloque Lippmann, held in Paris in 1938, Mises and Hayek countered these concerns by concluding that neoliberalism would be the best way forward.[52] In 1947, neoliberalism found its intellectual base during the first meeting of the Mont Pèrelin Society, which was held in a mountain resort in Switzerland. Prospective members were expected to embrace market-based approaches to political economy. From Switzerland, the neoliberal gospel shifted to America, finding a welcome home at the University of Chicago. From there, Mises, Hayek (the latter had joined the ranks of this university) and Friedman persuasively and consistently introduced neoliberalism's blessings, including some libertarian edges, in political and public policy circles. Gerstle observes: '….neoliberals wanted to be seen as the creators of a disciplined 'thought collective' with the ability to unleash a singularly fresh and coherent liberal ideology on the

[50] *The Rise and Fall of the Neoliberal Order*, 80.

[51] *Liberalism*, 109.

[52] Water Lippmann (1889–1974) was an influential American journalist who argued that the march of human freedom was grounded in the progress of economic freedom. He also understood that enjoyment of liberty required a certain level of political and economic order.

world.'[53] Stiglitz argues that neoliberal economists constructed a theory to support their views, not surprisingly called neoclassical economics.[54]

As already mentioned, when stagflation had exposed the incapacity of Keynesian policies, neoliberals grabbed the opportunity to propose theirs. They observed that since the 1930s, government interventions had gone too far. However, how neoliberalism should precisely be defined, was a challenge. Gerstle notes that: '.... these Mont Pèrelin crusaders would never succeed in imparting to American neoliberalism a singular shape or meaning.'

Neoliberalism's near-global triumph and decline is described along the lines of its history in the United States. After all, America embraced neoliberalism most solidly and shared the doctrine with many countries around the world. Neoliberalism was also propagated by the IMF and World Bank. Both international institutions had adopted the Washington Consensus, whose conditions were forced upon mostly Latin American and African countries in need of financial support.[55] Latin America, for instance, experienced a so-called Lost Decade in the 1980s. In many countries the rapid influx and then outflow of capital under the policies of capital market and financial market liberalization led to repeated crises. In Africa, the Washington Consensus policies triggered a process of deindustrialization, deepening poverty, and a quarter century of near-zero growth in per capita income.[56]

To illustrate neoliberalism's American history, President Reagan's neoliberal policies and those of President Clinton are summarized, demonstrating that neoliberalism in practice has indeed no uniform interpretation. Finally, President Trump first term's distancing from neoliberalism is presented as well.

[53] *The Rise and Fall of the Neoliberal Order*, 73–74.

[54] *The Road to Freedom*, 29. My understanding of neoliberalism and neoclassical economics is that neoclassical economics constituted the basis on which neoliberalism was constructed.

[55] The ten key points of the Washington Consensus are: a guarantee of fiscal discipline, and a curb to budget deficit; a reduction of public expenditures; tax reform; financial liberalization; competitive exchange rates; trade liberalization; promotion of foreign direct investment; privatization of state enterprises; deregulation of the economy; and protection of property rights.

[56] *The Road to Freedom*, 34.

Neoliberalism in America

Several varieties circulated of American neoliberalism. Gerstle identifies various strategies of reform, or clusters of policy initiatives, each having evolved during the period between the first meeting of the Mont Pèrelin Society and the late 1960s. I summarize their respective key characteristics below:

(i) Ensuring the functioning of free markets through firm regulation of property and exchange, and the circulation of money and credit. All this required the intervention of a strong government;
(ii) the application of market principles not just to work and production, as well as income and consumption, but also to all areas of human endeavour;
(iii) the renewal of personal freedom as professed by classical liberalism at the time.[57]

No wonder neoliberalism attracted people from both sides of the political spectrum—not just the Right but also the Left. Apart from different interpretations, neoliberalism also includes paradoxes. Hayek, for example, argued that the establishment of a firm economic order was a prerequisite for the liberty of individuals from government.

Politically attractive elements of neoliberalism were turned into neoliberal policies by American President Ronald Reagan and British Prime Minister Margaret Thatcher. President Bill Clinton implemented policies that were not much different from Reagan's. Labour leader Tony Blair's 'Third Way' did the same in Britain, followed by other European centre-left leaders, such as Dutch Prime Minister Wim Kok, French Prime Minister Lionel Jospin, and German Chancellor Gerhard Schröder. Their political agenda was aimed at the liberation of markets and deregulation of state-regulated economies around the world; a notorious example of a non-Western country embracing neoliberalism was General Pinochet's Chile.

Reagan's Neoliberal Policies

Returning to the Reagan era, CEOs of wealthy American corporations funded neoliberal research institutes and think tanks such as the Heritage Foundation, the Cato Institute and the American Enterprise Institute. All

[57] *The Rise and Fall of the Neoliberal Order*, 88.

of them worked with the Reagan administration to promote Reagan's *supply-side economics.* It focused on the reduction of tax rates while ignoring budget deficits. Lower taxes, it was thought, would stimulate economic growth. This in turn would broaden the tax revenues base.[58] This assumption helped Reagan to cut taxes while continuing funding the popular (but not a part of the neoliberal 'playbook') Social Security and Medicare programs.[59] It should be noted that Reagan's welfare programme linked welfare and race. He publicized the idea of the 'welfare queen'—'a stereotype of Black women claiming tax dollars of hardworking white people to raise delinquent broods.'[60] The Reagan administration applied a strategy of discipline and punish: Expand police forces, increase the volume of arrests, and imprison convicted offenders for long periods of time.[61]

'Reagan's greatest political achievement was to reconcile a politics focussed on restoring white supremacy and godliness with his own neoliberal market orientation, with its emphasis on personal freedom and antagonism to the New Deal state...... Reagan, seemingly, had found a way to draw on conservative racial and religious fury to propel his anti-government, neoliberal agenda.[62]

Reaganomics also included more defence spending in his pursuit to win the Cold War, which he did.[63]

Another central theme of the Reagan administration was small government. Government can never help, it can only hurt—markets were the solution and government was the problem. Nonetheless, the federal government became bigger. The 1985 Gramm-Rudman-Hollings Deficit Reduction Initiative (GRH) included targets that would help eliminate the deficit by 1991.[64]

[58] George H. W. Bush cynically called it 'voodoo economics'.

[59] However, the tax cuts Reagan implemented in his first term resulted in heavy revenue shortfalls that had to be offset by increasing taxes on corporate profits in his second term. Reagan refused to cut down federal government's deficits. Later, this was successfully done by President Clinton.

[60] *On Freedom*, 138.

[61] *The Rise and Fall of the Neoliberal Order*, 130.

[62] Ibid., 119–120.

[63] In 1983, Ronald Reagan and Congress established the National Endowment for Democracy (NED), whose principal objective was to fight the spread of communism. NED's backers argue that it helped bring about an end to the cold war by highlighting the lack of democratic legitimacy in the Soviet Union. Elon Musk, DOGE's boss, stated: 'That evil organisation needs to be dissolved'. Source: *The Economist*, 22 February 2025, 32.

[64] GRH was widely discussed in policy circles in the Global North, zooming in on the dangers that excessive government deficits could have on the world economy.

Regarding regulatory reform, Reagan diminished a large number of regulatory powers of government organizations, such as the Environmental Protection Agency. As for deregulation, sectors such as communications, transportation and banking benefitted from them. For example, the Airline Deregulation Act allowed competitive bidding for route destinations, resulting in a true explosion in the number of airlines and fights, and hence a surge in corporate profits. But not all went well. Deregulation of the Savings and Loan industry (S&L) did not work out well. After 1987's Black Monday stock market crash, quite a number of S&Ls collapsed. Their bailout did cost American taxpayers over $100 billion.

Compared with the achievements of President Bill Clinton, Reagan's record on free trade is rather mixed. His administration's finetuning and adjustments of existing trade deals in the agricultural and high technology sectors were about all. On the other hand, Reagan supported strong protectionist policies against Japanese car makers—not quite fitting neoliberal ideas. However, Reagan promoted global free trade, through his involvement in three important agreements: GATT, the Uruguay Round, and from there, initiatives to establish the WTO. The same applied to the Free Trade Agreement with Canada. Clinton would broaden this agreement by including Mexico into the North American Free Trade Agreement (NAFTA).

What Came After Reagan

After having lost various presidential elections, the Democratic Party realized that some neoliberal ideas went down well with the electorate. The party embarked on formulating a different variety of neoliberalism. The Democratic Leadership Council (DLC), which Clinton had joined, was established to do just that—old politics had to give way to new realities. DLC wanted to distance the party from its past philosophy and, instead, embrace business, free markets and high tech. DLC was also prepared to move the Democratic Party closer to what Republicans thought about social policies and morals. This was best done, it was thought, by bringing the poor into the economic mainstream so as to free them from welfare dependence. The Democrats maintained their politics, however, of inclusion, equal rights, and full citizenship. It was now time to conclude: 'That a new generation of Democrats had begun adopting neoliberal principles as their own was a sure sign of this ideology's ascent.'[65]

[65] *The Rise and Fall of the Neoliberal Order*, 140.

The collapse of the Soviet bloc gave neoliberal philosophy a boost, legitimatizing the neoliberal doctrine. Word has it that at the time, Prime Minister Thatcher said that there was no alternative to neoliberalism. After the Soviet Union's collapse, President Clinton concluded that there was no future for a nation seeking to resist market forces.

The End of History

Indeed, the fall of the Berlin Wall in 1989, and subsequent collapse of the Soviet Union in 1991, triggered a sense of triumph among liberal philosophers, such as Fukuyama. In 1992, he published his bestseller *The End of History And The Last Man*[66] celebrating liberalism's victory. Liberalism had won the competition with communism.

A 'peace dividend' ensued, in combination with a period of globalized bliss. International trade, foreign direct investment, and global economic growth blossomed. Poor countries were catching up; some former Third World countries joined the ranks of emerging economies. The number of extremely poor people more than halved and more people than ever before gained access to health and education.

Returning to *The End of History And The Last Man*, the book's title invites the curious reader to wonder what Fukuyama would have meant with 'the end of history', and—even more intriguing—what about 'the last man'? He had already presented his arguments in his 1989 article in *The National Interest* entitled: The End of History, in which he observes:

> … a remarkable consensus concerning the legitimacy of liberal democracy as a system of government had emerged throughout the world over the past few years, as it conquered rival ideologies like hereditary monarchy, fascism, and most recently communism. I argued that liberal democracy may constitute the 'end point of mankind's ideological evolution' and the 'final form of human government', and as such constituted the 'end of history'. That is, while earlier forms of government were characterized by grave defects and irrationalities that led to their eventual collapse, liberal democracy was arguably free from such fundamental internal contradictions.[67]

Fukuyama quite boldly concludes that the ideal of liberal democracy could not be improved. However, in his recent work *Liberalism and its*

[66] Fukuyama, F. (992) *The End of History And The Last Man*. London: Penguin Books.
[67] *The End of History*, xi.

Discontents, he is more modest about liberalism's virtues, and addresses a couple of challenges, presented in part IV.

What about 'the last man'. Why had Fukuyama added 'the last man' to *The End of History's* title? In explaining, the author first introduces the notion of man's desire for recognition—a familiar part of the human personality. This was first described by Plato in *The Republic*: Besides desire and reasoning, human beings seek recognition of their own worth.

> Hegel saw this urge [the desire for recognition; PdH] as the driving force of the whole historical process. He asserted that history comes to an end, because the longing that had driven the historical process, i.e., the struggle for recognition, has now been satisfied in a society characterized by universal and reciprocal recognition. No other arrangement of human social institutions was better able to satisfy this longing, and hence no further progressive historical change is possible.[68]

The question is whether the desire for recognition, available to citizens of contemporary liberal democracies, would be satisfied? The Left would say that recognition would be incomplete because capitalism creates economic inequality. Liberal democracy, they argue, continues to recognize equal people unequally. A more powerful reaction comes from the Right, referring to Nietzsche's thinking, because the typical citizen of a liberal democracy was a 'last man' who, schooled by the founders of modern liberalism, gave up prideful belief in his or her superior worth in favour of comfortable self-preservation.

The question then is: Would this 'last man' be devoid of any striving or aspiration? And, I wonder, would this last man not be terribly dull and devoid of any ambition? Fukuyama adds: 'Might not the fear of becoming contemptible 'last men' not lead men to assert themselves in new and unforeseen ways, even to the point of becoming once again bestial 'first men' engaged in bloody prestige battles, this time with modern weapons?'[69]

At the end of the book, Fukuyama concludes that ultimately, history itself will vindicate its own rationality. It is doubtful whether we have

[68] Ibid., xviii.
[69] Ibid., xxiii.

reached this point, for despite the recent worldwide liberal revolution, the evidence available to us now concerning the direction into which developments are moving remains inconclusive. But is there the danger, wonders Fukuyama, 'that we will be happy on one level, but still dissatisfied with ourselves on another, and hence ready to drag the world back into history with all its wars, injustice, and revolution?[70] My conclusion is that in 1992, Fukuyama was sensible enough not to declare liberalism's ultimate victory, but at the most a temporary one.

The collapse of communism, opened the world to capitalist penetration, so to speak, leaving little to no space for ideologies other than neoliberalism. This was initially well understood by President Clinton, Prime Minister Blair and other political leaders. 'When all this unfolded, neoliberalism went from being a political movement to a political order.'[71]

Clinton's Neoliberal Record

President Clinton repealed the Glass-Steagall Act, and introduced the Financial Services Modernization Act (aka Gramm-Leach-Billey Act), allowing investment and commercial banks to merge.[72] In hindsight, this opened the door for the financial crisis of 2007–2008. The Telecommunications Act allowed Silicon Valley to capitalize on its technical innovations.[73] Clinton deregulated the economy significantly. Freeing up markets was the animating spirit of the Clinton administration. During his 1996 State of the Union Address, Clinton announced that 'Big government is over'. Government would be made more flexible and efficient—more business-like, so to speak.[74] In many ways, Clinton continued what Reagan had set in motion.

[70] Ibid., 312.

[71] *The Rise and Fall of the Neoliberal Order*, 149. When is the tipping point? 'The true test of a political order ….is when the opposition acquiesces to an order's ideological and policy imperatives.' Ibid., 156. In the case of the neoliberal doctrine, towards the end of the 1990s it appeared to be a force too powerful for anyone to stop.

[72] And opening the doors to the so-called 'financialization' of the economy.

[73] However, Martin Kitman, a media columnist, warned that the Telecommunications Act would bring a new generation of robber barons to life. He proved to be right.

[74] No wonder that the philosophy of New Public Management, promoted by Vice President Al Gore, went down very well among state bureaucracies. Its six core characteristics are: productivity, marketization, service, orientation, decentralization, and accountability for results.

Clinton slashed expenditures in the social sphere, promoting welfare-to-work policies instead, combining labour skills training and public assistance for the unemployed. He attempted to introduce moderate social welfare provisions in tandem with greater corporate responsibility. Meanwhile, Clinton's health care reform proposals had failed dramatically. The Clinton administration did not forget the plight of the working poor. It raised the national minimum wage and expanded the Earned Income Tax Credit for lower wage earners. Meanwhile, the federal government was downsized.

Regarding globalization, Clinton strove after the introduction of a socially conscious market globalism that would include the entire world on the way to a golden age of technological progress and prosperity.[75] He believed that a sustained expansion of the American economy depended on economic growth of the global economy, including the Third World's, and emerging economies in particular. Clinton wanted to bring this about, not by way of force but through strengthening commercial ties and through popular culture. As noted, Clinton made NAFTA possible, and he successfully helped to conclude the GATT-inspired Uruguay Trade Round, which in 1994 was finalized when the WTO was established and China was welcomed as a member country. Clinton was instrumental in preventing Russia from bankruptcy in using his influence to convince the IMF to provide Russia with a massive loan. Gerstle concludes that Clinton 'became the Democratic Eisenhower, America's neoliberal president par excellence.'[76] As mentioned before, Clinton carried through the neoliberal policies that Reagan had started.

To be successful and popular, a politician needs luck, and Clinton had luck. Around the middle of the 1990s, the combination of neoliberal fiscal and monetary policies worked out well. The US budget deficit went down, long-term interest rates dropped without weakening the dollar or pushing inflation up. America attracted capital from East Asia. Some of these countries, and a number of Latin American countries, pegged their currencies to the dollar. Meanwhile, Silicon Valley (including its startups) was booming. American consumers invested in computers, cars and real estate. In short, neoliberalism Clinton-style appeared to work quite well.

[75] *Neoliberalism*, 36.

[76] *The Rise and Fall of the Neoliberal Order*, 156. President Eisenhower, who in 1952 introduced major education, infrastructure, and research programs in ten country. Succeeded Harry Truman, as president, introduced major education, infrastructure and research programs, partly funded from a progressive tax regime.

Dissent

Nonetheless, the downsides of neoliberalism became gradually visible. An IMF paper has this to say: The benefits in terms of increased growth seem fairly difficult to establish when looking at a broad group of countries. Second, the costs in terms of increased inequality are prominent. Such costs epitomize the trade-off between the growth and equity effects of some aspects of the neoliberal agenda. Third, increased inequality in turn hurts the level of sustainability of growth. Even if growth is the sole or main purpose of the neoliberal agenda, advocates of that agenda still need to pay attention to the distributional effects.[77] Regarding inequality, the authors make an additional observation: 'The increase in inequality engendered by financial openness and austerity might itself undercut growth, the very thing that the neoclassical liberal agenda is intent on boosting.'[78]

Dissenters expose the growing imbalance of power and income between the rich and the poor. This happened despite the fact that aggregate incomes had grown substantially. However, in the Global North, trickle-down theory had not worked, nor the idea that economic growth would rise the tide which 'would lift all boats'.[79] Fukuyama observes in this vein, '.......there was a deeper problem with the underlying economic theory itself.'[80] Also, neoliberals took to a relaxed government attitude towards large corporations. Fukuyama comments in this connection that there is no reason why economic efficiency needs to trump all other social values.[81] He cites an inspiring experience in this vein:

> And yet, many societies can and do protect small producers at the expense of economic efficiency, because they believe that there are social goods other than consumer welfare. This has been done by France and Japan, for example, both of which sought to block the entry of American corporations into their markets. Would France be better off if its thousands of cafes were driven out of business by Starbucks?[82]

[77] Ostry, J., Loungani, P., Furceri, D. Neoliberalism: Oversold? In: *Finance and Development*, June 2016, 39.

[78] Ibid., 40–41.

[79] However, Branko Milanović demonstrated that the income gap between rich and poor countries had shrunk. Source: Milanović, B. (2016) *Global Inequality; A New Approach for the Age of Globalization*. Cambridge; The Belknap Press of Harvard University Press.

[80] *Liberalism and its Discontents*, 31.

[81] Ibid., 36.

[82] Ibid., 35.

Financialization helped usher in the Great Recession. In its wake, independent small entrepreneurs who used to work in the 'gig economy' experienced hardship; they lost their clientele. They belonged to the so-called 'precariat'. They could not any longer afford social security payments, let alone contribute to a pension fund. Many houses were foreclosed; scores of home owners could no longer afford rising mortgage bill.

Obama and Growing Dissent

The Obama administration also met with dissent. The Tea Party emerged, which included various dissenters, ranging from those opposing Obama's Affordable Care Act to his alleged disproportionate bailouts during the Great Recession. In fact, the Wall Street bailout casted a shadow over his presidency. Another current voiced opposition to economic inequality with ethno-racial resentment. The argument was that the Democratic Party allied itself with the black poor to win their votes (and assisting them after the elections) while ignoring the needs of the country's 'best' citizens, including blue collar workers who had lost their job. They blamed globalized trade bringing cheaper competing goods into the American market. This sentiment was later ably exploited by populist British politicians promoting Brexit, and Donald Trump, who did not like the globalist dimension of neoliberalism. Indeed, Trump demonstrated anti-globalist tendencies, preferring bilateral (trade) deals, favouring America's manufacturing sector. Gerstle summarizes Trump's philosophy:

> Trump's politics challenged neoliberalism's commitment to the free movement of goods and people across national boundaries, its celebration of the diversity of people, and its confidence in the wisdom of highly educated and highly cultured globalized elites. To neoliberalism, he increasingly counterposed an ethnonationalist populism that resonated with an aroused Tea Party base eager to refocus America's identity around whiteness, manufacturing, and a plebeian cultural style designed to offend the country's 'social betters'.[83]

Dissent also erupted from America's multiracial—mostly young—leftists. Outraged by the 2008–2009 financial crises, their leaders decided to occupy Wall Street. Their immediate impact was limited as they lacked a

[83] *The Rise and Fall of the Neoliberal Order*, 248.

clear strategy, nor a list of demands. But it opened the opportunity for left-leaning politicians and scholars to expose the downsides of neoliberalism, in particular the issue of widening inequality. As a result, independent left-leaning Senator Bernie Sanders and economist Thomas Piketty made their fame. Both promoted democratic socialism. However, dissent was not voiced by the Left only. For example, during the 2019 National Conservative Conference in Washington, DC, Oren Case, a fellow of the conservative Manhattan Institute, concluded that the market—neoliberal's ideal of the self-regulating market—does not work. Neoliberalism was not so self-sustaining as was believed. The widespread dissatisfaction with neoliberal policies as applied by Clinton and Obama, led to the election of Donald Trump.

President Trump Ended Neoliberalist Policies but Not Entirely

Trump won the 2016 presidential elections; Hillary Clinton had lost. The Democrats had failed to acknowledge the damage done to white and black workers by neoliberal-inspired policies. As we saw, dissent had already erupted before Trump entered the political arena. The neoliberal order was bruised. It had left too many people behind. It triggered more inequality, and resulted in loss of wealth for minority homeowners.

Trump's first presidency embraced some neoliberal policies, but not all. As Gerstle observes: 'But there were, in fact, two such programs issuing from the Trump administration: One pointed in the direction of maintaining the liberal order, the other in the direction of dismantling it.'[84] Deregulation and tax cuts were combined with attacks on free trade and immigration. NAFTA was scrapped and replaced by the United States-Mexico-Canada Agreement (USMCA), however, retaining much of the original framework. Trump withdrew from the Trans-Pacific Partnership (TPP); but at the same time his administration offered many TPP members bilateral or multilateral trade deals.

Another neoliberal theme, i.e., tax cuts, was applied by the Trump administration. For example, the Tax Cuts and Jobs Act lowered the income tax rate, including the top marginal rate from 39.6% to 38%. It increased the standard deduction and family tax credits. Better even, that is for corporations, the new law lowered corporate tax rates from 35% to

[84] Ibid., 270.

21%, triggering a boost in corporate profits. The downside was that inequality further increased.

During his first term, Trump also signed a large number of Executive Orders. More than half of them concerned neoliberal themes, such as deregulation, privatization, downsizing government, weakening organized labour, and the reduction of public spending on social services. But Trump also favoured economic nationalism, serving narrow nationalist interests, as strongly suggested by his advisor Steve Bannon at the time. Trumpism justified economic nationalism by arguing that it protects ordinary people from the ravages of global capitalism.[85]

Gerstle argues that Trump belongs to a group of ethnonationalist leaders:

> They want the planet to be governed by force rather than by international law and multinational nongovernmental organizations. They seek a world divided into blocs—East Asia, North America, northern Eurasia, the Middle East, and South Asia among them—each controlled by a regional hegemon. This world would be far from flat: rather tall, jagged, and hard-to-scale walls would separate blocs.... from each other. In this imagined future, the United States would withdraw from its seventy-five-year role as the world's policeman and from its responsibility as the enforcer of liberal and neoliberal rules of global order. In words and deeds, Trump was making steps to make this vision a reality.[86]

During his first term in office, Trump also complained that countries like China, Mexico and Japan were subsidizing their (export) goods. What was in the offing happened in 2018, Trump launched his most spectacular illiberal tendency: A trade war with China and, later, with Mexico, Canada, Japan, and the European Union. All affected countries and he EU retaliated. The neoliberal order was broken.

When in 2020, the Covid-pandemic had broken out, followed by repeated lockdowns, the vulnerability of the neoliberal order of which small government constituted a major element, became again visible. Without robust government support, the economy would collapse. The

[85] *Neoliberalism*, 118. On p. 120, the authors observe: 'Trump's personal business activities went in the opposite direction.... visible in the US president's network of hotels (and other businesses) from Honolulu to Rio de Janeiro.'

[86] *The Rise and Fall of the Neoliberal Order*, 277.

Trump administration had no choice but to provide support to businesses, and families. Financial support was also provided to develop an anti-Covid vaccine. Trump's last act as outgoing president took place on 6 January 2001, when he suggested his followers to march to the Capitol Building, which ended in an ugly confrontation between police and Trump followers.

As this book goes to press, Donald Trump started his second presidential term with, again, a tsunami of Executive Orders and forays in the global domain which suggest that not just tariff hikes and protectionist trade policies will have the upper end, but also that traditional relations with friendly nations are put to the test. America's traditional bonds with Europe are under threat. This also applies to America's role in NATO. The Trump administration seems more concerned about what may happen in Asia (in particular China) than in Europe.

It seems as if President Trump is hitting the final nail in neoliberalism's coffin. Neoliberal pundits may observe that not all is lost; after all, the federal government will be downsized (which is part and parcel of the neoliberal order) under the dynamic leadership of Elon Musk. However, all other elements of neoliberal's philosophy seem to have been dumped.

The liberal order which the US created after WWII is no longer there. Given Trump's unpredictability, at this stage it is hard—and unwise—to make projections about the ideological direction the Trump administration may exactly take.

What Next?

As we do not know what will happen, only possible scenarios can be contemplated. The first one is that the popularity of current national populist politics, combined with economic nationalism, will be intensified. For consumers the consequence will be rising prices for many goods and services. Trade wars may also be intensified (i.e., *tit-for-tat* dynamics) which may affect the entire global economy.

Another scenario suggests that populism will lose popularity (i.e., not delivering the goods their voters expected). Voters may either return to political parties promoting (neo)liberal free market themes, or prefer a New Deal/Keynesian approach. This is what Stiglitz proposes:

> John Maynard Keynes and FDR saw an alternative way forward from classical economics.... their vision still stands as an alternative to the neoclassical and neoliberal economics that followed and the new Right that is emerging.

> The Keynes and FDR approach was a tempered capitalism with government playing a key but limited role ensuring stability, efficiency, and equity—or at least more than provided by unfettered capitalism. They laid the groundwork for a twenty-first-century progressive capitalism that supports meaningful human freedom.[87]

World Economic Forum leader, Klaus Schwab, sketches yet another scenario, inspired by his vison of a fourth industrial revolution.[88] He predicts a transformation of existing social structures in ways that would blur the lines between physical, digital, and biological spheres. Schwab argues that neoliberalism can be reformed by means of leading technologies, such as AI, autonomous vehicles, quantum computing, 3D printing, telecommuting and the Internet of Things. What he does not address in his vision, however, is the widening gap between the rich and the poor, the spread via social media of misinformation and reliance on robots and algorithms in many sectors of society.

Summing up, as for the different political-economic orders we have seen emerging since the end of the Great War, the New Deal order demonstrated that a strong central government was able to manage a dynamic capitalist economy in the public interest. Subsequently, the neoliberal order convinced many voters that free markets would unleash capitalism from state controls, spreading prosperity and personal freedom the world over. Neither the philosophy of the New Deal order nor the neoliberal one enjoys the popular support they used to have. What is in the offing, nobody knows.

Part IV Liberalism and Democracy

Liberalism is associated with democracy.[89] Yet the two are based on different principles and institutions. Democracy refers to rule by the people (through elections), while liberalism refers to the Rule of Law, which—among others—restricts the powers of the executive. Early liberals were

[87] *The Road to Freedom*, 42.

[88] Schwab, K. (2016) *The Fourth Industrial Revolution*. New York: Crown Business.

[89] Indeed, Paul Krugman combines liberalism and democracy. He argues: 'Liberalism, in other words, is not just about the welfare state: It's also about democracy and the rule of law. Source: *The Conscience of a Liberal*, 267.

wary of, what they called, the dangerous features of democracy; after all, democracy could fall prey to the tyranny of the majority.

Democracy is not just the pursuit of majority rule, it also involves fairness, tolerance, inclusivity, restraint, and self-criticism. These are all aspects of so-called soft power. They are fragile; no wonder former liberal Dutch Prime Minister Mark Rutte (Now NATO's Secretary General), compared democracy with a Delft-blue porcelain vase. What he meant to express was that although the vase is beautiful, it is, indeed, very fragile. His symbolism was spot on, but it was not understood much by the Dutch public.

It would not be an exaggeration to argue that the cultural features of political modernity—openness, reflectiveness, critical distance, scepticism, and experimentation—have taken their inspiration from a liberal mindset. All these features are no longer appreciated by an increasing number of voters. Leaders of autocratic regimes deliberately undermine the functioning of democratic societies. Scholars and commentators express concerns, as we shall see. According to them, liberal democracy is not delivering the goods the people expected. In short, liberal democracy is under attack.

Concerns

In *Democratic Capitalism*, Martin Wolf, *Financial Times*'s chief economic commentator, underscores that democracy and the market share a central notion: The idea of equality of status.[90] In a democracy, everybody has the right to a voice in public affairs, and in a free market everybody has the right to buy and sell what they own; in short: One cannot do without the other. Wolf therefore concludes that a market economy can only thrive in a stable democratic society.

Harvard professor of philosophy, Michael Sandel, agrees. In *Democracy's Discontent*, he argues that in the past, America found ways to hold economic power to democratic account. However, the strong connection between them is being eroded.[91]

Wolf, Sandel, but also Ingrid Robeyns and Bradford DeLong address shortcomings. Wolf, for example, concludes that democratic societies are under threat; the balance between the economic and political dimension

[90] Wolf, M. (2023) *The Crisis of Democratic Capitalism*. London: Allen Lane.

[91] Sandel, M. (2022) *Democracy's Discontent; A New Edition for our Perilous Times*. Cambridge: The Belknap Press.

of democracies is broken.[92] Some democracies become less liberal and more illiberal. In this realm, Ingrid Robeyns, Chair in Ethics of Institutions at Utrecht University, observes that '…the rights of minorities are no longer protected, and popularly elected leaders can enact the will of 'the people' as they interpret it. In illiberal democracies, those in power curtail the ability of the free press, independent thinkers, and political opponents to criticize the government; they also weaken the legal system.'[93]

Robeyns also observes that any contemporary capitalist system still has various elements of the mixed economy that was the dominant model in the Global North between 1945 and the 1970s. Unfortunately, argues Robeyns, the composition of the mix has changed considerably. Since the 1970s, a larger part of the provisioning of goods has shifted from the public to the private sector, and a lot of public property has been transferred to the private sector too. Meanwhile, regulation of private markets has weakened, while regulation of the public sector has intensified.[94]

A key destabilizing factor, as mentioned before, is that the economic system is not delivering the security and widely shared prosperity expected by a large part of society. In *Slouching Towards Utopia*, Bradford DeLong, economics professor at the University of California, Berkeley, writes this about the post-WWII near-utopian mixed economy: 'Perhaps the closest humanity got was the shotgun marriage of Hayek and Polanyi blessed by Keynes in the form of post-World War II North Atlantic developmental social democracy.'[95]

Unfortunately, this institutional setup was unsustainable. In *Growth Triumphant*, Richard Easterlin observes that the history of the ends human beings pursue demonstrates that they are ill-suited for utopia. He depicts humanity on a hedonic treadmill: 'Generation after generation thinks it needs only another ten or twenty percent more income to be perfectly happy….In the end, the triumph of economic growth is not a triumph of humanity over material wants; rather it is the triumph of material wants over humanity.'[96]

[92] *The Crisis of Democratic Capitalism*, xix.

[93] Robeyns, I. (2024) *Limitarianism; The Case Against Extreme Wealth*. New York: Astra Press, 73.

[94] Ibid., 209.

[95] DeLong, J. B. (2022) *Slouching Towards Utopia; An Economic History of the Twentieth Century*. London: Basic Books, 7.

[96] Easterlin, R. (1996) *Growth Triumphant; The Twenty-First Century in Historical Perspective*. Ann Arbor: University of Michigan Press, 154.

DeLong's sentiment about the postwar bliss is not just shared by Piketty, also Paul Krugman remembers that exceptional period as a 'paradise lost'. He explains why:

> Postwar America was, above all, a middle-class society. The great boom in wages that began with World War II had lifted tens of millions of Americans .... from urban slums and rural poverty to a life of home ownership and unprecedented comfort. The rich, on the other hand, had lost ground: They were few in number and, relative to the prosperous middle, not all that rich....... Most people in America lived recognizably similar and remarkably decent material lives...... the American political process was for the most part governed by bipartisan coalition of men who agreed on fundamental values. .... Now that America was all grown up, we thought, a relatively equal society with a strong middle-class and an equable political scene was its normal state.'[97]

Those were the good times, certainly compared with what happened after 2010. DeLong observes:

> The years following 2010 were to bring large system-destabilizing waves of political and cultural anger from masses of citizens, all upset in different ways and for different reasons at the failure of the system of the twentieth century to work for them as they thought that it should.[98]

To a large extent, governments were to blame as they mismanaged the situation, creating insecurity and dissatisfaction. In a rising number of countries, populist parties benefitted from the inflammable situation. Governments neither sufficiently regulated financial markets, nor delivered sufficient social services. They also failed to prevent the gap between the rich and the poor from widening. Both democracy and liberal values were weakened, thereby strengthening the hands of authoritarian political leaders.

Although DeLong's vantage point is economic, he underscores the interplay between the economic and almost everything else:

[97] *The Conscience of a Liberal*, 3–4.

[98] Ibid., 1. On page 4, DeLong subtly reminds the reader that the riches were vastly more unequally distributed around the globe in 2010 than they were in 1870.

> As nearly everything economic was transformed and transformed again—as the economy was revolutionized in every generation, at least in those places on the earth that were lucky enough to be the growth poles—those changes shaped and transformed nearly everything sociological, political and cultural.[99]

Not surprisingly, Fukuyama is also concerned about the rise of populist parties, driven by discontent with liberalism. He observes, however, that this trend does not have to do with the essence of the liberal doctrine, but rather with the way in which certain sound liberal ideas have been wrongly interpreted and pushed to extremes.[100] The answer to discontent, says Fukuyama, is not to abandon liberalism but to moderate it; rebuilding faith in classical liberalism, that is what should be done.

Anne Appelbaum's book *Autocracy, Inc.*, addresses the urgent issue of autocratic states undermining the liberal world order, that 'the West' had taken for granted. Applebaum argues that this world order no longer exists.[101] Autocrats (read: dictators) the world over, join hands to undermine the values the democratic world embraces. They do not like the checks and balances democratic states have, nor do they like terms like transparency and accountability. If these would have been allowed in their countries, their kleptocratic and criminal attitude would have been exposed.

The author describes autocrats helping one another. For example, when America slapped sanctions on Venezuela, Russian energy giants stepped in to invest in Venezuela's oil business. Cuba helped Venezuela to spy on its people and weaponize rations to starve the Venezuelan opposition. Another example: Zimbabwe's President endorsed Russia's invasion of Ukraine; he was rewarded with a Russian helicopter. At this time of writing, the media report that North Korea assists Russia with 10,000 troops to help fighting Russia's war with Ukraine. Other aspects are also worrying, such as the possible consequences of endless cyberattacks and the economic power of autocrats:

[99] Ibid., 5.

[100] *Liberalism and its Discontents*, xi.

[101] Applebaum, A. (2024) *Autocracy, Inc.*; *The Dictators Who Want To Run The World.* London: Allen Lane, 174.

> Europeans who aspire to a Fortress Europe also need to wake up to the reality that Russian influence campaigns and Chinese commercial interests are already shaping their politics and limiting their choices.[102]

Applebaum ends *Autocracy, Inc.*, with a passionate appeal:

> There is no liberal world order anymore, and the aspiration to create one no longer seems real. But there are liberal societies, open and free countries that offer a better chance for people to live useful lives than closed dictatorships do…. They can be destroyed from the outside and from the inside, too, by division and demagogues. Or they can be saved. But only if those of us who live in them are willing to make the effort to save them.[103]

Possible Remedies

The authors whose concerns I just presented also deal with the question what could be done to address them. Fukuyama says that liberalism should not be abandoned but be moderated. His aim is to rebuild faith in classical liberalism, because the alternatives proposed by the Right and the Left offer no realistic alternatives. Historically, liberal societies have been engines of economic growth, creators of new technologies, and producers of vibrant arts and culture. Fukuyama rhetorically wonders whether, for example, China's unfree political and economic model will be able to generate innovation, or will produce anything like an appealing global culture?

Fukuyama outlines a few general principles of classical liberalism which should guide the formulation of more specific policies. He adds that many of them will apply particularly, but not exclusively, to the US. When the social composition of a nation changes, it is wise for political parties to manage this social change. Do not restrict voting rights in the US, warms Fukuyama, as this will pose a threat to American democracy. Instead, follow Disraeli's action way back in nineteenth-century Britain. Disraeli managed social change by pushing through Parliament the Second Reform Bill, greatly expanding the franchise and laying the groundwork for Conservative domination of British politics through the remainder of the nineteenth century. This attitude would imply adherence to classical liberal principles: Accepting the fact of demographic diversity in America and

[102] Ibid., 174.
[103] Ibid., 176.

to make use of it to support conservative values.[104] Sandel has this to say on the issue of xenophobia: 'What has become of the left's traditional emphasis on solidarity, civic pride, and the mutual obligation of citizens? A healthy sense civic pride can offer an alternative to xenophobia and hyper-nationalism.[105]

For a modern liberal democracy to function well, there has to be a high level of trust in government; not a blind trust, but one recognizing that government serves critical public purposes. And it is not the size of government, the issue is the *quality* of government. A modern state needs to be impersonal and equipped with well-educated professionals with a strong sense of public purpose.

As I pointed out before, the downside of unequal wealth and income, has not been sufficiently addressed by liberals. Fukuyama warns that if inequality grows too extreme, aggregate demand stagnates, and political protests against the system will crop up. But he also brings under our attention that all modern states redistribute resources to greater or lesser degree. It has to be done in a balanced manner: 'The task is to set social protections of a sustainable level, where they do not undercut incentives and can be supported by public finance on a long-term basis.'[106]

Freedom of speech should be protected, says Fukuyama. Not by way of direct state regulation but rather the prevention of large accumulations of private power through anti-trust and competition laws. Regarding identity politics, He underscores that liberal institutions need to stay focused on the rights individuals rather than those of groups.[107]

Fukuyama concludes that successful liberal societies need to prioritize public-spiritedness, tolerance, open-mindedness, and active engagement in public affairs if they are to cohere. In addition, they need to prize innovation, entrepreneurship, and risk-taking, if they are to prosper economically.

[104] President Reagan once said that Americans with Latino roots are Republicans, but they didn't know it yet.

[105] Piketty, T.& Sandel, M. (2025) *Equality; What It Means and Why It Matters.* Cambridge, Polity Press, 102.

[106] *Liberalism and its Discontents*, 148.

[107] Snyder says about freedom: 'It is freedom that enables us to choose and combine values, including those thought to be progressive. Although the Left often concedes that language of freedom to the Right, people on the Left do propose policies that would further freedom. They just usually fail to make their case in those terms.' Source: *On Freedom*, 235.

Sometimes fulfilment comes from the acceptance of limits. Recovering a sense of moderation, both individual and communal, is therefore the key to the revival—indeed, to the survival—of liberalism itself.[108]

Rosenblatt's advice is—in line with Fukuyama's—that liberals should reconnect with the resources of their liberal tradition to recover, understand, and embrace its core values.[109]

References

Allen, R. (2017). *The Industrial Revolution: A Very Short Introduction*. Oxford University Press.

Applebaum, A. (2024). *Autocracy, Inc.; The Dictators Who Want to Run the World*. Allen Lane.

Bowles, S. (2016). *The Moral Economy; Why Good Incentives are no Substitute for Good Citizens*. Yale University Press.

Buchholz, T. (1999). *New Ideas from Dead Economists: An Introduction to Modern Economic Thought*. Penguin Books.

Burchell, G., Gordon, C., & Miller, P. (1991). *The Foucault effect: Studies in Governmentality*. The University of Chicago Press.

Caldwell, B. (2004). *Hayek's Challenge; An Intellectual Biography of F.A. Hayek*. The University of Chicago Press.

DeLong, J. B. (2022). *Slouching Towards Utopia; An Economic History of the Twentieth Century*. Basic Books.

Easterlin, R. (1996). *Growth Triumphant; The Twenty-First Century in Historical Perspective*. University of Michigan Press.

Freeden, M. (2015). *Liberalism; A Very Short Introduction*. Oxford University Press.

Fukuyama, F. (1992). *The End of History and The Last Man*. Penguin Books.

Fukuyama, F. (2022). *Liberalism and Its Discontents*. Profile Books.

Gerstle, G. (2022). *The Rise and Fall of the Neoliberal Order; America and the world in the Free Market Era*. Oxford University Press.

Gray, J. (1986). *Liberalism*. Open University Press.

Heilbroner, R. (1995). *The Worldly Philosophers; The Lives, Times and Ideas of the Great Economic Thinkers*. Penguin Books.

Keynes, J. M. (1964). *The General Theory of Employment, Interest and Money*. Harcourt Brace.

Krugman, P. (2009). *The Conscience of a Liberal*. W.W. Norton.

[108] *Liberalism and its Discontents*, 154.

[109] *The Lost History of Liberalism*, 277.

Leigh, A. (2024). *How Economics Explains the World; A Short History of Humanity.* Mariner Books.

Maddison, A. (2003). *The World Economy; Historical Statistics.* OECD Development Centre of the Organisation for Economic Development and Development.

McCloskey, D. (2019). Fukuyama was Correct: Liberalism Is the Telos of History. *Journal of Contextual Economics, 139*(2–4), 285–304.

Milanović, B. (2016). *Global Inequality; A New Approach for the Age of Globalization.* The Belknap Press of Harvard University Press.

Ostry, J., Loungani, P., & Furceri, D. (2016). Neoliberalism: Oversold? *Finance and Development, 53*, 38–41.

Piketty, T. (2014). *Capital in the Twenty-First Century.* The Belknap Press of Harvard University Press.

Piketty, T., & Sandel, M. (2025). *Equality; What It Means and Why It Matters.* Polity Press.

Polanyi, K. (2001). *The Great Transformation; The Political and Economic Origins of Our Time.* Beacon Press.

Reiss, J. (2013). *Philosophy of Economics; A Contemporary Introduction.* Routledge.

Robeyns, I. (2024). *Limitarianism; The Case Against Extreme Wealth.* Astra Press.

Rosenblatt, H. (2018). *The Lost History of Liberalism; From Ancient Rome to the Twenty-First Century.* Princeton University Press.

Russell, B. (1979). *A History of Western Philosophy.* Unwin.

Sandel, M. (2022). *Democracy's Discontent; A New Edition for our Perilous Times.* The Belknap Press.

Schumpeter, J. (1970). *Capitalism, Socialism and Democracy.* Unwin University Press.

Schwab, K. (2016). *The Fourth Industrial Revolution.* Crown Business.

Sen, A. (2021). *Home in the World; A Memoir.* Penguin Random House.

Smith, A. (2003). *The Wealth of Nations.* Bantam Classics.

Snyder, T. (2024). *On Freedom.* The Bodley Head.

Soll, J. (2022). *Free Market; The History of an Idea.* Basic Books.

Stedman Jones, D. (2012). *Masters of the Universe: Hayek, Friedman, and the British Neoliberal Politics.* Princeton University Press.

Steger, M., & Roy, R. (2021). *Neoliberalism; A Very Sort Introduction.* Oxford University Press.

Stiglitz, J. (2024). *The Road to Freedom; Economics and the Good Society.* Allen Lane.

Tong, R. (1989). *Feminist Thought: A Comprehensive Introduction.* Routledge.

Wolf, M. (2023). *The Crisis of Democratic Capitalism.* Allen Lane.

CHAPTER 4

Karl Polanyi's Critique of Market Liberalism

Prologue

The majority of the economists presented in this book were positively inspired by liberalism but Polanyi was not one of them. His critical analysis of how, over the past centuries, market liberalism (as he called it) evolved in Britain, other European countries, and America, is a thorough one. Anthropological, historical, political, and economic developments are presented in his magnum opus *The Great Transformation*. Before modern economists revealed the limitations of self-regulating markets, Polanyi's principal message was that market liberalism, after it took off in the nineteenth century, was doomed to fail and resulted in the political and economic disasters of the Great War, the Great Depression and the rise of fascism and communism. These evil political doctrines were reactions against market liberalism's inability to satisfy people's rights, said Polanyi.

In his youth, Polanyi embraced liberal ideals, which were soon replaced by reformist socialism, whose aim it was to transform capitalism into a socialist society by means of parliament-led alterations to existing institutions. Since then, Polanyi's intellectual formation was to a large extent moulded by the turbulent economic and geopolitical events of the twentieth century. As a result, he did not stubbornly stick to one philosophy. No, in the course of his life he warmed, as we shall see, to various philosophies.

P. de Haan, *Great Economists and the Evolution of Economic Liberalism*, https://doi.org/10.1007/978-3-031-93831-3_4

Polanyi rejected the self-regulating market doctrine, which is not surprising for a leftist scholar. Yet, at the same time he embraced another crucial value of liberalism—freedom.

He published *The Great Transformation* in 1944, when WWII was in its ending phase. Inspired by this bright perspective, he ended *The Great Transformation* in a hopeful spirit:

> Uncomplaining acceptance of the reality of society gives man indominable courage and strength to remove all removable injustice and unfreedom. As long as he is true to his task of creating more abundant freedom for all, he need not fear that either power or planning will turn against him and destroy the freedom he is building by their instrumentality. This is the meaning of freedom in a complex society; it gives us all the certainty we need.[1]

In 1944, another influential book came out: *The Road to Serfdom*, written by Friederich Hayek. In it, he warned against too much government intervention in the economy which would only lead to authoritarian rule and the loss of freedom. Since the 1970s, Hayek's ideas enjoyed overwhelming popularity among policy makers, while Polanyi's book was nearly forgotten.

However, *The Great Transformation* is now enjoying renewed interest. As Polanyi's biographer, Gareth Dale, observes, Polanyi offers 'an anticipatory and transformative guiding idea that can inspire collective action to change social reality, and it is in his defense of nonmarket utopia that Polanyi's legacy lies.'[2] Indeed, *The Great Transformation* is not just about what went wrong since the Industrial Revolution, but rather about what the future could bring in terms of political, economic, and social transformation, now that market liberalism's failures have again been exposed.

Part I Polanyi's Life and Work

Károly Polányi (1886–1964) was an economic historian, economic anthropologist, political economist, historical sociologist, and a social philosopher. Karl was born on 25 October 1886 in Vienna, into a well-to-do Jewish family. When Karl was in his infancy, the Polanyi' s moved to

[1] Polanyi, K. (2001) *The Great Transformation; The Political and Economic Origins of Our Time*. Boston: Beacon Press, 268.

Budapest, the second cosmopolitan capital of the Austrian-Hungarian double monarchy. His father was a successful contractor, specialized in railway and tunnel construction. He maintained unorthodox pedagogical ideas about his children's education; they were educated in strict isolation. They saw only their four tutors: one British, one Swiss-French, one Swiss-German, and one Hungarian. Each tutor was teaching one child a week in turn. Polanyi senior was bringing them up according to Jean-Jacques Rousseau's ideas, which demanded complete isolation from the hypocrisy and corruption of society. This helped Karl and his siblings to become polyglots. German and Hungarian were spoken at home, English was learned from the English tutor, and French was spoken at table. His mother was a feminist, and a regular guest at literary salons in both capitals. The good life was over when Karl's father had fallen on hard times.

As of the age of eleven, Karl attended Minta high school, one of Budapest's finest. Its alumni included physicist Edward Teller, economist Nicholas Kaldor and psychiatrist Thomas Sasz. In short, Minta was a nursery for the elite.

In *Adventures of a Bystander*, management guru Peter Drucker, who knew the Polanyi's well, observed that none of the children turned into an idiot, yet they turned out different and unusual.[3] Karl's younger brother Michael became a distinguished physical chemist and liberal philosopher. After the untimely dearth of their beloved father, Karl strengthened his bond with Michael. Karl acted as a stand-in father for Michael. However, after the 1920s, their relationship deteriorated. Especially when Michael started to deviate decisively from Karl's political and economic opinions, the latter had difficulties accepting them. However, towards the end of the 1950s, Karl's relationship with Michael became reconciliatory; in the end they agreed to disagree, as Dale observes.[4]

Young Karl's intellectual formation took place in Budapest. Hungary, and Budapest in particular, were booming. Average annual growth accelerated to 7% during Polanyi's childhood and went even up to 9% during

[2] Dale, G. (2018) *Karl Polanyi, A Life on the Left*. New York: Columbia University Press, 288.

[3] Drucker, P. (2007) *Adventures of a Bystander*. New Brunswick and London: Transaction Publishers.

[4] *Karl Polanyi*, pp. 256, 278. On p. 139 Dale writes about the two brothers' personalities: 'Those who knew Karl and Michael would be struck by their dissimilar personalities, the elder brother appearing outgoing, exuberant and cheerful, in contrast to the restrained and 'British' Michael."

his teenage years. No wonder Budapest, like Vienna, had attracted famous intellectuals and artists, such as mathematician John von Neumann, Edward Teller and Bela Bartok. It was in Budapest where Polanyi became inspired by socialism and later also by Christianity. While studying at the University of Budapest, Karl founded the radical and influential *Galileo Circle*, in which Michael also participated. He had intellectual encounters with philosophers such as Georgy Lukács and Karl Mannheim. In 1908, he earned a PhD in philosophy, and in 1914 he obtained a law degree. In 1914, loyal to his leftist ideas, he founded, together with Count Michael Karolyi, the Hungarian Radical Party. When he was 25, Polanyi was elected a member of the Hungarian Parliament.

During the Great War, Polanyi served as a cavalry officer in the Austro-Hungarian army. During the war he used his spare time to read Marx's *Capital*. After the war, he returned to Budapest where he resumed his political career. However, after the war had ended, political turbulence ensued in Hungary. In 1924 Béla Kun toppled the Karolyi government to create the Hungarian Soviet Republic.

Viennese Period

Polanyi left for Vienna, where he met Ilona Duczynska, an activist and communist. The couple married in 1923. They had one daughter, Kari. While in Vienna, he became associate editor of the prestigious Austrian Economist (*Der Őstterreichische Volkswirt*). Viennese intellectuals often met in *Kaffee Landtmann* (it still exists) to discuss the intricacies of psychoanalysis and Marxism. Sigmund Freud, Karl Popper, and Ludwig Wittgenstein lived in Vienna at the time, and so did economists Ludwig von Mises, Friedrich Hayek and, briefly, Joseph Schumpeter. Painters like Egon Schiele, Gustav Klimt, and Oskar Kokoschka also lived in this vibrant city The composers Arnold Schönberg and Gustav Mahler lived there, as well as the authors Arthur Schnitzler, Joseph Roth, and Stefan Zweig.

In *Adventures of a Bystander*, Drucker painted a lively portrait of the Polanyi's. Karl had invited Drucker to his house to share Christmas dinner with his family. As it turned out, the Polanyi family lived in a very poor Viennese neighbourhood and the food served was, according to Drucker, the worst meal of his life. This was not because Polanyi earned a meagre salary; it was because the Polanyi's gave most of their income to Hungarian refugees who had fled to Vienna without any means. What made the Polanyi family so remarkable, observed Drucker, was that they shared the same cause: to overcome the nineteenth century and to find a new society that would be free and yet not 'bourgeois', or 'liberal'; prosperous and yet not dominated by economics; communal and yet not a Marxist collectivism.

Inspired by the stimulating intellectual Viennese environment, but certainly also by the catastrophe of the Great War, Polanyi began criticizing the free market philosophy of von Mises. Mises argued that a centrally planned economy was infeasible since economic calculation is only possible with the existence of a price mechanism in an environment in which owners of property engage in free competition. Mises' theory would later be elaborated by Hayek (see Chap. 5). Polanyi vehemently opposed the liberal free market doctrine. He made the case for economic, social and regulatory reform in *The Great Transformation.*

Great Britain, Canada, and America

When in 1933, Hitler came to power in Germany, Polanyi left Austria for London, where he worked as a journalist and tutor at the Workers' Educational Association. Being an anglophile, Polanyi was looking forward to come to Britain.[5] In London he already started to collect documentation for *The Great Transformation,* the book he began writing in 1940 and completed in 1944 when he was a visiting scholar at Bennington College, Vermont. The book, although not an easy read, is considered one of the most influential books on modern economic history.

Thanks to the largely positive reviews of *The Great Transformation,* from 1947 to 1953 Polanyi was offered a teaching position in economic history at New York's Columbia University. His lectures at Columbia drew large crowds of students. His wife Ilona was refused a visa entry into the US (Senator Joseph McCarthy led the anti-communist witch hunt at

[5] 'He praised the British Constitution (alongside the American) as a beacon of liberty and hailed the democratic traditions Anglo-Saxon political culture as 'infinitely treasured asset(s) to the common fund of Universal peace and progress', albeit with the caveat that their long-term survival in Britain would require the introduction of 'genuine social equality' into its political institutions. Britain's 'most important contribution to the world of political thought' was the idea of tolerance, which he took to encompass not only the acceptance of nonconformity and minority opinions but also the conviction that its own political institutions should not be 'imposed' on other countries.' Source: *Karl Polanyi*, 153–154.

the time). The Polanyi's settled in Picketing, Ontario, Canada, from where Karl commuted to New York.

After Columbia, Polanyi received a grant from the Ford Foundation to study the role of money, trade, and markets in pre-capitalist societies, as well as economic systems of ancient empires, with a view to put the functioning of economic systems in historical perspective. In 1957 he published another acclaimed work: *Trade and Market in the Early Empires.* He died on 23 April 1964 in Picketing.

Polanyi's Work

Polanyi's central theme is that instead of the historically normal pattern of subordinating the economy to society, the system of self-regulating markets required subordinating society to the market. It means no less than the running of society as an adjunct to the market, instead of the economy *embedded* in social relations, as in antique societies.

In *The Great Transformation*'s introduction, Fred Block summarizes Polanyi's thinking well: 'For Polanyi the deepest flaw in market liberalism was that it subordinates human purposes to the logic of an impersonal market mechanism. He argued instead that human beings should use the instruments of democratic governance to control and direct the economy to meet our individual and collective needs.'[6]

Indeed, embeddedness is central to Polanyi's thinking. Before the nineteenth century, when sustained economic development took off, the human economy was always embedded in society. Polanyi described, for example, how the Trobriands in Melanesia went about their business in harmonious and balanced ways. Some anthropologists accused Polanyi of romanticizing primitive cultures, as he seemed to suggest that non-modern, non-Western people were different and would not have been as economically rational in their dealings as Westerners.

Economic historian and Economics Nobel Laureate, Douglass North, pointed out that it is easy to find fault with Polanyi's analytical framework. North noted that Polanyi selected a few historical examples which fitted into his thinking, while leaving out others that did not.[7] Polanyi observed

[6] *The Great Transformation*, xxxviii.

[7] North, D. (1977) Markets and Other Allocation Systems in History: The Challenge of Karl Polanyi. In: *Journal of European Economic History* 6 (Winter), 703–716.

that price-making markets never completely dominated economic decision-making throughout history. Even in the nineteenth century, a large percentage of allocative decisions did *not* occur in price-making markets; elements of reciprocity and redistribution played their part as well. North gave examples of this type of allocation of resources, such as cooperatives, trade unions, guilds, etc. All of them are institutions that allocate resources in place of markets. North concluded that further advance in economic history requires that economic historians succeed in defining and explaining the different allocative systems that have characterized economic organization in the past. Polanyi's intuitive genius, according to North, was that he saw the issue of allocative systems at hand.

Market liberalism triggered a response by society, Polanyi noted, which in turn meant that this system could not work completely free as intended. Efforts to bring about greater autonomy of the market would trigger societal tensions. Polanyi presented the idea of the *double movement*, in that a movement toward an unfettered market economy results in a counter movement to create stability. As Timothy Snyder succinctly observes: 'Markets should work for us, not the other way around.'[8] Polanyi's double movement was, as we shall see, inspired by Arnold Toynbee's Challenge-and-Response cyclical movement.

The gold standard that governed the global economy in the nineteenth century, created increasing tensions within and among nations. As we shall see, the functioning of the gold standard had the ironic effect of intensifying the importance of government in dealing with the gold standard's rules of the game. Polanyi argued that the simple rules of the gold standard imposed on people economic costs that were unbearable. This culminated in the catastrophe of the Great War and ensuing protectionism, followed by the Great Depression, which brought the preceding century of market liberalism to its end. Communism and fascism sprang up in some societies, while in others social democracy developed.

Polanyi and Keynes

Keynes and Polanyi were contemporaries. Although Polanyi agreed with much of Keynes's critique of market liberalism, including Keynes' opinion that government was much more than a mere nightwatchman, he was not a Keynesian. After all, Keynes was a liberal and Polanyi was not. Keynes,

[8] *On Freedom*, 220.

like Polanyi, criticized the neoclassical view on the functioning of economies. Keynes proposed—while accepting aspects of the neoclassical doctrine—a counterbalancing role through government intervention. Unlike his brother Michael, Karl rejected this doctrine as he argued that market liberalism had a disruptive effect on society—it was doomed.[9]

Polanyi also did not agree with Keynes's analysis of the causes of the catastrophic developments after the end of the Great War. In *The Economic Consequences of Peace* (1919), Keynes put the blame on the politically inspired greediness of the Allies (France, Great Britain, and America) over defeated Germany in demanding an impossible amount of war reparations, stipulated in the *Treaty of Versailles.* The allies' intention was to prevent Germany from politically and economically getting back on its feet. The consequences of the *Treaty* would destroy the economic system which had brought prosperity before the war, according to Keynes. Polanyi blamed the strain of the entire economic system for the post-war catastrophic developments.

Polanyi the Moralist

Polanyi emphasized that it was wrong to treat nature and human beings as objects whose price is determined by market forces. Such a concept, he maintained, violated the principles that have governed societies for centuries: nature and human life have almost always been recognized as having a sacred dimension. He pointed to the fact that when the natural environment is turned into economic commodities, one can be sure it leads to an environmental catastrophe. Polanyi as moralist (and romanticist, I add) can be characterized as an environmentalist well before it became fashionable.

During his younger days, Karl embraced liberal ideals. However, for Karl these ideals were shattered by the Great War, rising fascism and the Great Depression. As already mentioned, Polanyi became also inspired by socialism and he drew inspiration from the New Testament. No wonder Dale describes the contradictions in Polanyi's character:

[9] Michael shared Keynes's ideas, he was a Keynesian liberal. He observed that liberal capitalism had proved itself to be a spontaneously evolving functioning social tradition, one that, corrected by laws, and Keynesian interventions, provided an acceptable environment in which citizens could thrive. Michael even joined the Mont Pèrelin Society (more about it in Chap. 5).

> Such puzzles and paradoxes provided the initial impetus for the writing of this biography, in part because, to understand them requires a thinking through of Polanyi's life and times, but also because to understand it is the tensions and contradictions in his personal commitments and his oeuvre that give them their engagingly maverick character. Polanyi was, for example, in love with Bolshevik while spurning Bolshevism; he was a social democrat who disdained the social-democratic orthodoxy, and liberal who charged classical liberalism with full responsibility for the collapse of its dreams.… He was a Christian who rarely worshipped God, a modernist who immersed himself in study of the ancient world, and an ardent supporter of the peasant's cause who lived almost exclusively in sprawling conurbations.[10]

When Polanyi published *The Great Transformation*, he hoped to see a situation emerging in which both national economies *and* the global economy would be subordinated to democratic politics. Polanyi argued that human beings should use the instruments of democratic governance to control and direct the economy to meet their needs.

As for the global economy, the World Bank and the IMF had been established to serve the global economy, later broadened with the WTO. However, it must be doubted that they have been able to function as Polanyi wanted, i.e., that the logic of the market would be a subordinate of society. As regards national economies, perhaps the Nordic countries best reflected Polanyi's ideas when they applied a *Middle Way*, maintaining a fine balance between the exigencies of the market on the one hand and societal requirements on the other.

After The Great Transformation

The Great Transformation provided Polanyi's research agenda for the rest of his life. It was his task, he wrote to his wife Ilona, to lay a new foundation for understanding the meaning of life in an industrial civilization. This preoccupied him until the end of his life. Tragically, he was not successful in completing this herculean task. One analyst of Polanyi's work, Sally Humphreys, observed that the socialist aspect in Polanyi's later work had withered, in that during his American period his economic historiography no longer focused on the study of market society but on precapitalist societies. This represented a turn from politics, and it was illustrated by Polanyi's unwillingness to elaborate the implications of his theories for America's post-war problems.[11] However, it should be underscored that

[10] *Karl Polanyi*, 7–8.
[11] Ibid., 222–223.

Polanyi's research in precapitalist societies represented a logical progression of the concerns expressed in *The Great Transformation.*

Nonetheless, he was more successful in his work in economics and economic history, in which empirical research into primitive and archaic societies played an important part. His analysis of classical Athens and Dahomey, for example, revealed that—despite being separated by two millennia—they had both discovered ways of effectively reconciling economic planning with the requirements of markets.[12]

The Great Transformation

Karl Polanyi wrote *The Great Transformation* during WWII. He analysed the political and economic origins of nineteenth-century civilization which was affected by the Industrial Revolution. The Great War and the Great Depression of the 1930s hastened the destruction of that civilization. Among the institutions of the nineteenth century, the gold standard was crucial, and its fall was the proximate cause of the destruction of that civilization, according to Polanyi. He observed that: 'Nowhere has liberal philosophy failed so conspicuously as in its understanding of the problem of change.'[13]

The Great Transformation's main theme is still relevant: self-regulating markets do not always work. Unchecked they lead to excesses, as confirmed by the endless—and sometimes extreme—ups and downs of markets and entire economies. Economics Nobel Laureate Joseph Stiglitz, who is greatly inspired by Polanyi, writes in his *Foreword* to Polanyi's book that the deficiencies of self-regulating markets—not only in their internal workings but also in their consequences (e.g., for the poor)—are so great that government intervention becomes necessary.[14]

Composition of the Book

The Great Transformation consists of three parts. The first part: *The International System*, describes the 100 years peace, roughly encompassing the nineteenth century and ending in 1914, when the Great War broke out, followed by the Great Depression, and the revolutionary 1930s.

[12] Ibid., 228.

[13] *The Great Transformation*, 35. The book's reviews were on balance favourable. The most moving one was by Michael Polanyi, who summed up in a letter to Karl: 'It says 'pretty well all you had to say' and gives expression to 'the thought and passion of a lifetime'. So intensely personal is it, 'so passionate and eloquent in your own particular tone of sentiment', that it simply could not have been written by anybody else.' Ibid., 172.

[14] Ibid., vii.

Part two is entitled: *Rise and Fall of Market Economy*. Polanyi goes back to primitive and pre-nineteenth-century societies to demonstrate the balanced interplay between society and market. This part of the book also describes the political and economic developments in Britain from the fifteenth century to the 1795 *Speenhamland Law* (i.e., assuring a minimum income for the poor, irrespective of their earnings), followed by what the Industrial Revolution brought about in the realm of economic and social philosophies and their social and economic consequences. Capitalism had arrived unannounced, observed Polanyi. No one had forecast the development of a *machine* industry; it came as a complete surprise.

> The concept of the machine would play an important part in Polanyi's further elaboration of *The Great Transformation*'s concerns. This is what Dale observes: 'It included...what Polanyi regarded as core topics of 'socialist economics': the decline of the market system, its ideological legacy, how to reintegrate the economy into society and how to democratically control science and technology in the approaching stage of 'machine civilization'. In the process, he was groping toward a new way of construing the relationship between industrial and commercial society, centered on the concept of the 'machine'.[15]

Part three: *Transformation in Progress*, analyses the origins of the Great War, the Great Depression, the rise of fascism and communism in Europe, as well as President Roosevelt's New Deal in America, which Polanyi admired.[16]

Part I: The International System

Polanyi distinguished four institutions, crucial for the economic and political order that characterized the Western world in the nineteenth century: (i) a balance of political power, (ii) the gold standard, (iii) a self-regulating

[15] Ibid., 223.

[16] 'Most of all, Polanyi was mesmerized by Franklin Roosevelt ('a great leader') and the New Deal. Out of the depths of the Depression, he prophesied 'a great transformation in the USA is growing''. *Karl Polanyi*, 146.

market system, and, (iv) the liberal state. In particular, the self-regulating market was in Polanyi's own words: 'the fount and matrix of the system', and 'the innovation which gave rise to a specific civilization'.[17]

Of these four institutions, the gold standard was crucial; its fall was the proximate cause of the destruction of the nineteenth-century civilization. The breakdown of the international gold standard was the invisible link between the disintegration of the world economy, which started at the turn of the century, and the transformation of an entire civilization in the 1930s. By the time the gold standard failed in the early 1930s, most of the other nineteenth-century institutions had already been sacrificed in a vain effort to save it.

Polanyi argued that the market economy, free trade, and the gold standard were English inventions. During the 1920s, these institutions broke down everywhere. He concluded that:

> ...in Germany, Italy, and Austria the event was merely more political and more dramatic. But whatever the scenery and the temperature of the final episode, the long-term factors which wrecked that civilization should be studied in the birthplace of the Industrial Revolution, England'.[18]

Part II: Rise and Fall of Market Economy

At the beginning of the nineteenth century the markets functioned nearly free. This inspired economic thinkers to emphasize the blessings of the self-regulating market system as originally conceived by Adam Smith in *The Wealth of Nations* (1776). John Stuart Mill and David Ricardo elaborated Smith's ***invisible hand*** and the notion that economic actors' self-interest would also serve society at large. After all, any producer makes a living from selling his produce, and these products in turn serve consumers' demand. The market mechanism brings about equilibrium between supply and demand. In Polanyi's words: 'A market economy is an economic system controlled, regulated, and directed by market prices; order in the production and distribution of goods is entrusted to this self-regulating mechanism. An economy of this kind derives from the expectation that human beings behave in such a way as to achieve maximum money gains.'[19]

[17] *The Great Transformation*, 3.
[18] Ibid., 32.
[19] Ibid., 71.

Triggered by the economic progress made during the Industrial Revolution, liberal economic philosophy gained the upper hand. It became the organizing principle for the world economy at the time. It was as if market organization of economic activity was the natural state of human affairs. Indeed, the control of the economic system by the market was of overwhelming consequence to the whole organization of society.

There was, nonetheless, nothing natural about *laissez faire*; free markets could never have come into being merely by allowing things to take their course. *Laissez faire* was enforced by the state, which was endowed with a large bureaucracy able to fulfil the tasks set by the adherents of liberalism. In short, *laissez faire* was planned.

The downside was that the self-regulating market system disrupted society as it had existed hitherto. Polanyi observed:

> 'the control of the economic system by the market is of overwhelming consequence to the whole organization of society: it means no less than the running of society as an adjunct to the market'.[20]

So, instead of the economy being *embedded* in social relations, social relations are embedded in the economic system.[21] Polanyi admitted that there was material improvement for the exploited workers. Nevertheless, he concluded that human society became subordinated to the self-regulating market (SRM). For Polanyi, the modern economy had become disembedded from society.

The Great Transformation presents examples of economies that had been organized in ways other than through a SRM. Polanyi argued that the organization of production and distribution in many societies, on scales as small as a band of Kung bushmen or as large as Hammurabi's empire, or even as large as the planned economy of the Soviet Union, employed redistributive systems. In much of Western Europe a

[20] Ibid., 60.

[21] About embeddedness Polanyi typically observed that 'the journey from *gemeinnschaft* to *gesellschaft* had witnessed traditional socioeconomic practices recklessly cast asunder, as market capitalism 'disembedded' economy from society.' *Karl Polanyi*, 5. Not surprisingly, Polanyi distinguished the embedded economies of the past and the disembedded market society of nineteenth-century Britain. Disembedding of the economy from the social fabric was bound to wreak civilizational collapse, Polanyi argued in a lecture at the University of London. Ibid., 322.

combination of *redistributive and reciprocative systems* dominated through the end of the feudal and manorial era. These systems came to be increasingly supplemented by market trading, the control and encouragement of which was a major focus of medieval municipal and mercantilist national governments.

Polanyi emphasizes the *reciprocity and redistributive* nature of the way societies went about the exchange of goods. Take the Kula ring trade as practiced in the Trobriand islands:

> The Kula ring in western Melanesia, based on the principle of reciprocity, is one of the most elaborate trading transactions known to man ... there are, as a rule, individual partners in Kula who reciprocate one another's Kula gifts with equally valuable armbands and necklaces, preferably such as have previously belonged to distinguished persons. Now, a systematic and organized give-and-take of valuable objects transported over long distances is justly described as trade. Yet this complex whole is exclusively run on the lines of reciprocity.... Not the propensity to barter, but reciprocity in social behavior dominates.[22]

Mutual obligations in themselves, argued Polanyi, explain the absence of the notion of gain or even wealth other than that consisting of objects traditionally enhancing social prestige.[23]

Towards the end of the eighteenth century, and with full force in the nineteenth century, two things happened. First, the rapidly expanding factor system altered the relationship between commerce and industry. Production now involved large-scale investment of funds with fixed obligations to pay for those funds. And, second, it was the development of economic liberalism as a body of thought that provided justification of a new set of public policies that facilitated transformation of land, labour and capital into the 'fictitious commodities' of a self-regulating system; these three commodities were traded with complete freedom. Fictitious, according to Polanyi, because land, labour and capital, were *not* in fact produced for sale. Nor did

[22] *The Great Transformation*, 52–53.

[23] Ibid., 49. When making a distinction between (noneconomic) value and price, the difference between the market economy and traditional transactions such as applied by the Kula, illustrates this distinction well.

the available quantity of these three disappear when prices were low. He added that labour and land were no other than the human beings themselves of which every society consists and the natural surroundings in which it exists. To include them in the market mechanism means to subordinate the substance of society itself to the laws of the market.[24]

This sounds rather weird for most of us now, as the contemporary reader assumes that land, labour and capital each have a market price. Bradford DeLong helps to understand what Polanyi had in mind:

> 'With respect to land, people believe they have rights to a stable community. This includes the belief that the natural and built environment in which they grew up... is theirs, whether or not market logic says it would be more profitable if it were different—say a highway ran through it—or more lucrative if somebody else lived there. ... With respect to labor, people believe they have a right to a suitable income. After all, they prepared for their profession, played by the rules, and so believe society owes them a fair income.... And this holds whether or not the logic of the world market says otherwise. With respect to finance, people believe that as long as they do their job of working diligently, the flow of purchasing power through the economy should be such as to give them the wherewithal to buy.... People have not just property rights, but these other economic rights as well—rights that pure market economy will not respect. A pure market economy will lay down that highway, ignore years of preparation when doling out an income, and allow your purchasing power to dry up and blow away along with your job if someone thousands of miles away decides better returns on investments are to be found elsewhere.[25]

[24] Ibid., 75. On pp. 166–167, Polanyi made an interesting observation about the effects of colonialism and exploitation: 'Yet, it is precisely this emphasis put on exploitation which tends to hide from our view the even greater issue of cultural degradation. If exploitation is defined in strictly economic terms as a permanent inadequacy of ratios of exchange, it is doubtful whether, as a matter of fact, there was exploitation. The catastrophe of the native community is a direct result of the rapid and violent disruption of the basic institutions of the victim.... These institutions are disrupted by the very fact that a market economy is forced upon an entirely differently organized community; labor and land are made into commodities, which, again, is only a short formula for the liquidation of every and any cultural institution on an organic society.'

[25] DeLong, B. (2022) *Slouching Towards Utopia; An Economic History of the Twentieth Century*. London: Basic Books, 94–95.

Polanyi described how, in spite of the threat to social order, the *laissez faire* philosophy evolved into a true faith in man's secular salvation through a SRM. He referred to Thomas Malthus who accepted poverty as part of a natural order. Malthus projected a mismatch between population growth and the capacity of a society to feed its people. Because he failed to see that technological improvement could boost agricultural production, he concluded that once the population had outgrown the available agricultural potential, famine would ensue, after which equilibrium would be restored between people and the food supply.

Market liberalism also produced an inevitable response; a concerted effort to protect society from the market. Polanyi called the continuing tension and conflict between the efforts to establish, maintain, and spread the SRM, and the efforts to protect people and society from SRM's consequences: the *double movement*. This was illustrated by the developments in Britain. On one side was a concerted philosophical and legislative program there to establish the SRM from the enclosures of the 1790s, through the Poor Law Reform of 1834 (which halted government payments to able-bodied poor, unless they entered the workhouses),[26] to the Ricardian Bank Charter Act of 1844 (which restricted powers of British banks and gave exclusive note-issuing powers to the Bank of England), and the repeal of the Corn Laws in 1846 (introducing a decisive shift towards free trade in Britain). The other side was a widely varying, unorganized set of movements, legislative reforms, and administrative actions to limit the effects of self-regulation, from the Chartists through early legislation to limit the hours of work of women and children, through the growth of labour unions, and the re-imposition of tariffs on foodstuffs, to the first legislation presaging the welfare state.

[26] The original Poor Laws of 1601, which provided deserving poor meagre rations through parishes, but withheld these so-called parish-loaves from the undeserving poor.

Polanyi was impressed by the social philosophy and initiatives of entrepreneur Robert Owen (1771–1858). He grasped the fact that what appeared primarily as an economic problem was essentially a social one. In economic terms the worker was exploited: He did not get in exchange that which was his due. Owen justly pronounced that unless legislative interference and direction counteracted these devastating forces, permanent evils would follow. He believed that man should be his own employer; the principle of cooperation or 'union' would solve the problem of the machine without sacrificing either individual freedom or social solidarity, either man's dignity or his sympathy with his fellows. In New Lanark, Owen established a futuristic education scheme. Owenite Societies were associations designed to support plans of Villages of Cooperation. In hindsight, Owenism, concluded Polanyi, was the beginning of the trade union movement.[27]

What are the *double movement's* implicit tensions? As I mentioned before, the double-movement notion was inspired by Toynbee's Challenge-and-Response dialectic.[28] SRMs cannot function freely, precisely because of the correcting influence of the counter movement that was defending the principle of social protection. In this context, Polanyi's definition of socialism is interesting. He defines socialism as the tendency inherent in an industrial civilization to transcend the self-regulating market by consciously subordinating it to a democratic society. From the point of view of the community as a whole, socialism is merely the continuation of that endeavour to make society a distinctively human relationship of persons which in Western Europe was always associated with Christian traditions.[29] This definition allows for a continuing role for markets *within*

[27] *The Great Transformation*, 176.

[28] In Toynbee's *A Study of History*, the author presented a history of the rise and fall of civilizations, governed by sequences of Challenge-and-Response and Withdrawal-and-Return. Polanyi took a special interest in the former. 'Its premise was that the central explanatory events in any historical process are challenges that confront individuals and societies, putting their spiritual resources to the test....As ordeal follows ordeal, some civilizations fall by the wayside, others struggle on, while still others grow in wisdom and stature—in the process releasing new forces and institutions that are then tested by new challenges.' *Karl Polanyi*, 135.

[29] *The Great Transformation*, 242.

socialist societies. Polanyi noted that socialist working-class parties were, on the whole, committed to the reform of capitalism, not to its revolutionary overthrow.

At any event, Polanyi observed that not even radical adherents of economic liberalism could escape the rule which makes laissez-faire inapplicable to advanced industrial conditions; for in the critical case of trade union law and anti-trust regulations, extreme liberals themselves had to call for manifold interventions of the state in order to secure the preconditions for the working of a self-regulating market against monopolistic compacts. So, even free trade and competition required intervention to be workable.

The SRM was impaired in operation, and it meant that justification for international cooperation and the liberal state were weakened. In fact, increasing protectionism so impaired the SRM that it led to political intervention. When foreign debtors refused to pay, Polanyi suggested that governments should respond to the resulting strain. In an emergency, the unity of society would assert itself through the medium of government intervention.

More disruptive strains emerged. For example, under the gold standard, any measure that caused a budgetary deficit might start a depreciation of the currency. If on the other hand, unemployment was being fought by the expansion of bank credit, rising domestic prices would hit exports and affect the balance of payments. In either case, exchanges would slump and the country concerned would feel the pressure on its currency; in other words: A *catch-22* situation.

Protectionism, and the call for autarky, blocked free international trade. Within a few years, free trade was a matter of the past. Whether protection was justified or not, a weakness of the world market system was brought to light. Import tariffs of one country hampered the exports of another and forced it to seek markets in unprotected regions. Economic imperialism was mainly a struggle among the industrialized nations so as to extend their trade into politically unprotected markets. Yet, it was still felt that maintenance of the gold standard was imperative. At the heart of the transformation was the failure of the market utopia, concluded Polanyi.

When in the 1930s, the last of the nineteenth-century surviving institutions—the gold standard—collapsed, all of a sudden the stress within nations was diminished. Their responses were adjustments to the disappearance of the traditional world economy. Polanyi concluded Part II as follows:

…when it disintegrated, market civilization itself was engulfed. This explains the almost unbelievable fact that a civilization was being disrupted by the blind action of soulless institutions the only purpose of which was the automatic increase of material welfare'.[30]

Part III: Transformation in Progress
When in the 1920s the international system failed, the almost forgotten issues of early capitalism re-appeared. Popular government was one of them. The struggle to restore the nineteenth-century system by re-establishing the gold standard subsequently destroyed the international financial system.[31]

In Europe the charge of inflationism became an effective argument against democratic legislatures in the 1920s, with devastating consequences: Not cutting wages or social services were inescapably set by the mechanism of the market. Invariably, the danger was to the currency. And with equal regularity, the responsibility was fixed on inflated wages and unbalanced budgets—an unsustainable situation. Polanyi concluded that The *New Deal* never had a chance if America would not have gone off gold.

In other countries, going off gold meant dropping out of the world economy. Perhaps the only exception was Great Britain, whose share in world trade was so large that she had been able to lay down the modalities under which the international monetary system should work, thus shifting the burden of the gold standard to other shoulders. War reparations after WWI had a highly destabilizing effect on the currencies of the defeated countries; in particular Germany and Austria. The burden of the international credit mechanism was shifted first to the European victors and from there to America. The collapse of the American economy in October 1929 pulled the rest of the industrialized world into the Great Depression. The global political and economic system disintegrated conjointly.

[30] Ibid., 228.

[31] Re-establishment of the gold standard in Great Britain was disastrous: 'But under Britain's restored gold standard in 1925, the Bank of England was prevented from setting bank rates low enough to allow a level of investment equal to what the community wanted to save; the result was mass unemployment. Keynes had already predicted this in his 1925 essay 'The Economic Consequences of Mr. Churchill'. Winston Churchill was then the Chancellor of the Exchequer and reintroduced the gold standard at its pre-WWI level.' Source: De Haan, P. (2016) *From Keynes to Piketty; The Century That Shook Up Economics.* London: Palgrave Macmillan, 45.

Fear gripped the people and leadership was thrust upon those who offered a way out at whatever price. The time was ripe for radical solutions, concluded Polanyi. Fascism and communism sprang up as a response to the collapse of the SRM. Fascism has as little to do with the Great War as with the Versailles Treaty. After all, the movement also appeared in defeated countries like Bulgaria and in victorious ones like Finland and Norway, but also Italy and Spain. Polanyi concluded that the part played by fascism was determined by one factor only: The condition of the market system.

The Disarmament Conference (1932–1934) stopped meeting and in 1933, Germany left the League of Nations. The Nazis were banking on the final dissolution of the nineteenth-century economy. As a result, the political and economic system of the world disintegrated.

Russia's rise was also linked with her role in the transformation. The collectivization of the farms meant the supersession of the market economy by cooperative methods in regard to the decisive factor of land. Russia emerged as the representative of a new system which would replace the market economy. In short, the failure of the international system let loose the energies of history—the tracks were laid down by the tendencies inherent in the market society.

The conflict between the market and the elementary requirements of an organized society provided the century with the dynamics and produced the typical strains and stresses which ultimately destroyed that society. External wars only hastened its destruction. From the ensuing crisis a 'great transformation' commenced, one that was destined, Polanyi hoped, to *re-embed* economy in society.

Economic history reveals that the emergence of a national market was in no way the result of the gradual and spontaneous emancipation of the economic sphere from governmental control. On the contrary, the market has been the outcome of a conscious and often violent intervention on the part of government which imposed the market organization on society for noneconomic ends. Polanyi concluded that the weakness of nineteenth-century society was not that it was industrial but that it was a market society.

Polanyi was optimistic about the longer term results of the reaction to the nineteenth -century economic system. He hoped to see a situation emerging in which both national economies and the global economy would be subordinated to democratic politics and individual freedom. There are three facts in the consciousness of Western man: Knowledge of death, knowledge of freedom, and knowledge of society. Polanyi concluded that the discovery of society is either the end or the rebirth of freedom.

Part II Polanyi's Philosophical Inspirations and His Observations About Liberalism

How can Karl Polanyi be characterized in philosophical terms? This is not an easy question to answer, as he drew inspiration from various political philosophical and Christian sources. Dale has this to say: Polanyi can be understood as a synthesizer, a freethinking humanist on a quest for community. He was destined to tease out, and become entangled, in contradictions between liberal and communitarian (and socialist) thought that formed (and form) the dominant creative tension within political philosophy.[32] Polanyi argued that liberalism had failed society. Liberal political economy had sanctioned a 'denial of responsibility on the part of the well-to-do for the conditions of their fellows.'[33]

What about Polanyi's appreciation of Marxism? He is ambivalent on it. During his young adult years in Budapest, he became 'increasingly critical' of Marxism.[34] During that time Polanyi warmed to liberal socialism. He argued that Marxism sees the world from the outside and posits the inevitable collapse of capitalism. This way of thinking would lull individuals into a position in which their ethical stance counts for nothing. On the other hand, Dale observes that as the key to the creation of 'personal' economic relations, Polanyi's thought resembles that of Marx, among others. However, during his North American years, Polanyi's views became closer to non-Marxist left.

Regarding Polanyi's Christian inspiration, in his younger days he had read the New Testament with great attention. Once in Great Britain, he

[32] *Karl Polanyi*, 3.
[33] *The Great Transformation*, 106.
[34] *Karl Polanyi*, 49.

joined the Christian Left, whose philosophy was, among others, inspired by T.H. Green who, as we saw, criticized classical liberalism for neglecting the suffering of the impoverished classes. Polanyi contributed an essay to *Christianity and the Social Revolution* (1935), in which he set out his religious philosophy. Christianity's spiritual nature is individual freedom. He further argued that all humans are morally equal; they cannot act ethically without reference to their coexistence with others, and are thus destined to create a community. He then, typically, concluded that further moves towards community were inevitable, if humanity were to survive. However, he added, Christianity did not have the necessary strength indispensable to the coming transformation. Despite his earlier inspiration the New Testament had given him, Polanyi now argued that the New Testament was insufficient; he saw that a post-Christian age was dawning.

Returning to Polanyi's above observation about liberal political economy having sanctioned a denial of responsibility, one wonders whether the philosophy of new liberalism had not had any influence on Polanyi's thinking. After all, Green had argued that the individual can only come to fruition within the life of a community. Government had a moral duty to concern itself with the good life of the citizenry as a whole. Green radicalized liberal political theory at the time. His philosophy inspired younger thinkers such as Arnold Toynbee who, as alluded to, introduced the Challenge-and-Response model. Toynbee had been groomed in Whiggish promises of progress but had drastically changed his mind after the Great War, revealing the potential collapse of Western civilization. *The Great Transformation* echoes Toynbee's thinking rather than Green's.

Another 'modern' new liberal was Keynes. Before arriving in England, Karl had written Michael that he was looking forward to meeting Keynes. His initial appreciation of Keynes gradually evaporated. In this connection, Dale observes: 'Polanyi identified several political forces and actors that were attempting to derail Britain's socialist trajectory. There was Wall Street and its 'ruthless Republican' allies, whose fingerprints were all over Bretton Woods alongside those of Keynes, who had 'destroyed his life's work by pledging himself to the interests of Republican big business''. It must be concluded that, in the end, new liberalism—in its different guises—had not influenced Polanyi.

Polanyi is best known for his critique of classical liberal political economy, and he died believing that its errors would never be repeated; this is what institutional political economist Jamie Peck concluded.[35] Indeed, it

[35] Peck, J. (2010) *Constructions of Neoliberal Reason*. Oxford: Oxford University Press, 27.

seemed as if during the *trente glorieuses* the sharp edges of the market economy, as Polanyi laid bare, had disappeared. From the 1940s to the 1980s considerable achievements of social democratic governments, particularly in Scandinavia, show that Polanyi's vision could be put into practice. De Long sums it up quite lucidly: 'A social democratic government needed to enable the market economy in order to generate growth and prosperity. But it also needed to check the market and keep the 'market economy' from turning into a 'market society' that people might reject, a society where employment was not stable, incomes were not commensurate with what people deserved, and communities were being continually upended and transformed by market fluctuations.'[36] But this social-democratic near-utopia did not last.

The Great Transformation is a critique of one of economic liberalism's major aspects: The SRM doctrine. Before market liberalism took off, the economy was embedded in society. Polanyi reminded the reader that not just the market economy, but also free trade and the gold standard were English inventions. Polanyi observed that British philosophers/economists, among them, Adam Smith and David Hume—and the British Liberal party at the time—had promoted these liberal economic notions, be it that the Liberal party never was a whole hearted supporter of free trade.

Polanyi argued that SRM was the 'fount and matrix of the entire system'. It was also the innovation that gave rise to a specific civilization. In other words, the control of the economic system by the market was of overwhelming consequence for the organization of society. Subsequently, he concluded with a statement which to this day is closely associated with Polanyi: The running of society became an adjunct to the market, rather than the other way round. He told his students that if economic liberalism were to fully take hold of society's material life, it would surely destroy it.[37] Fair enough, there was material improvement for the exploited workers. Nonetheless, the system was bound to collapse; this is the central message of *The Great Transformation*.

In his Introduction to *The Great Transformation*, Fred Block argues: 'Polanyi's analysis of the three fictitious commodities [land, labour and capital; PdH] teaches that the neoliberal vision of automatic market

[36] *Slouching Towards Utopia*, 399.
[37] *Karl Polanyi*, 156.

adjustment at the global level is a dangerous fantasy. Just as national economies depend on an active governmental role, so too does the global economy need strong regulatory institutions.... Without such institutions particular economies—and perhaps the entire global economy—will suffer crippling economic crises.'[38] More fundamentally, Block observes, is that market liberalism makes demands on ordinary people that are simply not sustainable. He had poor people in developing countries in mind, but, as it later turned out, also scores of formerly employed factory workers in industrial areas in rich countries who were laid off. They turned their backs to traditional political parties and voted for populist parties instead.

It must be underscored that Polanyi did not reject liberalism altogether; after all, he embraced freedom—a central notion of liberalism. What did he mean with this term? At the end of *The Great Transformation*, he observed that the dividing line between liberalism on the one hand, and fascism and socialism on the other, is not principally economic—it is moral and religious. Even where they profess identical economics, they are not only different but are embodiments of opposite principles. The ultimate on which they separate is freedom. Power and compulsion are a part of the reality for fascists and socialists. However, the issue on which they divide is whether, in the light of this knowledge, the idea of freedom can be upheld or not; in other words, is freedom an empty word, or can man reassert his freedom in the face of that knowledge and strive for its fulfilment in society without lapsing into moral illusionism?[39]

The book's final paragraph says it all:

> Uncomplaining acceptance of the reality of society gives man indominable courage and strength to remove all removable injustice and unfreedom. As long as he is true to his task of creating more abundant freedom for all, he need not fear that either power or planning will turn against him and destroy the freedom he is building by their instrumentality. This is the meaning of freedom in a complex society; it gives us all the certainty we need.[40]

[38] *The Great Transformation*, xxxiv.

[39] Ibid., 267.

[40] Ibid., 268.

References

Dale, G. (2018). *Karl Polanyi, A Life on the Left*. Columbia University Press.

De Haan, P. (2016). *From Keynes to Piketty; The Century That Shook Up Economics*. Palgrave Macmillan.

DeLong, B. (2022). *Slouching Towards Utopia; An Economic History of the Twentieth Century*. Basic Books.

Drucker, P. (2007). *Adventures of a Bystander*. Transaction Publishers.

North, D. (1977). *Markets and Other Allocation Systems in History: The Challenge of Karl Polanyi*. Journal of European Economic History.

Peck, J. (2010). *Constructions of Neoliberal Reason*. Oxford University Press.

Polanyi, K. (2001). *The Great Transformation; The Political and Economic Origins of Our Time*. Beacon Press.

CHAPTER 5

Keynes and Hayek: Both Liberals but Economic Adversaries

Prologue

Karl Polanyi's principal message was that market liberalism was doomed to fail and resulted in political and economic disasters. Polanyi's contemporaries, John Maynard Keynes, born in 1883, and Friedrich August Hayek in 1899, were—like Polanyi—both 'children' of the *Belle Epoque*. Keynes and Hayek, as we shall see, differed from Polanyi's interpretation of the political and economic consequences of what had happened, and what should be done. As this chapter's title suggests, Keynes and Hayek did not agree at all between them what the problems were, let alone how to address them.

The Belle Epoque, the period of unprecedented economic bliss, inspired Keynes to write this about a fortunate Londoner, benefitting from the riches: 'The inhabitant of London could order by telephone, sipping his morning tea in bed, the various products of the whole earth, in such quantity as he might see fit, and reasonably expect early delivery upon his doorstep'[1] The *Belle Epoque* was free market economics at its best.

This exceptional period of economic progress came to an abrupt end in 1914, when the Great War broke out. Towards the end of 1919, immediately after the end of the peace negotiations in France, Keynes published

[1] Keynes, J.M. (2005) *The Economic Consequences of Peace*. New York: Cosimo Classics, 11.

P. de Haan, *Great Economists and the Evolution of Economic Liberalism*, https://doi.org/10.1007/978-3-031-93831-3_5

The Economic Consequences of Peace, about the dramatic consequences of the Treaty of Versailles; consequences, which very few people at the time foresaw. The consequences were disastrous; there is simply no other word for it: Dangerous political instability, combined with hyperinflation in Germany and Austria.

During the war, Hayek had served as a spotter in Austria's air force. Hailing from a relatively well-off noble family, Austria's hyperinflation caused the Hayek family's capital to evaporate. The great British historian Arnold Toynbee observed, with foresight, that men and women all over the world were seriously contemplating the possibility that the Western system of society might break down and cease to work. Germany and Austria were broke, while other European countries owed the United States enormous sums of money from the costly war. Unemployment shot up, and so did malnutrition.

In America, the brief post-war period, better-known as the *Roaring Twenties*, led to an unjustified overoptimism about ever-rising stock prices. The Wall Street crash of October 1929 eventually led to the Great Depression. Counterproductive protectionist trade policies were adopted. Monetary and fiscal austerity measures only worsened the situation. Economists wrung their hands, as classical economic approaches only worsened the depression. New theories were required to explain the situation, but they were not yet at hand.

During the 1920s, Keynes already bade farewell to one of classical economics' central themes: *laissez faire*. He was also discovering that the basic problem with economic depressions was a shortage of aggregate demand. When aggregate demand fell short, as it did during the Great Depression, the government had to step in to fill the demand gap and restore a balance in the economy; this is what Keynes proposed. Hayek, on the other hand, stuck to conservative classical economic theory. He fiercely defended that the free market system should be left to itself. One should have confidence in the market's natural self-regulating system, Hayek argued. Tinkering with it would make a difficult situation, such as a depression, only worse.

Hayek and Keynes called themselves liberals. Both felt that ideas and freedom were essential elements of liberalism. Yet they differed regarding other aspects. Keynes moved into the direction of what new liberalism added to liberalism's classical notions, while Hayek remained to the end of his long life the more conservative liberal.

This chapter presents the development in the thinking of both game-changers, their differences, their clashes, but also their mutual intellectual respect. Keynes and Hayek provided the basis of the two dominant mainstream schools of thought in economics: Keynesianism and neoclassical economics. Both have not lost relevance; on the contrary. The debate between Keynes and Hayek was continued, with fresh inputs from Paul Samuelson and Milton Friedman, and—after them—by scores of other economists.

Introduction

Keynes and Hayek were two towering figures in economics. Their interests reached beyond the economic science. Hayek made forays in social science methodology, physiological psychology, the history of ideas, and political philosophy. Keynes, who had not even graduated in economics (his dissertation was about probability), invented modern macroeconomics and revolutionized economics. He was also a philosopher, statesman, polemicist, and protector of the arts. Both collected antiquarian books.

Their contributions to economics, using little mathematics, provided the foundation for the development of modern economics; therefore, their theories are presented in some detail. Keynes was the most famous economist of the first half of the past century. Hayek was arguably the economist who contributed most widely and deeply to the preservation of neoclassical economics along Austrian School lines.[2]

Hayek strongly disavowed the Keynesian Revolution. Although both claimed to have been inspired by liberalism, they differed regarding its interpretation. Despite their radically different opinions on economics, and the spirited debate on them, they maintained a long and courteous correspondence and friendship.[3] In a condolence letter to Keynes's widow, Lydia Lopokova, Hayek wrote that Keynes was the most intelligent and most original thinker he had known.

[2] Economics professor at Cambridge university, Ha-Joon Chang, rightly noted that there are differences between the Austrian School and neoclassical economics. 'Not all neoclassical economists are free-market economists….The adherents of the Austrian school are even more ardent supporters of the free market than most followers of the Neoclassical school.' Source: Chang, H.-J. (2014) *Economics: The User's Guide*. London: Pelican Books, 138.

[3] Laurence Hayek's obituary of his father mentions that Keynes and Hayek took shifts on the roof of King's Chapel on fire-watch during the War. Source: *King's College, Cambridge, Annual Report 2008*, 142. Later research proved that this did not happen.

Part I: Keynes and Hayek: Their Life and Work and Debate on the Business Cycle

Keynes's Life and Work

John Maynard was the son of John Neville Keynes, a Cambridge logician and economist, and Florence Ada Brown who was Cambridge's mayor for some time. As young Maynard was a brilliant pupil, he won a scholarship to Eton. His father helped him to gain another scholarship; this time to King's College, Cambridge, where he studied mathematics during his undergraduate years. He was tutored by Alfred Marshall (1842–1924) who persuaded him to study economics, to no avail. Keynes's doctoral thesis was about probability. As for the use of mathematics in economics, Keynes's scepticism grew rather than diminished with age. His scepticism equally applied to econometrics. This had to do with his understanding of the complexity of social life which simply cannot fully be captured by mathematics and equations.

Keynes started his professional career in London as a civil servant at the India Office. In his spare time he wrote his thesis. He did not like working at the India Office much, and so returned to Cambridge to take up a teaching post and the editorship of the *Economic Journal*. He was invited to become a member of the Bloomsbury Group, a nonconformist group of intellectuals, authors, and painters.[4] Some say that Keynes developed his sense of superiority there. Indeed, philosopher Isaiah Berlin (1909–1997) once observed that Keynes was equipped with an indestructible superiority complex. He was invariably the cleverest person in any meeting, knew it, and showed it. Another commentator, who served with Keynes on the Council for the Encouragement of Music and the Arts during WWII, complained that Keynes used his brilliance 'too unsparingly…he never dimmed his headlights.'[5]

Keynes made his fame after the end of the Great War. This is how it happened. He represented the Treasury during the peace negotiations. Before the Treaty of Versailles was signed, he resigned in disgust, as he correctly felt that the treaty could only result in more misery and political instability in Europe. In record time he wrote *The Economic Consequences*

[4] American poet/satirist Dorothy Parker wrote that the Bloomsbury Group lived in squares, painted in circles and loved in triangles.

[5] Skidelsky, R. (2003) *John Maynard Keynes 1883–1946: Economist, Philosopher, Statesman*. London: Pan Books, 471.

of Peace, which came out at the end of 1919. It became an instant best-seller, not just in Europe but also in the US. As for Keynes's fame, this is illustrated by this anecdote: 'He worked in various roles for the British government and advised politicians, who had to put up with a lot from him. Apparently, when Keynes arrived with Prime Minister Herbert Henry Asquith at a function near Oxford, a butler announced them as 'Mr. Keynes and another gentleman.'[6]

He returned to Cambridge to lecture, wrote for the *Manchester Guardian*, and other widely read newspapers. He became bursar of King's College and guided the finances of an insurance company. He also found the time to write books. One of them is *A Tract on Monetary Reform* (1923), in which he warned for the dangers of inflation.[7] Corrective measures were called for, argued Keynes, to redress the situation and prevent hyperinflation, as experienced by Austria and Germany after the war had ended. In 1930, he published *A Treatise on Money*, which is best seen as a precursor to his masterpiece *The General Theory of Employment, Interest and Money* (1936). The *Treatise* emphasized the role of investment and saving. Keynes maintained that there is no automatic mechanism in a credit-money economy to keep saving and investment in equilibrium.

In hindsight, Keynes was not happy with *A Treatise* as it did not explain how an economy could remain in a state of prolonged depression. Something else must hold the economy back, he thought. He provided the answer in *The General Theory*. The essence of *The General Theory* is that the economy is not, as neoclassicals argued, self-regulating. He explored the problem and dangers of capitalist instability. The economy needed to be managed to redress or prevent imbalances and to ensure full employment. Mass unemployment was Keynes's principal concern. Insufficient aggregate demand caused the depression—this was Keynes's fundamental insight. The government had to stimulate aggregate demand through fiscal policies to get the economy out of a slump. The book radiated hope. 'What we got was joyful revelation in dark times', observed a student at the time.[8]

[6] *In the Long Run We're all Dead*, 82.

[7] Milton Friedman, the most famous economist of the second half of the past century, took inspiration from this book in developing his monetarist policy proposals, as explained in Chap. 6.

[8] Skidelsky, R. (2010) *Keynes A Very Short Introduction*. Oxford: Oxford University Press, 2. On the same page Skidelsky quotes Lorie Tarsis, another economics student, who wrote: 'And finally what Keynes supplied was hope: hope that prosperity could be restored and maintained without the support of prison camps, executions and bestial interrogations.'

In his analysis, Keynes applied an entirely new *macroeconomic* approach.[9] An economy was best understood by grasping the big picture: Looking down from the top at aggregate demand and supply, aggregate savings and investment, etc. Robert Heilbroner said of this exceptional book that it 'was revolutionary; no other word will quite do. It stood economics on its head, very much as *The Wealth of Nations* and *Capital* had done.'[10] The book triggered the Keynesian Revolution. Keynes said that *The General Theory*'s purpose was to save capitalism from its demise, although he had a moral distaste for capitalism, yet he felt that it could survive under improved management.

The General Theory is not an easy read; the book combines inconsistencies with brilliant insights. This is how Paul Samuelson (1915–2009) assessed tit:

> It is a badly written book, poorly organized; any layman who, beguiled by the author's previous reputation, bought the book was cheated of his 5 shillings…Flashes of insight and intuition intersperse tedious algebra. An awkward definition suddenly gives way to an unforgettable cadenza. When it finally is mastered, we find its analysis to be obvious and at the same time new. In short, it is a work of genius.[11]

Another fan of Keynes was the Canadian economic adviser of Roosevelt, Laughlin Currie (1902–1993) who was taken aback upon reading *The General Theory*. He observed: 'All too often we find that familiar things are being described in unfamiliar language, that concepts cannot be given statistical meaning, and that precision and definiteness are being purchased at the expense of reality.'[12] This unfamiliar language was in fact Keynes's most lasting contribution to economics.

[9] Keynes introduced a new macroeconomic approach. Why new? Eighteen's century French Physiocrat François Quesnay (1694–1774) had depicted the economy in a macroeconomic circular manner, starting with farmers (the creators of wealth), who handed their net produce to landowners, who in turn spent it on consumer goods.

[10] Heilbroner, R. (2000) *The Worldly Philosophers; The Lives, Times and Ideas of the Great Economic Thinkers*. Seventh Edition. London: Penguin Books, 270.

[11] *In the Long Run We're all Dead*, 79–80.

[12] Source: Burns, J. (2023) *Milton Friedman; the Last Conservative*. New York: Farrar, Straus and Giroux, 96.

As always in economics, the book did not just receive praise, it was also criticized by, among others, Joseph Schumpeter (1883–1950) and members of the Stockholm School, but not by Hayek. *The General Theory* inspired Keynesians and their critics to continue the debate, as this book shows.

Whenever economies enter into a recession, such as during the Great Recession and, more recently, the global Covid-pandemic, Keynes's policy tools are dusted off and applied once again. These recent experiences made it abundantly clear that government has to play a stabilising and growth-promoting role in the management of an economy.

Towards the end of WWII, Keynes again played an important role. He had prepared a paper in anticipation of the Bretton Woods Conference, held in July 1944, hosted by American President Roosevelt. The aim of the conference was to establish global monetary stability after the war, and to create an institution to help affected countries with post-war reconstruction and economic development.

Keynes proposed to prevent a repeat of the mistakes made by the Allies after the Great War. He was in favour of an international Clearing Union, including the establishment of a new international reserve currency, the *bancor*. This clearing union was to assist countries with trade deficits with temporary credits, and to penalize countries running trade surpluses (in particular the US at the time), in order to prevent the international economic system from sinking into another depression.

Keynes was invited to chair the meetings tasked with the establishment of the International Bank for Reconstruction and Development (i.e., the World Bank). His American counterpart, Henry Dexter White (1892–1948), presided over the meeting to establish the International Monetary Fund. The Americans did not like Keynes's *bancor* idea of penalizing surplus countries. Since America was by far the world's richest country, it called the shots. Keynes's bancor idea was not accepted. Instead, the dollar became the global reserve currency, backed by a fixed exchange rate between the dollar and gold.

In August 1945, the British government requested Keynes to negotiate a grant, or an interest-free loan, deal with the US, as the British government was almost broke. The strain involving tough negotiations and repeated trips across the Atlantic took their toll. After having suffered a second heart attack, Keynes died on 21 April 1946; at the age of 63.

Life and Work of Hayek

Friedrich August Hayek hailed from a prominent Viennese family. His father was a medical doctor and his mother was related to the Wittgenstein's; Friedrich (Fritz for friends) was a cousin of philosopher Ludwig Wittgenstein. During the Great War, Hayek was enlisted in an Austro-Hungarian artillery regiment, and worked as spotter in an air force plane. Once the war had ended, Austrians—including the Hayek family—were suffering from hyperinflation. This traumatic experience may explain why inflation and monetary stability were Hayek's lifelong preoccupations.

After the war, Hayek studied law, but after having completed his law studies, he took up economics under Friedrich von Wieser (1851–1926), who had developed the idea of diminishing marginal utility. Inspired by utilitarianism, this led to the proposal of redistribution of income so as to bring about a greater utility for mankind at large. Young Friedrich was attracted to socialism, not least inspired by the lively discussions he had with other young Viennese intellectuals at café Landtmann. Hayek was one of the organizers of the Geist-Kreis, where subjects ranging from logical positivism to literature were hotly debated.

Hayek underwent his economic formation from leading scholars of the Austrian School. Apart from his marginal utility ideas, Wieser argued that prices were the key to understanding how markets work. Wieser introduced Hayek to Ludwig von Mises (1881–1973), an impressive figure of the Austrian School, who was a strong proponent of the self-regulating role of markets. In *Economic Calculation in the Socialist Commonwealth* (1920), Mises explained that a centrally planned economy lacked the necessary data to calculate prices that would bring supply and demand into balance. It was Mises who cured Hayek from his socialist sympathies.

After a brief career in Austria as director of the Institute for Business Cycle Research, Hayek was invited to visit the UK in 1931. The invitation was inspired by the contents of Hayek's *The Paradox of Saving* (1929), in which he argued that there was a direct relationship between savings and demand. It was Lionel Robbins of the London School of Economics (LSE) who invited Hayek to come to Britain. Robbins felt that Hayek was the perfect candidate to, as elaborated below, attack Keynes's *Treatise on Money* (1930). He was offered a LSE professorship in 1931. In that same year, Hayek published *Prices and Production*. After the Austrian *Anschluss* in 1938, Hayek adopted British citizenship.

His *Monetary Theory and the Trade Cycle* came out in 1933. Recessions are caused by imbalances, argued Hayek. There was no longer a direct relationship between savings and investment, like in the old days when entrepreneurs used their savings to invest. The balance between saving and investment had to be restored. Too much money in circulation was another factor causing recessions, as it triggered too much consumer demand, leading to inflation. Hayek's remedy was: Cut down consumer demand so that extra savings be freed up to finance fresh investments. Keynes's remedy, as pointed out before, was the opposite: Depressions and unemployment were caused by a drop in aggregate demand.

After the end of WWII, Hayek visited the United States, to undertake a speaking tour resulting from the successful publication of *The Road to Serfdom* (1944) in *The Reader's Digest*.[13] In this booklet, Hayek grilled central planning, and the overarching role of government in the economy, which was detrimental to economic development and to individual liberties. State intervention would trigger even more state intervention and it would raise the chances of fascism. Needless to say Hayek's opinion was not universally accepted.[14]

In 1945, the prestigious *American Economic Review* published Hayek's article: The Use of Knowledge in Society. Reflective of his Austrian School influence, Hayek observed that the price system, based upon competition, provides the information necessary to take economic decisions by individual investors and consumers. Hence the system facilitates *decentralized*, from the bottom-up, decision-making which central planning cannot provide. There are other types of information, much of which is specific to individuals. Possession of such tacit, and thus largely unmeasurable, information gives practically every individual some advantage over all others. However, this information cannot be captured by economic planners, But, concluded Hayek, the price system, that includes all the information, can!

Hayek compared the price system with *a system of telecommunications*. Distortions of this system, for example caused by inflation or wage and

[13] A cartoon version of *The Road to Serfdom* had been published as well.

[14] '*The Road to Serfdom* was less a work of economic theory than a declaration of total libertarian faith in individuals, in their leading role in market mechanisms, and in the absolute dangers of any and all government involvement in the economy. With hindsight and a knowledge of the role of government in economic growth since the end of World War II, the book stands out for its total lack of engagement with the realities of postwar growth period and its fanatical vision of the state as a force of evil.' Soll, J. (2022) *Free Market; The History of an Idea*. New York: Basic Books, 248.

price controls, give the wrong signals. Prices would no longer reflect the most efficient modes of production. Chances are then great that resources will be employed in areas that are the most optimal neither for firms nor for the economy as a whole. This reduces efficiency and a society's standard of living.

In 1947, after having returned to Europe, Hayek initiated the Mont Pèlerin Society, a community of like-minded liberals, such as von Mises, his Geist-Kreis friend Fritz Machlup (1902–1983), and Americans, among them George Stigler (1911–1991) and Friedman. Philosopher of science Karl Popper (1902–1994) also participated. The society advocates freedom of expression, free market economic policies and the political values of an open society. It also seeks to discover ways in which free enterprise can replace government entities in providing public functions.

In 1950, Hayek accepted an invitation to teach at the University of Chicago. During his Chicago tenure, he wrote *The Constitution of Liberty* (1960). This book is more a work on political philosophy than an economic treatise. Initially, the book did not sell well as it came out during the height of Keynesianism. Two decades later, however, Hayek's message went down very well in America and Europe; it inspired American President Reagan and British Prime Minister Thatcher's neoliberal policies.

The Constitution of Liberty presents principles of a society in which citizens enjoy freedom. The book describes how it can be achieved and explains what its realization means in practice. Hayek's objective for the reader was to restate the traditional doctrines of classical liberalism. The coercive power of government should be limited as much as possible. Yet, he acknowledged that government had a role to play in well-defined fields, such as the provision of a monetary system, the setting of standards of weights and measures, as well as education, sanitary and health services. Markets should be allowed to function as freely as possible, thereby providing the right price signals for consumers and producers.

In 1962, Hayek returned to Europe where he was appointed professor at the University of Freiburg, West Germany. After some time, he returned to Austria to spend his last active years at the University of Salzburg. In 1974, he was awarded the Nobel Prize in Economics. After his term had ended in Salzburg, Hayek went back to Freiburg, where he died in March 1992.

The Debate Between Keynes and Hayek

How It Started

In 1929, Keynes was appointed to the Macmillan Committee on Finance and Industry. He defended import duties and export credits, much to the chagrin of another vocal member of the committee, Lionel Robbins, an LSE free trader. Robbins wanted his dissenting opinion, as an annex, included in the committee's report. Keynes tried very hard to block it, but in the end he gave in.

One of the central themes of Keynes's *A Treatise on Money* was, as I have pointed out, a distinction between savings and investments, not necessarily being of equal value. One group of people saved but quite another invested, Keynes argued. Their intentions differed, resulting in imbalances. The monetary authorities had to make sure that savings and investments were kept in equilibrium. Robbins, however, strongly disagreed and, triggered by the contents of *A Treatise on Money*, he very much wanted to continue the debate between Keynes's Cambridge and Robbins's LSE, so as to teach Keynes a lesson. Robbins had invited Hayek to deliver a few lectures at the LSE on Hayek's *Paradox of Savings* (1929), in which he criticized Keynes's thinking. Robbins felt that Hayek was the ideal candidate to write a scathing attack on Keynes's *Treatise*. Hayek consented and wrote a very long, vitriol review entitled *Reflections*, which appeared in LSE's journal *Economica*.[15]

Hayek argued that *A Treatise* was extremely difficult, unsystematic, and obscure. His main criticism, however, was that Keynes had ignored Austrian notions of capital theory. Hayek suggested that Keynes was an amateur in economics; a reputation Keynes indeed had in some circles. Hayek did not agree with Keynes's rejection of the need for an equilibrium between saving and investment. Hayek maintained, in line with Austrian School's theory of capital, that when savings and investments were not in equilibrium, it was the result of banks offering inappropriate 'unnatural' levels of credit.

[15] Hayek, F. A. (1932) Reflections on the Pure Theory of Money of Mr. J.M. Keynes. *Economica*. No. 35, February, 22–44.

Anybody familiar with Keynes's self-esteem[16] and temper would not be surprised to learn that he was furious. He sat down and dipped his pen in blood-soaked ink, so to speak. In responding, Keynes took the opportunity to characterize Hayek's recently published *Prices and Production* as one of 'the most frightful muddles he had ever read.' Keynes had not been entirely happy with *A Treatise*; he said that it was at best a reflection of 'work in progress'. At the time of Hayek's review, he had already distanced himself from some of the contents. Keynes's reaction also referred to new insights he was to elaborate in *The General Theory of Employment, Interest and Money*. About this book, he wrote to his friend and playwright George Bernard Shaw:

> ....you have to know that I believe myself to be writing a book on economic theory which will largely revolutionise—not, I suppose at once, but in the course of the next ten years—the way the world thinks about economic problems.[17]

At any event, as Nicholas Wapshott observes, Robbins and Hayek were grateful that Keynes had 'taken the bait', and happy that the great man was prepared to engage in a detailed discussion that would pit new Keynesian ideas against those of the Austrian School.'[18]

The ensuing exchange, printed in *Economica*, and later followed by personal correspondence between Hayek and Keynes, did not result in a shared understanding. In a correspondence with Piero Sraffa (1898–1983), one of his favourite pupils, Keynes remarked about Hayek's opinion: 'I feel that the abyss yawns—and so do I. Yet, I can't help feeling that there is something interesting in it.'[19] Would this last remark not suggest that Keynes recognized Hayek's brilliance? I believe it did, as confirmed in Hayek's later works.

[16] Russell once admitted that Keynes's intellect was the sharpest and clearest that he had ever known. When he argued with Keynes, he felt that he took his life in his hands, and he seldom emerged without feeling something of a fool. Nonetheless, Russell got on very well with Keynes. Let me add an anecdote. Being a workaholic, Keynes suffered from constant fatigue. As a young man he went to spend a restful weekend with the Russell's, and twenty-six unexpected guests arrived, most of them, Russell implied, summoned by Keynes.

[17] *The Worldly Philosophers*, 269.

[18] Wapshott, N. (2011) *Keynes Hayek; The Clash That Defined Modern Economics*. New York: W.W. Norton, 101.

[19] Ibid., 106.

Keynes and Hayek's Analyses of the Great Depression and Business Cycles
During the Interbellum, the Great Depression constituted economists' central challenge. As mentioned before, after the end of the Great War, a peace treaty was signed between the warring parties in the Hall of Mirrors, Versailles, France. Countries that had lost the war, such as Germany and Austria, had to pay the victors enormous 'reparation' payments to compensate for material and human losses during the war. This triggered political unrest and runaway inflation in both countries. The political result was that Adolf Hitler won the German elections in 1932. Well before that year, in 1917 a communist revolution ousted the Russian Czar, and Communism was ushered in. Fascism became the leading political philosophy in various European countries. Aggravated by the Great Depression, which started in October 1929, resulting in mass unemployment, poverty, and misery, the capitalist system became under grave threats. Keynes wanted to save the capitalist system by solving the problem of persistent mass unemployment.[20] Hayek also reacted to the challenge; however, in quite a different manner.

Keynes analysed the Great Depression from a completely new, top-down macroeconomic vantage point, in which the government played an active part in countering lost aggregate demand. His remedy was to increase total aggregate demand. There were a number of ways in which this could be done: Through monetary means, by lowering the interest rate and funnelling new money into the economy, or through fiscal means by tax breaks, and by public works. Government's actions would boost demand, triggering renewed production and employment. However, in a severe depression, such as the Great Depression, monetary policy would not work, concluded Keynes, as prices fell faster than interest rates. Once nominal rates fell to zero, there was nothing further the central bank could do to make borrowing cheaper, or to ease the debt burdens, and thus to stimulate the economy. When monetary policy does not work, the only remedy to shore up demand was through fiscal means, i.e., cutting taxes and government getting money into the hands of those who would spend it—in other words, government as spender of last resort. All this he presented in *The General Theory*. The book became arguably the past century's most influential publication in economics.

[20] In 1925, Keynes had visited the Soviet Union, and was not impressed by what he saw there. Moreover, he had become alarmed about young undergraduates in Cambridge turning to communism.

Now, what was Hayek's analysis of the business cycle? Well before *The Road to Serfdom*, in which he criticized central planning,[21] he had studied the business cycle in depth, applying a bottom-up, microeconomic approach, banking on the free functioning of the market and the role played by capital in the economy. Hayek observed that because no one could know what was in the minds of every member of society, and that the best indicator of their conflicting needs was market prices, all attempts to manipulate an economy were misplaced. After all, the myriad different prices agreed in all individual transactions made up the economy. Contrary to Keynes, who wondered how high unemployment and slack capacity could persist for a long time, Hayek tried to find out how, after a boom (caused by excessive money creation and low interest rates, triggering a misallocation of capital), the economy had turned into a depression. He argued that after a boom period, the economy would, after some time, reach a state of equilibrium, thanks to the 'invisible hand' and the essential role of the price system. The logic behind his reasoning was as follows: Competition among workers and among lenders should drive down wages and interest rates until it was once again profitable to hire workers and invest. Hayek added that the creation of artificial demand would do nothing to undo the misallocation of capital and would thus only lead to another burst of inflation—for Hayek a horror scenario.

Hayek wanted, in the traditional liberal fashion, state power to be as limited as possible. He challenged the state's monopoly of setting interest rates by the central bank. Such manipulation of the economy, Hayek argued, would bring about grave disturbances of the economic system as a whole. Instead, he proposed that the issuance of money by private banks was the key to ending the business cycle.[22]

For those who would like a more entertaining, yet accurate, presentation of the differences between Hayek and Keynes on the business cycle, I suggest to watch on YouTube *Fear the Boom and Bust*; *The Original Keynes* versus *Hayek Rap Battle*.

[21] Keynes wrote Hayek that he found himself deeply in agreement with *The Road to Serfdom*. Yet, he wrote: 'I should… conclude rather differently. I should say that what is not no planning, or even less planning, indeed I should say we almost certainly want more. But the planning should take place in a community in which as many people as possible, both leaders and followers, wholly share your own moral position.' Source: *Worldly Philosophers*, 278.

[22] In an interview Hayek said: 'I believe that if it were not for government interference with the monetary system, we would have no industrial fluctuations and no periods of depression.' Source: Interview of Hayek by Thomas W. Hazlett, 1977.

The Time Was Ripe for Keynes's Ideas

Keynes's approach to ending mass unemployment had an irresistible appeal. Politicians and the public at large loved it. After all, mass unemployment was on the top of politicians' agenda, and the prospect of solving it was obviously popular among the public. It helped a great deal that Keynes was good at promoting his ideas. His access to politicians, publishers, and influential newspapers certainly helped. In 1933, he published *The Means to Prosperity*; a collection of articles he had written for *The Times*, a British newspaper, about his most recent thinking on employment creation, which he included in *The General Theory.* On 31 December 1933, he published an 'Open Letter to Roosevelt' in *The New York Times*, in which the gist of *The General Theory*'s contents was presented.[23] Before *The General Theory* came out, he had met President Roosevelt twice.

In 1933, Keynes's new ideas were already applied by Adolf Hitler and Franklin Roosevelt; so three years before the publication of *The General Theory.* In other words, Keynes's ideas were already 'in the air' and being applied by both of them. By 1936, unemployment had virtually disappeared in Germany, while the depression in Germany had even been deeper than the one in the US.

Immediately after he had been elected Germany's *Reichskanzler* in January 1933, Hitler launched large public works programs, including rearmament. A few months later, across the Atlantic, Franklin Roosevelt had been inaugurated as President of the United States. To counter the deep slump, Roosevelt launched the *New Deal*—a broad range of public works, agricultural subsidies, and employment programs.

[23] In his open letter, Keynes applied a style of writing that was not particularly one to endear. A commentator observed in this vein, that this open letter sounded like a letter from a school teacher to the very rich father of a very dull pupil. Source; *Keynes A Very Short Introduction*, 8–9. Nonetheless, in his letter, he wrote, for example, that 'The stimulation of output by increasing aggregate purchasing power is the right way to get prices up; and not the other way around.' Another quote from the letter could have come straight from *The General Theory*, which appeared three years after Keynes sent his letter to Roosevelt: 'Thus as the prime mover in the first stage of the technique of recovery I lay overwhelming emphasis on the increase of national purchasing power resulting from governmental expenditure which is financed by loans and not by taxing present income.

Keynes's Changing Ideas

Various new ideas presented in *The General Theory* had been developed by Keynes and his *Cambridge Circus* collaborators well before the book came out. Other ideas, such as liquidity preference, the multiplier, and animal spirits were new. Richard Kahn (1905–1989) had developed the employment *multiplier*, which Keynes gratefully integrated into *The General Theory*, be it as the investment multiplier. In essence, the employment multiplier means that every job created by the government would add a further job to supply that new worker with goods. Keynes's investment multiplier (k) tells us that, when there is an increment of aggregate investment, income will increase by an amount which is *k* times the increment of investment.[24] Kahn was a member of the Cambridge Circus, together with other loyal Keynes disciples, such as James Meade (1907–1997), Austin Robinson (1897–1993), Joan Robinson, and Piero Sraffa. This group of young, brilliant economists influenced Keynes's thinking.

As briefly mentioned in Chap. 3, new liberal philosopher-economist and anti-imperialist John Hobson had launched an idea which was later taken over by Keynes. Hobson introduced the idea of under-consumption, which later appeared in Keynes's work as inadequate aggregate demand. Hobson had observed that over-saving and the unequal distribution of wealth restricted the purchasing power of the British population. The poor ended up with insufficient income to survive in dignity, concluded Hobson, and their consequent under-consumption created economic crises. Hobson's ideas had been included in a 1926 pamphlet of the Independent Labour party entitled *The Living Wage*. Hobson's ideas must sound familiar to Keynesians. Initially, Keynes did not entirely accept Hobson's under-consumption idea.[25] Later, Keynes told Hobson that their shared point was that depressions could be cured by encouraging spending; indeed, exactly the opposite of the medicine that traditionalists extolled.

[24] Keynes, J. M. (1964) *The General Theory of Employment, Interest and Money*. Orlando: Harcourt Brace, 115.

[25] In a letter to a journalist, he wrote: 'If in existing circumstances we could do something, orthodox or unorthodox, to stimulate demand, from whatever quarter, that demand would call forth an increased supply, which in turn would maintain and intensify the demand, and so on. But all the same it is not quite what Hobson has in mind I think.' Source: *John Maynard Keynes 1883–1946*, 378.

Regarding liquidity preference, Keynes denied Say's law, which said that supply creates its own demand. He disagreed with the classical idea that if people do not spend their money in one way they will spend it in another; i.e., an act of individual saving inevitably leads to a parallel act of investment. His denial led Keynes to the notion of liquidity preference, explaining why savings do not automatically translate into investments. People save not necessarily inspired by the rate of interest; other motives are also at play.

Animal spirits has become an established expression in economics. What did Keynes mean with the term? He described it as a spontaneous urge to action rather than inaction. When entrepreneurs are optimistic about the future, they will invest more and the economy will grow faster; the economy could even develop into a boom. However, when their mood is pessimistic, they will not invest, incomes will drop and unemployment will rise.

Laissez Faire or Not Laissez Faire, That's the Question

Throughout his life, Hayek remained a defender of the liberal laissez faire doctrine. He strongly believed that interfering with the free market would lead to unforeseen, inefficient, and destabilizing consequences, such as depressions. Keynes characterized Hayek as 'a misguided disciple of the free market'.

During his student days, Keynes was tutored by Alfred Marshall in the classical tradition. However, in the course of time, Keynes changed his mind. He voiced strong doubts about the free market and laissez faire before *The General Theory* came out. In 1925, Keynes had already concluded that classic economic liberalism along laissez faire lines would not work any longer, given the enormous economic changes that had taken place since Adam Smith's days. In 1926, Keynes published an essay entitled *The End of* Laissez-Faire, the essence of which is summarized in the box below.

> It is not true that individuals possess a prescriptive 'natural liberty' in their economic actions. ...The world is *not* so governed from above that private and social interests always coincide... It is *not* a correct deduction from the *Principles of Economics* that enlightened self-interest always operates in the public interest. Nor is it true that self-interest generally *is* enlightened; more often individuals acting separately to promote their own ends are too ignorant or too weak to attain even these. .... We cannot, therefore, settle on abstract grounds, but must handle on its merits in detail, what Burke termed 'one of the finest problems in legislation, namely, to determine what the State ought to take upon itself to direct by public wisdom, and what it ought to leave, with as little interference as possible, to individual exertion.'[26]

Government's Role

With a few exceptions, Hayek was opposed to government intervention in the economy; the market would eventually correct economic disturbances. Keynes did not agree. Given his insight that the economy was not automatically returning to an equilibrium, Keynes concluded that there was a logical—and necessary—role for the state to play in situations of economic disturbances. Hayek argued, instead, that the state simply did not have the knowledge to effectively intervene. The market offered the necessary information. Government is only there to establish the rules of the game and to protect the Rule of Law, argued Hayek.

Way back in 1929, Keynes supported David Lloyd George's Liberal party in the election campaign. He wrote a pamphlet entitled *Can Lloyd George Do It?* In it, Keynes argued that public works could bring back life to the sluggish economy and create employment. And in 1933, he published four articles in *The Times* entitled *The Means to Prosperity*, in which he proposed to tackle Britain's persistent unemployment through countercyclical public spending. In *A Treatise*, Keynes had proposed this 'priming the pump' policy to boost industrial production as well. Public works reappeared in full force in *The General Theory*, which served as the

[26] Keynes, J. M. (1931) The End of Laissez Faire. In: *Essays in Persuasion*. London: Macmillan, 312.

theoretical justification for interventionist policies to address unemployment he had already advocated for some time. Who does not remember Keynes's famous quote in *The General Theory*:

> If the Treasury were to fill old bottles with bank-notes, bury them at suitable depths in disused coal-mines which are then filled up to the surface with town rubbish, and leave it to private enterprise on well-tried principles of laissez-faire to dig the notes up again…. there need be no more unemployment and with the help of the repercussions, the real income of the community would probably become a good deal larger than it is. It would, indeed, be more sensible to build houses and the like; but if there are practical difficulties in the way of doing this, the above would be better than nothing.[27]

Hayek, on the other hand, maintained that investing with borrowed money would make matters worse. The only way to mobilize all available resources was *not* to use 'artificial stimulants', but to leave it to time to bring about a permanent cure.[28] There was no easy way out of a depression, said Hayek; there are no simple solutions for solving complex problems. Time and again, Hayek argued that the free market would in the end restore the economy to an equilibrium in which everyone was employed.

The Role of Money and Inflation

In Hayek's thinking, the supply of money, and the speed with which it passed from one to another, played a key role in the functioning of an economy. The economy would function most effectively when money operated as a neutral factor.[29] Later, money and monetarism provided the foundation for Friedman's monetarist counterrevolution, challenging Keynesianism, elaborated in Chap. 6.

[27] *The General Theory*, 129.

[28] Keynes's pupil Richard Kahn concluded: 'If Hayek believes that the spending of newly printed currency on employment and consumption will worsen our current terrible depression, then Hayek is a nut.' *Keynes Hayek*, 108. Libertarian Ayn Rand was also not impressed by Hayek. She dismissed him as a compromiser, and worse: a total complete, vicious bastard. Ibid., 205.

[29] Yet Hayek admitted: 'It is probably an illusion to suppose that we shall ever be able entirely to eliminate industrial fluctuations by means of monetary policy.' Ibid., 79.

Having analysed consumers' behaviour, Keynes's consumption function demonstrated that as incomes grow, a smaller portion of income growth will be spent on increased consumption and a larger portion on saving. This implied that, as the economy grows and people get richer across the board, *aggregate* consumption would diminish over time. Keynes concluded that to keep the economy and employment going, a little inflation was needed to compensate for gradually decreasing aggregate demand in a growing economy.

Abhorring runaway inflation, Hayek could not possibly agree. In *Prices and Production* he had argued:

> The most we may hope for is that the growing information of the public may make it easier for central banks both to follow a cautious policy during the upward swing of the cycle, and so to mitigate the following depression, and to resist the well-meaning but dangerous proposal to fight depression by 'a little inflation.'[30]

In sum, Keynes was dealing with busts, Hayek was concerned about the negative effects of booms.

Liquidity Preference

The opening section of *The General Theory* said that the author targeted classical economics: It was too theoretical, hardly reflective of 'the economic society in which we actually live.'[31] One of the classical principles was, as we saw, that individual saving leads to an equal amount of investment. This was not so, according to Keynes.

Keynes introduced the term 'liquidity preference'. In the classical understanding, the interest rate depended on what people wanted to save; i.e., if they wanted to save more, the interest rate would fall and this would encourage people to invest. If they wanted to save less, the rate would increase, thereby discouraging investment.

Keynes observed that the motivation of savers was not strictly dependent on the rate in interest. At times—and this was the liquidity preference—people preferred to keep their savings in cash, allowing them to

[30] *Prices and Production*, 298. Wapshott observes: 'Hayek concludes that the price was roaring inflation, and having witnessed hyperinflation destroy civil order in Vienna and undermine his family's savings, he believed it a price too high to pay.' *Keynes Hayek*, 111.

[31] *The General Theory*, 3.

quickly take advantage of sudden changes in the economy. Hence, Keynes concluded that because of this liquidity preference, interest rates were higher than necessary because banks had to offer savers something 'extra' to put their money in a savings account.

Keynes had sent Hayek a copy of *The General Theory*, expecting a thorough reaction. Hayek wrote Keynes a letter to thank him and told him that, not surprisingly, he was puzzled by two issues: Keynes's account of the supposed relationship between saving and investment, and by his liquidity preference. He said that he would respond in more detail, to be published in the *Economic Journal*, of which Keynes was the editor.

Was the Debate Continued After The General Theory's Publication?

In February 1936 *The General Theory* appeared. In that same year, Hayek was working on the question of people's economic behaviour. Hayek concluded—and this was a new insight—that an economy rarely, if ever, came to rest. In November 1936, he presented his findings in an address entitled *Economics and Knowledge*, to the London Economic Club. On the subject of economic behaviour, he argued that an equilibrium in the economy could only be expected if the intentions of all participants are known, and they have perfect knowledge. Indeed, this is impossible; these participants do not have perfect knowledge (at best they have partial knowledge) and, therefore, a perfect market does not exist.

However, the decisions of all participants together create a moving picture of the real market. Hayek then concluded that prices reflect what was going on in the market. He observed that it was impossible to understand the full weight of the countless individual economic decisions made by all individuals that make up an economy, yet their knowledge was reflected in ever-fluctuating prices. It was Hayek's *eureka moment*. He described this exciting notion as 'the one enlightening idea which made me see the whole character of economic theory in, what to me was, an entirely new light.[32] But if an outside force, say the government, would try to regulate the economy, it would frustrate the wishes (and curtail the happiness and liberties) of the market's participants, i.e., the people in whose interest government claimed to act.[33]

[32] *Keynes Hayek*, 181.
[33] Ibid., 180.

He was elated having arrived at this insight. However, Hayek's bliss was short-lived, as more and more students and collaborators, such as Nicholas Kaldor (1908–1986) John Hicks (1904–1989), and Aba Lerner (1903–1982) left him, joining the ranks of a growing group of devout Keynesians.

In *Free Market*, Jacob Soll has this to say: 'What is remarkable is that, in spite of so many failures, economists, philosophers, politicians, and others still cling to the dream that the economy can be completely self-regulating and express shock when they find that it is not...... In the end, free markets cannot liberate humanity from itself.'[34]

In the end, Hayek did not review *The General Theory*. Why not? He did not really give a clear answer. He felt that Keynes's new work was hard to confront because it was a macroeconomic (rather than a microeconomic) account of the working of the economy. Later in life, Hayek admitted that he should have reviewed the book. He felt, however, that he would have to elaborate aspects Keynes had disregarded, such as (again) Keynes's still inadequately developed theory of capital. This would have been a prerequisite for a thorough disposal of Keynes's argument.[35] Instead of confronting Keynes, Hayek put all his efforts into writing *The Pure Theory of Capital* (1940), that was to serve as an antidote to *The General Theory*. There is a section in *The Pure Theory of Capital* that hinted at the role of monetary policy, which would later be elaborated by Friedman:

> There is little ground for believing that a system with the modern complex credit structure will ever work smoothly without some deliberate control of the monetary mechanism, since money by its very nature constitutes a kind of loose joint in the self-equilibrating apparatus of the price mechanism which is bound to impede its working. The aim of any successful monetary policy must be to reduce as far as possible this slack in the self-correcting forces of the price mechanism, and to make adaptation more prompt so as to reduce the necessity for a later, more violent, reaction.[36]

[34] *Free Market*, 10.
[35] Keynes Hayek., 175.
[36] *The Pure Theory of Capital*, 440.

Part II Keynes and Hayek: Their Liberal Philosophies

Keynes's Philosophy in Brief

Keynes strongly believed that economics was a moral science. It is no surprise that his biographer, Robert Skidelsky, observes that philosophy provided the foundation of Keynes's life.[37] So, the question is what Keynes's understanding was of morality, and other philosophical notions?

Let me first touch upon Keynes's early beliefs. In his monumental biography, Skidelsky devotes a brief chapter on them. On 9 September 1938, Keynes read a paper to Bloomsbury's Memoir Club on this theme. He had developed the ideas in the period 1903–1906, when Keynes was in his early 20s. At the time, he was a member of the Cambridge Conversazione Group. Later, some group members joined the equally exclusive Bloomsbury Group, including Keynes.

Principia Ethica

It was *Principia Ethica* (1903) written by G.E. Moore (1873–1958) which influenced Maynard's philosophical outlook. Keynes said that this book was the most important book in his life. An important aspect of Moore's philosophy was the notion of 'good', and in particular 'the good life' which could not really be defined well. The only things valuable in themselves, argued Moore, were "states of mind', of which the most valuable were the pleasures of human intercourse and the enjoyment of beautiful objects….it is only for the sake of these things …that one can be justified in performing any public or private duty.' Regarding intercourse, Moore certainly had not sexual intercourse in mind. Skidelsky wrote that Moore 'confessed to the society that when he came to Cambridge he did not know that there would be a single man there who fornicated, or that sodomy was ever practised in modern times.'[38]

Keynes also accepted Moore's doctrine of organic unity. This is the view that a whole consists of interdependent parts, so that its value—as in a work of art—can be greater or smaller than the sum of those parts. This is in line with his rejection of methodological individualism as a generally valid method of economic analysis. After all, Keynes once observed, macroeconomy is not equal to the sum of individual choices.

[37] *John Maynard Keynes; 1883–1946*, 85.
[38] Ibid., 88.

During the time Keynes studied in Cambridge, Moore was very popular among the newly enlightened student community, freed from Christian 'hocus pocus'. In their attempt to shed Victorian values and mores, Keynes and his contemporaries had been looking for an alternative value system, which they found in Moore's philosophy. Moore had taught Keynes to value friendships above almost all else. After all, isn't material life ultimately insignificant in comparison to intellectual pleasure?

Regarding Moore's term 'the good life', Keynes's conception of it influenced the way he lived his own life, and his public aims. He tried to combine a personal ideal of civilized living with causes that would bring the good life within reach of others. A principal cause for him was, of course, management of the economy, but he also advocated liberal moral codes and supported the arts out of his own pocket.

It helped that Moore had charisma and that he radiated a strong dedication to the pursuit of truth; the motto of *Principia Ethica* was: Everything is what it is, and not another thing. Skidelsky concludes that it was hard to see how Moore's philosophy could have survived the process of growing up.[39] In *The History of Western Philosophy*, Russell —who had known Moore (he found that Moore had an intellect as passionate as Spinoza's)— only mentions Moore while describing Berkeley's philosophy.[40] At any event, what Moore did for acolytes was to provide a standard of value against which to measure the aims of life. It continued to be Keynes's ideal.

Robert Skidelsky and his philosopher son Edward, present their understanding of 'the good life' in *How Much is Enough; Money and The Good Life*.[41] The authors argue that the long-term goal of economic policy should not be growth, but the structuring of our collective existence so as to facilitate the good life—what it is to live well.

(*continued*)

[39] Moore's star faded relatively rapidly. The Fabian philosophy eclipsed Moore's among later student generations at Cambridge.

[40] Russell, B. (1979) *A History of Western Philosophy*. London: Unwin, 631.

[41] Skidelsky, R., and Skidelsky, E. (2012) *How Much Is Enough; Money and The Good Life How Much is Enough*. New York: Other Press, 145–179.

(continued)

Do the Skidelsky's present us a clearer picture of the good life than G.E. Moore and Keynes did? They indeed elaborate the term, and make a case in its favour. From the outset they say that they do not follow Rawls's notion of primary goods, or Martha Nussbaum and Sen's capabilities (see Chap. 7 on Sen).

The authors propose the notion of basic goods: These goods are not just means to a good life, they *are* the good life! Their goal is not confronting poverty (like Sen and Nussbaum do) but countering obscene wealth (like Piketty and Robeyns do).

The authors apply four criteria in choosing their basic goods: (i) These goods must be universal; they belong to the good life as such, (ii) they must be final; they are good in themselves, and not just a means to some other good; (iii) they are *sui generis*, meaning that they are not part of some other good; (iv) they must be indispensable; anyone who lacks them may be deemed to have suffered a loss.

After the criteria had been established, seven basic goods ensued. The first one is *health*; i.e., the full functioning of the body, like French physician Rene Leriche so wonderfully remarked: Life in the silence of the organs. *Security* is the authors' second basic good. A person's justified expectation is that his life will continue more or less in its accustomed course. *Respect* is basic good number three. This is a necessary condition for other basic goods, but it is also a basic good in itself. Number four is *personality*; i.e., the ability to execute a plan of life reflective of one's tastes, temperament, and conception of the good. *Harmony with nature* is yet another basic good. This sounds rather romantic,[42] if not anachronistic, given the urbanized lives we lead. Therefore, the authors argue that we should strive to ensure that cities are not alienated from their natural surroundings. *Friendship* is one but the last basic good which is also a part of Moore's understanding of the good life. Friendship in a relationship is only possible between two people who love one another for what they are, not for what they can offer. The seventh basic good is *leisure*; a special form of activity in its own right, in the absence of external compulsion. These seven basic goods help us, and society at large, to bring about the good life for all.

[42] Longing for what once was, does not make sense, suggest the authors: 'Changes cannot always be rectified simply by being reversed, any more than a man flattened by a steamroller can be restored to life by being run over backwards.' Ibid., 179.

Keynes elaborated Moore's philosophy in his own *Miscellanea Ethica*. Apart from dealing with one of Moore's central themes, the notion of 'good', he criticized some of Moore's other themes. For example, Keynes argued that Moore had failed to establish a rational basis for altruistic behaviour; there was no necessary connection between individual and universal goodness. Another criticism was that it was impossible to tell what kinds of action would increase goodness of the universe as a whole.

Skidelsky brings up another aspect. There was Moore's class of so-called mixed goods, meaning that good states of mind would depend on the existence of bad states of affairs. A little elaboration helps to explain this point. Feelings of pity, courage, justice, etc., which have positive ethical value, could be said to depend on the existence of suffering, danger, injustice. To the extent that social reform rids the world of bad states of affairs, it may also be decreasing the total of ethical goodness. Skidelsky then concludes that the fact that Keynes was alert to them shows his intellectual honesty and that it also explains his limited passion for social reform.[43]

Probability

Keynes thought and worked long on the notion of probability. In 1921, he presented his insights in *A Treatise on Probability*. The book was philosophical in nature. He had come to the conclusion that probabilistic knowledge was a variety of logical knowledge which had to do with the bearing of evidence on conclusions. It was about the rationality of beliefs and not the conjuncture of events. Keynes claimed that the mind could often reduce uncertainty to probability; in his words 'intuiting' that some outcomes would be more or less likely than others'. This perception sanctioned a degree of belief in the conclusions.

His probability theory is both optimistic about the power of human reason, and pessimistic about the ability of reason to understand the secrets of the universe. Keynes devoted attention to two more terms: The weight of argument and, number two, moral risk. The former means roughly the amount of evidence which supports a probability judgement. This does not alter the probability, but it can alter the amount of confidence one has in one's judgement. As regards moral risk, Keynes argued

[43] *Keynes; A Very Short Introduction*, 40.

that it is more rational to aim for a smaller good which seems more attainable, than to aim for a larger one which seems less, when the two courses of action have equal probable goodness. This argument provided the philosophical basis for Keynes's rejection of revolutionary change, which he shared with the founder of British conservatism Edmund Burke.

Edmund Burke

In 1904, Keynes had written a large piece about Edmund Burke (1729–1797), the conservative political philosopher. Keynes commended Burke as the first utilitarian having consistently espoused the greatest happiness principle, which Jeremy Bentham would further develop. Keynes agreed with Burke that this was a political principle. Another aspect of Burke's doctrine of prudence (i.e., opposed to present evil for the sake of future benefits) also met with Keynes's appreciation. He, like Burke, rejected revolutions. Burke's appreciation of expediency also met with Keynes's approval. He argued: 'It is fatal for a capitalist government to have principles. It must be opportunistic in the best sense of the word, living by accommodation and good sense. If a monarchical, plutocratic, or other analogous form of government has principles, it will fail.'[44]

Burke defended property rights. First of all, redistribution of property would not make a real difference to the poor, as they far outnumbered the wealthy. Reason number two was that it would reduce the numbers who could enjoy the benefits of wealth. Keynes felt that Burke's opinion about property rights made sense. However, it was less valid if directed against any attempt to influence the channels in which wealth flows, and the relief of starvation or poverty.

Keynes was not impressed with Burke's timidity. Burke, for example, denied the value of the pursuit of truth on the ground that it might disturb the peace. Keynes argued, in the spirit of John Stuart Mill, that whatever the immediate consequences of a new truth may be, there is a high probability that truth will in the long run lead to better results than falsehood.[45] Yet, Keynes summarized Burke's political legacy, of which one aspect (i.e., the academic reasoner and philosopher) is particularly interesting:

[44] Ibid., 45.
[45] Ibid., 46–47.

> But whether or not the great political ideals that have inspired men in the past are madness and delusion, they have provided a more powerful motive force than anything which Burke has to offer .... For all his passions and speechmaking, it is the academic reasoner and philosopher who offers us these carefully guarded and qualified precepts, not the leader of men. Statesmen must learn wisdom in the school of Burke; if they wish to put it to any great and difficult purpose, the essentials of leadership they must seek elsewhere.[46]

Regarding Keynes's political philosophy, he integrated elements of Burke's philosophy, i.e., contentment as the aim and risk avoidance, and two key elements in reforming liberalism, i.e., a commitment to truth and belief in the possibility of rational individual judgement. Below, his rejection of conservatism and socialism is described.

What Type of Liberal Was Keynes?

In August 1925, Keynes delivered a speech entitled *Am I a Liberal?* to the Liberal Summer School in Cambridge.[47] In the UK at the time, there were three political parties, whose philosophies Keynes analysed in his speech. Not being a 'party man', and in identifying a party to his liking, Keynes followed the principle of *repulsion*—he selected the party he disliked least. He took the audience by the hand to explain, in an ironic—if not sarcastic—manner, where he arrived at applying this negative attitude. The Conservative party was certainly not to Keynes's liking. He concluded: 'It leads nowhere; it satisfies no ideal; it conforms to no intellectual standard; it is not even safe, or calculated to preserve from spoilers that degree of civilization which we have already attained.'[48]

Next, the Labour party was grilled. Superficially, observed Keynes, this party was more attractive. But taking a closer look, there are great difficulties. It is a class party, and Keynes did not belong to it—you would find him on the side of the educated *bourgeoisie*. The real repulsion (the word he indeed used) which kept him away from Labour, was that too much would always be decided by those who did not know what they were talking about. Moreover, if the control of the party would be seized by an

[46] *John Maynard Keynes, 1883–1946*, 98.

[47] Keynes, J. M. (1931) Am I a Liberal? In: *Essays in Persuasion*. London: Macmillan, 323–338.

[48] Ibid., 324.

autocratic inner ring, this control would be exercised in the interests of the extreme Left Wing. It would then become the Party of Catastrophe which could only flourish in an atmosphere of social oppression. Keynes believed that beyond 1925, questions about the economic framework of society would be by far the most important political issue.

Then, the Liberal party. Keynes argued that the leadership of a political party ought, in essence, to be autocratic. The Conservatives were in the best position in this respect. Traditionally, the management of the Liberal party was also sufficiently autocratic. But recently, lamented Keynes, there were ill-advised movements in the direction of democratizing the contents of the party programme. Yet, Keynes concluded that the Liberal party was still the best instrument (least repulsive) of future economic progress, if only it had strong leadership and the right programme.

Keynes then approached the question from a *positive* angle: What would attract him to a party rather than to what repelled him? Much of what the Liberal party had proposed in the past (such as social reforms, or progressive taxation of incomes and wealth) was now common ground of all parties. So, what would remain? The so-called Drink Question and Free Trade, suggested Keynes. I will only deal with free trade.

Keynes said that he no longer believed in the *political* philosophy of the Doctrine of Free Trade. Yet he believed in free trade, because, in the long run it is the only policy which is technically sound and intellectually tight. Having discussed free trade—a central theme of economic liberalism—Keynes then presented his ideas about what a Liberal party should look like—what should its philosophy and practice be? This party's programme must not deal with the nineteenth-century issues of liberalism, but with those matters which were of urgent importance now.

Keynes then mentioned five questions,[49] of which I elaborate the Economic Question. He introduced a distinction in three epochs, as proposed by American institutionalist economist J.R. Commons (1862–1945). They were: (i) the Era of Scarcity, (ii) the Era of Abundance, and (iii) the Era of Stability. During the seventeenth and eighteenth century, humanity fought its way out of the bondage of scarcity into abundance. In the nineteenth century, this epoch culminated in the victories of *laissez faire* and classic economic liberalism.[50] Now, the era of Stabilization was the actual

[49] Peace Questions, Questions of Government, Sex questions, Drug Questions, and Economic Questions.

[50] Keynes ironically observed that it was not surprising that the veterans of the party cast backward glances on that easier age.

alternative to Marx's communism. Commons argued that in this period there was a diminution of individual liberty, enforced in part by governmental sanctions, but mainly by economic sanctions through concerted action, whether secret, semi-open, open, or arbitrational of associations, corporations, and other collective movements of manufacturers, merchants, labourers, farmers, and bankers.

Keynes concluded that the transition from economic anarchy to a regime which deliberately aims at controlling and directing economic forces in the interests of social justice and social stability, would present enormous difficulties both technical and political. Nonetheless, Keynes suggested that the true destiny of New Liberalism was to seek their solution!

No longer, the free play of supply and demand (the idea of the old-world party) would bring about the necessary economic adjustments. In typical Keynesian style, he observed that one can, for example, alter the value of money and then leave the consequential adjustments to be brought about by forces of supply and demand. This belonged to the days of fifty or a hundred years ago when trade unions were powerless, and when the economic Juggernaut was allowed to crash along the highway of progress without obstruction and even with applause. In economic terms, continued Keynes, this means that one must find new policies and new instruments to adapt and control the working of economic forces, so that they do not intolerably interfere with contemporary ideas as to what was fit and proper in the interest of social stability and justice.

Keynes ended *Am I a Liberal?* as follows: 'We have changed, by insensible degrees, our philosophy of economic life, our notions of what is reasonable and what is tolerable; and we have done this without changing our technique or our copybook maxims. Hence our tears and trouble. A party programme had to be developed....under the pressure and the stimulus of actual events.... But if the Liberal party is to recover its forces, it must have an attitude, a philosophy, and a direction.'[51]

Keynes proposed a *modern* version of liberalism. Classic liberalism would not work any longer, given the enormous economic changes that had taken place since Locke's and Smith's days—laissez faire would not do any longer. He also referred to *moral* aspects when he argued that

[51] *Am I a Liberal?*, 337–338.

economic forces ought to be adjusted in the interests of social justice and social stability. Having a job and a decent income was a matter of social justice, ensuring social stability. He proposed that new liberalism should be helpful in bringing this about.[52]

In his later writings, Keynes favoured birth control and the use of contraceptives, marriage laws, and treatment of sexual offenders. In line with J.S. Mill, he favoured improvement of the position of women. In all these matters he admitted compatibility between Labour (much of Labour's heart was in the right place, Keynes said) and liberal aspirations. Keynes positioned himself in the middle between the Liberals and Labour.

Keynes was brought up as a classical liberal, but we have seen that, especially after the Great War, he increasingly became a new liberal. His change of mind was partly inspired by dramatic political and economic developments and partly by philosophers of new liberalism. Keynes, however, should also be appreciated as the economist who presented an effective and unorthodox approach to the Great Depression. Unorthodox, because he gave a much larger interventionist role to the government in tackling the crisis than classical economists would even think of. This is another important element of new liberalism.

Hayek's Political Philosophy

Keynes explained what his position was in the changing British political environment during the Interbellum. He looked ahead, facing new challenges and proposed a new liberalism to counter them. Often characterized as a political conservative, Hayek felt the need to clarify where he stood in the political spectrum. He explained his position in a postscript to

[52] George Katiforis (935–2022), former member of the European Parliament on behalf of the Panhellenic Socialist Party, argued that Keynes had not really answered the question whether he was a Liberal or not. According to Katiforis, Keynes was in fact a bourgeois Marxist, as some of his ideas, reflected above, were strikingly similar to Marx's, such as his plea for social justice and social stability, let alone the social ownership of the means of production. Yet, Keynes prescribed a cure for capitalism while no such prescription could ever be effective in the eyes of Marx. Source: Katiforis, G. Keynes as a Bourgeois Marxist. In: Ed.: Aretis, P. & Sayer, M. (2004) *The Rise of the Market; Critical Essays on the Political Economy of Neo-Liberalism*. Cheltenham: Edward Elgar, 181–222. On p. 222, Katiforis made a final, eloquent and moving, observation about Keynes: 'Rather than despair that heaven is not all, he strove to conjure up in the barricaded lives of his contemporaries, there and then, a small patch of heaven. How could any one of us claim to be civilized and regard the obnoxious Etonian with anything else but gratitude.'

The Constitution of Liberty,[53] that appeared in 1960. The postscript's title is *Why I am not a Conservative*. Unlike Keynes, he went back to the origins of liberalism.

The postscript started with the observation that in matters of current politics, liberals generally have little choice but to support conservative parties. Conservatism proper is a legitimate, probably necessary, and certainly widespread attitude of oppression to drastic change. Until the rise of socialism, its opposite was liberalism. Hayek's major objection to conservatism is that it cannot offer an alternative to the direction in which we are moving.

Conservatives, liberals, and socialists can be depicted in a triangle, with the conservatives taking up one corner, with the socialists pulling towards the second, and the liberals towards the third. But, as the socialists have been able to pull harder, the conservatives have tended to follow them rather than into the liberal direction, and have adopted—at appropriate intervals of time—their ideas, made respectable by radical propaganda. It has regularly been the conservatives who have compromised with socialism.

One of the fundamental traits of the conservative is a fear of change, while the liberal position is based on courage and confidence, on a readiness to let change run its course. The conservative is inclined to use the forces of government to prevent change. Conservatives are fond of authorities and lack understanding of economic forces. A conservative does not object to coercion of arbitrary power as long as it is used for what he regards as the right purposes, and—like the socialist—he regards himself entitled to enforce the values he holds on other people.

For the liberal, neither moral nor religious ideals are proper objects of coercion, with the exception of the Rule of Law. Both the conservative and the socialist recognize no such limits. This may explain why it seems to be easier for the repentant socialist to find a new spiritual home in the conservative fold than in the liberal.

Regarding the superiority and the role of elites, the liberal—though fully aware of the important role that cultural and intellectual elites have played in the evolution of civilization—believes that these elites have to prove themselves by their capacity to maintain their position under the same rules that apply to all others.

[53] Hayek, F. (2006) *The Constitution of Liberty*. London: Routledge Classics, 343–355.

Conservatives usually oppose collectivist measures in the industrial field. At the same time, however, they are also usually protectionist and have frequently supported socialist measures in agriculture. Conservatives feel instinctively that it is new ideas more than anything else that causes change. Though the liberal certainly does not regard all change as progress, he does regard the advance of knowledge as one of the chief aims of human effort and expects from it the general solution of such problems and difficulties which need to be solved.

Hayek finds that the most objectionable feature of the conservative attitude is its propensity to reject well-substantiated new knowledge because it dislikes some of the consequences which seem to follow from it. Connected with the distrust of the new is its hostility to internationalism and its proneness to strident nationalism.

There is one respect in which there is justification for saying that the liberal occupies a position midway between the socialist and the conservative, and that is that he is as far from the crude rationalism of the socialist, who wants to reconstruct all social institutions according to a pattern prescribed by his individual reason, as from the mysticism to which the conservative so frequently has to resort.

What Hayek calls 'liberalism' has little to do with any political movement that goes under the name today. Freeden argues that whether Hayek is considered a liberal, a conservative, a libertarian, or a hybrid among those, is itself a question of ideological and scholarly interpretation.[54] Hayek himself maintained that he was a liberal, be it of a particular flavour, so to speak. What he wanted is a word which describes the party of life, the party that favours free growth and spontaneous evolution. *Whiggism* is historically the correct name for the ideas in which Hayek believed. Whiggism's philosophy was inspired, as we saw, by Locke. Conservatism may sometimes be a useful practical maxim, but it does not provide any guiding principles which can influence long-range developments. Hayek's political philosophy is more forward-looking than his conservative version of neoclassical economics. Hayek's political philosophy was more optimistic, more trusting in reason and new ideas, and less respectful of inherited or traditional institutions.

[54] Freeden, M. (2015) *Liberalism, A Very Short Introduction*. Oxford: Oxford University Press, 90.

Hayek's Whiggism

An intriguing question is where Hayek's preference for Whiggism came from? In *The Constitution of Liberty*, he answered the question. The development of the theory of liberty, Hayek wrote, took place in England and France. The British theory was empirical and unsystematic, while the French version of liberty was rationalistic and speculative. Hayek preferred the British version, since it was inspired by the interpretation of traditional institutions which had evolved spontaneously. The French version aimed at creating a utopia. Moreover, the British philosophers had given us an interpretation of the growth of civilization that is still the foundation of the argument for liberty. They found the origin of institutions in the survival of the successful. Their view is expressed in terms of 'how nations stumble upon establishments which are indeed the result of human action but not the execution of human design.'[55]

The British version of liberty was never a complete laissez faire. The British understood that it was the evolution of well-constructed institutions where the rules of contending interests would be reconciled. In addition, they maintained that a successful free society would always be a tradition-bound society. The system of liberty is an ideal that will only be preserved if it is accepted as an overriding principle governing all particular acts of legislation. The other side of the liberty coin is responsibility. The term responsibility is not just a legal term; it has a strong *moral* dimension as well. When people are allowed to act as they see fit, they must also be held responsible for the results of their actions.

The Growth of Civilization

Hayek argued that growth of the human mind is part of the growth of civilization, and the mind can never foresee its own advance. Ways of doing things, traditions, and institutions are the products of cumulative growth of civilizations without ever having been designed by any one mind. So, concluded Hayek, individual liberty is essential to leave room for the unforeseeable and the creation of great ideas. Freedom means renunciation of direct control of individual efforts so that a free society can make use of much more knowledge than the mind of the wisest ruler could comprehend by itself. As Keynes had said earlier on, it is ideas that

[55] *The Constitution of Liberty*, 51.

govern evolution. Hayek lamented that what was lacking were abstract liberal principles, together a program of truly liberal radicalism! Hayek gradually moved into the direction of libertarianism,[56] but he did not favour anarchy. Yet, like libertarian Robert Nozick, he proposed that private companies carry out communal duties.[57]

The Spontaneous Order

One of Hayek's principal themes was the spontaneous order. He may well have borrowed the term from the philosopher Michael Polanyi (1891–1976), who observed: 'When order is achieved among human beings by allowing them to interact with each other on their own initiative—subject to the laws which uniformly apply to all of them—we have a spontaneous order in society.'[58]

Hayek had an implicit warning about autocratic states. He argued that there was something seriously lacking in a society in which all the intellectual, moral, and artistic leaders belong to the employed class, especially if most of them are employed by the government. He was afraid that there was the tendency to move into that direction, which would mean that autocratic states, applying central planning, would not benefit from the information and knowledge that the market provides.

The Constitution of Liberty

According to Hayek, constitutionalism means that all power rests on the understanding that it will be exercised according to commonly accepted principles. The American Constitution is *a constitution of liberty*; a constitution that protects the individual against all arbitrary coercion. It puts limits to the powers of legislation, and provides individuals with a domain of clearly defined property to make decisions based upon their own wishes and knowledge.

[56] 'He rejected the alternative of libertarian, as it carried the flavour of 'a manufactured term and of a substitute'.' Source: Gerstle, G. (2022) *The Rise and Fall of the Neoliberal Order; America and the World in the Free Market Era*. Oxford: Oxford University Press, 106, 529–530.

[57] Nozick's philosophy is summarized in Chap. 6.

[58] *The Constitution of Liberty*, 140.

Hayek wondered what the essential conditions of liberty under the law would be. First, the limitation on the powers of all government, including the powers of the legislature. The Rule of Law is more than constitutionalism; it requires that all laws conform to certain principles. The Rule of Law is, therefore, not a rule of the law, but a rule concerning what law ought to be—a meta-legal doctrine or political ideal. It is important to remember that the Rule of Law restricts government only in its *coercive* activities. Laws ought to be known and be certain. Hayek argued that there is probably no single factor which has contributed more to the prosperity of the West than the relative certainty of the law which has prevailed there. Other chief requirements of true law are equality and that the law must be just.

The Rule of Law and the State

Now, what about the relationship between the Rule of Law and the role of the state in economic affairs? The proper functioning of a market economy presupposes certain activities on the part of the state, as long as they are compatible with the market. Government is in charge of a monetary system; setting standards of weights and measures; statistics; and basic education. Then there is the provision of public services such as health and sanitation, and the construction and maintenance of roads which will not be provided by the private sector, as it would be difficult to charge the individual beneficiary for them. This does not imply that the government should implement these services; they can be done by competent companies, or even voluntary associations, while the financial responsibility would remain in government hands.

What About the Poor?

Hayek did not pay much attention to poverty. This does not mean that he would not have been in favour of the eradication of absolute poverty in the world. This was best done, he argued, through the market, as the past few decades had demonstrated. He was open to the idea of making provisions for people in extreme poverty or starvation, due to circumstances beyond their control. However, these provisions should be made outside the market, as the market does not serve the objective of social justice. In fact, the market does not have objectives, added Hayek.

Compulsory public social insurance managed by state organizations was unacceptable as it blocks competition from private insurers and it turns into a tool of redistribution. As for national health insurance, Hayek argued that 'it is probably in the interest of all that under a free system those with full earning capacity should often be rapidly cured of temporary and not dangerous disablement at the expense of some neglect of the aged and mortally ill.'[59] Hayek proposed a gradual transformation of sickness and unemployment allowances systems into systems of true insurance under which the individuals pay for benefits offered by competing institutions.

What he, however, did not address was the fact that the market does not necessarily result in a just income distribution. The market allows for wide differences in income and wealth. Hayek was not a fan of income redistribution by way of taxes or subsidies. He argued that redistribution would in the end result in levelling of incomes. So, concluded Hayek, do not strive after justice when it comes to income distribution, but accept an efficient market outcome.[60] In Hayek's thinking, market failures were acceptable to a large extent; government failure was not.

Taxation

Hayek was not in favour of progressive taxation. He observed that a majority should not be entitled to apply to a minority a rule which it does not apply to itself. This was an infringement of a principle much more fundamental than democracy itself. Hayek proposed a flat rate applied to all tax payers. After all, in a flat-rate system the rich would proportionally pay more than the poor. The poor could be compensated for the indirect taxes they pay on top of the flat income tax rate.

On the last page of *The Constitution of Liberty*, Hayek summarized, in a passionate way, his convictions and philosophy:

> Nowhere is freedom more important than where our ignorance is greatest—at the boundaries of knowledge, in other words, where nobody can predict what lies a step ahead….But the ultimate aim of freedom is the enlargement of these capacities in which man surpasses his ancestors and to which each generation must endeavour to add its share—its share in the growth of knowledge and the gradual advance of moral and aesthetic beliefs, where no

[59] Ibid., 260.

[60] Chapter 7 on Sen's philosophy and Chap. 9 on Thomas Piketty's insights, present their respective thinking on income and wealth distribution.

> superior must be allowed to enforce one set of views of what is right or good and where only further experience can decide what should prevail. It is whenever man reaches beyond his present self, where the new emerges and assessment lies in the future, that liberty ultimately shows its value.[61]

The Lasting Influence of Keynes and Hayek

Keynesianism remained popular until the early 1970s. What then happened was something Keynesians had not foreseen—stagflation did them in, so to speak. Keynesians had believed in the Phillips Curve, named after LSE economist William Phillips (1914–1975). He had studied the development of employment and inflation in the UK over a long period of time. Phillips concluded that there was an inverse relation between inflation and unemployment—a bit of inflation went together with less unemployment. However, as of the beginning of the 1970s, this was no longer the case; both unemployment and inflation went up—stagflation was the result. This could not happen according to Keynesians. They were at a loss to explain it. But Friedman could!

Emeritus professor of economics, Edmund Phelps had invented the term 'natural rate of unemployment'. If governments wanted to push the unemployment rate below this natural rate, the result was that this would not just trigger inflation but also unemployment. The reason being that workers demanded higher wages which in turn would be included in the price of goods and services, causing a *wage-price spiral*, followed by hyperinflation. Friedman borrowed this natural rate of unemployment notion in explaining stagflation. Friedman also explained that there was too much money in the economy, which also had an upward push on inflation, further discussed in Chap. 6.

After the necessary anti-stagflation measures had been implemented, a fairly stable period, starting around the beginning of the 1980s, ensued: The Great Moderation. Conservative liberal-minded economists Hayek and Friedman had won the day. Indeed, for quite some time, they did. However, things were beginning to go wrong in 2007–2008. A financial crisis in America, quickly spilling over into a large part of the world, triggered the Great Recession. The financial crisis proved, once again, that the popular belief in self-regulating markets was illusory. In addressing the

[61] *The Constitution of Liberty*, 340.

ensuing deep recession, Keynesian stimulus measures were taken by most governments, ranging from tax rebates to loan-financed public spending, in combination with Quantitative Easing (QE), a new, unorthodox monetary policy. Together, these measures brought back a sense of equilibrium in the economy.

The same applied in early 2020 when the Covid-pandemic brought the global economy to a halt. Again, governments that could afford it, took Keynesian and monetary measures to keep their economies afloat. In sum, governments did what the market was unable to do—Keynes had returned with a vengeance.

A fair conclusion would be that in good times, Hayek's (and Friedman's) market-based philosophy is useful. But when an economy is facing a recession, Keynesian remedies have an important corrective part to play.

From a theoretical point of view, Keynes's macroeconomic approach became a universally applied approach. Central in Hayek's thinking is the role of the market.[62] Hayek maintained that decentralized production processes and democracy would minimize the power exercised by man over man—it would safeguard freedom. This view is challenged by technology, illiberal democratic regimes, and autocracies. Today, the most efficient systems may be centralized ones, in which big data, and Artificial Intelligence (AI) play a crucial role. After all, big data and AI can allow large tech firms to 'capture' significant parts of the economy and, subsequently, manage it far more efficiently than any autocratic bureaucracy ever could. However, this does not imply that big-tech, illiberal democracies, or autocratic regimes, would have *all* the necessary knowledge to control the market. Living economies, including markets, evolve and economic actors adapt to the ever-changing economic environment. Some will be successful in this process, others not. Hayek constantly urged that unless power is dispersed it is always dangerous. Given the contemporary context, Hayek's unrelenting defence of freedom is as relevant then as it is today.

[62] 'I've come to believe that both the aim of the market order, and therefore the object of explanation of the theory of it, is to cope with the inevitable ignorance of everybody of most of the particular facts which determine this order. By a process which men did not understand, their activities have produced an order much more extensive and comprehensive than anything they could have comprehended, but on the functioning of which we have become utterly dependent.' Source: Hayek, F.A. Coping with Ignorance. In: *Imprimis*, July 1978, Volume 7, Issue 7.

References

Burns, J. (2023). *Milton Friedman; the Last Conservative*. Farrar, Straus and Giroux.

Chang, H.-J. (2014). *Economics: The User's Guide*. Pelican Books.

Frank, B. (2023). *In the Long Run We're all Dead; The Lives and Deaths of Great Economists*. Haus Publishing Ltd.

Freeden, M. (2015) Liberalism, A Very Short Introduction. : Oxford University Press

Gerstle, G. (2022). *The Rise and Fall of the Neoliberal Order; America and the World in the Free Market Era*. Oxford University Press.

Hayek, F. (2006). *The Constitution of Liberty*. Routledge Classics.

Hayek, F. A. (1932). Reflections on the Pure Theory of Money of Mr. J.M. Keynes. *Economica*.

Hayek, F. A. (1940). *The Pure Theory of Capital*. University of Chicago Press.

Hayek, F.A. Coping with Ignorance. In: *Imprimis*, July 1978

Heilbroner, R. (2000). *The Worldly Philosophers; The Lives, Times and Ideas of the Great Economic Thinkers* (7th ed.). Penguin Books.

Katiforis, G. (2004). Keynes as a Bourgeois Marxist. In P. Aretis & M. Sayer (Eds.), *The Rise of the Market; Critical Essays on the Political Economy of Neo-Liberalism*. Edward Elgar.

Keynes, J. M. (1931a). The End of Laissez Faire. In *Essays in Persuasion*. Macmillan.

Keynes, J. M. (1931b). Am I a Liberal? In *Essays in Persuasion*. Macmillan.

Keynes, J. M. (1964). *The General Theory of Employment, Interest and Money*. Harcourt Brace & Company.

Keynes, J. M. (2005). *The Economic Consequences of Peace*. Cosimo Classics.

King's College, Cambridge Annual Report 2008

Russell, B. (1979). *A History of Western Philosophy*. Unwin.

Skidelsky, R. (2003). *John Maynard Keynes 1883–1946: Economist, Philosopher, Statesman*. Pan Books.

Skidelsky, R. (2010). *Keynes A Very Short Introduction*. Oxford University Press.

Skidelsky, R., & Skidelsky, E. (2012). *How Much Is Enough; Money and The Good Life How Much Is Enough*. Other Press.

Soll, J. (2022). *Free Market; The History of an Idea*. Basic Books.

Wapshott, N. (2011). *Keynes Hayek; The Clash That Defined Modern Economics*. W.W. Norton.

CHAPTER 6

Friedman and Samuelson at Odds on Keynes

Prologue

It seemed as if Keynes had found the answer to the question how to overcome booms and busts. Indeed, Keynesianism reigned from the 1930s onwards, not just in economics but in economic policy making as well. Keynes underscored the crucial role that governments had to play in overcoming economic depressions. Hayek strongly disagreed with Keynes's views, as we saw in the previous chapter. During the early 1930s, Hayek and Keynes started an intellectual debate about the respective roles of the market and government, which was continued by Paul Samuelson and Milton Friedman in their *Newsweek* columns, and beyond, which greatly influenced the public debate at the time.

Samuelson remained a Keynesian, while Friedman, also a Keynesian in his younger days, was won over by conservative liberal and libertarian thinkers. As of the late 1960s, Friedman exposed Keynesianism's weaknesses, while developing a monetarist theory, as well as new insights in the consumption function. Like Hayek, he influenced economic policymaking of the United States, Great Britain, and scores of other countries, such as Chile, which became known as neoliberalism. Samuelson gradually accepted some of Friedman's new insights. Both lived long enough to witness that Keynesianism had not been buried forever; but not long enough to witness neoliberalism's decline.

P. de Haan, *Great Economists and the Evolution of Economic Liberalism*, https://doi.org/10.1007/978-3-031-93831-3_6

Introduction

Friedman once observed that there was no such thing as a purely economic issue; it is often mingled with political and philosophical ones. This is probably why people sometimes think that economics is little more than ideology dressed up in scientific garb. Economists do not often share their philosophical or ideological inspiration. When invited to do so, most of them stay close to economics and methodological issues. Only few would refer to great philosophers, such as Plato, Aristotle, Hegel, Locke, Kant, or Wittgenstein. One economist even declined an invitation to share his philosophical inspiration as he admitted not having one. This did certainly not apply to 'wunderkind' Samuelson or to Friedman.

On 8 December 1995, Samuelson wrote Friedman a rather sentimental letter. It said that 'it was 62 years ago……that we first met. I was a lowly sophomore [at the University of Chicago; PdH] and you were already spottable as a scholar of destiny.'[1] In his letter, Samuelson stressed that the many aspects in life and work they shared were more important than their differences: 'I hope it will be said of us that, though we disagreed on much, we understood wherein our logical and empirical differences were based and that we were pretty good at preserving the amiability, friendship, and respect throughout.' It was also a remarkable letter as Friedman consistently loved to smash idols. Pigou, Keynes, and Samuelson were his targets, according to Friedman's biographer Jennifer Burns. Friedman responded by saying that he, and his wife Rose, were very touched by Samuelson's letter and that he agreed about the early years together in Chicago. Yet Friedman corrected Samuelson in one aspect. He noted that it must have been either 63 or 61 years ago that they first met.

Samuelson and Friedman had a lot in common. Both belonged to the same generation. They knew the horror and misery the Great Depression had inflicted upon fellow Americans having lost their job, business, or savings. Both were sons of Jewish immigrants. Both studied at the University of Chicago, and married young women of their university class, joining them in their academic work. And both had a brilliant mind; both were awarded the Nobel Prize in Economics.

However, there were also differences between them. As for their family background, Samuelson's father was a pharmacist belonging to the

[1] Wapshott, N. (2021) *Samuelson Friedman; The Battle Over the Free Market*. New York: W.W. Norton, 254.

American middle class, while Friedman's father had not been successful in the successive small businesses he ran. Samuelson's literary style, as Nicholas Wapshott notes, 'betrayed his personality. His were the contributions of an established, confident leader in his field',[2] often resorting to irony in discussing the work of his contemporaries. Friedman's style was, in my words, more a street fighter's; he was after scoring points. He wanted to influence politics, not just in America but also in other countries such as the UK and Chile during the Pinochet years. Not condemning Pinochet's repressive dictatorship had cost Friedman a lot of popular goodwill.

After working at Harvard and, as a consultant to the National Resources Planning Board during WWII, Samuelson wanted to return to Harvard but was not accepted, on account of antisemitic tendencies there. He went across the street in Cambridge, so to speak, and established the top-ranking Economics Department at the Massachusetts Institute of Technology (MIT). Friedman, after having moved to wartime Washington DC, returned to Chicago, after one year teaching at the University of Minnesota, where his contract was not extended; word has it that also Friedman was a victim of antisemitism.

Friedman's groundbreaking contributions to economics were based on extensive empirical analyses of the relationship between the money supply and economic booms and busts, as well as his analysis of consumption and saving patterns. In other words, he applied an inductive approach to economics. Samuelson made his fame by doing economics in a new way by unifying economic theory (he was primarily a theorist) through mathematical analysis and deriving operational theorems; he approached economics in a deductive manner.[3] There was yet another difference between

[2] Ibid., 10.

[3] On 10 May 1996, Deirdre McCloskey delivered her inaugural address entitled *The Vices of Economists; The Virtues of the Bourgeoisie,* to the faculties of Erasmus University of Rotterdam. In a rather ironic (if not polemic) manner, she observes this about Samuelson: 'The Samuelsonian vice is that of staying always in a world of theory, spending an academic career imagining alternative worlds in which the sea is boiling hot and pigs have wings. In other words, the Vice in question is ….theorizing endlessly and without a point…. Though Samuelson was philosophically speaking a positivist, and therefore committed to testing theories against the facts of the world, he never did.' 6–7. Regarding the bourgeoisie, mentioned in the title of her address, McCloskey observes: 'The claim that I make about modern economics, and about a lot else that is modern, such as modern jazz, modern architecture, modern painting, modern poetry, is that it has an aristocratic, not a bourgeois, ethos.' 12. To prevent misunderstandings, McCloskey admires Samuelson a great deal as he often brought up economic issues that turned out having great scientific relevance.

them. They held different opinions about methodological aspects, an example of which is presented in a box below.

Part I contains a brief overview of economic developments since the end of WWII and the extent to which Keynesianism and neoclassical economics influenced them. The following section describes Friedman's distancing from Keynesianism and Samuelson's reactions.

In Part II Samuelson's philosophy is summarized, followed by Friedman's conservative liberal convictions and the inspirations he drew from philosophers ranging from Locke to Nozick. The chapter concludes with Samuelson's and Friedman's legacies.

Part I Keynes Called the Shots, but Did He?

Economic Developments After the End of World War II

As young economists, Friedman and Samuelson witnessed the rise of Keynes, who in 1936 created a revolution in economics after *The General Theory* had come out.

Chapter 5 presents *The General Theory* in some detail; therefore, a very brief summary would suffice. Keynes looked at the aggregate picture, thereby ushering in a new field: macroeconomics. He emphasized the stabilizing role of government's fiscal and monetary intervention in a depressed economy to help restore economic growth and full employment. Based on his interpretation of the consumption function, which says that lower-income earners spend relatively more of extra income than higher-income earners, Keynes's investment *multiplier* was an important mechanism to boost consumption in a depressed economy. This increased consumption would in turn promote investment, which would result in more income and spending, and so on.

Keynesianism was applied in most advanced economies up to the early 1970s, when stagflation could not be explained by Keynesians. But Friedman explained why inflation had skyrocketed and why unemployment rose simultaneously. In *From Keynes to Piketty* I wrote:

> Keynesianism wasn't equipped to solve stagflation in the 1970s, while neoclassical recipes only deepened the Great Depression of the 1930s. This suggests that the popularity of economic schools of thought depends on

> what is happening in the real world; one of the two main schools—Keynesianism or neoclassical economics—flourished when the time was ripe.[4]

After stagflation had been brought under control through restrictive monetary measures, interest rate hikes, and strict controls on government budgets, neoclassical economics regained popularity. A fairly long period of economic progress and stability ensued: the Great Moderation. During the 1990s and early 2000s, deregulation, low interest rates, cheap money, and the aggressive introduction of irresponsible financial instruments saw the light. In 2007, this resulted in a catastrophic financial freeze and, subsequently, the Great Recession.

Ben Bernanke, Fed Chairman at the time, had understood Friedman's lesson of the Great Depression: Don't let credit dry up! As elaborated in Chap. 2, the Fed, supported by a helpful American Congress, approved huge dollar injections into the financial system and the economy at large Yet, Bernanke argued that conventional monetary policy alone was not enough, additional monetary injections (called Quantitative Easing (QE)) *and* fiscal support were required as well. The Obama Administration quickly pushed a large fiscal program through Congress. What was done to counter the Great Recession in America was also applied in Europe, Japan, China and other countries that could afford it.

Wapshott rightly concludes: 'The treatment applied in the 2008 financial crisis was in part Keynesian, but also in part a vindication of Friedman's money-supply notions.'[5] In good times, the general principles of a market economy were useful. But when an economy started heading towards a recession, which happened again when the Covid-pandemic had broken out, Keynesian remedies had an important part to play.

[4] De Haan, P. (2016) *From Keynes to Piketty; The Century that Shook up Economics*. London: Palgrave Macmillan, 225. Friedman formulated the succession of schools of thought in a more comprehensive way: 'Only a crisis—actual or perceived—produces real change. When that crisis occurs, the actions that are taken depend on the ideas that are lying around. That, I believe, is our basic function: to develop alternatives to existing policies, to keep them alive and available until politically impossible becomes politically inevitable.' Source: Burns, J. (2023) *Milton Friedman; the Last Conservative*. New York: Farrar, Straus and Giroux. Burns used Friedman's text as the motto of her book.

[5] Samuelson *Friedman*, 280.

Methodological Issues

In 1953, Friedman published a thought-provoking book *Essays in Positive Economics.* One essay stood out; it was entitled The Methodology of Positive Economics. Therein he referred to an article written by John Neville Keynes (indeed, Maynard's father). Keynes Sr. made a distinction between a positive science, being a body of systematised knowledge, like a physical science, concerning *what is*, and a normative, or regulative, science, being a body of systematized knowledge discussing criteria of *what ought to be.* The challenge, argued Keynes Sr. (supported by Friedman) was how to decide whether a suggested hypothesis or theory should be tentatively accepted as part of the body of systematised knowledge concerning what is.

Friedman characterized economics as a positive science being a body of tentatively accepted generalisations about economic phenomena that can be used to predict the consequences of changes or circumstances.[6]

Regarding hypotheses, Friedman argued that a hypothesis is important if it explains much by little; i.e., if it abstracts the common and crucial elements from the mass of complex surrounding the phenomena to be explained and permits valid predictions on the basis of them alone. As for assumptions, theories should be evaluated not on the basis of realism of their assumptions, but exclusively on the basis of the accuracy of their predictions. Friedman then made the following rather blunt observation. He said that a hypothesis must be descriptively false in its assumptions; it takes account of none of the many attendant circumstances, since its very success shows these assumptions to be irrelevant for the phenomena to be explained. For Friedman economics was a positive science, as 'an engine of analysis'.[7]

(*continued*)

[6] Rose Friedman observed that her husband's *Newsweek* columns fell into two categories: positive economics and normative economics. The first group deals with the purely scientific question of the effects that can be expected from specific stimuli. The second class includes columns about specific issues or problems that apply his general philosophy as set forth in *Capitalism and Freedom*, i.e., his fervent belief that the promotion of individual freedom should be the prime objective of social arrangements. Source: Friedman, M., and Friedman, R. (1998) *Two Lucky People.* Chicago: Chicago University Press, 357–358. In 1976, Friedman repeated his opinion about economics becoming a positive science like physics or chemistry in his Nobel Prize acceptance speech.

[7] Ebenstein, L. (2007) *Milton Friedman; A Biography.* London: Palgrave Macmillan, 157.

(continued)

Samuelson called Friedman's version of positive economics peculiar. He also challenged Friedman's opinion about assumptions. He argued that on the basis of the principles of logic, true assumptions can only produce true conclusions. Samuelson also observed that false assumptions can produce both true and false conclusions, and he stressed that economics needed true conclusions. Even Hayek, Friedman's philosophical comrade-in-arms, felt that *Essays in Positive Economics* was in a way a dangerous book, which he should have let known around the time it came out.[8]

How Samuelson and Friedman Differed on Keynes

After WWII, Keynesianism was further developed by Samuelson, Alvin Hansen and Lawrence Klein (1920–2013), among others, and became known—and popular—as New Economics.[9] Their approach to economics was largely based on quantifiable macro-aggregates, that, they believed, could provide them with the information that governments and economists need to direct and manage the economy. This seemed to run smoothly until in the 1970s, as mentioned, stagflation broke out, and 'old economics' represented by Hayek and Friedman, won the day.

In 1966, *Time* magazine ran a cover story about New Keynesianism, arguing that while Keynes was interested in pulling the economy out of the Great Depression towards prosperity, New Economics economists were interested in making an already prospering economy even more

[8] 'In his actual work, then, Friedman often did not follow the methodological dictums that he had laid out in his methodology article'. Source: Caldwell, B. (2004) *Hayek's Challenge; An Intellectual Biography of F.A. Hayek*. Chicago: The University of Chicago Press, 386.

[9] After Keynes had died in April 1946, Samuelson contributed a commemorative article to *Econometrica* (July 1946) in which he confessed that '*The General Theory* was an obscure and badly written book. It was arrogant, bad-tempered, polemical, and not overly generous in its acknowledgments. It was not well-suited for classroom use. Yet, it was a work of genius, its analysis both obvious and new.' Later, Samuelson came round to the view that although Keynes's work was characterized by numerous logical flaws and omissions but that his tools represented an important addition to our economic knowledge… It provided a new system, and that was what was needed to defeat the classical theory. Samuelson presented Keynes as having brilliant intuitions but leaving a gap that Samuelson was to fill with the 'Keynesian savings-investment-income cross.' Source: Backhouse, R. (2017) *Founder of Modern Economics: Paul A. Samuelson*. Vol. I. Oxford: Oxford University Press, 526, 530.

prosperous. Ironically, *Time* quoted Friedman as having said 'We are all Keynesians now'; a statement often attributed to President Nixon. Needless to say, Friedman felt misreported. What he had said was: 'In one sense, we are all Keynesians now; in another, nobody is any longer a Keynesian.'[10]

His analysis of the important role of the money supply was one step away from Keynes; the others were his refutation of Keynes's consumption function and the Phillips Curve. Friedman triggered a counterrevolution in economics and became the most influential economist of the second half of the twentieth century. He strongly advocated freeing up markets, small government, and monetarist policies.

Friedman's attacks on Keynes in his *Newsweek* columns prompted Samuelson to defend Keynes's legacy. The debate in their columns was at times rough. Friedman's wife Rose confirmed that Milton considered Samuelson to be his chief contemporary rival. Wapshott observes that Samuelson described Friedman's challenge to Keynesianism as a man with a foil attacking a battleship. But Samuelson did not underestimate his rival: 'He is about as smart as a guy as you'll meet. He's as persuasive as you hope not to meet.'[11] Friedman's friend, former American Secretary of State, and Secretary of the Treasury George Schultz once quipped: 'Everybody loves to argue with Milton, particularly when he isn't there.'[12] Friedman's most recent biographer, Jennifer Burns, observes about their relationship: 'Schultz's tenure at Treasury marked the high-water mark of Friedman's influence. In many ways, Schultz became Friedman's 'instrument of policy.'[13]

[10] *Samuelson Friedman*, 75–76. Friedman later explained that all economists use Keynesian language and apparatus; however, none of us any longer accepts the initial Keynesian conclusions. Hayek once admitted that Friedman was in important respects closer to Keynes than to him. Friedman's biographer, Jennifer Burns, argues that Friedman had never been a Keynesian, not even in his younger days. When preparing new tax proposals for the Treasury, Friedman was not applying Keynesian economic policy. He observed: 'Taxation represented a less intrusive and more intrinsically conservative approach.' *Milton Friedman*, 120.

[11] Ibid., 58. Burns mentions that Samuelson had turned down an offer from the University of Chicago 'because he dreaded facing Friedman day in day out. 'It would polarize me, it would radicalize me'.' Ibid., 159.

[12] Ibid., 59. Burns describes the first encounter Shultz had with Friedman and Samuelson at MIT: 'The evening consisted of a back and forth between the two of them, and one of them could say one word and the other would know where they're going and say another word, and it was back and forth, and you got an evening where you came away saying, I just watched two of the most brilliant people I ever heard of talk.' Ibid., 328.

[13] Ibid., 344.

Arguably the essential bone of contention between Samuelson and Friedman was the assault of Keynesian economics on the free market's functioning. This will be dealt with first, after which their different thinking on monetary issues, the consumption function, and the Phillips Curve follow.

Free Markets

For neoclassical economic liberals, the functioning of free markets is a near-religious issue. It goes down to their fundamental beliefs how economies best function, and about self-interest serving the public interest. Friedman abhorred regulation, while Samuelson thought of regulations as correcting market failures. For free market economists, such as Hayek, Friedman, and their academic allies assembled in the Mont Pèlerin Society, the market system was a virtuous phenomenon in which buyer and seller mutually agree on a price for a good or service without any outside interference.[14] Samuelson, on the other hand, saw prices merely as a means of rationing scarce resources. He argued that capitalist societies operated under an unwritten social contract, based on manners, traditions, conventions, and laws that allowed people to live together in peace. Social mobility is an important aspect of a market economy, allowing people to economically and socially improve themselves.

The market, prices, and equilibrium between supply and demand are central themes of microeconomics. Burns observes that Samuelson had not wandered far from the price theory he had learned at the University of Chicago, but since then expressed in advanced mathematics.[15] But he had let go of this microeconomic price theory in favour of Keynesian macroeconomic concepts when thinking about aggregate demand and supply. In this case, markets might not clear unless the state stepped in. Samuelson called this the neoclassical synthesis—a blend of traditional price theory on the micro level and Keynesian analysis on the macro level.[16] Samuelson provided a humorous, explanation of the difference between macro- and microeconomics:

[14] The origin and purpose of the Mont Pèlerin Society is described in Chap. 3.

[15] *Milton Friedman*, 140.

[16] 'The neoclassical synthesis continued the project of making economics more quantitative and theoretical, but newly welded this quest to the acceptance of government intervention that was once characteristic of the institutional school. In turn, universities stopped offering courses in business cycles, replacing them with macroeconomics.' Ibid., 140.

> The most interesting and important thing about economics as a science is precisely that almost everything that is true for the individual is wrong for the society and almost everything that is true for society as a whole is wrong for the individual. One individual can affect the price of hardly anything he buys. Yet, all individuals together make the price what it is.[17]

The role of government was in Keynes's view not just an economic matter, it was also one of morality.[18] Like Keynes, Samuelson defended government's role in a mixed economy. Time and again, he explained how a modern, mixed economy functioned. Friedman, as we will see, presented a *liberal* society in which the government played a minimal role,[19] and one in which the central bank would be strictly limited to the creation of money.

Money Mattered

Keynesian economists believed that by fiscal means (taxation and spending) they could manage the economy. Money did not play a prominent part in their thinking. However, according to Friedman money *did* matter a lot. He argued that the erroneous management of the quantity of money (i.e., tightening instead of broadening the money supply) had caused the Great Depression. Wrong handling of the money supply also explained why in the 1970s, inflation ran out of control.

Friedman got his ideas from reading Keynes's collection of articles entitled *A Tract on Monetary Reform* (1923), which Keynes had meanwhile discarded. Keynes had argued, much to Friedman's liking, that the general price level was directly linked to the amount and velocity of money in the economy. So, if the money supply could be controlled, e.g., by banks rationing the supply of credit, inflation and economic growth could be managed. Friedman argued that central banks should play a key role in the management of the money supply.

[17] *Samuelson Friedman*, 142. When debating the virtues of the market with pro-market colleagues, I like to bring under their attention that the market can also be unforgiving.

[18] In a letter to Hayek, dated 28 June 1944, congratulating him with his bestseller *The Road to Serfdom*, Keynes wrote: 'What we need is the restoration of right moral thinking—a return to proper moral values in our moral philosophy. If only you could turn your crusade in that direction you would not look or feel quite so much like Don Quixote.'

[19] However, Friedman admitted that only between the American Civil War and the First World War, the US resembled a laissez faire and free enterprise society as close as one could hope to observe in practice.

In 1963, together with Anna Schwartz, Friedman published *A Monetary History of the United States 1867–1960*, in which they demonstrated that money indeed did matter in the management (or mismanagement) of the economy. However, their insights did not have the impact they had hoped for, with the exception of Fed Chairmen Volcker's and Greenspan's policies during the 1980s, late 1990s and early 2000s, respectively.[20] Friedman observed that under Greenspan's leadership, the rate of growth in the money supply had been more stable than in almost any previous administration.

Volcker and Friedman had opposite temperaments; Friedman liked straight talk, while Volcker cultivated mystique. In addition, Volcker was not a fan of Friedman, he knew him as a perpetual irritant—a gadfly of the Fed. Initially Volcker, well aware of Friedman's thinking, applied his monetarist policy: Strictly manipulating the money supply; not the interest rate. He observed that the Fed would control the quantity of money (the money supply) rather than the price of money (the interest rate). However, during the course of his Fed-chairmanship, Volcker also dramatically increased the Fed's interest rate to help tame the runaway inflation and double-digit interest rates in the real economy, partly the result of deregulation of market interest rates, which eclipsed the inflation rate. He realized that this move, 'the Volcker shock', would increase market interest rates even more. This in turn triggered a deep, but brief, recession in the US. But it was unavoidable, Volcker said. Friedman was dismayed about Volcker's move. Friedman argued in his widely read *Newsweek* columns, that it would undermine his monetarism. He predicted that the fight against inflation would only be temporary. This did not happen. With inflation tamed at 5%, Volcker announced that the Fed would return its attention from money supply and interest rates to strictly the latter. Friedman and Schwartz's monetarist policy advice had been based on data from a world that no longer existed. The monetarist era was over; that is for the time being.[21]

[20] 'Greenspan deeply admired Friedman. He liked to joke that the diminutive economist had 'the world's biggest brain per square inch of body'. Source: *Milton Friedman*, 442.

[21] *Milton Friedman*, 406–429.

Now, what was Samuelson's opinion on the matter? He must have wrecked his brains in countering Friedman, as the latter's monetarist insight was quiet persuasive. Time and again, Friedman proclaimed that inflation was always and everywhere a monetary phenomenon. Samuelson challenged Friedman to explain how money (and exactly *what* money) in an economy could be measured accurately. This was an essential prerequisite for a central bank to intervene in the market. Such a measurement would be very difficult, argued Samuelson, even for monetarists. Regarding former Fed Chairman Alan Greenspan's monetarist policies, Samuelson blamed the latter of lacking morality in his actions.[22]

The opponents could not come to grips on the issue; that is initially. When asked to name his most interesting blunder, Friedman replied that it was his attempt to sell Keynesians his monetary framework. He admitted to have been naïve to think that by putting his ideas in Keynesian language he would have made a dent on the Keynesians.[23] Samuelson later admitted that Friedman, together with Anna Schwartz, had provided an impressive mass of data in making monetarism a movement to reckon with. Samuelson also said that the revival of the quantity theory of money had made economists more willing to recognize that monetary policy could stimulate, stabilize, or depress a modern economy, fully coordinate with fiscal policy as a macroeconomic control instrument.[24] As a result, Samuelson paid more attention to monetarist theories in future editions of his textbook *Economics*.

[22] In an interview in *The Atlantic* of 17 June, 2009, Samuelson said: 'The trouble is that he had been an Ayn Rander. You can take the boy out of the cult, but you can't take the cult out of the boy. He actually had instructions, probably pinned on the wall: 'Nothing from this office should go forth which discredits the capitalist system. Greed is good.' Ayn Rand (pseudonym of Alissa Rosenbaum), was a Russian immigrant into the United States, after her family lost everything resulting from Russia's 1917 October Revolution. Once in America, she studied cinematography. Besides a controversial celebrity, Ayn Rand was a screenwriter and novelist. Her books *The Fountainhead* and *Atlas Shrugged* were bestsellers. The main character in both novels were men of uncommon ability, drive, vision and with high levels of testosterone, unfortunately surrounded by weak persons and their enablers. Rand rejected the label libertarian, criticizing American libertarians as the 'hippies of the right'. She argued that libertarians are a monstrous, disgusting bunch of people. Nonetheless, Rand's philosophy of *Objectivism* is similar to libertarianism. But there are slight differences. For example, 'objectivist' followers espouse egoism while libertarians would not necessarily endorse selfishness. Although she was never accepted by academic philosophers, Rand enjoyed recognition and popularity among libertarians. After 2009, she became an iconic figure in the anti-government Tea Party.

[23] *Samuelson Friedman*, 103.

[24] Samuelson, P. (1970) *Readings in Economics*. New York: McGraw Hill, 146.

Yet Samuelson revenged himself when he observed that Friedman was doing little more than agreeing with Keynes, who had suggested that at full employment there was a direct link between the increase in the supply of money and a rise in prices. Keynes believed that, if—in the long-term—the interest rate could be brought down low enough, monetary policy could play an effective role in curing depression and stagnation.[25] It was not just, as Friedman suggested, an oversupply of money that caused inflation, Samuelson argued that changes in people's saving behaviour, or entrepreneurs' *animal spirits* could equally alter prices.

The Consumption Function

Friedman's second anti-Keynesian salvo concerned the consumption function; again, Friedman begged to differ. But let me first summarize Keynes's consumption function: The larger a person's income, the more likely that person would save the new income than spend it.

Keynes's consumption function was important to the *multiplier*, suggesting that every extra dollar injected into the economy through public spending or tax cuts, would be spent many times over. So, this extra dollar would give the economy a boost much larger than just the extra dollar. It was best to direct the stimulus to the poorer sections of society, for the simple reason that they spend more of the extra dollar, than richer sections.

Friedman had analysed decades of American families' budgets, on the basis of which he concluded that people did not make decisions about spending on the basis of their recent income but on their, as Friedman called it, 'permanent income'.[26] This permanent income was the amount of income a person expected to earn in the long run. Hence, Friedman concluded that Keynes's assumption about how more of the extra income the less well-off would be spending than the rich was wrong. Friedman's insight undermined the expected multiplier effect of a stimulus injection. In addition, Friedman's permanent income also implied that higher incomes did not necessarily lead to higher savings. With the permanent income incorporated in his analysis, Friedman argued that this triggered an inherently cyclically more stable system.[27]

[25] *Samuelson Friedman*, 135.

[26] 'The permanent income hypothesis is elegant, but it does a poor job of describing how people actually behave. Either because people aren't perfectly rational or because they believe that government stimulus will grow the tax base, government spending can boost total economic activity.' Source: Leigh, A. (2024) *How Economics Explains the World; A Short History of Humanity*. New York: Mariner Books, 127.

[27] *Milton Friedman*, 228.

Samuelson had presented his own revealed preference theory.[28] He refuted the idea of consumption being based on discounted future earnings and questioned whether households could be seen as utility maximizers.[29]

He also developed the multiplier-accelerator model. This model combines the Keynesian multiplier with the investment accelerator, in which the multiplier could be used to determine the *level* of income, while the acceleration principle was needed to explain *fluctuations* in the level of income.[30]

The Phillips Curve

Keynesians maintained that there was a stable and measurable *inverse* relationship between inflation and unemployment. So when inflation was rising, unemployment would decrease, and the other way round. LSE researcher, William Phillips (Bill, for friends) had analysed British employment figures over the period 1861–1957. Phillips concluded that, indeed, there was such an inverse link. But when, in the early 1970s, not just unemployment rose, but also inflation; the result was *stagflation.*

At the time, Keynes had concluded that a bit of inflation was needed to ensure full employment, given the fact that a society with growing incomes, had the tendency to underspend. In addition, governments had invested heavily in the rising welfare costs. Both factors triggered double-digit inflation. Friedman should be credited for the fact that already in his 1967 Presidential Address to the American Economic Association (AEA), he had pointed out that governments wanting to push the unemployment rate below the 'natural rate of unemployment' would not just trigger inflation but also more unemployment. Crucial in Friedman's analysis was the distinction between nominal wages and real wages. Workers realized that their nominal wages did not keep pace with inflation. Their real wage became smaller; hence their demands for higher wages. Friedman's recipe was: limit the money supply. Although he had won the battle against the Keynesians, but in the end, he would not win the war.

[28] Revealed preference theory is a method of analysing choices made by individuals, mostly used for comparing the influence of policies on consumer behaviour. In the post-war period, the so-called life cycle theory became popular, according to which households save to provide consumption in old age; the idea Samuelson was to popularise as the overlapping-generations or consumption-loan model. *Founder of Modern Economics*, 214.

[29] Ibid., 214.

[30] Ibid., 264.

Samuelson and other Keynesians, such as Robert Solow, had endorsed the validity of the Phillips Curve. So, what was Samuelson's reaction to Friedman on this issue? He said that in the longer term the relationship between employment and inflation might indeed not hold. After all, expectations about future price rises would begin to inflate wage demands, triggering higher inflation. Samuelson wrote to Friedman: 'My book's [*Economics*; PdH] discussion of the Phillips Curve problem makes all the points that you so properly made and many more.... It discusses short run, long run, opposing views about natural rates of unemployment, about expectations, about variable leads and lags, and multi-dimensional relations, etc.'[31] In short, Samuelson was not really at odds with Friedman on this issue.

Part II Samuelson and Friedman: Their Philosophical Inspirations

Introduction

Although both can be called liberals, Samuelson was one with traits of new liberalism, while Friedman gradually became a conservative liberal, however one with libertarian stripes, so to speak.[32] Samuelson wrote an entertaining essay entitled My Life Philosophy, which was one of the twenty-two essays published in Michael Szenberg's *Eminent Economists; Their Life Philosophies.* In his contribution, Samuelson mentioned Karl Popper and Thomas Kuhn (1922–1996).[33] Szenberg had not invited Friedman, admitting that the number of economists and their selection had been quite arbitrary. I guess that Friedman's contribution would have been quite a bit more spicy than Samuelson's.

Samuelson was surely influenced by liberalism and by new liberal Keynes. His thinking about the role of government, taxes, and the market is more nuanced than Friedman's. I summarize what Samuelson had to say about his life philosophy.

[31] *Samuelson Friedman*, 115.

[32] Burns characterized Friedman as the 'last conservative'. Burns observes that in the twenty-first century, the synthesis that Friedman represented, based in free market economics, individual liberty, and global cooperation, has fallen apart.

[33] Szenberg, M. (1993) *Eminent Economists; Their Life Philosophies*. Cambridge: Cambridge University Press. I checked which philosophers were mentioned by these twenty-two economists (among them nine Nobel Prize laureates). Only few philosophers were mentioned: Bergson, Berlin, Hegel, Kuhn, Mill, Plato, Popper, Russell, Spinoza, and Wittgenstein.

Friedman's philosophy (including libertarian shades) is presented and compared with liberal philosophies of Locke, Smith, and Mill, plus Robert Nozick's libertarian propositions. Ayn Rand (1905–1982) also gave Friedman libertarian inspiration.[34]

Samuelson's Inspiration

This is what Samuelson wrote about his life philosophy: 'I was the proverbial tabula rasa as far as political economy was concerned: nothing to unlearn in that bloody sponge called my brain. Aaron Director's laissez faire conservatism got first crack at me. I marvel that the worst virulences of that particular system got worked out of my system early.'[35] Samuelson's parents were 'liberals' in the American sense of the term, and he was moulded in that *weltanschauung*.

In *My Life Philosophies*, Samuelson does not refer to ancient philosophers, or early representatives of liberalism who would have given him inspiration. But he engagingly wrote about methodological issues. Never far from his consciousness was a concern for the ethics of the outcome. Indeed, his was a simple ideology favouring the underdog and (other things equal) abhorring inequality, probably inspired by Mill and new liberalism's ideas. As a science, Samuelson argued that economics can concern itself only with the best means of attaining given ends; it cannot prescribe the ends themselves. But, at the back of his mind, he was concerned about the ethics of the outcome.

He did not go along with Friedman's opinion about the close relationship between economic and political freedoms. Indeed, Samuelson begged to differ: 'I was taught at the University of Chicago that business freedoms and personal freedoms have to be strongly linked, as a matter both of brute empirical fact and of cogent deductive syllogism… Gradually I had to acknowledge that the paradigm could not fit the facts. By most Millian criteria, regimented Scandinavia was freer than my America—or certainly

[34] Although Friedman does not refer to Ayn Rand in his work (he seldomly invoked his political inspirators), in their memoir, among the intellectual sources for the libertarian movement in the immediate post-war decades, Rose and Milton mentioned Hayek's ***Road to Serfdom***, Ayn Rand's *Fountainhead* and *Atlas Shrugged*, as well as Friedman's own *Capitalism and Freedom*. *Milton Friedman*, 151.

[35] *Founder of Modern Economics*, 62–63.

at least as free.'[36] Samuelson confessed that he had a dream:'…I have a dream of a humane economy that is at the same time efficient and respecting of personal (if not business) freedoms. Much of producing and consuming decisions involve use of the market mechanism. But the worst inequalities of condition that result from reliance on market forces—even in the presence of equality of ex ante opportunity—can be mitigated by the transfer of powers of the democratic state.'[37] He called this economics with a heart.

The notion of *truth* is popular among philosophers; after all, what exactly is truth? Samuelson argued that truth has many facets. Precision in deterministic facts or in their probability laws can at best be only partial and approximate. 'But still…. it is forced upon one that what ultimately shapes the verdicts of the scientist jury is an empirical reality out there.'[38]

When in 1962, Kuhn's *The Structure of Scientific Revolutions* came out, Samuelson made two predictions:

> … one, that in the physical and life sciences its thesis would have to be modified to recognize that there is a cumulative property of knowledge that makes later paradigms ultimately dominate earlier ones, however differently the struggle may transiently look; two, that Kuhn's doctrine of incommensurability of alternative paradigms would cater to a strong desire on the part of polemical scientists who will be delighted to be able to say, 'That's all very well to say that we'uns have to agree with you'uns'. Kuhn has correctly discerned the warts on the countenance of evolving science. His readers must not lose the face from the warts.[39]

Samuelson gradually recognized the limitations of laissez faire which Keynes had described in *The End of Laissez Faire*. And, like Keynes, Samuelson also saw the merits of government's corrective role in the economy, not just in addressing booms, busts, and market failures, but also in promoting social justice and social stability.

[36] *Eminent Economists*, 239.

[37] Ibid., 240.

[38] Ibid., 244. Winston Churchill is reported to have once remarked about truth: Men often stumble over the truth, but most manage to pick themselves up and hurry off as if nothing had happened.

[39] Ibid., 244.

Friedman's Inspiration

Introduction

Two of Friedman's publications reflect his philosophy very well. As I already mentioned, in 1963, Friedman and Schwartz published *A Monetary History of the United States, 1867–1960.* The second book is *Capitalism and Freedom*, which had come out a year earlier. The former is a scholarly analysis, while the second is, in essence, a political and philosophical polemic work, in liberalism's tradition. One of Friedman's biographers, Lenny Ebenstein says about *Capitalism and Freedom*: 'The work is something of a departure from his main work in academic economics. In fact, it is the beginning of his career as an advocate of less government and freer and more competitive markets as the principle by which to order society.'[40]

A Monetary History

Let me first deal with *A Monetary History of the United States.* The conventional wisdom about the Great Depression is that as the American economy developed, the depression was caused by excess saving and a declining propensity to consume. However, Friedman and Schwartz arrived at quite a different conclusion.

Based upon a thorough analysis of a century of American monetary policies, the authors concluded that the Fed had applied inappropriate monetary policies. Instead of lowering the interest rate and supplying banks with money to prevent more bank failures, and to counter the declining quantity of money in the economy, the Fed kept the interest rate high and contracted the money supply, thereby deepening the depression. If the Fed would have done what Friedman and Schwartz suggested, the Great Depression would only have turned into a 'garden variety' depression. Since the Fed was a government institution, it was not the market which was to blame for the crisis, but government—'government failed tragically.'[41]

Capitalism and Freedom

Friedman's scathing criticism of government's role, is one of the central themes of *Capitalism and Freedom.* He strongly felt that in the Western world, governments had expanded far too much and, with a few

[40] Ebenstein, L. (2007) *Milton Friedman; A biography.* London: Palgrave Macmillan, 138.
[41] *Two Lucky People*, 233.

exceptions, failed to achieve their objectives. The book is in fact a *manifesto*, containing Friedman's liberal political and economic philosophy, which he would, with varying success, press upon prominent American and British politicians, ranging from Barry Goldwater, Richard Nixon, Ronald Reagan, to Margaret Thatcher.

Capitalism and Freedom's main thrust is that economic freedom is not just an end in itself; it is an indispensable means towards achieving political freedom. The book clearly revived the liberal laissez-faire view of the economy as a self-regulating mechanism. To ensure an effective allocation of scarce resources, the government had to be kept small. Friedman acknowledged that government was necessary to protect individuals' freedom. However, by concentrating power in the hands of politicians, government posed a threat to freedom.

Friedman bluntly argued that almost nothing good could be achieved by government. He gave examples, such as the fact that progressive taxes had not limited the gap between rich and poor; social welfare had only exacerbated poverty; and public housing had only worsened the housing conditions of the poor. Taxes should be brought down to an across-the-board *flat rate* (as also proposed by Mill); while the poor should benefit from a negative income tax rate so as to provide them with a basic income.[42] Finally, the exchange rate should be freed up.

The book went far beyond economics. The author proposed to do away with the military draft system (a very popular proposal among youngsters at the time, as the Vietnam war was intensified). Friedman also proposed to introduce education vouchers for parents who could choose the desired (and thus best-performing) school for their children. While Smith and Mill advocated government to provide schooling, Friedman proposed parents to choose a public or private school of their liking for their children. Medical licenses should be abolished. And he advocated the legal sale of drugs, saying that we have no right to use force to prevent a fellow man from committing suicide, or from drinking alcohol or taking drugs, again, reminiscent of what Mill had proposed.

[42] Friedman's negative income tax idea goes all the way back to his thinking in the late 1930s, when he proposed a universal basic income. Daniel Patrick Moynihan was appreciative of Friedman's concern. 'He remembered, the Republicans 'had almost no thinkers, almost no writers, almost no reputation for a sophisticated or even compassionate view of social policy.' Friedman aside, anti-poverty policy was the near exclusive province of the Democratic Party.' *Milton Friedman*, 280.

Some of Friedman's proposals were quite radical. Take his proposal to abolish medical licenses. Fellow economist, Kenneth Arrow (1921–2017) did not agree. He argued that for any patient it was crucial to find a good doctor and not an incompetent one. Government licenses ensured that medical doctors had the necessary professional qualifications. Also Hayek observed that Friedman was simply too radical in some of his proposals.

There is a strong connection between economic and political freedom, argued Friedman. History demonstrated that political freedom came about with the development of the free market and liberal market institutions. For Friedman, economic freedom constituted the base, while political freedom was the superstructure. He underscored that a socialist society simply cannot be democratic. However, in *Capitalism and Freedom*'s fortieth anniversary edition, Friedman admitted that there is not a mutual relationship between the two freedoms. In some countries (i.e., China) there was a fair degree of economic freedom while political arrangements were far from free. He, therefore, would replace the dichotomy of economic freedom and political freedom with the trichotomy economic freedom, civil freedom, and political freedom.[43]

In 1958, philosopher Isaiah Berlin delivered a lecture entitled *Two Concepts of Liberty*, in which he presented negative and positive liberty. Negative liberty, or freedom *from*, is a person's ability to do as he or she wished, without the interference of others, echoing the ideas of Locke and Mill. It means the right to property, religion, and speech beyond the control of the state. By contrast, positive liberty, or freedom *to*, is about self-mastery, said Berlin; it is the triumph of a person's 'higher nature' over low impulses and outside influence. Positive freedom reflects a deeper sense of autonomy—a doer; deciding; self-directed free from external influences.

(*continued*)

[43] Friedman concluded that one of the major shortcomings of his book was the inadequate treatment of the role of political freedom, which under some circumstances promotes economic and civic freedom, and under others inhibits both. Source: *Capitalism and Freedom*, fortieth edition, ix.

(continued)

Berlin concluded, however, that liberating people's true will would invariably mean the state placing constraints on what they could legally do for their own benefit, just as children are compelled to go to school, even if they do not understand why. Berlin then observed that negative and positive freedom were in conflict. Jean-Jacques Rousseau had argued that one could force people to be free. This, Berlin argued, was the logic of paternalists, tyrants, and Marxists.

Friedman maintained that the private sector, unlike government, was the stable sector in the economy. As long as there were no major shocks in the economy, production and employment would develop gradually. This view is, as we saw, contrary to the Keynesian analysis in which government intervention is required to redress shocks caused by the private sector.

It is not easy to establish what type of liberal Friedman really was. In their memoir, Friedman confessed that he had forgotten how thoroughly Keynesian he was. However, in her monumental biography of Friedman, Burns could detect nothing in Friedman's views at the time which could be meaningfully understood as Keynesian.[44] Nor can Friedman's philosophy be exclusively associated with liberalism, or libertarianism. Wapshott, observed that Friedman was not just an evangelist of capitalism, he gradually changed from a liberal into an ideologue of 'radical libertarianism.'[45] Samuelson once wrote, tongue in cheek, that 'Professor Friedman is an able scholar and a forceful spokesman for the libertarian form of conservative economics.[46]

Burns characterizes Friedman as 'the last conservative', although Friedman himself would have rejected this label. He thought himself being a liberal—meaning the classical sort; i.e., a believer in limited, representative government, free trade, and individual rights. Why then the label conservative? In America the term 'liberal' is associated with Roosevelt's New Deal order; while this was also rejected by Friedman.[47] In

[44] *Milton Friedman*, 119.

[45] *Samuelson Friedman*, 49. Wapshott argues on the same page that 'Friedman's libertarianism ran counter to traditional conservative principles.... old conservative prejudices, such as race hatred, had no place in capitalism, which was a disinterested system that treated all people alike.'

[46] Ibid., 55.

[47] Although Friedman cast his first vote for Roosevelt and took his first job in the Roosevelt Administration.

other countries than the US, Friedman might have been called a neoliberal, but—adds Burns—this term gained little purchase in America.

Then, there is the libertarian label, as mentioned by Wapshott and, to some extent, by Samuelson. I mentioned before that Friedman got some inspiration from libertarian philosophy. Yet, he would not call himself a libertarian, although libertarianism shared his strong interest in liberty and his celebration of individual freedom. Burns observes, however, that Friedman could at best be labelled as a conservative libertarian, since he remained attached to the state's management of money, unlike many other libertarians, who maintain very minimalist opinions about the role of the state. Finally, why was Friedman then the 'last conservative'? Burns observes that in the twenty-first century, the synthesis that Friedman represented, based in free market economics, individual liberty, and global cooperation, has fallen apart.[48]

Libertarianism

Libertarianism upholds liberty as a core principle. Libertarians seek to maximize autonomy and political freedom, emphasizing free association, freedom of choice, individualism and voluntary association. Libertarianism is the theory that asserts that states of affairs are just to the extent that they are the outcome of a process in which individuals act voluntarily and in which their rights are not being violated.

Actions are right as long as they do not violate anyone's freedom or liberties. Fukuyama argues that libertarianism is a peculiar doctrine founded on hostility to government as such.[49] Libertarians typically maintain that the only relevant consideration in political matters is individual liberty—acts and policies are just only if they do not violate anyone's rights. The duties that rights imply are typically 'negative' duties not to interfere. For example, the right to life is one *not* to be killed, that is all.

In appraising economic institutions, libertarians focus on rights and liberties. In particular, property rights are strongly defended by libertarians. Von Mises and Hayek expressed libertarian ideas in their respective work. As described in Chap. 3, modern libertarianism started in Austria, before moving to the United States. A prominent libertarian philosopher in America was Robert Nozick.

[48] *Milton Friedman*, 14–16.

[49] Fukuyama, F. (2022) *Liberalism and its Discontents*. London: Profile Books, vii.

Robert Nozick

Robert Nozick was the only son of Russian immigrants. Young Robert transformed himself from an obese, anxious, but precociously clever boy into a prominent twentieth-century political theorist. After graduating from Columbia College in 1963, he got his PhD in philosophy at Princeton. He lectured philosophy at Princeton, Rockefeller, before becoming a full professor in 1969 at Harvard, when he was only 30 years old. He would stay at Harvard for the rest of his academic career. During his graduate studies, he moved from the politically left to right-wing libertarianism. What had driven him to libertarianism was the coerciveness of socialism. He argued that socialism violates people's rights by outlawing capitalist acts between consenting adults.

In his work, the individual, and his or her right to life, liberty, and property, are fundamental. He argued that respect for individual rights is the key criterion for assessing state action. The only legitimate state is a *minimal state* that restricts its activities to the protection of the rights of life (indeed, the right not to be killed), liberty, property, and contract.

Nozick remains best-known for his *Anarchy, State, and Utopia*.[50] This book became the philosophical manifesto of the New Right in America. In *Anarchy, State, and Utopia*, Nozick focuses on the idea of self-ownership. He advocated, for example, decriminalisation of prostitution and, like Friedman, drugs. Nozick rejected the notion of inalienable rights of life, liberty, and property as developed by Locke. The latter, as touched upon before, wondered whether people could be justified in appropriating a previously unowned resource. Locke argued that they could, however, under certain conditions: Individuals could acquire ownership over a resource by mixing their labour with it. But Nozick asked:

> ......why isn't mixing what I own with what I don't own a way of losing what I own rather than a way of gaining what I don't? If I own a can of tomato juice and spill it in the sea so its molecules...mingle evenly throughout the sea, do I thereby come to own the sea, or have I foolishly dissipated my tomato juice?[51]

The key libertarian starting point, argued Nozick, is that people have a stringent set of rights, giving them the kind of control over themselves

[50] Nozick, R. (1974) *Anarchy, State, and Utopia*. Oxford: Basil Blackwell.
[51] Ibid., 174.

that one might have over possessions they own. According to Nozick's, what he called, entitlement theory of justice, a transaction is just if it arises from just acquisition of what was unowned or by voluntary transfer of what was justly owned. It includes: (i) Rights to control the use of the entity, (ii) rights to transfer these rights to others, (iii) immunities to the loss of these rights, (iv) compensation rights in case others use the entity without one's consent, and (v) enforcement rights. As rights are to secure liberty and to permit people to pursue their own affairs, welfare considerations would never justify interferences with individual rights.[52]

Nozick's entitlement of justice consists of three principles: (i) the Principle of Justice in Acquisitions, (ii) the Principle of Justice in Transfers, and (iii) the Principle of Rectification of Injustice. Needless to say, Nozick was not a supporter of 'distributive justice', implying that society had resources to distribute. No, said Nozick, only individuals do, and they are entitled to hold or transfer them. Regarding transfers, he regards them as voluntary if they do not violate any rights. Only remedying or preventing injustices justifies redistribution or other interferences with voluntary action.

Regarding distributive justice, he distinguished between historical and end-result principles of distributive justice. The former applies when the justice of a distribution depends upon how it came about. By contrast, current time-slice principles of justice say that justice is determined by how things are distributed (i.e., who has what) as judged by structural principles. End-state principles comprise all unhistorical principles of distributive justice, such as current time-slice principles.

Nozick also distinguished between patterned and unpatterned principles. Patterned principles require that distributive shares vary with a combination of natural dimensions such as moral merit or usefulness to society. He observed that most principles of distributive justice are patterned. However, the requirement that a distribution of justice be patterned will result in violations of people's liberties. Nozick illustrates this observation with a famous example. Suppose that the holdings in a society are in complete accordance with some favoured patterned principle of distributive justice: D1. Nozick apparently loved basketball because he presented then famous Los Angeles Laker's player Wilt Chamberlain. Suppose also that in

[52] Although a strong supporter of the idea of a minimal state, Hayek addresses welfare concerns, as presented in Chap. 5.

that society Chamberlain signs a contract with his team, stipulating that 25 cents of the price of each ticket of each home game goes to Chamberlain. Now, suppose that during one year no transfers occur except from 1 million persons attending the games, resulting in making Chamberlain $250,000 richer. Nozick called this situation: D2. However, if D1 was just and people voluntarily moved from D1 to D2, the question then is how can D2 not be just? If D1 is regarded as the only just distribution under the favoured principle, in order to preserve justice either Chamberlain's rights have to be violated by taking $250,000 away from him or by forbidding contracts such as that between Chamberlain and the Los Angeles Lakers, and between his team and fans. The conclusion is that neither option seems attractive.[53]

Regarding the role of the minimal state, Part I of *Anarchy, State and Utopia* is to rebut the individualist anarchist's claim that no state can be justified. Part I is devoted to what Nozick considers to be the fundamental question of political philosophy; i.e., whether there should be any state at all. Nozick shows how a minimal state—in essence a 'night watchman' state limited to the protection of the rights of life, liberty and property—could arise without violating rights, inspired by social contract theory, such as Locke's.

A minimal state is justified because it would arise spontaneously among people living in a hypothetical 'state of nature'. Again, in line with Locke, Nozick assumed that everyone possesses the natural rights to life, liberty, and property. Everyone also has the natural right to punish those who violate one's own natural rights. As it is difficult to defend for anyone to do this on his own, individuals band together to form 'protection associations' in which members defend each other's rights and punish rights violators. Some of these associations would develop into *private* businesses offering protection and punishment services for a fee. Eventually, only one dominant firm (or a confederation of firms) would control all the protection and punishment business in the community, in return for protection of the members of the community. Because this firm would have a monopoly, it would constitute a minimal state in the true libertarian sense. And because this minimal state would come about without violating anyone's natural rights, a state with these powers is justified. Nozick added that

[53] This illustration is taken from Reiss, J. (2013) *Philosophy of Economics; A Contemporary Introduction*. London: Routledge, 260.

every group would enjoy the same freedom to realize their own idea of a good society. In this way, concluded Nozick, the minimal state constituted a framework for utopia.[54]

Nozick refuted modern forms of (new) liberalism that, in addition to the role of the minimal state, it should have powers to (i) regulate economic activities of citizens, (ii) redistribute wealth, and (iii) provide social services such as education and health care. In short, Nozick argued against the welfare state, but admits that even a minimal state can only function if properly funded by taxes.

He had more to say about taxes. Taxation is the most coercive restraint. Nozick compares taxation to some extent with forced labour. An example: if the income tax is 25%, a person working 40 hours a week, works 10 hours for other people. These 10 hours are forced labour according to Nozick, akin to slavery, he added. Yet, as mentioned, he was not opposed to all taxation. He writes in *Anarchy, State and Utopia* about the minimal state that it is limited to the narrow functions of protection against force, theft, fraud, enforcement of contracts, and the level of taxation necessary to uphold it. However, by defining what this minimal state should do, Nozick opens the door to a much larger degree of state involvement, and thus taxation. In this context, Reiss wonders whether there would not be many more market imperfections that require state interventions?[55]

What would Nozick, had he still been alive, say about the gig economy? Hausman, McPherson and Satz present an interesting thought experiment: 'The main business of companies in the gig economy is matchmaking, connecting people who have a service to sell with interested buyers, and doing that quickly and efficiently via the Internet. These companies facilitate 'capitalist acts between consenting adults' (in Robert Nozick's memorable phrase) and surely appeal strongly to libertarian sentiments.'[56]

[54] Not surprisingly, *Anarchy, State and Utopia*, generated a host of critical observations from other scholars, such as about Nozick's notion of exclusive property rights. Suppose that there is overwhelming evidence that in the past many violations of people's rights have occurred, it is not clear why today's holdings should be protected by the state. Since an enormous amount of historical information is needed in order to determine the just state, there is no way to move from the current state to the one that is just. Reiss concludes: 'Within the Nozickian system it is very hard to see, however, why an unjust distribution of property rights should be defended.' *Philosophy of Economics*, 264. Nozick did not defend or revise his political views in his published work.

[55] Ibid., 263.

[56] Hausman, D. McPherson, M, and Satz, D (2017) *Economic Analysis, Moral Philosophy, and Public Policy*. Cambridge: Cambridge University Press, 321.

The Legacies of Friedman and Samuelson

Samuelson was in many ways a game-changer. He was 'infected' by Keynesianism (he quipped: 'You either caught it or you did not'), while formalizing economic research using mathematics. He reshaped and improved the theoretical foundations of the economic science, and co-developed New Economics. The many editions of his textbook taught millions of aspiring young economists all over the world. As Samuelson's biographer Roger Backhouse wrote, 'Samuelson' had become an institution in world economics.[57] He established the prestigious Economics Department at MIT. He enriched economic theory with the Stolper-Samuelson theorem, his revealed preference notion, the multiplier-accelerator model. His neoclassical synthesis[58] remains the most widely acknowledged guide to how macroeconomics can be made to avoid catastrophe. In this vein, Samuelson once quoted Thorstein Veblen's bon mot: There is no reason why theoretical economics should be the monopoly of the reactionaries.

When, in the early 1970s, Keynesianism was on the defence, Friedman's fame started to rise and he became the most influential economist of the Western world. He also was a game-changer, as he offered new ways to tackle old problems.[59] Friedman firmly established himself as a principal critic of Keynesianism (his consumption function differed greatly from Keynes's and he proved that the implications of the Phillips Curve were wrong) and became the major protagonist of market stability, government inefficiency, and monetarist policies. Although libertarians and classical liberals claim Friedman, he belonged to neither. Unlike some libertarians, Friedman accepted the legitimacy of the state. As for classical liberalism, he was critical of doctrinaire, laissez faire philosophy that assigned almost no role to the state.

Gradually, Friedman became more a conservative philosopher and less an accomplished economist. He proposed the US army staffed by volunteers instead of conscripts, educational vouchers, floating exchange rates, and a universal basic income. Above all, Friedman was a strong defender of freedom in the political as well as in the economic realm.

[57] *Founder of Modern Economics*, xx.

[58] Joan Robinson called the neoclassical synthesis 'bastard Keynesianism'. Source: Robinson, J. (1979) *The Generalisation of the General Theory*. London: Macmillan, xiv.

[59] *Milton Friedman*, 480.

Friedman's star rose in Washington DC. Successive American Presidents listened to his advice. During his lifetime, he influenced, with limited success, the Fed's monetary policies. He was more successful in the United Kingdom, where Prime Minister Margaret Thatcher took over his monetarist doctrine—she was delighted by its simplicity.[60] Nonetheless, by 1981 monetarism was abandoned in Britain because none of the targets set by the then Chancellor of the Exchequer had been met. When Joe Biden was running for office in 2020 he declared that 'Milton Friedman isn't running the show anymore'. But Biden was wrong about Friedman's lasting influence.

When the Great Recession broke out, Keynesianism made a comeback. Keynes was included in the list of the most influential economists, published by *The Economist* in February 2011; while Friedman was not, but his disciple, former Fed Chairman Ben Bernanke was, in recognition of Quantitative Easing, inspired by Friedman's insights. When in early 2020 the Covid-pandemic broke out, Keynesian fiscal policies were again widely applied along with monetary policies to keep affected economies afloat.

Samuelson took on board some of Friedman's new insights, such as the latter's monetarist theory. New Keynesians portray a Keynesian vision of what to do in a recession, but they accept the neoclassical rational expectations hypothesis, invented by Robert Lucas. Their models do not exclude the possibility of frictions resulting from market imperfections. New Keynesians include rigidities (such as price stickiness) to modify the assumption of frictionless rationality. They allow policy interventions in the short term if there is a crisis.

During a recession, Samuelson, would propose, like Keynes, effective aggregate demand management. Keynes, however, would not have included a large role for money as suggested by monetarism. Friedman would have strongly promoted monetarist policies in a crisis situation, including the central bank printing money, as these measures would restore economic equilibrium.

[60] Thatcher's predecessor Edward Heath was less enthusiastic. He acidly wrote: 'The Conservative Party had rightly criticized socialists for their attachment to doctrinal, impractical ideas. The purpose of politics is to bring benefit to one's country, not to experiment with academic theories. Monetarism, the idea that inflation is a purely monetary phenomenon, the product of nothing more than an increase in the money supply, is perhaps the most deceptively simplistic of all economic theories. As such, it was always likely to be especially attractive to those whose understanding of economics was limited.' *Samuelson Friedman*, 236.

Regarding liberalism's influence, both Samuelson and Friedman were groomed in the economic liberal tradition. Samuelson was a liberal with traits of new liberalism, while Friedman gradually moved into conservative economic liberalism, however one with libertarian influences.

References

Backhouse, R. (2017). *Founder of Modern Economics: Paul A. Samuelson* (Vol. I). Oxford University Press.

Burns, J. (2023). *Milton Friedman; the Last Conservative*. Farrar, Straus and Giroux.

Caldwell, B. (2004). *Hayek's Challenge; An Intellectual Biography of F.A. Hayek*. University of Chicago Press.

Ebenstein, L. (2007). *Milton Friedman; A Biography*. Palgrave Macmillan.

De Haan, P. (2016). *From Keynes to Piketty; The Century that Shook up Economics*. Palgrave Macmillan.

Friedman, M. (1953). The Methodology of Positive Economics. In *Essays in Positive Economics*. Chicago University Press.

Friedman, M., & Friedman, R. (1998). *Two Lucky People*. Chicago University Press.

Friedman, M. (2002). *Capitalism and Freedom. Fortieth Anniversary Edition*. Chicago University Press.

Fukuyama, F. (2022). *Liberalism and Its Discontents*. Profile Books.

Hausman, D., McPherson, M., & Satz, D. (2017). *Economic Analysis, Moral Philosophy, and Public Policy*. Cambridge University Press.

Leigh, A. (2024). *How Economics Explains the World; A Short History of Humanity*. Mariner Books.

McCloskey, D. (1996). *The Vices of Economists; The Virtues of the Bourgeoisie*. Erasmus University.

Nozick, R. (1974). *Anarchy, State, and Utopia*. Basil Blackwell.

Reiss, J. (2013). *Philosophy of Economics; A Contemporary Introduction*. Routledge.

Robinson, J. (1979). *The Generalisation of the General Theory*. Macmillan.

Samuelson, P. (1970). *Readings in Economics*. McGraw Hill.

Szenberg, M. (1993). *Eminent Economists; Their Life Philosophies*. Cambridge University Press.

Wapshott, N. (2021). *Samuelson Friedman; The Battle Over the Free Market*. W.W. Norton.

CHAPTER 7

Amartya Sen: Economist-Philosopher

Prologue

After the end of WWII, economists began feeling that economics should stay away from philosophical reflections. They felt that they best limited themselves to facts. As a result, much of economics became neat and elegant, as Amartya Sen observes. Jokingly, Sen adds that some of modern economics seems indeed to be based on the corset-maker's old advice: If madam is entirely comfortable in it, then madam most certainly needs a smaller size.

Sen did not want to 'stick to facts'; on the contrary, he wanted to probe deeper than the facts only. He was lucky, as during his student says in the early 1950s, Kenneth Arrow's *Social Choice and Individual Values* had just come out. Young Amartya studied Arrow's book with gusto. Social choice and welfare economics would remain Sen's main interests.

In 1971, John Rawls published *A Theory of Justice*, a most influential liberal political philosophical treatise, dealing with justice in the distribution of income and wealth. Rawls applied contractarian notions, as originally developed by Thomas Hobbes. While Sen admired Rawls's work, he also laid his theory's shortcomings bare. But Rawls's theory also inspired Sen to develop his capability approach, reflective of his economic and philosophical concerns, one of them being people's freedoms, or rather lack thereof. Sen argues that the increase in real freedoms is the true measure of a good society.

P. de Haan, *Great Economists and the Evolution of Economic Liberalism*, https://doi.org/10.1007/978-3-031-93831-3_7

Apart from being an economist, Sen is also a celebrated philosopher. His interests and contributions cover a much wider field than just economics. Sen brought philosophical notions back into economics, in particular those concerning liberal political philosophy. Sen confronted scholars, who had presented new ideas, such as Arrow's social choice theory, with probing observations. Also Rawls, could not escape Sen's critical analysis, which may have given the addressees sleepless nights.

Sen broadened the scope of economics in joining development economists, arguing that economic analyses of mature economies should not any longer be the standard; what was happening in developing countries should form an integral part of their work.

Sen practiced what he preached. As Robert Solow remarked: Sen is the conscience of our profession. Sen is one of the game-changers presented in this book, precisely because of his global view, his contributions to welfare economics, and the inclusion of philosophical notions into economics, and the other way round.

Introduction

Amartya Sen cannot easily be put into one spot. He is more a cosmopolitan than an Indian citizen. The Sens have a house in Cambridge, Massachusetts; the base from which Sen taught at Harvard during the academic year. They also have a home in Cambridge, England, where Sen was a Fellow of Trinity College and his wife, Emma Rothschild, a Fellow of Magdalene College. They usually spend their winter holidays at their home in Santiniketan in West Bengal, India.

In his books and articles Sen refers to Western philosophers but equally so to Asian philosophers, such as Buddha and the enlightened emperor Ashoka. He also introduced terms, such as *niti* and *nyanya* in his academic work. Both terms stand for justice in classical Sanskrit.

When first in Cambridge, England, young Amartya had taken a keen interest in philosophy and ethics. His tutor Joan Robinson told him to 'give up all that rubbish'. Luckily, he did not follow her advice. Later he explained, in a humorous fashion, why ethics appealed to him: To escape pogroms and poverty a large group of Eastern European Jews sailed to America via Liverpool. Somebody asked why Jews were doing much better in America than in England. The reason was that a small group of passengers decided to disembark in Liverpool. Sen then remarked that he disembarked to take up ethics while the remainder of the economist passengers continued their voyage.

Sen can also be characterized as a gadfly. He once observed that, as just mentioned, much of economics was neat and elegant. But he added that some of it was not. Indeed, he challenged central assumptions of economic and philosophical theories, undermining their consistency and elegance, while giving the inventors of these theories headaches in attempts to rescue them.

Part I of this chapter is devoted to Sen's life and work. Part II zooms in Sen's contributions to the philosophy of economics.

Part I Sen's Life and Work

In 1933, Amartya Kumar Sen was born in his mother's home town Santiniketan, located north of Calcutta (now Kolkata), on the campus of Rabindranath Tagore's Visva-Bharati, consisting of a school and college. Tagore gave Sen his first name which means destined for immortality. Soon after Amartya's birth, mother and son returned to Dacca (now Dhaka), at the time a sleepy city but now Bangladesh's sprawling and overcrowded capital, where Amartya's father had taken up a chemistry professorship at Dacca University.

Amartya was sent to St. Gregory's School, a strict and ambitious American missionary school, which he did not like and, as a result, performed well below average. His parents then sent him back to his birth place. He enjoyed the progressive pedagogical approach of Visva Bharati. Grades were seen there as unimportant. Sen remembers one teacher having commented on a class mate's performance: 'You know, she is really quite original, even though her grades are very good.'[1] On the school's curriculum Sen had this to say:' …they combined learning about India's own traditions with many opportunities to learn about other countries too and their cultures right across the world.'[2] It made a lasting impression on Sen's academic work. Another fruitful inspiration was given by his maternal grandfather Kshiti Mohan Sen, a distinguished Sanskrit scholar, and a

[1] Sen, A. (2022) *Home in the World; A Memoir.* London: Penguin Random House, 52.
[2] Ibid., 17.

close associate of Tagore's.[3] Amartya was the only grandchild who had the sense of academic vocation, so he was destined 'to carry the mantle'.

In 1942, Gandhi launched the 'Quit India' movement. The Bengal famine of 1943 took the lives of between 2 and 3 million people, mainly poor fishermen and landless workers. They perished from starvation. The famine was the consequence of various causes: Wartime inflation, censorship and imperial indifference.[4] This famine destroyed the last remnants of respect for the British. Later in life, Sen studied this man-made disaster in detail. He concluded that at the time there was an adequate food supply in Bengal, but that particular groups of people, including landless workers, did not have the means to buy food as its price rose rapidly due to acquisitions by the military, panic buying, hoarding and price gouging. All of these factors were connected to the war in the region. Sen's research ultimately resulted in 1981 in the publication of his influential book *Poverty and Famines.*

Before India's independence in 1947, violent clashes between Hindus and Muslims erupted. Amartya witnessed a tragic accident right in front of his grandfather's home: 'One afternoon in 1944, a man came through the gate screaming pitifully and bleeding profusely. The wounded person, who had been knifed on his back, was a Muslim daily labourer, called Kader Mia. He had come for some work in a neighbouring house and was going home after some work in a nearby house—for a tiny reward—and had been knifed on the street by a communal thug in our largely Hindu area. As he was being taken to the hospital by my father, he went on saying that his wife had told him not to go into a hostile area during the communal riots. But he had to go out in search of work and earning because his family had nothing to eat. The penalty of that economic unfreedom turned out to be death, which occurred later in the hospital.... Kader Mia need not have come to a hostile area in search of income in those troubled times if his family could have managed without it.'[5] The experience made

[3] Sen lamented the wrong impression the British public had of Tagore: 'Tagore soon became thought of in Europe as a sage with a message—a message of peace and goodwill from the East—which ... could save Europe from the dire predicament of war....This was a far cry from the many-sided creative artist and careful reasoner that people at home found in Tagore.... When an otherwise sympathetic writer such as Bernard Shaw jokingly transformed Rabindranath Tagore into a fictional character called Stupendranath Begorr, there was not much hope that Tagore's real ideas would receive the attention they deserved.' Ibid., 89–90.

[4] The British Viceroy had written about the famine to Prime Minister Churchill, to no avail.

[5] Quote from *Les Prix Nobel. The Nobel Prizes 1998.* Stockholm: Nobel Foundation, 1999.

a deep impression on Amartya. It made him aware of the dangers of narrowly defined identities, and of the divisiveness in communitarian politics. It taught him that economic unfreedom, in the form of extreme poverty, makes a person a helpless prey in the violation of other freedoms.

Sen initially intended to study physics, but in the end he opted for economics, as he felt that it had greater societal relevance. At Calcutta's prestigious Presidency College he was introduced to Marshall's *Principles of Economics*, Samuelson's *Foundations of Economic Analysis*, and other economics classics. At the time, the College was a political hotbed. Sen remembers that the student community was politically very active, and political issues were hotly debated in tea stalls on nearby College Street. Though the egalitarian commitment of the 'left' appealed to him, he admitted not having enough enthusiasm to join any political party. Nonetheless, for a while Amartya had a leading role in the Student Federation, a broad alliance of leftist students, with close links with the communist party. He sensed, however, that there was something disturbing about standard left-wing politics, in particular its scepticism about democratic procedures that permitted liberty-respecting pluralism. Sen recalls in his Nobel Prize speech that: 'As I look back at the fields of academic work in which I have felt most involved throughout my life .... they were already among the concerns that were agitating me most in my undergraduate days in Calcutta.'[6]

Just before he turned nineteen, Amartya had to undergo serious medical treatment. It turned out that he was suffering from stage two squamous cell carcinoma. He underwent a truly unpleasant radiation therapy, which was very new and dangerous at the time. His convalescence lasted six months. Having had cancer made him feel polluted, powerless and outcast. But on the other hand, conquering cancer made him also stronger. He resumed his studies with renewed energy, resulting in a First, and winning all sorts of prizes. In 1953, he successfully applied to Trinity College, Cambridge, where Jawaharlal Nehru also had studied.

Amartya had to find lodgings in Cambridge. He rented a room in the house of his landlady Mrs. Hanger. This is what he wrote about her: 'Mrs Hanger ...was enormously kind and interested in the world. However, she confessed, she was very worried about having me in the house since she had never met a non-white person before.... It turned out that Mrs.

[6] Ibid.

Hanger's fear of coloured people had some rational basis in her understanding of science. On my first day, after welcoming me warmly, she popped the question. 'Will your colour come off in the bath—I mean in a really hot bath?....... during the year of my stay she had transformed herself into a crusader for racial equality... by the time I left she was lecturing everyone in the neighbourhood on the need to understand that 'all people are equal".[7]

In Cambridge, he encountered strong disagreements between Keynes's disciples and their critics, and he fell under the spell of the brilliant but vigorously intolerant Joan Robinson, who supervised his thesis *The Choice of Technology*, which was critical of India's government planning.

> Initially, Sen wanted to work on welfare economics, inspired by Arrow's *Social Choice and Individual Values*, which he had already read at Presidency College. When he told Robinson about his intention, she said: 'Don't you know that this is a busted subject? She told me the story that clever economists were trying to do welfare economics, but that cleverest of them all, Jan Graaff, showed that all this is nonsense.' I told Joan she might be mistaken in her interpretation of Graaff's work; first, Graaff didn't in fact show that welfare economics was nonsense; second, he himself never claimed that he had. Joan was not only unpersuaded, she had no interest in listening to my thoughts on the subject. She told me that I had better work on something more useful.'[8]

Meanwhile, Sen was anxious to learn what exciting developments were taking place in India. He applied for a two-year leave from Cambridge to work on his doctoral thesis. This was granted, and off he went. Soon after his return to India, at the age of 23, Sen was invited to establish a new

[7] *Home in the World*, 257, 282.

[8] Ibid., 292. Economics laureate Edmund Phelps neither had a pleasant encounter with Robinson: 'Professor Robinson was a formidable presence, and it was with some trepidation that I went to see her over tea one afternoon. Wasting no time on pleasantries, she launched into an exposition of her recent thought. I didn't understand her and asked a question, but I didn't understand her answer either. I tried again, but she gave up. 'You could understand', she said, 'if you wanted to.' Source: Phelps, E. (2023) *My Journeys in Economic Theory*. New York: Columbia University Press, 48.

department of economics at Jadavpur University. In 1963, he joined the newly formed Delhi School of Economics (DSE), which turned out to be a most challenging period of his academic life, and a golden period in the history of DSE. By the time Sen left Delhi in 1971 to join the London School of Economics (LSE), he and his colleagues had succeeded in making DSE India's pre-eminent centre of education in economics.

Around the early 1970s, Sen started to take an interest in academic fields beyond economics, in particular philosophy. He explained his choice as follows: 'The broadening of my studies into philosophy was important for me not just because some of my main areas of interest in economics relate quite closely to philosophical disciplines (for example social choice theory makes intense use of mathematical logic and also draws on moral philosophy, and so does the study of inequality and deprivation), but also because I found philosophical studies very rewarding on their own.'[9] This was possible thanks to the lucky fact that he won a Prize Fellowship at Trinity College. In casting his intellectual net wider, he made the acquaintance with philosophers such as Arrow, Rawls, and Nozick. Later in life he lectured together with them. In a plane journey to San Francisco, Sen was asked by the person sitting next to him whether, as a teacher at Harvard, he had heard of an 'apparently interesting' course taught by 'Kenneth Arrow, John Rawls, and some unknown guy.'[10]

After his return to England in 1971, Sen's life did not continue smoothly. His marriage to Nabaneeta Dev ended in divorce. In addition, he had to undergo treatment for bone necrosis resulting from his radiation treatment in Calcutta. After having undergone an operation of nearly seven hours, and a subsequent convalescence period, Sen was cured.

In 1978, he married Eva Colorni, an Italian economist. Sen started a particularly productive period in his professional life in which he contributed to the theory of social choice and the theory of justice. He also analysed the phenomenon of famines and developed his capability approach. All of these subjects added to his academic prestige.

She also supported him in broadening the framework of social choice theory in a variety of applied problems: To assess poverty; to evaluate inequality; to clarify the nature of relative deprivation; to develop distribution-adjusted national income measures; to clarify the penalty of

[9] *Les Prix Nobel. The Nobel Prizes 1998.*
[10] Source: *Les Prix Nobel. The Nobel Prizes 1998.*

unemployment; to analyse violations of personal liberties and basic rights; and to characterize gender disparities and women's relative disadvantage. This is quite a handful of important, mainly developmental, themes. Nonetheless, the results of Sen's analyses were put together in two collections of articles: *Choice, Welfare and Measurement* and *Resources, Values and Development*.[11]

Harvard and Trinity

After Eva Colorni died in 1985, Sen returned to America and settled in Cambridge,[12] to join Harvard as the Thomas W. Lamont University Professor of Economics. At Harvard, Sen further developed his capabilities approach. Capabilities, elaborated below, depend not just on physical but also on mental characteristics as well as on social opportunities and influences. As such, they can serve as the basis of an assessment of personal advantage but also of governments' efficiency and equity of social policies. In *Commodities and Capabilities*,[13] Sen applied his theory to empirical exercises.

In 1998, after having accepted the position of Master of the College, Sen returned to Trinity College, Cambridge. He confessed that his return to Cambridge was also inspired by the fact that his wife Emma Rothschild (whom he had married in 1991) was a Fellow of next-door's King's College, where she was the Director of the Centre for History and Economics. To briefly complete Sen's academic life, in 2004, he returned to Harvard. From 2012 to 2015 Sen was the first chancellor of India's newly established Nalanda University.

Apart from the Nobel Prize, Sen can be proud of the characterization given of him by another Nobel laureate and fellow-economist, Robert Solow: Sen is the conscience of our profession![14]

[11] Sen, A. (1982) *Choice, Welfare and Measurement*. Oxford: Basil Blackwell.

Sen, A. (1984) *Resources, Values and Development*. Cambridge: Harvard University Press.

[12] During the early 1960s, Sen briefly taught at the Massachusetts Institute of Technology.

[13] Sen, A. (1983) *Commodities and Capabilities*. Hennipman Lecture. Amsterdam: North Holland.

[14] Another characterization of Sen as 'the Mother Teresa of economics', was not much appreciated by him as he admitted never having tried to follow a lifestyle of dedicated self-sacrifice.

Social Choice Theory

While at LSE, Sen worked on social choice theory triggered by Arrow's *Social Choice and Individual Values*.[15] The book contained the so-called Impossibility Theorem.[16] This theorem says that, except when there was complete consensus, all voting procedures yielded outcomes that were, one way or the other, undemocratic. Sen, being an Indian citizen, and his young country being the world's largest democracy, feared that Arrow's theorem would be a rationale for dictatorship.

After having taken an in-depth look at the theorem, Sen argued that one of Arrow's axioms—which ruled out comparisons between different citizens' well-being—was not essential, further elaborated in the second part of this chapter. If such comparisons were indeed allowed, Sen concluded, with a sigh of relief, that the impossibility result no longer held.

Sen accompanied many PhD theses at LSE and, from 1977 to 1988, at the University of Oxford. They led to formal results and informal understandings emerging from these theses. As a result, the gloom of 'impossibility results' ceased to be the exclusive prominent theme in the field. In his Nobel Prize speech, Sen said that the 1970s were probably the golden years of social choice theory across the world. In 1998, Sen received the Nobel Prize in Economics for his contributions to welfare economics.

Theory of Justice

After having worked on social choice, Sen analysed utilitarianism, inspired by John Rawls's *A Theory of Justice*,[17] which was widely seen as a philosophical justification for the modern welfare state. Utilitarians maintain (together with many economists, by the way) that society needs only to take care of the welfare of its citizens. In utilitarian thinking, rights only play an indirect role in contributing to happiness. One of Rawls's central themes is his 'difference principle', which states that a just society should maximize the welfare of the worst-off group, echoing a utilitarian

[15] Arrow, K. (1951) *Social Choice and Individual Values*. New York: John Wiley and Sons.

[16] Development economist and Harvard professor Dani Rodrik developed a different Impossibility Theorem for the global economy. His theorem says that democracy, national sovereignty, and global economic integration are mutually incompatible. 'We can have at most two out of three.' Source: Rodrik, D. (2011) *The Globalization Paradox; Democracy and the Future of the World Economy*. New York: W.W. Norton, 200.

[17] Rawls, J. (1971) *A Theory of Justice*. Cambridge: Harvard University Press.

principle. Rawls argued that socio-economic institutions had to be arranged in such a way as to benefit the worst off in society relative to a situation of greater equality.

Rawls's primary focus was on individual rights, which takes precedence over material well-being, which many scholars ignored, but not Sen. In his *Journal of Political Economy* article: The Impossibility of the Paretian Liberal, Sen made the case for paying attention to rights and welfare, emphasizing the potential conflict between the two.[18] When people define their own welfare in terms of *restricting* the freedom of others (e.g., Muslim clerics are happier if schooling is prohibited for girls), free choice conflicts with Pareto optimality. After all, Pareto argued that in the optimal state, no one can be made better-off without someone else made worse off. However, Pareto optimality does not address *distributional* considerations regarding utility. In *On Ethics and Economics*, Sen observes: 'A state can be Pareto optimal with some people in extreme misery and others rolling in luxury, so long as the miserable cannot be made better off without cutting into the luxury of the rich.'[19] In 2009, Sen published *The Idea of Justice*, which contains not just a criticism of Rawls's theory of justice, but also his own theory.

Poverty, Famines, and Development

In 1981, Sen published *Poverty and Famines.*[20] In this book, he presents famines as economic problems, i.e., concentrating on how poor people can buy food, thanks to e.g., food-for-work programs, or otherwise get entitled to it, rather than in terms of the undifferentiated picture of aggregate food supply for the economy as a whole. Sen's point is that famines don't occur from a lack of food, but from inequalities. He draws an interesting comparison with Britain's limited food supplies during WWII:

> Surprisingly, in the difficult years of food shortage during the Second Word War there was actually a sharp reduction in the incidence of undernourishment in Britain. Faced with the prospect of a diminution in total food sup-

[18] Sen, A. The Impossibility of the Paretian Liberal. *Journal of Political Economy*, 78 (1970): 152–157.

[19] Sen, A. (1987) *On Ethics and Economics.* Oxford: Basil Blackwell, 32.

[20] Sen, A. (1981) *Poverty and Famines: An Essay on Entitlement and Deprivation.* Oxford: Clarendon Press.

plies in the 1940s (partly because of transport difficulties and dangers during the war), the government put in place a system for more equal sharing out of what was available—through rationing and price control. The result was that suddenly the chronically undernourished could afford to buy enough food for their needs—more than they had ever been able to before.[21]

In *The Idea of Justice*, Sen reminds us that no major famine has ever occurred in a functioning democracy with regular elections, opposition parties, basic freedom of speech and a relatively free media, even when a country is poor and in a seriously adverse food situation. This understanding has now become widely accepted, even though, initially, there was much scepticism about it.[22]

Capability

Development economists gradually understood that, in the utilitarian tradition, Gross Domestic Product (GDP) growth, does not necessarily benefit everybody in an equal manner, nor does it contribute to an equal distribution of well-being among citizens. Utility is equally misleading, argues Sen, because deprived individuals typically tailor their aspirations to their impoverished circumstances. Hence, economic growth alone is an inadequate measure of welfare, precisely because it does not reveal how well (or badly, for that matter) deprived individuals are doing. Sen argues that GDP leaves out individuals' opportunities—they may be even more important than income. To get around these difficulties, Sen proposed a new way of thinking about the goals of development: the *capability* approach.[23]

[21] *Home in the World*, 389.

[22] Sen, A. (2009) *The Idea of Justice*. London: Allen Lane, 342.

[23] Stiglitz presents a comparable way of looking at capability. 'But there is an important positive sense of freedom that I have already noted: freedom to live up to one's potential. People who are living on the edge have, in some sense, no freedom. They do what they must to survive. But to give them the resources they need to live decent lives, let alone to live up to their potential, requires taxing the whole community.' Source: Stiglitz, J. (2024) *The Road to Freedom*. London: Allen Lane, 3.

'While these were intensely practical matters, I also got more and more involved in trying to understand the nature of individual advantage in terms of the substantive freedoms that different persons respectively enjoy, in the form of the capability to achieve valuable things. If my work in social choice theory was initially motivated by a desire to overcome Arrow's pessimistic picture by going beyond his limited informational base, my work on social justice based on individual freedoms and capabilities was similarly motivated by an inspiration to learn from, but go beyond, John Rawls's elegant theory of justice, through a broader use of available information. My intellectual life has been much influenced by the contributions as well as the wonderful helpfulness of both Arrow and Rawls.'[24]

True, income is important because of the opportunities it creates. However, actual opportunities also depend on other factors such as a person's life span, health, and literacy. Sen underscores that these factors should definitely be considered when measuring welfare.

In 1999, Sen elaborated and expanded the capability approach in his book *Development as Freedom*,[25] in which he presents five specific types of freedoms: political freedoms, economic facilities, social opportunities, transparency guarantees, and protective security. Sen argues that not opulence per se, but the increase in real freedoms is the true measure of a good society. He adds that the increase in *real* freedoms should be both ends and the means of development. In this context, Sen discusses the correlation between social opportunities of education and health and how both complement economic and political freedoms. After all, a healthy and well-educated person is better suited to make informed economic decisions and better equipped to take part in political discussions.

Sen argues that individuals' capabilities constitute the principal dimension in which societies should strive for greater equality. Together with his old friend Mabub ul Haq (1934–1998), he designed the Human

[24] *Les Prix Nobel. The Nobel Prizes 1998.*

[25] Sen, A. (1999) *Development as Freedom*. Oxford: Oxford University Press.

Development Index (HDI).[26] The United Nations Development Programme applies this HDI instrument in their annual World Development Reports.[27]

India

Finally, what about India? Together with Jean Drèze, Sen published *India: Development and Participation*.[28] The conclusion was that the ambitious goals included in Nehru's speech on the occasion of India's independence from Great Britain in 1947, remained largely unaccomplished. Surely, much had changed for the better in the Third World: Life expectancy had expanded and real per capita income had more than tripled. Yet, Sen and Drèze conclude that the 1 billion citizens of the world's biggest democracy were still among the world's most deprived. At the time of the book's publication in 2002, India's economic and social performance paled in comparison with China's. So, the challenge was to nudge India's economy along China's stunning economic performance, without sacrificing India's democracy.

In a 1999 article in *The Atlantic*, Sen recommends for India a middle path between the tough development policy that creates wealth at the expense of civil liberties, and radical progressivism that only seeks to protect civil liberties at the expense of development.

Sen only proposed to reform the current development model, rather than create a new theory of ethical development. He argues that local conditions are decisive for economic development. Ultimately nations themselves control their destiny. He was in favour of deregulation and the opening of India's economy to foreign trade and investment. But, not surprisingly, he underscores the importance of government intervention on behalf of the poor, especially in health, education, and nutrition.

[26] The Human Development Index (HDI) is a summary measure of average achievement in key dimensions of human development: A long and healthy life, being knowledgeable, and having a decent standard of living.

[27] Sen got to know Mabub ul Haq during their undergraduate student days at Cambridge. They complained about mainstream economics taking so little interest in the lives of human beings. Source: *Home in the World*, 265.

[28] Sen, A., and Drèze, J. (2002) *India: Development and Participation*. Oxford: Oxford University Press.

Sen's re-appraisal of India's performance since the publication of Drèze and Sen's book would have been interesting, because India has, since 2002, undergone massive changes in political, economic and social aspects. Unfortunately, in his 2021 memoir, Sen does not comment on India's breathtaking economic developments or on Prime Minister Narendra Modi's slightly weakening grip on India's society.

Part II Sen's Contributions to the Philosophy of Economics

Introduction

Sen's contributions to philosophy, often together with his critical analysis, range from liberal themes, such as welfare economics, social choice theory, to economic and social justice. He developed and added ethical notions to his theory of famines, the capability approach and measurement of countries' well-being. He was inspired by many philosophers ranging from Hobbes, Hume, Smith, Locke, Condorcet, Rousseau, Kant, Mill, and Marx, to Gautama Buddha and emperor Ashoka. He also found inspiration in ancient Sanskrit stories.

Sen re-introduced the notion of ethics and moral issues into economics. He once observed that moral acceptance of rights—especially rights that are valued and supported, and not just respected in the form of constraints—call for systematic departures from self-interested behaviour. Even a partial and limited move into the direction of actual conduct, Sen argues, would shake the behavioural foundations of standard economic theory.

In her wonderful biographical story about Sen, Sylvia Nasar presents three questions on which Sen proposed answers: Can society make choices in a way that reflects individual citizens' preferences? Can individual rights be reconciled with economic welfare? And, question number three, what is the measure of a just society? Although not all of Sen's contributions can be dealt with, his answers to some of these questions are presented below. His analysis of Rawls's Theory of Justice is one of them. Sen's capability approach, is subsequently dealt with. Finally, Sen's analysis of Arrow's Impossibility Theorem concludes Part II.

Rawls's Theory of Justice

Markets often produce a high degree of inequality. This triggers various philosophical questions: is inequality necessarily unfair, or should we strive after more efficiency at the cost of allowing some people to be treated unfairly? And, not least important, to what extent can government measures be justified to correct market outcomes through redistribution? These questions are not just philosophical and political in nature, they also involve methodological issues which economists found hard to deal with.

A Theory of Justice is considered to be the most important book in political philosophy of the past century. The literature on Rawls is exceptionally large. Rawls does not analyse justice as such; his vantage point is *justice as fairness*, which has implications concerning principles of distributive justice. Julian Reiss summarizes Rawls's principles:

(i) Each person has an equal right to the most extensive scheme of equal basic liberties compatible with a similar scheme of liberties for all.
(ii) Social and economic inequalities are to satisfy two conditions: they must be (a) to the greatest benefit of the least advantaged members of society; and (b) attached to offices and positions open to all under conditions of fair equality of opportunity.[29]

The first principle concerns the political institutions of a society, and the second principle society's socio-economic institutions. Rawls puts the first principle above the second. This implies that deviations from the most extensive possible scheme of basic liberties[30] cannot be justified or

[29] Reiss, J. (2013) *Philosophy of Economics; A Contemporary Introduction*. London: Routledge, 264–265.

[30] As regards liberty, it may be that the liberty of some individuals may conflict with that of others. The extensiveness of liberties that can be granted is limited by the requirement to grant the same liberties to everyone. In other words, one will demand only such liberties everybody can enjoy, such as the liberty of conscience and freedom of association, the freedom of speech and the rights to vote, to hold public office, and to be treated in accordance with the rule of law.

compensated for by greater socio-economic opportunities. The principles of justice determine the basic social institutions that should govern the society they are about to create.

The first principle is called the 'Priority of Liberty' principle. Rawls requires equality of the value of political liberties. This means that citizens should have the *same* opportunities not just to hold office, but also to influence elections, regardless of their income and social position in society. Before dealing with the second principle, other crucial aspects of Rawls's theory are presented, including Sen's observations on some of them.

Social Contract

Rawls's theory goes back to social contract theories, as originally developed, by Hobbes, and further elaborated by Locke and Rousseau, elaborated in the Annexe. The state, in Hobbes's view, can help overcome the downside of 'the state of nature', in which the life of citizens, in his oft-quoted words, can be 'solitary, poor, nasty, brutish and short'. Rawls, however, adds a dimension to this notion, borrowed from Immanuel Kant (1724–1804)—Reason: 'I shall regard Locke's *Second Treatise of Government*, Rousseau's *The Social Contract* and Kant's ethical works beginning with *The Foundation of Metaphysics of Morals* as definitive works of contract tradition.'[31] He adds that: 'My aim is to present a conception of justice which generalizes and carries to a higher level of abstraction the familiar theory of the social contract as found, say, in Locke, Rousseau, and Kant.'[32]

Rawls argued that people have the capacity for reasoning from an impartial standpoint. Rawls replaces the original state of nature with a

[31] Rawls, J. (1971) *A Theory of Justice*. Oxford: Oxford University Press, 11.
[32] Ibid., 11.

thought experiment, what he called, the 'original position'.[33] This is central to his theory of justice. In this vein Rawls argued: 'The merit of the contract terminology is that it conveys the idea that principles of justice may be conceived as principles that would be chosen by rational persons, and that in this way conceptions of justice may be explained and justified.'[34] Sen observes that the use by Rawls of the social contract limits the involvement of participants in the pursuit of justice to the members of a given polity, broadly similar to that of a nation-state in the standard political theory.[35]

In this original position, people are placed behind a 'veil of ignorance'. This term begs an explanation. Rawls introduced this term to let us forget everything about ourselves that is irrelevant from the point of view of justice. In other words, we don't know our race and class, gender and possessions, our natural talents, and willingness to work. What we also do not know is our conception of the good. For example, we do not know whether we are religious or whether we value freedom higher than equality. In short, we do not seem to know much about anything.[36] But we *do* know, Rawls added, a lot about general psychological tendencies, about human behaviour, how markets work, and about biological evolution and the capacity of humans to develop ideas of justice and rationality. About these latter aspects Rawls observed: 'Once the powers of understanding mature, and persons come to recognize their place in society and are able to take up the standpoint of others, they appreciate the mutual benefits of establishing fair terms of social cooperation.'[37]

[33] 'Rawls's method of investigation invokes 'contractarian' reasoning, involving the question: what 'social contract' would be accepted by everyone unanimously in the original position? The contractarian method of reasoning is broadly in the Kantian tradition.' Source: *The Idea of Justice,* 69. Nozick had this to say on the original position: 'Rawls's contribution may lie in the construction of a thought experiment that shows how a particular set of assumptions leads to a particular conclusion.' Source: Meadowcroft, J. (2011) Nozick's critique of Rawls: Distribution, Entitlement, and the Assumptive World of A Theory of Justice. In: *Cambridge Collection on Line.* Cambridge University Press, 170–171.

[34] *A Theory of Justice*, 16.

[35] *The Idea of Justice*, 71.

[36] Snyder observes this about the veil of ignorance: 'It asks you to bracket what you know about your place in society behind this 'veil', so as to look at the world more objectively and make better policy.' Source: Snyder, T. (2024) *On Freedom.* London: The Bodley Head, 240.

[37] *A Theory of Justice*, 459–460.

When resources are scarce, there is a point in competing for them. Only when we are not fully altruistic, would we compete for them. Under these competitive circumstances some security and a more stable society can be gained from cooperation. It is important in Rawls's view, unlike Hobbes's for example, that resources should not be too scarce because in situations of serious scarcity, or during wars or famines, proposals for acting justly do not stand a chance. So, the circumstances of justice are such that cooperation is possible.

One may not have a specific conception of 'the good', but Rawls assumes that we all share some desires, what Rawls calls 'comprehensive preferences'. Regarding desires, Rawls introduced the term 'primary goods': All-purpose means necessary to exercise morality and to a variety of conceptions of the good. They include rights and liberties, powers and opportunities, income and wealth and the social basis of self-respect. Rawls assumes that in the original position we do not have other preferences, i.e., people are mutually disinterested. Sen observes that the primary goods approach seems to take little note of the diversity of human beings.[38]

Rawls's Second Principle

Returning to his second principle, the first part of it, i.e., the greatest benefit of the least advantaged members of society, this is the 'Difference Principle', meaning that the socio-economic institutions must be arranged in such a way as to benefit the worst off in society relative to a situation of greater equality. 'Social and economic inequalities....are just only if they result in compensating benefits for everyone, and in particular for the least advantaged members of society.'[39] In other words, social and economic institutions would be designed to advance the interests of the worst-off group, to the extent that an increase in inequality is only justified if this improves the material position of the poor.[40] This principle aims to trade off equality and efficiency considerations.

[38] Sen, A. *Equality of What? The Tanner Lecture on Human Values*. Stanford University, 22 May, 1979, 215.

[39] *A Theory of Justice*, 15.

[40] 'Rawls' ideal society would, however, rely only minimally on redistributive taxes and transfers as an equalizing measure. On grounds of efficiency, liberty, and opportunity, Rawls emphasized efforts to equalize the *starting points* of members of successive generations in preference to redistributing unequal outcomes.' Source: Hausman, D., McPherson, M. (1996) *Economic Analysis and Moral Philosophy*. Cambridge: Cambridge University Press, 157. Freeden has this to say about liberal egalitarianism: '....liberal egalitarianism usually falls short of the radical equalization of socialist schemes. It rests content with ensuring minima for a human life, and with reducing the gap between the fortunate and the disadvantaged through a mix of public and private redistributive measures—the state, employers' codes of

Table 7.1 Four economic systems

Society	*Least advantaged*	*Middle class*	*The rich*	*Gross product*
Egalitarianism (North Korea)	2000	2000	2000	6000
Social market economy (Germany)	15,000	20,000	65,000	100,000
Market economy, Scandinavian model	20,000	35,000	45,000	100,000
Hong Kong capitalism	5000	30,000	115,000	150,000

Source: *Philosophy of Economics*, p. 265

An example, borrowed from Reiss, may clarify what Rawls meant. Let us compare four economic systems, ranging from one extreme egalitarian economy (i.e., North Korea), a social market economy (Germany), a Scandinavian market economy, and the other extreme: pure capitalism (Hong Kong). Provided that these are the only possible institutional arrangements, and interpreting the numbers as representing the value of primary goods, applying the difference principle results in the unique choice for a Scandinavian market economy system. True, inequality exists in Scandinavia, but compared with other arrangements, the least disadvantaged benefit the most there. In sum, between Germany and Scandinavia, two societies with comparable mid-range products, the more equal arrangement, Scandinavia, is preferred (Table 7.1).[41]

The second part of the second principle, i.e., fair equality of opportunity, requires that citizens with the same talents and willingness to put an effort have the same cultural, political and economic opportunities, independently of whether they were born rich or poor.

Fair equality of opportunity has priority over the difference principle. What does this mean? Those inequalities that benefit the least advantaged in society are admissible only to the extent that everyone has the same degree of access to socio-economic goods. A key point of Rawls's is that citizens will not agree to have equality. Justice requires, adds Phelps in *My Journeys in Economic Theory* on p. 77, that the differences between the rewards of the more advantaged and the least advantaged are to be allowed up to the point at which any *larger* differences, or disparities, would *reduce* the reward of the least rewarded (i.e., the lowest earners).[42] This

conduct, and voluntary associations such as charities But it is prepared to permit discrepancies in wealth that will nonetheless influence life-chances.' Freeden, M. (2015) *Liberalism; A Very Short Introduction*, 98.

[41] *Philosophy of Economics*, 265–266.

[42] Phelps, E. (2023) *My Journeys in Economic Theory*. Columbia University Press, 77.

distributive policy came to be called 'maxi-min', since the lowest reward was to be lifted up to the maximum possible level.[43]

> 'The choice of basic principles of justice is the first act in Rawls's multi-staged unfolding of social justice. The first stage leads to the next, 'constitutional', stage in which actual institutions are selected in line with the chosen principle of justice, taking note of the conditions of each particular society. The working of these institutions, in turn, leads to further social decisions at later stages in the Rawlsian system, for example through appropriate legislation.... The imagined sequence moves forward step by step on firmly specified lines, with an elaborately characterized unfolding of completely just social arrangements. The whole process of this unfolding is based on the emergence of what he describes as the 'the two principles of justice' in the first stage that influence everything else that happens in the Rawlsian sequence.'[44]

Some Observations

Sen underscores that *A theory of Justice* transformed contemporary liberal political philosophy in a radical way. Nonetheless, he observes that the main planks of Rawls's theory were seriously defective, elaborated below.[45] Indeed, Rawls's theory also triggered criticisms from others as well, exposing its limitations. Some terms used by Rawls encounter difficulties when it comes to defining or clarifying them. Take fairness: Can the question what is fair? be addressed by asking what would be fair in ideal conditions X? For social scientists this is a difficult and unattractive question to

[43] Phelps adds: '.... Rawlsian justice does *not* eliminate inequality, however defined; it may decrease it—depending on conditions—or it may increase it. What is crucial is it increases to the maximum the rewards of the workers who are the least advantaged.' Ibid., 78. On page 79, Phelps writes that he urged Rawls to explain again that his theory of justice is about rewarding the work of the least advantaged, not the poor in general.

[44] *The Idea of Justice*, 56.

[45] During the early 1960s, Sen and Garry Runciman already wrote an article which appeared in 1965 in *Mind* in which they argued against Rawls's assumption (who was developing his theory of justice at the time) that in a state of impartial choice only one particular choice would emerge as being favoured by all. Source: *Home in the World*, 319.

speculate about, because the remoteness of these speculations from everyday experiences makes the results of such speculations unreliable.[46]

Reiss mentions the following difficulties regarding Rawls's principles of justice:

- 'The principles are established using a method that doesn't have the best credentials and whose results aren't regarded as binding by everyone.
- Rawls' 'veil of ignorance' makes peculiar assumptions about what people know and do not know that do not seem compelling and that, arguably, are designed just as to yield Rawls' principles as a result.[47]
- The principles will not be convincing to those who come from radically different starting points, such as proponents of desert-based theories of justice or libertarians.'[48]

What More Sen Had to Say

We already saw that, young Amartya was confronted with dire poverty in West Bengal and East Pakistan (now Bangladesh). So it is understandable that he analysed Rawls's principles with poverty and destitution in mind. Indeed, Sen's vantage point differs from that of Rawls. The latter's theory was widely seen as a philosophical justification for a modern welfare state.[49] Sen then wonders—while broadly in agreement with the Rawlsian reasoning underlying the first principle—why any violation of liberty must invariably be judged to be more crucial for a person—or for a society—than suffering from intense hunger, starvation, epidemics and other calamities?[50] Sen thus disputes the priority given by Rawls of rights and liberties above all else: 'Why should the status of intense economic needs, which can be of life and death, be lower than that of political liberties?'[51] Sen concludes that Rawls's theory cannot have universal validity as his assumed society is not quite the same as the Indian society, or any other society plagued by poverty and destitution.

[46] *Philosophy of Economics*, 268.

[47] This is what Freeden observed in this vein: 'For a Rawlsian philosophical liberal, there is an inevitability about human rationality that is morally compelling: being irrational is not an ethical option.' Source: *Liberalism*, 100.

[48] *Philosophy of Economics*, 269.

[49] Rawls was aware of the limitations of his theory, as he restricts its application to societies where economic issues are not matters of life and death.

[50] *The Idea of Justice*, 300.

[51] Sen, A. (1999) *Development as Freedom*. Oxford: Oxford University Press, 64.

Thomas Piketty has the following observations to make about Rawls's difference principle and Sen's capability approach: '...the capabilities approach favored by the Indian economist Amartya Sen is not very different in its basic logic. At a purely theoretical level, there is in fact a certain (partly artificial) consensus concerning the abstract principles of social justice. The disagreements become clearer when one tries to give a little substance to these social rights and inequalities and to anchor them in specific historical and economic contexts. In practice, the conflicts have to do mainly with the means of effecting real improvement in the living conditions of the least advantaged, the precise extent of the rights that can be granted to all ....and exactly what factors are within and beyond the control of individuals.[52]

Aside from this general observation, Sen has more to say. Rawls identified some specific principles of justice that would determine the choice of just institutions for the basic structure of a society. In the *four economic systems* box above, the unique choice of principles is presented. Sen expresses his scepticism about this unique choice of one particular set of principles. He argues that there are genuinely plural, and sometimes conflicting, general concerns that bear on our understanding of justice, including Rawls's priority of liberty.

Rawls's 'veil of ignorance' leaves out the perspectives and reasonings by anyone whose assessments are relevant because, for example, their way of thinking about issues throw a different light on particular judgements. Sen then introduces Adam Smith's 'impartial spectator'. This spectator would 'broaden the discussion to avoid local parochialism of values, which might have the effect of ignoring some pertinent arguments, unfamiliar in a particular culture.'[53] Inspired by Smith, Sen then proposes a different approach, casting the net wider. He argues that there are genuinely plural, and sometimes conflicting, general concerns that bear on the understanding of justice. Plurality of unbiased principles can reflect the fact that impartiality can take different forms.[54]

[52] Piketty, T (2014) *Capital in the Twenty-First Century*. Cambridge: The Belknap Press of Harvard University Press, 480.

[53] *The Idea of Justice*, 45.

[54] Ibid., 56–57.

> Sen gives a well-known example in which one has to decide which of three children—Anne, Bob and Carla—should get a flute about which they are quarrelling. Anne claims the flute on the ground that she is the only one of the three who knows how to play it, and that it would be quite unjust to give the flute to either Bob or Carla. However, Bob defends his case for having the flute by pointing out that he is the only one among them who is so poor that he has no toys whatsoever; the flute would give him the toy. But now Carla points out that she has been working diligently for many months to make the flute with her own hands and just when she finished her work, Bob and Anne came along intending to grab the flute from her.
>
> Having heard all three and their different reasoning, there is a difficult decision one has to make. Theorists of different persuasions, such as utilitarians, economic egalitarians, or no-nonsense libertarians, may each take the view that there is a straightforward just resolution. Bob would get the support from the economic egalitarian, while Carla would receive sympathy from the libertarian. The utilitarian hedonist may face the hardest challenge, but he or she would tend to give weight to the fact that Anne's pleasure is likely more stronger. The point is that it is not easy to make a decision. The different resolutions all have serious arguments in support of them, and one may not be able to identify any of the alternative arguments as being the one that must invariably prevail.[55]

Sen concludes, rather bluntly, that if there is no unique emergence of a given set of principles of justice that together identify the institutions needed for the basic structure of the society, then the entire procedure of 'justice as fairness', as in Rawls's theory, would be hard to use.[56] He reminds us that Rawls's original basic claim of the emergence of a unique set of principles of justice was a bit softened in his later writings.[57] Sen

[55] Ibid., 12–15.

[56] Ibid., 57.

[57] 'Indeed in his *Justice as Fairness, A Restatement,* Rawls notes that 'there are indefinitely many considerations that may be appealed to in the original position and each alterative conception of justice is favored by some consideration and disfavored by others', and also that 'the balance of reasons itself rests on judgment, though judgment informed and guided by reasoning'. When Rawls goes on to concede that 'the ideal cannot be fully attained', his reference is to his ideal theory of justice as fairness.' Source: *The Idea of Justice*, 58.

concludes, however, that if Rawls's second thoughts are really saying what they seem to be saying, then his earlier stage-by-stage theory of justice as fairness would have to be abandoned.

Sen's conclusion must have been a difficult pill for Rawls to swallow. Nonetheless, Sen concludes that Rawls's original theory was important in clarifying various aspects of the idea of justice, and that a great deal of the enlightenment from Rawls's pioneering contribution would remain, and continue, to enrich political philosophy.[58]

Sen's Capability Approach

Contrary to Rawls who assumes a society where economic issues are not matters of life and death, Sen must have had India in mind when conceiving his capability approach. In his own words, the capability approach is a general approach, focusing on information on individual advantages, judged in terms of opportunity rather than a specific 'design' for how a society should be organized.[59] In doing so, Sen proposes a new way of thinking about the goals of development. The capability perspective underscores the central relevance of the inequality of capabilities in the assessment of social disparities. Sen provides a telling example in this vein: 'The deprivation of girls is more readily—and more reliably—assessed by looking at capability deprivation reflected, for example, in greater mortality, morbidity, under-nourishment or medical neglect, than can be found on the basis of comparing incomes of different families.'[60]

As I already pointed out, Rawls puts liberty above all other considerations, giving precedence to maximal liberty over economic and social equity. But liberty functions alongside other concerns in determining a person's overall well-being. Sen argues that Rawls, by focusing on primary goods, gives *indirect* acknowledgment of the importance of human freedom in giving people a real opportunity to do what they would like with their own lives. The fit between a person's holding of primary goods and the freedoms that the person enjoys, can be very imperfect as a result of this person's poverty, deprivation, poor health, what have you. This tension can be addressed, proposes Sen, through focusing on the *actual*

[58] Ibid, 58.
[59] Ibid., 232.
[60] Ibid., 257.

capabilities of people. Moving from focusing on Rawls's primary goods to Sen's capability approach would bring the theory down to the actual patterns of behaviour in any real society.

When addressing questions of justice and welfare, Sen wonders what kind of information one needs. Income per capita is certainly important, but there are other factors that reveal how prosperous, or deprived, people really are. After all, some people simply lack the opportunities to improve their situation, because of destitution, oppression, or even their personality. Along the way they may have come to terms with their unfortunate circumstances. What they then do is to survive by *adapting* to their situation, because not doing so would result in even more misery. In other words, these people tailor their aspirations to their impoverished circumstances.

Sen argues that income should be valued as a *resource* and, as we saw, different people have different abilities to convert this resource into well-being. Again, compare this with Rawls's primary goods. In Sen's thinking these primary goods are resources. Their usefulness to an individual would depend on his or her characteristics and on a conducive, or not so conducive, environment. Rawls emphasis on liberty is fine, but this may not be enough for some people to achieve the kind of life they would like to live; something crucial is missing. The capabilities approach captures this missing element. In sum, and this is Sen's crucial point, individuals' capabilities constitute the principal dimension in which societies should strive for greater equality.[61]

Functionings and Capabilities

Looking a bit closer at capabilities, Sen makes a distinction between functionings and capabilities. Functionings include people's doings and beings. People like to *do* things: read, move about, have fun with friends, voice their opinions. But people also want to *be* things: healthy, fed, clad, and respected. Capabilities on the other hand are alternative *combinations* of functionings that are feasible for a person to achieve.[62] An example: In the

[61] 'The capability approach has been enormously successful in drawing economists', philosophers' and political and other social scientists' attention to it in recent years but much work needs to be done before it can be accepted as a viable alternative to utilitarianism, libertarianism or Rawls's theory of justice.' *Philosophy of Economics*, 275.

[62] Ibid., 271.

United States citizens have a right to vote. In order for citizens to have a capacity to vote, they must have functionings. They can range from the availability of education, to the very specific, such as transportation to the polls. Only when such barriers are removed can the citizen truly be said to act out of personal choice.

Now, if one wishes to compare various levels of economic and social development, including poverty, one has to know what the relevant functionings would be. The problem, however, is that Sen is not very specific. By contrast, Martha Nussbaum provides a well-defined and intriguing list of core functionings, ranging from life, health, bodily integrity all the way to being able to live with and toward others and having control over one's material and political environment. Nussbaum is of the opinion that every human being should be entitled to these functionings. However, her list and opinion smack of patronizing. Reiss rightly wonders why anyone should accept her preferred long list of functionings.[63]

The Human Development Index

Together with Mabub ul Haq, Sen designed the Human Development Index (HDI), combining measures of life expectancy at birth, years of schooling and gross national income. The inspiration for HDI's development was that gross national income is not always a proper indication of people's well-being. Sen observes, for example, that in the US, inner city African Americans as a group frequently have no higher—often a substantially lower—chance of reaching an advanced age than do people born in many poor regions, such as Costa Rica, Jamaica, Sri Lanka or large parts of China and India.[64]

All told, the capabilities approach is not a complete theory of justice. But it greatly helps social researchers and development economists to think deeper about matters of inequality, well-being, and social justice and how to eventually capture them in measurable and evaluative terms.

The Impossibility Theorem

Sen argues that a theory of justice must have something to say about the *choices* that are actually on offer, and not just keep us engrossed in an imagined and implausible world of unbeatable magnificence. Regarding

[63] Ibid., 273.

[64] *The Idea of Justice*, 226.

choices, way back in 1951, Arrow created quite a stir among economists and, I add, political philosophers. What happened? In *Social Choice and Individual Values*, Arrow presented his Impossibility Theorem. He was concerned with the difficulties of group decisions and the inconsistencies to which they might lead.

Now, what is this Impossibility Theorem; how can it be described? This theorem seemed to be a logically rock-solid proof that no voting system could produce results that reflected the preferences of individuals. Sen presents a more precise description of the term: This theorem is an elegant and powerful mathematical presentation showing that even some mild conditions of reasonable sensitivity of social decisions to what members of a society want, cannot be simultaneously satisfied by any rational and democratic social choice procedure.[65] As a result, one is left with the *gloomy* prospect of having a dictatorial method of social judgement.

Arrow modernized social choice theory. He was the one to put the discipline of social choice, including axioms, in a structured and analytical form, demanding that social decisions satisfy certain minimal conditions of reasonableness, from which the appropriate social rankings and choices of social states would emerge. This led to the birth of the modern discipline of social choice theory. In short: 'In general, social choice theory as a discipline is concerned with arriving at overall judgements for social choice based on a diversity of perspectives and priorities.'[66]

For many, including Sen—who already red Arrow's groundbreaking book during his student days at Presidency College—the implications of Arrow's theorem were disquieting. After all, did this theorem not imply that India's young democracy was doomed and would be overtaken by authoritarian rule? Sen observes that '.... so far as Arrow's own axioms were concerned, Arrow dramatically deepened the pre-existing gloom by establishing an astonishing—and hugely pessimistic—result of apparently ubiquitous reach, which is now known as Arrow's impossibility theorem.'[67] Indeed, a sobering perspective.

Sen took a closer analytical look at Arrow's Impossibility Theorem, in particular its axioms. The 'impossibility' could be overcome, argues Sen, by applying some small but effective extensions, that could serve as the

[65] Ibid., 92–93.

[66] *The Idea of Justice*, 109.

[67] Ibid., 92. Arrow himself gave his theorem a less-gloomy name: General Possibility Theorem.

basis of a constructive social analysis as well.[68] He discovered that, while impossibilities can indeed arise with considerable frequency, they can also be largely resolved by making the social decision procedures more *informationally* sensitive. In fact, information on interpersonal comparisons of well-being and relative advantages turned out to be particularly crucial. Sen then concludes that democracy could be saved—authoritarian rule was by no means unavoidable.

Let me explain. Arrow took the viewpoint that *interpersonal* comparison of utilities had no meaning, since his theory required *collective* rationality. Now, by dropping this collective rationality, Sen proposes a way out. He arrives at the insight that denying any use of *interpersonal comparison* of utilities, as Arrow did, had a decisive role in precipitating the impossibility theorem. This sounds rather abstract; again, a little elaboration may help. In Arrow's framework, we cannot be guided by any equity considerations (no interpersonal comparisons!) that would require the identification of the rich viz-a-viz the poor. If being rich or being poor is defined in terms of income, then that is a non-utility characteristic of which one cannot take any direct note in Arrow's system, precisely because of the exclusive reliance on utilities. But nor can one identify a person's being rich or being poor with having a high or a low level of happiness, since that would involve interpersonal comparison of happiness or utilities which is also ruled out. In short, equity considerations lose their applicability in this framework.

> If three voters, 1,2 and 3 respectively rank in descending order three alternatives as [x, y, z], [y, z, x] and [z, x, y], then in a majority vote x would defeat y, while y defeats z, and z defeats x, so that there would not be a majority winner at all. Hence it would be impossible to find a cogent resolution to the problem through majority rule; majority voting fails to satisfy the collective rationality condition. In this case, making a democratic choice is impossible, if one were to insist on certain firm rules of consistency.

[68] Sen was not the only one seeking a way out of the impossibility. In his *On Ethics and Economics*, he refers to an impressive number of other scholars having done the same.

The extent of happiness as an indicator of a person's situation is applied to each individual *separately*, so without any comparison *between* levels of happiness of two different people. Hence, to assess inequality and to take note of the demands of equity, no use can be made of the happiness metric. These informational restrictions leaves one with a variant of *voting methods*, like majority decisions. The box above contains an example. As mentioned, in situations like these, making a democratic choice is impossible; a dictator determines the social rankings.

Now, broadening the informational basis of social choice is an important necessity for overcoming the negative implications of an information-starved decisional system. Sen emphasizes that interpersonal comparisons of the advantages and disadvantages of individuals have to be given a central role in these social judgements. If utility is the chosen indicator of individual advantage, then it is interpersonal comparison of utilities that become a crucial necessity for a viable system of social assessment.[69] Hence, using utility as the only criterion for the basis of social evaluation is too limited. A typical Sen observation is that one of the major limitations is the fact that the same collection of individual welfares may go with a very different overall social picture, with different societal arrangements, opportunities, freedoms, and personal liberties.

It is indeed difficult to accept that no importance is given to anything other than utility or happiness in the assessment of alternative states of policies.[70] And informational limitation is made even stronger by the particular utilitarian interpretation (i.e., in terms of happiness) of individual welfare. Sen demonstrates that this narrow view of individual well-being can be particularly restrictive when making interpersonal comparisons of deprivation. The framework used by Arrow, with some small but effective extensions as suggested by Sen, can be the basis of constructive social analysis. Nasar suggests: 'Sen's 'comparative metrics of well-being'

[69] *The Idea of Justice*, 280.

[70] 'If one believes, as many economists do, that preferences are reliable indicators of individual well-being and that the value of social policies depends exclusively on the extent to which they enhance individual well-being, then the social value of policies should depend on individual preferences. But we have argued that these beliefs are false. Preferences are often not reliable indicators of well-being, and the evaluation of social policies depends on many factors apart from their consequences for individual well-being.' Source: *Economic Analysis, Moral Philosophy, and Public Policy*. Cambridge: Cambridge University Press, 253.

launched his pursuit of yardsticks that could prod democratic governments to adopt social reforms, and launched a long-running debate over the best ways to define and measure poverty.'[71]

Conclusion

Sen is 'the conscience of economics', as Solow observed. Like Joan Robinson and Mariana Mazzucato (see next chapter), Sen demonstrates the inadequacy of the utility notion, not just in economics but also in philosophy. He brought ethics back to economics. I would argue that Sen could justly have accepted—although he rejected—the honourable title of 'Mother Teresa of Economics', as he consistently had the poor and deprived in mind when analysing economic and liberal political philosophical theories, such as Rawls's theory of justice, and Arrow's Impossibility Theorem. Together with Ul Haq, he developed the Human Development Index in which income is only one of various criteria in the measurement of development. The other HDI criteria were inspired by Sen's capability approach.

In sum, Sen consistently attempted to integrate economists' traditional concern for material well-being with liberal philosophers' concerns with individual rights and justice. And in this attempt he was quite successful. Sen is the philosopher who brought more discipline and reach in the work of political philosophers *and* economists working in the liberal tradition.

The philosopher Sen ended *The Idea of Justice* as follows:

> Philosophy can—and does—produce extraordinarily interesting and important work on a variety of subjects that have nothing to do with the deprivations and inequities and unfreedoms of human lives. This is as it should be, and there is much to rejoice in the expansion and consolidation of the horizon of our understanding in every field of human curiosity. However, philosophy can only play a part in bringing more discipline and greater reach to reflections on values and priorities as well as on the denials, subjugation and humiliations from which human beings suffer across the world. A shared commitment of theories of justice is to take these issues seriously and to see what they can do in terms of practical reasoning about justice and injustice in the world.[72]

[71] Nasar, S. (2011) *Grand Pursuit; The History of Economic Genius*. London: Fourth Estate, 456.

[72] *The Idea of Justice*, 413–414.

Annexe

Social contract theories go all the way back to the sixteenth century when Thomas Hobbes introduced the term social contract. Hobbes lived in a rather brutal period, which he famously characterized as *solitary, poor, nasty, brutish and short*. Philosophers after him, beginning with John Locke, took Hobbes's social contract model on board, be it that Locke analysed social contract in a more conducive environment than Hobbes's. Jean-Jacques Rousseau had a different environment in mind than Locke's; his temperament was also quite different from Locke's. This annexe provides more information about their life and work, concluding with some observations about them.

Hobbes, Locke, and Rousseau

Social contract theories all build on the idea that the state of nature is undesirable and that political institutions, such as the state, can help prevent, or overcome, anarchy. Hobbes, Locke, and Rousseau believed that humans living without central authority were facing uncertain conditions in a state of mutual competition.

Hobbes observed that civil government was the result of a contract between individuals belonging to a particular society in a competitive state of nature, 'protecting them from continual fear, and danger of violent death—the life of man was 'solitary, poor, nasty, brutish and short.'[73] For the sake of peace, Hobbes argued, men must make a contract to renounce their natural liberty, and authorize an absolute sovereign to govern them. Rousseau, however, believed that there was no explanation for why this would be the case, as he argued that in the state of nature there would have been no conflict or property. Again, contrary to Hobbes, Rousseau held that, as we shall see, in the state of nature 'uncorrupted morals' prevailed.

Social Contract

As mentioned in Chap. 3, the Renaissance vision of society was hierarchically led by absolute monarchs and the Church. This vision gradually lost political and philosophical credibility. As of the seventeenth century,

[73] Thomas Hobbes, *Leviathan*, Ed. Richard Tuck Cambridge; Cambridge University Press, 89. Hobbes had a grotesque vision of the state: A human Leviathan whose vast body was made up of an infinite number of human bodies.

philosophers promoted the notion of a voluntary social contract as the basis of social norms and political obligations.

Apart from Hobbes, Locke's and Rousseau's social contract thinking are presented. The history of social contract theory was not over after Hobbes, Locke, and Rousseau. Modern philosophers Rawls and Nozick drew inspiration from their predecessors.[74] Rawls, for example, put his theory squarely in the liberal political tradition. He observed that: 'The content of a liberal political conception of justice has three main elements: a list of equal basic rights and liberties, a priority for those freedoms, and an assurance that all members of society have adequate all-purpose means to make use of these rights and liberties.'[75]

In sum, social contract philosophy lives on. Most contract theorists draw conclusions regarding matters of interest to economics, such as the justification of property rights and the legitimacy of redistribution.

The Essential Locke

Life

Locke, as mentioned in Chap. 3, is generally regarded as the father of liberalism. He became the most influential philosopher of constitutional politics and individual rights of his time. Besides being a philosopher, Locke was also a medical doctor. In this latter capacity Locke became part of Lord Ashley's retinue.[76] As Ashley was one of the founders of the Whig movement, he exerted great influence on Locke's political thinking. Locke became the Whigs' intellectual hero.

In 1683, Locke and Lord Ashley fled to the Netherlands, as they had been involved in a political plot to exclude James (King Charles II's brother) from succession. Lord Ashley died in exile; Locke lived in Holland for six years. After the Glorious Revolution—the first modern liberal revolution which resulted in parliamentary sovereignty—he returned to England. While in Holland, he mingled with freethinking members of

[74] Recently, in the Netherlands a new political party was established with the name New Social Contract, inspired by a romantic longing for more social cohesion in Dutch society. Dutch newspaper NRC's edition of 26 September 2024, included an article observing that during the 1950s, there were various groupings in Dutch society, each having different political, economic and moral convictions; yet, the leaders of these groups maintained a dialogue. This is no longer the case, the article concluded, as there is no longer a widely shared community spirit.

[75] *Liberalism*, 11.

[76] Locke miraculously cured Lord Ashley of a liver infection.

Protestant groups such as Spinoza's small group of loyal confidants. Locke was receptive to Spinoza's ideas; in particular to his plea for political and religious tolerance and the need to separate Church and State.

Locke gave Hobbes's social contract a new meaning. He influenced political philosophy, and in particular modern liberalism, by tempering Hobbes's absolutist thinking and the separation of Church and State. His name remains closely associated with the notion of liberty and, indeed, social contract theory.

Work

A well-known work of Locke is *Two Treatises of Government.* In it, Locke argued against *absolute* monarchy and in favour of individual consent as the basis of political legitimacy. Drawing on a mix of Ciceronian and Christian inspiration, as presented in Chap. 3, Locke argued that private property was the linchpin of both political liberty and a functioning market. It should not surprise us that the Whigs, close to Locke's political heart, mainly consisted of land owners at the time. Regarding the market, private property gave all landowners the possibility of maximizing their economic production according to personal choice. In other words, they were free to choose what to buy and whom to do business with, thus creating favourable market conditions. Locke's ideas greatly influenced the Scottish Enlightenment, to which Adam Smith belonged.

In addition to what I just explained, Locke redefined subjectivity, or self, which influenced modern Western thinking of the self. His theory of association also influenced modern psychology, in that his recognition of ideas simple and complex, and their interaction, promoted the revision and expansion of this theory so as to explain how humans gain knowledge in the physical world.[77]

Now, what did Locke have to say about the social contract? Central to his theory is the contrast between the state of nature and a civil (read: political) society. Regarding this state of nature, Locke observed that the fact that the natural state of humanity without a government did not mean that it was lawless. Human beings, continued Locke, were still subject to the laws of God and nature. He argued that this state of nature, which had

[77] Locke's *Of the Abuse of Words,* is still an enjoyable read in which he shows his philosophical approach to the meaning of words and ideas. The booklet is reprinted in the Penguin *Great Ideas* series.

existed, was a historical phase preceding the establishment of government (and not a political tyranny), which had acquired the consent from the governed. Such a government did not have, unlike Hobbes's, a supernatural basis.[78]

In *Limitarianism; the Case Against Extreme Wealth*, Ingrid Robeyns refers to Hobbes's social contract, i.e., that it was rational for human beings to agree on a set of rules that govern public life, in order to make life better for all. Taxing wealth is one of Robeyns's proposals to limit the gap in the income and wealth distribution. She underscores the fundamental philosophical point that secure ownership of property cannot exist without taxation.

'It is a state's responsibility to implement the social contract, providing a set of rules that protect our basic rights and liberties, and preventing people from taking power into their own hands ...... Key to this is its protection of our property rights, which are central to our freedoms, our security, and our well-being; as well as its provision of public goods—from roads and railways to firefighters and nurses—that enable us to safely pursue our own endeavors. Yet for the government to exist and to exercise these functions, it must have resources—it must collect tax. Without tax, the government couldn't protect our property, and enable transactions in the market..... The fundamental philosophical point is that secure ownership of property cannot exist without taxation. There is no property without the state, and there is no state without tax.'[79] There is no property, and there are no markets without governments, and there is no government without taxes, there is no way to decide on what constitutes our property without first thinking about societal rules.[80]

[78] In other words: In the liberal understanding there are no citizens within a regime who can claim to rule by natural or supernatural right, without the consent of the governed.

[79] Robeyns, I. (2024) *Limitarianism; the Case Against Extreme Wealth*. New York: Astra House, 119–120.

[80] Ibid., 118.

Let us look a bit closer at Locke's state of nature. Nobody in the natural state has the political power to tell others what to do. Locke emphasized the good aspects of this state of nature. This is how Locke put it in the *Second Treatise of Government*:

> The State of Nature has a Law of Nature to govern it, which obliges every one: And Reason, which is that Law, teaches all Mankind, who will but consult it, that being all equal and independent, no one ought to harm another in his Life, Health, Liberty or Possessions.[81]

Unlike Hobbes, Locke believed that human nature was characterized by reason and tolerance. Yet he agreed with Hobbes that human nature resulted in people being selfish. To prevent or resolve conflicts in a decent manner, argued Locke, people transfer their rights to a political body—to a government.[82] They have done so in the majority of cases, and this is the origin of legitimate government. Locke argued that private and public interests are identical in the long run, though not necessarily over short periods. Russell had this to say about the character of government:

> Government, we are told, is a remedy for the inconveniences that arise, in the state of nature, from the fact that, in that state, every man is the judge of his own cause. But where the monarch is a party to the dispute, this is no remedy, since the monarch is both judge and plaintiff. These considerations lead to a view that governments should not be absolute, and that the judiciary should be independent of the executive.[83]

In sum, the proper alternative to the natural state is a government established with the consent of the people, through a social contract. Government provided effective protection of basic human rights to *life, liberty, and property* (Locke's famous trinity of natural rights) under the Rule of Law. However, the power of the government should be limited to the public good.[84]

[81] Locke, J. (1690) *Second Treatise of Government*, Section 6.

[82] 'Separation of government from business, in John Locke's sense, was achieved in an exemplary fashion in the charter of an independent Bank of England in 1694. Commercial capital had won its tilt against the Crown.' Source: Polanyi, K. *The Great Transformation*, 233.

[83] Russell, B. (1979) *A History of Western Philosophy*. London: Unwin Paperbacks, 607.

[84] Liberals generally believed in limited government, while several liberal philosophers decried government outright.

Locke had influenced his fellow countryman Thomas Paine (1737–1809) who wrote—quite radically—that government, even in its best state, was a necessary evil. Paine was a staymaker, like his father. However, his true talent was writing passionate political pamphlets which had a considerable influence at the time. Benjamin Franklin had persuaded Paine to visit the American colony. In 1774, Paine landed in Pennsylvania. In January 1776, he published *Common Sense*. His revolutionary essay greatly helped to shift the colonists' political sentiment to independence. *Common Sense* did not just bring Lockean liberalism to America, Paine also brought English radicalism to the colony. 'It was not Tom Paine's common sense but his rage that turned hundreds of thousands of Americans to thoughts of independence in the winter of 1776.'[85]

As Locke explained in *Two Treatises*, government is a power that has no other end but preservation and cannot justify killing, enslaving, or plundering citizens. Libertarian analysts interpret this statement as suggesting that governments exist *only* to protect people from infringements on their rights.

Private Property

As for economic aspects, Locke defended the *natural* right of private property. Arguably, this is the best-known and, at the same time, most controversial aspect of his philosophy. He argued that private property arises when human beings settle on uninhabited land and mix their labour with this land to create property that is useful to human beings. This can result in inequality of private possessions, which Locke accepted, and had to be protected by law. As most land was in the hands of the landed gentry, Locke can be portrayed as the philosophical spokesman of the Whig landowners at the time.[86] Nonetheless, Locke did not rule out state intervention in private property so long as it was done through Parliament following a constitutional representative process.

[85] Paine, T. (1986) *Common Sense*. London: Penguin Classics, 45.
[86] Lessnoff, M. (1986) *Social Contract*. London: Macmillan Education, 64.

Institutions of property rights and contract enforcement originated from classical liberalism. During the nineteenth century, the right of property and its accumulation was enhanced as a necessity for social and national growth; beyond what Locke had initially envisaged. Nonetheless, private property was the linchpin of both political liberty and the functioning of the market. We saw in Chap. 6 that Friedman argued, in line with Locke, that there is a connection between economic and political freedom. Regarding the institution of property rights, these rights and their protection play a fundamental role in explaining economic growth or stagnation in new institutional economics.

I mentioned that Locke had, besides a Ciceronian, also a Christian inspiration. In this vein, as Soll observes, God made the earth as a flawed home for fallen man. This is why Locke saw the need for property and government, to make sure that economic life neither collapsed nor strayed into immorality. It is important to underline that Locke defended the separation of church and state, while promoting religious toleration.

Regarding the notion of tolerance and pluralism, later liberal philosophers argued that the proliferation of opinions and beliefs was characteristic of a stable social order. Their efforts have been geared towards establishing a governing framework that would harmonize and minimize conflicting views but that would still allow varying views to exist and flourish. In short, pluralism would trigger tolerance.

Jean-Jacques Rousseau

Life

Swiss-born philosopher Jean-Jacques Rousseau was, besides philosopher, a very popular writer, and composer. His ideas worried the wealthy landowning classes at the time. *Le Contrat Social* shook up politics, paving the way for the French Revolution.[87] Apart from his immensely popular novel *Julie* (1761) which included beautiful descriptions of the Swiss

[87] The American Revolution was triggered by the British colonizer's tax policy for its American colony, which was not accepted by the latter. This led to the Seven Year's War over the issue of 'taxation without representation'. In turn this resulted in the formulation of the Constitution of the United States, establishing a federal government. At the time, the constitution was a republican and liberal document. It remains the oldest liberal governing document worldwide.

countryside, Rousseau's *Confessions* (1782) initiated the modern autobiography. Before *Confessions*, Rousseau published *Emile, or On Education* (1762). It is a work on the nature of education and the nature of man. He considered it to be the best and most important of all his writings. Due to a section of the book entitled 'Profession of Faith of the Savoyard Vicar', *Emile* was banned and it was publicly burned in 1762; the year of its first edition. It was forbidden by the Church, being listed on the Index. During the French Revolution *Emile* served as the inspiration for what became a new national system of education. His opera *The Village Soothsayer* was well received; in fact so well that King Louis XV attended a performance in 1752.

Kant was influenced by Rousseau. 'Kant was a man of such regular habits that people used to set their watches by him as he passed their doors on his constitutional, but on one occasion his time-table was disrupted for several days; this was when he was reading *Emile*. He said that he had to read Rousseau's book several times, because, at a first reading the beauty of the style prevented him from noticing the matter.'[88]

Rousseau had a troubled youth: His mother died soon after his birth and his father left him when Jean-Jacques was only ten years old. Undeterred, Rousseau managed to become one of Europe's most influential philosophers at the time. He met famous French writers such as Diderot and Voltaire, and British ones, such as Burke, Hume, and Boswell. Rousseau must have been a controversial person, as he regularly fell out with friends and he had to flee cities and countries in which he had intended to settle.[89]

[88] *A History of Western Philosophy*, 678.

[89] On one occasion, Frederick the Great of Prussia defended Rousseau. He wrote the governor of Neuchâtel, that Rousseau's only offense was that he had strange opinions which he thought were good ones. Philosopher-economist David Hume, after he ended his position at the British embassy in Paris, persuaded Rousseau to join him to Britain and found him a refuge from persecution in a country house in Staffordshire. However, Rousseau suspected a plot against him and fled back to France, spreading a report about Hume's bad faith.

Work

Rousseau is best-known for *Le Contrat Social* (1762) and, not least, its opening paragraph: 'Man was born free, and he is everywhere in chains. Those who think themselves the masters of others are indeed greater slaves than they. How did this transformation come about? I do not know. How can it be made legitimate? That question I believe I can answer.'[90]

Rousseau was outraged by the staggering inequality in France; he valued inequality even more than liberty. In order to address injustices, Rousseau designed a philosophy, beginning with the earliest human settlements. Initially people learned the advantages of social cooperation, and families were established. This period, lamented Rousseau, must have been the happiest and most stable of epochs, as in this state of nature property did not exist and there were no feelings of envy or distrust; in short, uncorrupted morals prevailed.[91] Once collections of settled families formed communities, private property and the division of labour were introduced triggering inequality. This was not a natural outcome; it was the result of human choice. Social hierarchies ensued which had a corrupting influence on human beings. Men became one another's enemies.

Perpetual conflicts ensued and lead to a horrible state of war. This made government necessary. Rousseau then concluded that the rich (who suffered most from this state of war) took the initiative in introducing government. And although government was decided by general agreement, that same agreement was achieved by cunning on the part of the rich. The result, Rousseau observed, gave them [the rich; PdH] new powers, destroyed natural liberty, fixed the law of property and inequality, and subjected almost all mankind to perpetual labour, slavery and wretchedness.

To put things right, Rousseau called for radical and republican democracy. Democratic politics would have to tear down the established hierarchy and build a more just society through a better political system. By joining together into a civil society through the social contract, and abandoning their claims of natural right, people could both preserve themselves and remain free. This is because, argued Rousseau, submission to the authority of the *general will* of the people as a whole would guarantee individuals against being subordinated to the will of others. He added that without the supreme criterion of equality, the general will would be

[90] Rousseau, J. (2004) *The Social Contract*. London: Penguin Books Great Ideas, 2.

[91] It should not surprise us that Rousseau observed: 'Nothing is more gentle than man in his primitive state.'

meaningless. This opinion, however, contained authoritarian implications. In this vein, Rousseau's concept of the social contract appears less analogous to Locke's and more to that of Hobbes.

Rousseau formulated the conditions for a legitimate state; i.e., the terms of the legitimate social contract, in which equality and liberty constituted central parts. Representatives of the government (i.e., magistrates) would not be the people's masters but its officers. In Rousseau's philosophy, the sovereign is the Rule of Law, decided by direct democracy in an assembly.

Some Observations

University of Glasgow academic researcher, Michael Lessnoff, took a closer look at *The Social Contract*. He observes that Rousseau is the great proponent of the 'democratic' social contract.[92] As mentioned, Rousseau introduced the concept of the general will, meaning that each associate puts his person and all his power under the supreme direction of the general will. Each associate would thus become a member of a collective body, capable of acting through an assembly of the associates, who would thus collectively exercise sovereign political authority, and the right to make laws governing the state.

Rousseau was in fact projecting an *ideal* state.[93] The ideal social contract constituted an exchange of natural liberty for civil liberty. And civil liberty means rule by a sovereign body in which each citizen has an equal share, and which expresses the general will. Regarding the general will Rousseau wrote:

> '…that anyone who refuses to obey the general will shall be forced to do so by the whole body; which means nothing more or less that *he will be forced to be free*…. Along with the civil state, man acquires moral liberty, which alone makes him truly master of himself; for the impulse of mere appetite is slavery, and obedience to self-imposed law is liberty.'[94]

Rousseau deviated from Hobbes and Locke, in that he argued that society and property constituted the real original sins.[95] He observed that

[92] *Social Contract*, 82.

[93] Ibid., 80.

[94] Rousseau, J. J. (1968). *The Social Contract*. Harmondsworth: Penguin, 68. Italics in the quotation are mine.

[95] Curiously, Locke is not mentioned once in *The Social* Contract, but Hobbes is: 'Of all Christian authors, the philosopher Hobbes is the only one who saw clearly both the evil and the remedy [monarchs being the head of the church and head of the state, PdH], and who dared to propose reuniting the two heads of the eagle and fully restoring the political unity without which neither the state nor the government will ever be well constituted.' *The Social Contract*, 159.

inequality was the product of self-love and pride. In the quest to satisfy people's pride, the wealthy and powerful created unnatural conventions and privileges to distinguish and celebrate themselves in a hierarchy. Rousseau concluded—in an anti-Lockean fashion—that the chains of mankind were private property and elite, minoritarian political and economic rule. Property, argued Rousseau, was a corrupting vice to be fought with empathy, but supported by a political push for economic equality.

Contrary to Locke's ideas about land ownership, Rousseau felt that the first man who found a piece of land exclaiming 'this is mine', was an imposter, responsible for the misery and inequality of the human race. Worse, the recognition of property, Rousseau added, was the first step on the road to feudalism and tyranny, as human beings gave up their individual rights to nobles and kings. Law making should not come from property owners but from the democratic, communal decisions of the majority of society. He observed in this connection that 'It was manifestly contrary to the law of nature .... that a handful of people should gorge themselves with superfluities while the hungry multitude goes in want of necessities.[96]

Rousseau concluded:

> There is only one law which by its very nature requires unanimous assent. This is the social pact: for the civil association is the most voluntary act in the world; every man having been born free and master of himself, no one else may under any pretext whatever subject him without his consent. To assert that the son of a slave is born a slave is to assert that he is not born a man.
>
> If then, there are opposing voices at the time when the social pact is made, this opposition does not invalidate the contract; it merely excludes the dissenters; they are foreigners among the citizens. After the state is instituted, residence implies consent: to inhabit the territory is to submit to the sovereign.[97]

References

Arrow, K. (1951). *Social Choice and Individual Values.* John Wiley and Sons.

Freeden, M. (2015). *Liberalism; A Very Short Introduction.* Oxford University Press.

Hausman, D., & McPherson, M. (1996). *Economic Analysis and Moral Philosophy.* Cambridge University Press.

[96] *Free Market*, 193.

[97] *The Social Contract*, 126.

Hobbes, T. (1996). *Leviathan*. R. Tuck (Ed.). Cambridge: Cambridge University Press.
Lessnoff, M. (1986). *Social Contract*. Macmillan Education.
Locke, J. (1690) Second Treatise of Government
Locke, J. Of the Abuse of Words. : Penguin Books Great Ideas
Meadowcroft, J. (2011). Nozick's critique of Rawls: Distribution, Entitlement, and the Assumptive World of A Theory of Justice. In *Cambridge Collection on Line*. Cambridge University Press.
Nasar, S. (2011) *Grand Pursuit; The History of Economic Genius*
Paine, T. (1986). *Common Sense*. Penguin Classics.
Phelps, E. (2023). *My Journeys in Economic Theory*. Columbia University Press.
Piketty, T. (2014). *Capital in the Twenty-First Century*. The Belknap Press of Harvard University Press.
Polanyi, K. *The Great Transformation; The Political and Economic Origins of Our Time*. Beacon Press.
Rawls, J. (1971). *A Theory of Justice*. Harvard University Press.
Reiss, J. (2013). *Philosophy of Economics; A Contemporary Introduction*. Routledge.
Robeyns, I. (2024). *Limitarianism; The Case Against Extreme Wealth*. Astra House.
Rodrik, D. (2011). *The Globalization Paradox; Democracy and the Future of the World Economy*. W.W. Norton.
Rousseau, J. (2004). *The Social Contract*. Penguin Books Great Ideas.
Russell, B. (1979). *A History of Western Philosophy*. Unwin Paperbacks.
Sen, A. (1979). *Equality of What? The Tanner Lecture on Human Values*. Stanford University.
Sen, A. (1981). *Poverty and Famines: An Essay on Entitlement and Deprivation*. Clarendon Press.
Sen, A. (1983). *Commodities and Capabilities. Hennipman Lecture*. North Holland.
Sen, A. (1984). *Resources, Values and Development*. Harvard University Press.
Sen, A. (1999a). *Development as Freedom*. Oxford University Press.
Sen, A. (1999b). *Les Prix Nobel. The Nobel Prizes 1998*. Nobel Foundation.
Sen, A. (2009). *The Idea of Justice*. Allen Lane.
Sen, A., & Drèze, J. (2002). *India: Development and Participation*. Oxford University Press.
Sen, A. (2022). *Home in the World; A Memoir*. Penguin Random House.
Snyder, T. *On Freedom*. The Bodley Head.
Stiglitz, J. (2024). *The Road to Freedom*. Allen Lane.

CHAPTER 8

Mariana Mazzucato Attacks the Philosophy of Neoclassical Economics

Prologue

The financial crisis of 2007 will certainly have contributed to Mariana Mazzucato's thinking about what had gone wrong and how it could have happened. In dealing with these questions, she delved deeper than exposing the dangers of deregulation, financialization, wrong economic policies, and immoral behaviour of bankers. She went all the way back to the origins of the economic science, starting with classical economists Adam Smith and David Ricardo to the emergence of neoclassical economics, which replaced classicals' notion of value by utility. From then on, the problem started, as Mazzucato extensively explains. She observes that the term 'public value' does not exist in economics any longer. Mazzucato's mission is to put value back where it belongs, and having done so, to put right what is wrong in the economy as we know it.

Mazzucato is in the good company of, among others, Joan Robinson, Keynes, Schumpeter, and Polanyi. Robinson argued that, since neoclassical economics had introduced the term utility, the moral dimension of economics had been thrown overboard. Neoclassical economics simply says that the value of goods is determined by their price. The consequence is that there are economic sectors, such as the financial sector, adding value to the economy, while government investments do not. This is wrong, argues Mazzucato; *the rules of the game* should be radically changed. But attempts to address these anomalies will not work until grounded in a

P. de Haan, *Great Economists and the Evolution of Economic Liberalism*, https://doi.org/10.1007/978-3-031-93831-3_8

proper theoretical understanding of the process by which economic *value* is created.

Mazzucato has eloquently exposed neoclassical economics' flaws. From a theoretical point of view, the central problem is the way in which value had changed its meaning, with far-reaching and destabilizing consequences. She did not stop there; she also proposed solutions. In doing so, she passionately offers an economics of hope. Mazzucato is one of the exceptional game-changers presented in this book. Her analyses and proposals for fundamental theoretical and policy change received praise from commentators and political leaders the world over. Mazzucato is one of the few economists who are global celebrities.

Part I Life and Work

Mariana Mazzucato was born in June 1968 in Rome, Italy. Together with her parents she moved to Princeton, USA, where her father had accepted a senior position as a physicist at Princeton University. After having completed her high school in Princeton, she started her undergraduate studies in history and international relations at Tufts University. After having obtained an MA from the New School for Social Research in 1994, she there earned her PhD in economics in 1999. Not surprisingly, when doing TED talks, she speaks with an American accent.

Career

During the period 1975 to 1998, Mazzucato was adjunct professor of economics at New York University. The next two years she taught at the University of Denver. The year before she gained her PhD, Mazzucato was a Marie Curie Research Fellow at the London Business School.

In 1999, she became a lecturer at the Open University, and in 2005, she was appointed full professor. Together with Paul Geroski, she established the Innovation, Knowledge and Development Research Centre.

During the period 2008–2014, Mazzucato was a visiting professor at various universities in Italy and Australia. Between 2011 and 2017, she combined these responsibilities with the RM Phillips Chair in the Economics of Innovation at the University of Sussex, England. In 2017, Mazzucato was appointed professor in the Economics of Innovation and Public Value at University College, London (UCL), where she founded the Institute for Innovation and Pubic Purpose.

Academic Work

Her books and articles focus on the interaction between public policy, innovation, markets, and inclusive economic growth from the micro level upwards. As regards growth as an evolutionary process, she was inspired by the thinking of Joseph Schumpeter. This inspiration shone through in her early research work on the origin and evolution of persistent differences between firms and the implications for industry life-cycle differences in the structure of sectors.

Mazzucato combines her empirical work with theoretical studies. In *The Value of Everything*, she blames, as mentioned, neoclassical economics for taking out the moral dimension of value, which created a lot of damage to the economy and society at large. Another aspect of Mazzucato's work is a forceful reappreciation of the role of government in innovation and value creation, as argued in *The Entrepreneurial State*. Governments can undertake so-called 'mission-oriented projects', elaborated in her *Mission Economy*. Government's bold action can drive and coordinate early stages of innovation (from which private investors initially shy away) to solve challenges ranging from health issues to climate change. In *The Big Con*, Mazzucato and co-author Rosie Collington, take aim at big accounting and consultancy firms. These firms do not create value, argue the authors, they hollow out the public sector's capacity.

Advisory Work and Board Memberships

Mazzucato advises many governments, political parties and institutions such as the British Labour Party, the European Commission, the OECD, the G-7, the World Economic Forum, and UN agencies. She served on the European Space Agency's High-Level Advisory Group on Human and Robotic Space Exploration for Europe. As for her advice to governments, Brazil, the UK, Finland, Sweden, Scotland, South Africa, and her home country Italy, benefitted from her insights in innovation, mission-oriented projects, and industrial strategies. In short, she is an influential and persuasive advisor, having spread her influence and thinking across the globe.

Media

After she established herself globally with *The Entrepreneurial State*, economists and the general public enjoy her lively TED lectures, and spicy op-eds in *The Guardian, Financial Times* and *The New York Times.* Mazzucato also regularly contributes columns to Project Syndicate.

Mazzucato's biography and her academic achievements, remind me of what Max Weber once observed that material interests may drive the trains down the tracks, but *ideas* are the switchmen! Mazzucato is such a 'switchman'.

The Value of Everything, The Entrepreneurial State, Mission Economy, and The Big Con

Mazzucato's thinking is consistently woven into her academic work, including her bestsellers. What follows intends to capture this consistency, centred around her analysis of value through time. She applies her interpretation of value to economic theory, the production boundary, and a variety of value-creating—and value-extracting—economic entities, ranging from multinational corporations, finance, big-tech and big-pharma, as well as large consulting firms, all the way to the value-creating activities of government. Mazzucato's critical analyses do not end in a doomsday scenario; on the contrary, she presents solutions, and—in her own words—'the economy of hope'.

The Value of Everything, includes Mazzucato's most comprehensive economic analysis. Therefore, this book is summarized in detail, while the gist of the other three books is woven into it.

The Value of Everything

The Value of Everything, starts with a crucial observation: 'We cannot understand economic growth if we do not go back to the beginning: What is wealth and where does wealth come from? Are we sure that much of what is passing for value creation is not just value extraction in disguise?'[1]

[1] Mazzucato, M. (2018) *The Value of Everything; Making and Taking in The Global Economy*. London, Allen Lane, xi. The book's title is in fact a reference to Oscar Wilde's line: A cynic is a man who knows the price of everything and the value of nothing.

The first story she tells is about GDP growth of the American economy between 1975 and 2017. GDP roughly tripled from $5.49 trillion to $17.29 trillion, and productivity grew by about 60%. However, from 1979 onwards, real hourly wages for the majority of American workers stagnated or even fell. So, who gained? A tiny elite captured all the gains. The winners argued that they were productive members of society, taking risks and hence deserving a higher income than people who simply benefitted from the spill-overs. But is it correct, Mazzucato wonders, what Lloyd Blankfein, then CEO of Goldman Sachs, claimed that his staff were among the most productive workers in the world? Perhaps Blankfein had forgotten that his investment bank, together with many others, had caused the 2007 financial crisis.

Something had changed since the 1960s, when finance was important in transferring existing wealth, but *not* creating it. During the 1960s, finance entered into GDP only as an intermediate input; i.e., a service contributing to the functioning of industries that were real value creators. This changed around 1970, when national accounts started to include the financial sector in their calculations. This change coincided with deregulation of the financial sector: Relaxing controls on bank lending; the interest rates they could charge; and the products they were allowed to sell.

The financial sector became a fast-track for smart people to get rich quickly. This sector outperformed the growth of the non-financial economy; large parts of the economy became 'financialized'. Rather than investing in the long-term health of the business, bank managers preferred spending a greater proportion of profits on share buy-backs, boosting stock prices, stock options, and top-executives' pay. Bank CEOs call this, like Blankfein, value creation. But it is not, argues Mazzucato, it is immoral value extraction.

Not just the financial sector is grilled, this also applies to big pharma, large consultancy firms, and Silicon Valley's big-tech firms. These latter businesses have the tendency to ignore government's pioneering role in the development of new technologies, from which Silicon Valley greatly benefitted. After all, the development of the Internet, GPS, touchscreen, SIRI and the algorithm behind Google have all been funded by public institutions, as described in *The Entrepreneurial State*.[2]

[2] Mazzucato, M. (2013) *The Entrepreneurial State; Debunking Public Vs. Private Sector Myths*. London: Anthem Press.

Instead of depicting government as a drain on the economy, a reappreciation of who exactly creates value, and who extracts it, is called for. Now, if the goal is—and this is one of Mazzucato's central objectives—to produce growth that is more innovative, inclusive, and sustainable, we need a better understanding of genuine value creation and a more confident and leading role of government.

The History of Value

In essence, value involves the production of goods and services. The question is whether the produced goods and services increase (or decrease) the resilience of the productive system. Value creation happens when different types of resources (human, physical, and intangibles) create *new* goods and services. By contrast, value extraction happens when activities are focused on moving *existing* resources and outputs around.

Across the history of economics, notions about value creation have been influenced by historical shifts in the economy: From agricultural to industrial, and from a mass-production-based to the contemporary platform economy. Until the middle of the nineteenth century, value was closely connected with labour input. Smith, Ricardo, and Marx measured the market value of a product in terms of the amount of labour that had gone into it. This is an objective measurement of value; rather than neoclassical economists' subjective interpretation of value. i.e., the market price.

In Smith's thinking there is a connection between value and productivity. Simply put, adding value in any branch of production is productive; not adding value is unproductive. Despite the fact that government had a number of duties in society, i.e., infrastructure, defence, and the Rule of Law, Smith put government on the unproductive side.[3] He was a free trader *par excellence*—a free market was one free of rent![4] In his view, rent belonged to the unproductive domain.[5]

[3] Ricardo also argued that government was by its very nature unproductive. Marx shared this opinion. In his analysis, the production boundary was defined by how profits were generated; i.e., whether an occupation was carried out in a capitalist production context.

[4] Ricardo and Marx redefined the theory of rent to make it clear that rent is income from *redistributing* value and not from creating it.

[5] Ricardo and Marx refined the theory of rent to make it clear that rent is income from *redistributing* value and not from creating it.

Neoclassical economists changed the meaning of value; they emphasized scarcity and the preferences of consumers and producers—value became a *subjective* notion. The value of goods and services was only determined by their market price, opening up economics to pervasive quantification. Any good or service being sold at an agreed market price was, by definition, value-creating. This change coincided with economists' wish to make economics more scientific, like physics and chemistry. Indeed, as Robinson observed: 'Economics is not only a branch of theology. All along it has been striving to escape from sentiment and to win for itself the status of a science.'[6] She concluded—well before Mazzucato—that economic theory had done away with the moral aspect of economics.[7]

A New Theory of Value

Since the Industrial Revolution, societies underwent structural changes, as epitomised by the emergence of labour unions, mass production, new institutions, and technological progress at large. The natural sciences also spread their wings; new theories emerged and innovations changed nearly everything. Economists were obviously not blind for these developments. They wanted to put economics on a scientific footing. A new theory of value was in the offing!

[6] Robinson, J. (1974) *Economic Philosophy*. Harmondsworth: Pelican Books, 25.

[7] Market values, as Michael Sandel argues, are coming to play a greater role in social life. 'Today, the logic of buying and selling no longer applies to material goods alone but increasingly governs the whole of life. It is time to ask whether we want to live this way.' Sandel, M. (2013) *What Money Can't Buy; The Moral Limits of Markets*. London: Penguin Books, 6. Sandel presents examples how markets reach into spheres of life erstwhile governed by moral, nonmarket, norms. A well-known example concerns fines instituted for parents picking up children late from a day care centre. Before the fine, parents made sure to be on time to pick up their child. But after the fine had been instituted, parents did not mind paying a fine. The fine crowded out nonmarket norms. Sandel challenges economists to figure out whether putting a price on an activity will crowd out nonmarket norms: 'To do so, they have to investigate the moral understandings that inform a given practice and determine whether marketizing the practice (by providing a financial incentive or disincentive) will displace them.' Ibid., 90. Sandel argues that there are fairness and corruption objections to what the market can or cannot buy. Fairness refers to inequality of market partners, in that one partner is not voluntarily parting with an object (e.g., a desperately poor person selling one of his kidneys). Regarding the corruption argument, Sandel mentions that it points to the degrading effect of market valuation and exchange on certain goods. According to this objection, certain moral and civic goods are diminished in value or corrupted if bought and sold.

Leon Walras (1834–1910) and Stanley Jevons (1835–1882) created the basis for a new theory of value. Also, Carl Menger contributed, arguing that the value arising from *utility* set the cost of production. The utility theory completely changed the concept of productive and unproductive labour. The distinction falls away in the new theory, since every sector that produces for the market exchanges value.

Alfred Marshall developed the term 'marginal utility' applied to value. Now, what does marginal utility mean? It is based on the notion of utility and scarcity.[8] Unlike the classical notion, it is *subjective*: the value of products is measured by their usefulness to the consumer who is prepared to pay for them. Changes in the marginal utility of a product results from changes in consumer preference. As for the marginal dimension: Utility decreases as the amount of a product that is held or consumed increases. Marginal utility increases when a product is scarce. The same principle applies to producers; we then talk of marginal productivity—the effect that an extra unit of produced goods has on the costs of production. Marginalism borrowed key concepts from physics, including the idea of equilibrium.

> The concept of marginalism lies at the heart of…. 'neoclassical' theory—the set of ideas that followed the classical theory developed by Smith and Ricardo and was extended by Marx. The term *neo*classical reflected how the new theories stood on the shoulders of giants but then took the theory in new directions. Microeconomic theory, the theory how firms, workers, and consumers make choices, is based on the neoclassical theory of production and consumption which rests on the maximization of profits (firms) and utility (consumers and workers)…. The inclusion of concepts like equilibria in the neoclassical model had the effect of portraying capitalism as a peaceful system driven by self-equilibrating competitive mechanisms.[9]

[8] Scarcity became ever more important to economics. In the early 1930s, it prompted Lionel Robbins to define the study of economics in terms of scarcity: the study of the allocation of resources, under condition of, indeed, scarcity.

[9] *The Value of Everything*, 63. Apart from laissez faire, equilibrium is another key notion of the neoclassicals. Robinson had this to say about equilibrium: '… the soothing harmonies of equilibrium supported *laissez faire* ideology and the elaboration of the argument kept us all too busy to have any time for dangerous thoughts.' *Economic Philosophy*, 70.

Price was now the ultimate measure of value. Marginal utility applies two assumptions: (i) All humans are one-dimensional utility calculators; they make *rational choices*, and (ii) there is no interference in price setting; equilibrium is arrived at under a system of *perfect competition*. Government should never intervene in the economy unless there are *market failures*. Who has not heard of Pareto's optimum, which depicts competitive markets where no one can be made better off without somebody else being made worse off? If markets happen to be *not* Pareto optimal, then everyone could be better off thanks to government correcting market failures.

Production Boundary

Mazzucato introduces the term 'production boundary'. This boundary is where the distinction is made between productive and unproductive activities. Within the boundary one finds the wealth creators; outside it one finds those who receive an income by way of transfers, such as subsidies to companies or social security payments to citizens.

She applies this boundary model to the financial sector and government. While she admits that the financial sector is important for buyers and sellers to do business with each other, the key question is how these activities are producing value. According to the prevailing economic theory, government is outside the production boundary and, consequently, it is unproductive. However, can government also make the economy grow, or does it only establish the rules of the game so that value creators can do their job efficiently? Modern economic thought has restricted government to fixing market failures rather than—again, this is an important aspect in Mazzucato's thinking—actively shaping markets.

The analysis of what value really is, is also important for the debate about the distribution of income. When value is determined by price, the level and distribution of income seem justified as long as there is a market for the goods and services generating that income. It is of no importance to ask whether the activity involved is productive or not. The classical concept of unearned income, such as rent, has vanished. 'Indeed, for economists there is no longer any story other than that of the subjective theory of value, with the market driven by supply and demand.'[10] But the distinction between productive and unproductive activities is not made on

[10] *The Value of Everything*, 13.

purely scientific grounds. Ascribing value has always involved flexible socio-economic arguments inspired by a particular political philosophy. Hence the definition of value is as much about politics as it is about particular views on how society ought to be constructed, and about narrowly defined economics.

Mazzucato then argues: 'On the basis of contemporary economic assumptions, we can no longer reliably say who creates value and who extracts it and therefore how the proceeds of production—income—should reasonably be distributed.'[11] This is regrettable, as it is important to the understanding of value extraction and hence the ability to limit it.

Smith argued that rent was unearned income. The neoclassical approach to rent, which prevails today, lies at the heart of Mazzucato's criticism. If value derives from price, income from rent must thus be productive. She concludes:

> 'Our understanding of rent and value profoundly affects how we measure GDP, how we view finance and the financialization of the economy, how we treat innovation, how we see government's role in the economy, and how we can steer the economy in a direction that is propelled by more investment and innovation, sustainable and inclusive.'[12]

Changing GDP Measurement and Its Consequences.

If income is not necessarily a sign of productivity but rather of something else—for example the classicals' notion of rent—then, when measuring GDP, something may creep in which is not creating value. What are the implications for GDP as a reliable measure of an economy's productiveness? Anything that fetches a price on the market is included in GDP, irrespective of the fact whether it contributes to value or extracts it, and, says Mazzucato, this applies in particular to the extractive activities of the financial sector. This calls into question how value is allocated across the economy.

Value theory has been a leading source of national accounting. As income tax statistics became more readily available, it was easier to construct estimates based on income data. In addition, Marshall's successor, Arthur Pigou (1877–1959) introduced the welfare concept into national

[11] Ibid., 71.
[12] Ibid., 74.

income accounting. He argued that activities generating welfare should be included, even if they were not paid for, such as subsidized government services. Simon Kuznets (1901–1985), who was in charge of calculating America's first national income, included all items that improved the material standard of living, barring items that did not. Neither Pigou nor Kuznets won the day; those who maintained that the national product is the sum total of market prices prevailed.

Keynes, who changed the perspective, invented, as described in Chap. 5, the notion of government spending to stimulate the economy. Government spending was now seen as directly increasing output. Keynes's ideas quickly gained acceptance: Government indeed contributed to the national product. This was a decisive moment in value theory. In other words:

$$\text{GDP} = \text{Consumption by households}(\text{C}) + \text{Investment by companies and by residual investment in housing}(\text{I}) + \text{Government spending}(\text{G}).$$

However, G is assumed to be unproductive, so it is outside the production boundary. Indeed, government is rarely acknowledged as a creator of value, despite the fact that, as Mazzucato will demonstrate, it does! And by not having a way to capture the value created by government, the national accounts contribute to the myth that government is only *facilitating* the creation of value rather than being a lead player in creating it.

Something extraordinary happened after the 1970s. From being perceived as only transferring existing value and 'rent' in the sense of unearned income, finance was transformed into a producer of new value. Commercial bank activities were now treated as financial intermediation, and investment bank activities as risk-taking. The result: The financial sector's contribution to GDP swelled considerably. What about the distinction between profits and rents? As long as the services of a landlord or a hedge fund manager (including pay) are treated as productive, as the marginal utility doctrine says, they became an integral part of GDP.

To date there is no rigorous underlying value theory based upon which national accounts are being put together. Mazzucato concludes:

> Making decisions about which goods and services to include in GDP involves returning to the concept of the production boundary at the centre of classical economic thought—distinguishing productive from unproductive activities—and the theory of value that justifies such a distinction....

> .The marginalist theory of value underlying contemporary national accounting systems leads to an indiscriminate attribution of productivity to anyone grabbing a large income, and downplays the productivity of the less fortunate.[13]

Hence, the way in which growth is defined and measured, is in the end determined by how value is being *interpreted.* In so doing, it justifies excessive inequalities of income and wealth and turns value extraction into value creation.

The Financial Sector

In some high-income countries the financial sector has outgrown their home economies. The sector's prime objective of taking in savings and providing credit to entrepreneurial initiatives, is more and more being eclipsed by circulating huge amounts of money *within* the sector; i.e., making money from moving existing money around. Only 15% of the funds generated in the sector go to businesses in non-financial industries. The rest is traded between financial institutions in ever more risky investments, underestimating the possibility of defaults. But defaults happened in 2008. And this resulted in contagion, i.e., defaulting banks, such as Lehman Brothers, affecting other banks, triggering the financial crisis, demonstrating the grave danger of 'excessive financialization'.[14]

Mazzucato proposes, as we already saw, not just to redefine *value*, but also to fundamentally transform the financial sector into a genuine value-creating one. If one were to strictly apply the value-added formula (i.e., wages plus profits), one finds that the financial sector, far from contributing 7.2% of GDP to the British economy, and 7.3% to that of the US, would in fact contribute zero, or even less, to output. By this yardstick, the sector is profoundly and fundamentally unproductive.[15]

[13] Ibid., 99–100.

[14] Ibid., 133. 'Society at large bears the costs of the speculative mania: unemployment rises and wages are held down, especially for those left behind during the previous economic expansion. In other words, value is extracted from labour's share of earnings in order to restore corporate profits.' Ibid., 110.

[15] Ibid., 106.

Despite the embarrassing and worrying events during the 2007 financial crisis (a 'Minsky moment'),[16] the American and British financial sectors—although weakened—are still dominant in both economies. Resulting from insufficiently adjusted regulations, the sector's capacity for value extraction is hardly diminished.

A new phenomenon is the appearance of asset management firms. These firms manage capital on behalf of the growing number of billionaires. There is also the appearance of Private Equity (PE) firms. Critics say these firms' aim is to cut costs in the short run, for example by firing workers and reducing investment, in order to make a quick profit and, subsequently, selling the business at the expense of long-term corporate health.

Financial intermediation services indirectly measured (FISIM) are calculated based on the extent to which banks can mark up their customers' borrowing rates over the lowest available interest rate. FISIM are included in national accounts as a contribution to GDP. This also applies to household borrowing, also known as 'privatized Keynesianism'; instead of government taking on debt to stimulate the economy, households and individuals now do so.

In sum, the financial sector has greatly diversified and grown in overall size. The production boundary is redrawn: finance is now within the boundary's productive side. This implies that ever-expanding finance would not harm the economy; on the contrary, it facilitates the circulation of goods and services.

Value Extraction

How does the financial sector extract value? It does so: (i) By inserting a wedge, (ii) in the form of transaction costs, and (iii) through high charges relative to risks. As for wedges, the costs of financial services rose, while at the same time the sector grew fast. Customers have not benefitted from the sector's economies of scale. How come? Banks form oligopolies, and thus control price setting. Much of fund management is a massive exercise in rent-seeking, as actively managed funds frequently fail to beat the

[16] Hyman Minsky developed a theory about the self-destabilizing dynamics of finance. He presented a 'big government, big bank' theory, in which government creates jobs by being 'employer of last resort', and underwrites distressed financial operators by being 'lender of last resort.'

performance of passive funds. Hence, financial actors should not make excessive amounts of money. A financial transaction tax would help redress this anomaly.

Financial regulation can help reform the sector, for example by helping to direct finance towards the real economy. What about the real economy? And what about value extraction and the widening gap between the haves and have-nots? As for the real economy, Carlota Perez argues that decoupling of finance from the real economy is not 'natural' but an artefact of deregulation and an excess belief in the power of the free market.[17]

This is what Mazzucato would like to see happening: The private sector must be rewarded for making decisions that target the long-term. Companies investing in training of staff, introducing new and risky technology, should be rewarded for investing in the long-term. Reinvestment of profits back into the real economy should be a condition to any type of government support. And executive pay should be held in check, realizing that there are other stakeholders who are also critical to value creation—workers, government, and civil society at large.

Widening Gap

Finance has both benefitted from and caused an ever widening inequality of income and wealth. Rising inequality might be justified if it promotes faster economic growth that also raises basic and average incomes. However, recent increases in inequality have been associated with slower economic growth. The financial sector contributed to widening this gap. Real wages have fallen or stagnated for many low and middle-income earners; household debts increased. Income distribution is skewed towards very high incomes. In the period 2010–2015, the wealth of the sixty-two richest individuals increased by 45%. Over the same period, the wealth of the bottom half fell by just over a trillion dollars—a drop of 38%. The annual OXFAM reports on this subject confirm this perverse trend. The

[17] Perez, C. The Double Bubble at the Turn of the Century: Technological Roots and Structural Implications. In: *Cambridge Journal of Economics*, 33(4) (2009), 801.

2024 OXFAM report says that, since 2020, the world's five richest men doubled their wealth, while 5 billion people worldwide became poorer.

Value, Innovation, and the Public Sector

The early decades of each of the industrial revolutions have been times of financial mania and increasing inequality. But after the financial bubbles collapse, governments rein in finance and promote the expansion of production which benefits society more broadly and makes finance serve its *real* purpose: providing credit for productive investment. However, when government does not step in and plays its part, financialization has a free rein. Can value extraction be limited, the income and wealth gap be shrunk, and will government's role be reappreciated?

Not just entrepreneurs invest in innovation; far from it. Where the risks are high and the costs are large, not the entrepreneur but government provides necessary long-term finance. Just a few examples: The Internet and SIRI were funded by the US Defense Advanced Research Projects Agency (DARPA).[18] The Internet and html code behind the worldwide web were developed by CERN, a government-sponsored laboratory in Geneva, Switzerland.

Apple, Google, Microsoft, Meta, and Amazon, together with China's Baidu, dominate the global desktop search market. These companies maintain that their profits are justified because they create value. However, they ignore government's leading role in innovation from which all of them benefitted greatly. In pursuit of innovation, governments have been willing to invest in areas with high risk, demonstrating greater patience and lower expectations of future returns. Government-sponsored innovations have not received the rewards they ought to have gotten. In fact, the risks are socialized while the rewards are privatized.

[18] One does not know in advance whether investment may eventually result in innovation. Hence it is understandable that a *spray gun approach* is applied by DARPA. However, now and again this approach is too wide. An example: DARPA funded the design of a website that would enable users to place a bet on the possible assassination or overthrow of foreign leaders, or on where the next terrorist attack would take place. The assumption of the designers was that betting would yield valuable information that the government could use to protect national security. Congress denounced the whole idea. Source: *What Money Can't Buy*, 149–150.

'Apple is a paradigmatic example here. ...Apple received its early stage funding from the US government's SBIR [Small Business Innovation Research; PdH] programme, and all the technologies which make the iPhone 'smart' are also State funded (with links to US programmes): the Internet, wireless networks, GPS, microelectronics, touch-screen displays and the latest voice-activated SIRI personal assistant.'[19] Apple's innovative products are the result of long years of US federal government support for innovation.

There is more. The US National Institutes of Health developed the basis for the development of the most innovative drugs, such as new molecular entities with priority rating. After the outbreak of the Covid-pandemic, governments subsidized the development of anti-Covid vaccines. German manufacturing is closely related to the strong links between science and industry fostered by e.g., the German Fraunhofer Institutes.

In *The Entrepreneurial State*, Mazzucato also mentions that Japan's Ministry of Trade and Industry, and Brazil and China's development banks were not just providing countercyclical lending, they were directing that lending towards the most innovative parts of the 'green' economy. In other words, the investments done were 'mission-oriented'.[20] Regarding the transformation into a sustainable green industrial system, key in this process will be building of innovative ecosystems that result in symbiotic (rather than parasitic) public-private partnerships.

It is only *after* high-risk public funds have been invested when risk-averse private financial funds enter, often venture capital (VC) entities. In biotechnology, nanotechnology, and the Internet, VC arrived 15–20 years after the most important investments were made by public sector funds.[21]

[19] Mazzucato, M. (2013) *The Entrepreneurial State; Debunking Public Vs. Private Sector Myths.* London: Anthem Press, 188.

[20] '...in 2003/2004 mission-oriented R&D made up more than 60 percent of public R&D spending in South Korea, the US, the UK, France, Canada, Japan, and Germany.' Ibid., 61.

[21] Ibid., 23. A quotation which explains industry's lack of appetite in upfront investing in nanotechnology: 'It is difficult for industry management to justify to their shareholders the large investment in long-term, fundamental research needed to make nanotechnology-based products possible. Furthermore, the highly interdisciplinary nature of the needed research is incompatible with many current *corporate* structures.' Ibid., 84. Mazzucato took this quote from an article written by Motoyama, Appelbaum and Parker, published in 2011, in *Technology and Society*, 33, nos. 1–2.

In other words, an entrepreneurial state invests in areas that the private sector would not invest in even if it had the resources, echoing Keynes's words when he said, way back in 1926: 'The important thing for Government to do is not to do things which individuals are doing already, and to do them a little better or a little worse, but to do those things which at present are not done at all.'[22] VC funds tend to be concentrated in areas of high potential growth, low technological complexity and low capital intensity. VCs reap the profits, while the public fund investor's direct share of the proceeds is almost nothing. Successful Silicon valley start-ups, benefitting from public investment in innovations, made fortunes.[23]

When, in 1984, former French President François Mitterrand visited Silicon Valley, an exchange of words ensued between Paul Berg, a winner of the Nobel Prize in Chemistry, and Tom Perkins, director of a VC fund, who boasted VCs role in biotech innovation. Berg responded: 'Where were you guys in the '50s and '60s when all the funding had to be done in the basic science?'[24]

An example: Apple benefitted greatly from innovations funded by the US government. In August 2012, Apple's market value stood at $623 billion. In 2011, Apple's nine top executives received a total of $440.8 million, and in 2012 $411.5 million. In 2011, these top executives together

[22] *The Value of Everything*, 229. In this context, Robert Skidelsky says this about Keynes's thinking regarding government's role: 'A greater role for government in turn requires the intellectual rehabilitation of the state as a potentially rational economic actor, rather than a mere vote-seeker. It is decades since anyone was able to write, as Keynes did in 1936, of the state being 'in a position to calculate the marginal efficiency of capital-goods on long views and on the basis of the general social advantage'. We need to think about a structure of the state which allows its investment function to be separated from the political incentives facing politicians.' Skidelsky, R. (2010) *Keynes, A Very Short Introduction*. Oxford: Oxford University Press, 168–169.

[23] '....when the appropriation of rewards outstrips the bearing of risks in the innovation process, the result is inequity; when the extent of inequity disrupts investment in the innovation process, the result is instability; and when the extent of instability increases the uncertainty of the innovation process, the result is a slowdown or even decline in economic growth. A major challenge is to put in place institutions to regulate the risk-reward nexus so that it supports equitable and stable economic growth.' *The Value of Everything*, 185.

[24] Ibid., 199.

earned the same amount as 17,600 Apple retail staff, and 15,000 in 2012. Regarding taxes, Apple designed various practices across the globe with one objective in mind—to pay less taxes. It is difficult to calculate how much Apple has exactly managed to save through its global tax-shuffling scheme. One researcher calculated that, if Apple were to report half of its profits in the US as opposed to only 30%, in 2011 Apple's tax liability would have been $2.4 billion higher than it actually was.[25]

Platform Capitalism

Platform capitalism is the contemporary way in which goods and services are produced, shared, and delivered, with less intermediation by old-fashioned companies such as travel agencies. Using the Internet provides a very sizeable concentration of market power. Google, for example, is a de facto monopolist.

What about value creation or value destruction by platform companies? First, these companies, who owe their favourable market position to government investment, should be repaying the taxpayer, instead of seeking tax breaks. Second, income from advertisements is considered to contribute to national income. But this income does not really increase the value of what is produced, whereas the services provided by these firms to users are not contributing to national income. This is a rather paradoxical situation, as these services *do* increase value! So, instead of us, users, paying Amazon a fee to use its AI capabilities (built with our data, by the way) Amazon should pay that fee to the users.

Innovation

Innovation is more and more the result of a collective process, whereby many smart people and organizations, including government, are involved. Ignoring this collectively produced social system, certain individuals feel justified in earning a much higher proportion of a nation's income than their own contribution warrants. Innovation has affected policies on taxes, patents and prices, adding to more inequality. What can be done about it? Mazzucato suggests (i) capping prices of publicly developed medicines; (ii) attaching conditions to public support, such as the requirement that

[25] *The Entrepreneurial State*, 188.

profits be reinvested back into production rather than spent on share buy-backs; (iii) allowing public agencies to retain equity or royalties in technologies for which they provided downstream funding; and (iv) by making income-contingent loans to businesses, as is being done in the case of student loans.

Innovation can lead to success but also to failure. Tesla, for example, received $465 million government investment support. The solar panel manufacturer Solyndra received a comparable amount. Tesla repaid the loan, and that was it; no royalties for government's innovative investments from which Tesla greatly benefitted. Solyndra went bankrupt and could not repay anything. This little story tells us that government fully pays for failures but does not get any benefit from the profits of successful investments.

Government Failure

Apart from 'market failure', there is also 'government failure', an offshoot of Public Choice theory. The theory calls for government to intervene as little as possible in the economy. This theory's assumption is that government is inevitably prone to corruption and laziness because agent and principal are too close to each other. So policy must make sure that gains from government intervention outweigh the costs of government failure.

During the early 1980s, Public Choice theory gained popularity among political leaders, notably Prime Minister Margaret Thatcher and President Ronald Reagan. The latter famously claimed that outside of its legitimate function, government does nothing as well, or economically, as the private sector. A decade later, this policy was adopted by so-called Third Way leaders Tony Blair and Bill Clinton (see Chap. 3). They were inspired by David Osborne and Ted Gaebler's book *Reinventing Government* (1992). The authors proposed a government that should 'steer more, row less'. The result was the introduction of a wave of consultants into the public sector, heavy outsourcing and privatization of public sector functions, thereby hollowing out the public sector's capacity.

Consultants and Value

What do consultants do? They are experts who transfer knowledge between organisations, use particular management frameworks to help clients to achieve their objectives, or provide additional skills. Yes, consultants are expected to create value by leveraging expertise and brokering technical or managerial knowledge. This is why they are hired by governments and businesses. But consultants are sometimes also contracted to propose tough measures which the management of the institution concerned is afraid to take, without the backing of the consultant's report.

In *The Big Con*, Mazzucato and Rosie Collington critically analyse the consulting industry.[26] The authors admit that it would be foolish to blame consultancies for all the problems that capitalism has created, from the financialization of our economies and the hollowing out of public organizations, yet they are critical of the Big Four accountancy firms (Deloitte, KPMG, Ernst & Young, and PwC) and the Big Three consultancy firms (Bain, Boston Consulting Group and McKinsey). They accuse them of incompetence, opportunism, costliness, and criticize their attitude to secure new contracts after a first consultancy.[27] In some instances initial consultancies are offered at an attractive low rate, to facilitate subsequent contracts.

Arguably, most damaging is consultants' substantial involvement in the public sector and businesses, as this erodes public sector capacity and that of businesses. As regards outsourcing, it seldom results in better public service delivery. Studies confirm that increased outsourcing was associated with a significant decrease in public services, a reduction in quality, and increased costs being propped up by the public sector.[28] It has proven very difficult to wind the clock back, i.e., to 're-insource' lost public sector capacity. *The Big Con* presents a variety of consultancies gone wrong.[29] One example is summarized in the box below.

[26] Mazzucato, M., and Collington, R. (2023) *The Big Con; How the Consulting Industry, Weakens Our Businesses, Infantilizes Our Government and Warps Our Economies.* London: Allen Lane.

[27] 'But across consultancies' work with governments, a systemic conflict of interest also exists. Because most consultancies, including McKinsey, want to secure future contracts from clients in the private sector—which remains a far bigger market than government contracting—there is a disincentive to provide advice that may harm key clients and industries, even if this is the appropriate course of action to achieve the government's goals or for society as a whole.' Ibid., 189.

[28] *The Value of Everything*, 255.

[29] The authors do present a few positive interventions of smaller specialised consultants firms.

To improve Stockholm's health system, the city's County Assembly decided to rebuild most of the Karolinska University Hospital. The new hospital, Nya Karolinska Solna (NKS) would be equipped with the latest medical technologies. The hospital's energy needs would be provided by renewable sources. The County Assembly decided to use a public-private partnership for building and managing the hospital. Despite various warnings against the anticipated high costs involved, the Assembly went ahead and contracted Swedish Hospital Partners (SHP), a consortium of a Swedish contracting firm and a British investment fund. The actual implementation costs turned out to be much higher than originally budgeted. Along the way, more consultants' firms had been hired, among them Boston Consulting Group (BCG), to implement 'value-based healthcare', a controversial management approach, based upon the philosophy of value in health care as cost-effectiveness. The *British Medical Journal* described the project as 'chaotic, prompting harsh criticism from the medical staff, an IT breakdown, and patient death during an emergency stop, as well as many logistical issues.' Meanwhile, BCG billed the hospital £22 million over six years, the equivalent of more than £60,000 a month for each of the nine consultants employed—many times more than Swedish public sector managers earned. BCG was succeeded by another consulting firm, underscoring the fact that NKS kept relying on private consultants to deliver the project. Overexpenditures continued; as a consequence, 250 doctors and 350 nurses at the hospital had been warned that they could lose their jobs. This would have involved extraction of value in the hospital. In the end, NKS became one of the most expensive buildings in the world, according to the County Assembly's leader of the opposition.[30]

It is no surprise that Mazzucato and Carrington conclude that the consultancy industry does, on balance, not create value.

The consulting industry has ....simultaneously shaped and benefited from it [market-driven economics; PdH], surfing the waves of the underlying

[30] *The Big Con*, 150–157.

> trends. The huge rents accrued match neither the value of its overall contribution nor the distribution of the risks....Public sector organizations in particular face challenges in overcoming the Big Con. The financial pressures that result from budget cuts and austerity programmes mean that public sector capacity is often limited.[31]

Thinking Big Again: Mission-Oriented Investments

Mazzucato argues that the time is more than ripe for government to regain confidence and take matters in its own hands. She argues that government must row so it can steer! Government should think big again, like President Roosevelt's New Deal, and President Kennedy's ambition to have an American walking the surface of the moon before 1970. As Kennedy said: 'We choose to go to the moon in this decade and do the other things, not because they are easy, but because they are hard.'[32]

Mission Economy devotes inspiring words to the achievement of Kennedy's ambitious aim.[33] It describes leadership by a government that had a clear vision. Government was stepping outside its traditional market-fixing role and into a market-shaping one. NASA was in the lead and demonstrated that it was able to combine centralized planning with decentralized project execution. It was an enormous undertaking, involving over 300,000 people, 20,000 contractors, and 200 universities. NASA was given the freedom to encourage risk-taking and attracting the best and brightest. Unexpected spill-overs resulted: The development of computing hardware and software for Apollo fuelled the IT revolution. Much of the technology in smartphones, such as the camera, telecommunications software, and integrated circuits, originated from the moon landing and related missions. The program also led to innovations in other sectors such as food, medicine, biology, microbiology, geology, and even toilets.

> Imagine the transformation: from a bureaucratic top-down administration to a goal-oriented stimulator of new ideas from the ground up.... If we could think and act in this way, we could realize a new vision for sustainable cities or inspire business investment in the social infrastructure and health-

[31] Ibid., 235.

[32] Part of the 1962 speech Kennedy delivered at Rice University. It must be mentioned that US policy makers were fearful that they were losing the technological battle with the USSR, after the Sputnik-launch in 1957. So, there was a strong geopolitical impulse at play.

[33] Mazzucato, M. (2021) *Mission Economy; A Moonshot Guide to Changing Capitalism*. London: Allen Lane. Chapter 4: *Lessons From Apollo: A Moonshot Guide to Change*, 59–102.

> care innovations required for a new understanding of well-being, or tackle the greatest challenges of our time such as climate change and health pandemics.[34]

In 1956, Robert Solow demonstrated that productivity gains can mostly be attributed to technological change, due to the *collective* effort behind some of the most radical technical changes where the public sector has historically taken a lead role. Mazzucato then makes a fundamental observation: 'What is required is a new and deeper understanding of public value, an expression found in philosophy but almost lost in today's economics.'[35] This value is to be created by the entire society, and it is also a goal to shape markets. The idea of public value then becomes broader than the term public good.

Once government has regained confidence, public institutions can expect success and, consequently, will be able to recruit and retain top-quality employees to replace consultants who had taken over their jobs. In this new perspective the two sectors (public and private), and all the institutions in between, nourish and reinforce each other in pursuit of the common goal of economic value creation. The sectors' interactions would then be less marked by hostility, and more infused with mutual respect.

Just as the IT revolution was chosen and directed at the time, Mazzucato suggests that now we can choose and direct 'green' and 'care' as the new paths for innovation. There are also lessons to be a learnt from mission-oriented investments, in particular America's 1960s moon project, and the climate change mission initiative taken by twenty-two European ministers and the European Union.

The Public Sector's Value

Mazzucato laments that governments are losing their self-confidence in claiming what they ought to get from their contributions to growth. What is the public sector's contribution to economic growth; in other words, what public value does it create? We saw that in the national accounts, government is lumped together with households as 'final consumers'. This suggests that it simply cannot make a surplus, earn returns, increase its

[34] Ibid., 101–102.

[35] *The Value of Everything*, 265.

productivity, or raise value added through market production. But this obscures the true importance of government in the economy. For example, value that government businesses do add is *not* shown in official statistics, nor is the value that education or health generates. The sentiment is that 'unproductive' government has to take (i.e., taxes) before it can spend. It is this false sentiment that underpins the theory of austerity—make sure to keep government small.

Keynes argued that markets were unstable and remained so in a chronic equilibrium condition of involuntary unemployment. In these circumstances, government had to act by spending money to get the economy going again. Keynes recognized government as spender of last resort, allowing the economy to produce more goods and services; in other words, government created value! Moreover, Keynes's *multiplier* suggests that an original amount injected into the economy would be multiplied, because the demand this original injected amount would lead to several rounds of additional spending. IMF studies suggest that government's multiplier spending has a positive effect on output.[36]

But what about government's role in good times? Paul Samuelson argued, as presented in Chap. 6, that in bad times government has a very useful role to play. But in normal economic times there is no role for government as a stimulator of the economy. If it would do so, it would only lead to higher inflation. During the early 1970s, Keynesian and Beveridge-inspired policies did overheat the economies of Europe and the United States, resulting in runaway inflation. Keynesianism got the blame and Milton Friedman's small government and monetarist philosophies were adopted instead, as described in Chap. 6. Mazzucato underscores that government can also create value through bailing out banks, investing in infrastructure, funding education and basic science, as well as funding radical, innovative technologies which help transform societies.

The Economics of Hope

To bring about real change we must, says Mazzucato, go beyond fixing isolated problems, and develop a near-utopian new type of economy—one that will work for the common good. The challenge is defining and

[36]One of them is IMF. (2010) *World Economic Outlook*. Washington DC: International Monetary Fund.

measuring the *collective* contribution to wealth creation, so that value extraction is less able to pass for value creation.

The notion that price determines value has had all kinds of negative consequences. First, this notion emboldened value extractors in finance, consulting firms, and other sectors of the economy. The contributions that governments made to technological breakthroughs were not recognized as value creation. Second, the metrics used to measure the contribution of the public sector and the influence of Public Choice theory, convinced many civil service workers that they were second-best. Third, with the little understanding of where value comes from, politicians and many government employees are like putty in the hands of consultancy firms claiming to be value creators. Not having a clear view of the collective value creating process, the public sector is entranced by stories about wealth creation which have led to regressive tax policies that increase inequality. Fourth, if anything that catches a price has value, then the way national accounting is done will not be able to distinguish value creation from value extraction. Only with a clear debate about the meaning of value can rent-extracting activities in every sector be better identified and deprived of political and ideological strength.

In *The Great Transformation*, Polanyi emphasized how the capitalist market has, from the start, been heavily shaped by state action. Polanyi concluded that the neoclassical notion of self-regulating markets was a myth.[37] Instead, markets are deeply embedded in social and political institutions. Keynes introduced the vital role government plays in overcoming economic depressions. Piketty warns against the dangers of inequality. Mazzucato proposes to fashion markets in ways that produce desirable outcomes such as green growth or a more equitable and caring society. Policymakers must be emboldened to broker 'deals' that generate symbiotic public-private partnerships.

The digital revolution requires participatory democracy, keeping citizens—not big business or big government—at the centre of technological change. All this requires a new understanding of policy and a new narrative as actively shaping and creating markets that achieve public value, benefitting society at large. Finally, young ambitious people might start choosing electoral politics, or careers in the civil service, over jobs in the

[37] Polanyi, K. (1944) *The Great Transformation; The Political and Economic Origins Our Time*. Boston: Beacon Press.

City or business—but only if they see that such choices are valuable and valued.[38]

Now, what direction should the economy take? Government spending and investment should create long-term growth. What counts is not just the rate of growth but in particular the *direction* of growth. For example, a green transformation requires a vast increase in the production of renewable energy and getting rid of fossil fuels; developing greener technologies; drastically decreasing the number of livestock. It also means that we develop a clear vision of what living a green life would mean. It means transforming all sectors. A green revolution will require deliberate changes in social values; i.e., a redirection of the entire economy, transforming production, distribution, and consumption in all sectors. What is needed, concludes Mazzucato, is to stir a new debate, putting value back where it belongs. We should develop a more dynamic understanding of what making and taking both mean in the context of the social objectives we share. It is badly needed for the creation of a new economics; an economics of hope!

Praise and Criticism

Given Mazzucato's outspoken progressive ideas, it is no surprise that apart from praise, she also received criticism. As for praise, *Financial Times*'s chief economic commentator, Martin Wolf, wrote about *The Entrepreneurial State* that the book is 'brilliant' and offers 'a controversial thesis' but that it is 'basically right'. Wolf also warns that the 'failure to recognize the role of government in driving innovation may well be the greatest threat to rising prosperity.'[39] Also *The Economist* (like Wolf not particularly left-leaning), congratulated Mazzucato for highlighting the state's 'central role in producing game-changing breakthroughs', and its 'contribution to the success of technology-based business', although, the newspaper added, Mazzucato is 'too hard on business.'[40] All told, *The Entrepreneurial State* was well-received.

[38] *The Value of Everything*, 277.

[39] A much-maligned engine of innovation. In: *Financial Times*, 4 August 2013.

[40] *The Entrepreneurial State*. In: *The Economist*, 24 May, 2022.

The Value of Everything was also well-received. Martin Wolf underscores Mazzucato's question: What creates value? *The Financial Times* wrote that the book will reignite a long-needed debate about what kind of world we really want to live in. If we want to replace the current parasitic system with a type of capitalism that is more sustainable, more symbiotic—that works for all, we need to ask ourselves critical questions: Where does wealth come from, which activities create it, which extract it, and which destroy it.

Mission Economy and *The Big Con* were not as enthusiastically received as her previous two books. As for *Mission Economy*, some reviewers praised Mazzucato's enthusiasm about the application of the Apollo-11 project to modern challenges. Nonetheless, it was felt that the author was a bit over-confident in government's ability to implement very large innovation-oriented projects. Governments are not always quick movers, hindered by bureaucratic rules and regulations, political influence, risk-aversion, and corruption. Possible failure must be considered in recommending these multi-faceted and costly projects. As liberal Swedish author John Norberg observes: 'such projects tend to be failures because political direction of innovation would have led to absence of objective feedback, whereas efficient progress tends to require very competitive markets with incremental innovation and power decentralized to individual entrepreneurs with their independent visions.'[41]

Perhaps a reason for the mixed reception of *The Big Con* was that its approach is polemic; it is, for example, wanting in highlighting successful consultancies that *did* add value to clients and the economy at large. After all, it is hard to understand why the consultancy sector has been able to grow so fast, if its track record would be as unimpressive as *The Big Con* suggests. In this vein, Norberg accuses Mazzucato's method of using anecdotes and stories—which say nothing of overall effects—instead of rigorous analysis.[42]

Reviewing books is one thing, what happens on the ground is another. The Apollo project, as so enthusiastically described by Mazzucato, was technical in nature, but proved to be very complex in its execution.

[41] Mission Economy by Mariana Mazzucato -could moonshot thinking help fix the planet? In: *Financial Times*, 13 January, 2021.

[42] Norberg, J. (2023) *The Capitalist Manifesto: Why the Global Free Market Will Save the World*. London: Atlantic Books, 182.

Imagine the complexities involved in Apollo-like social programs; they may turn out to be too complex to implement.

Government is reclaiming its position as value creator. Governments had taken the lead in countering the 2007 financial crisis and subsequent Great Recession. When the worldwide Covid-pandemic was raging, again, governments acted decisively in preventing their economies from sliding into a recession, in which value creation would have suffered greatly. During lockdowns, governments financially supported businesses, employees, and deserving households. Also, governments heavily subsidized development and production of anti-Covid vaccines. When in 2022, Russia closed its gas taps, affected European Union governments subsidized energy consumption of factories and consumers alike. True, these interventions were not in the spirit of Mazzucato's *Mission Economy*, but were triggered by urgent economic-financial and geopolitical challenges of the governments involved. The point is that government acted where the private sector could not.

Regarding another phenomenon criticized by Mazzucato, i.e., tax evasion by multinationals, which since 2008 had dropped significantly. Towards the end of 2021, the Organisation of Economic Cooperation and Development (OECD) agreed that 136 countries and jurisdictions, representing 90% of global trade, will ensure that multinational companies with a turnover of at least $750 million, would be subject to a minimum 15% tax rate as of 2023. This is a major reform of the international tax system, as it will result in multinational companies paying a fairer share of tax wherever they operate and generate profits.

Part II Mazzucato's Philosophical Inspiration

Introduction

Political philosopher Hannah Arendt (1906–1975) influenced Mazzucato's work. But there are also three 'worldly philosophers', to borrow Robert Heilbroner's term, who had a great influence on her ideas about the role of the state, the market, and innovation: Keynes, Polanyi, and Schumpeter. Mazzucato does not just apply their respective insights, she also expands them in her work. Arendt's life and work will be presented, focusing on its relevance for Mazzucato's work. Since Polanyi's and Keynes's life and work are presented in Chaps. 4 and 5, respectively, attention is paid to their influence on Mazzucato's work, and how the latter expands the formers' insights. Finally, Schumpeter's life and work will be briefly presented together with the influence he had on Mazzucato.

Hannah Arendt's Life and Work

Hannah Arendt was born in 1906 in Hannover, Germany. She was the only child of Jewish parents. Hannah professed no religious affiliation. She became an American citizen in 1951. Arendt died of a heart attack in 1975.

After completing her undergraduate work, Arendt continued her studies at the University of Heidelberg where she majored in philosophy under Karl Jaspers. After Hitler came to power in 1933, she left Germany and went to Paris. After the Nazi's invaded France in 1940, Arendt fled to America.[43] Upon arrival in the US, she was appointed research director of the Conference on Jewish Relations, followed by the chief-editorship at Schocker Books. After the war, she became executive secretary of Jewish Cultural Reconstruction whose objective was to recapture and redistribute cultural property looted by Nazi's from European Jews.

Initially, Arendt had difficulties finding an academic position. But in 1953, after she had been awarded a Gugenheim Fellowship the year before, she was invited to deliver the Christian Gauss lectures at Princeton University (in 1959, she returned briefly to Princeton as a visiting professor of politics[44]) which helped to kick-off her academic career. She subsequently lectured at the University of California, Berkeley, the University of Chicago, Columbia, Northwestern, Cornell and, finally, the New School in New York, where she taught political philosophy.

After the publication of *The Origins of Totalitarianism* in 1951, Arendt became a celebrated political philosopher. In 1958, she published *The Human Condition*, in which she introduced the term *vita activa*, elaborated below. In 1963, Arendt triggered a lot of controversy with the publication of *Eichmann in Jerusalem; a Report on the Banality of Evil.* The book contains the collection of essays Arendt contributed to *The New Yorker* magazine. The controversy Arendt stirred was that, contrary

[43] Varian Fry's organization helped many Jewish artists and academics, including Arendt, to escape from Europe, as depicted in the Netflix series *Transatlantic.*

[44] Arendt was the only woman to hold the rank of full professor at Princeton. When asked by an interviewer about this exceptional position, she replied: I am not at all disturbed about being a woman professor, because I am quite used to being a woman.

to expectations, she made a balanced, yet critical, analysis of Eichmann and the trial. She pointed out that Eichmann's actions were driven by blind dedication to the Nazi regime and his need to belong. Arendt also observed that Eichmann's addiction to clichés, and use of bureaucratic and law-abiding morality, clouded his ability to question his actions. She concluded that this taught us the lesson of the fearsome, word-and-thought-defying *banality of evil*.[45]

Also in 1963, she published *On Revolution*, in which she argued that the French Revolution turned out to be a disaster, while the American Revolution was a success—the leaders never lost sight of the importance of freedom. The liberal notion of freedom constitutes a crucial element in Arendt's philosophical work. In 1978, *The Life of the Mind*, consisting of three parts, saw the light. She had intended to write about the mental activities of thinking, willing, and judging. Her most recent work had focused on the first two, but went beyond this in terms of vita activa. It remained incomplete; she had just started the third part, when in 1975 she suddenly died of a heart attack. Her last work reflects her thinking on moral philosophy, to which she returned after the Eichmann process.

Mazzucato and Arendt

Robinson had observed, as we saw, that with the notion of utility in economics came mathematics, promising a new dawn for economics as a truly scientific subject. She added, however, that in an effort to become more rigorous, neoclassical economists stripped moral questions from their analysis.

Arendt had also something to say about mathematics. In *The Human Condition*, Arendt argued that 'The second key feature of science that leads to depoliticization—or, better, to a failure to engage in 'thinking what we are doing'—is science's reliance on math.'[46] For scientists have

[45] Israel was blamed of making the trial a show-trial in which Eichmann's crimes were portrayed as crimes against the state of Israel. As for Eichmann, she did not describe him as a monster and an agent of totalitarianism, but as a rather ordinary man; a bourgeois sales clerk who found a meaningful role for himself as well as a sense of importance in the Nazi movement. He was, in Arendt's words, terribly and terrifyingly normal.

Arendt was also criticized for her opinion about the role played by Jewish leaders who cooperated with the Nazi's during the war. She characterized this cooperation as a disintegration of Jewish morality. This created an uproar and animosity toward her in Israel and the Jewish community at large.

[46] Arendt, H. (2018) *The Human Condition* (Second edition). Chicago: Chicago University Press, xii. The first key feature of scientific thinking was a focus on cause and effect, on how things work that makes human reasoning substitutable by machines.

been forced to adopt a 'language' of mathematical symbols which now contains statements that cannot be translated into speech. This created a rupture in the linguistic fabric that human beings depend on, while human beings are political animals precisely because they are equipped with words.[47]

Arendt argued that the 'truths' of the modern scientific world view, though they can be demonstrated in mathematical formulas, will no longer lend themselves to normal expression in speech and thought. *The Human Condition* intends to help the reader to recognize the dangers of depolitization and explain why politization is such a good thing. After all, science tempts us into thinking that we can put an end to politics and transform the human condition into a series of technical problems that scientists would be able to solve.

Arendt simply proposed to, as mentioned, 'thinking what we are doing'. The challenge is to restore human authority over science's temptations and dangers. The same applies to the onslaught on political freedom. Citizens should take an active interest in public affairs, since this is the only way to escape totalitarianism and alienation in mass-production capitalism.

The Human Condition elaborates three fundamental human activities: labour, work and action, included in Arendt's term vita activa, in which labour is what we do out of biological necessity: feeding, procreation, and child-rearing. Work is what we do out of creative effort; to build the things that shape the world we live in and establish our social connections with others. Labour and work overlap to some extent, since loving another person is the result of social intercourse and creates the environment in which reproduction takes place. Now, what about the third fundamental human activity—action? Action identifies the effort we make together as political creatures, struggling in an environment of pluralistic diversity in pursuit of collective decisions about our polity's future course of action.[48] While labour and work belong to the social realm, action clearly belongs to the political realm.

Vita activa is a hopeful notion, said Arendt. Let me explain. Of the three human activities, action has the closest connection with the human condition of natality: 'the new beginning inherent in birth can make itself felt in the world only because the newcomer possesses the capacity of beginning something anew, that is, of acting.'[49] Arendt elaborated

[47] Ibid., xii.
[48] Ibid., xv.
[49] Ibid., 9.

natality's relevance: 'Moreover, since action is the political activity par excellence, natality, and not mortality, may be the critical category of political, as distinguished from metaphysical, thought.'[50] It is, in other words, the birth of the new men and the new beginning, the action they are capable of by virtue of being born.'

Arendt argued that vita activa can—and must—counter the inherent dangers of science and the onslaught on political freedom, by promoting the common good and public value through active citizens' participation.

Mazzucato agrees; she regrets that economic theory does not think about participation, which is left to those areas of political science focused on participatory institutions. This is an omission on the art of economics argues Mazzucato, since '……. vita activa also means the need for society to be open to real debate, the contestation of ideas and explicit conflicts over value.'[51] Participation is vital in reimagining the future together. After all, it is through democratic participation that the political and economic shortcomings laid bare in her books can be put right.

Arendt's vita activa is aimed at promoting the common good. The objective of Mazzucato's economics of hope is also the common good: To shape a near-utopian new type of economy—one that will work for the common good. This is the more urgent as electoral abstention is a concern.

Neoclassical Economics Revisited

As we saw, in the course of time economic liberalism has undergone changes, among others influenced by Hayek and Friedman. Their conservative neoclassical thinking boiled down to the view that the market was the exclusive creator of value. The market was the ideal mechanism to promote efficiency, growth, and economic stability. Government failure was thought to be much more damaging than market failure. Government should be kept as small as possible and state companies should be privatized.

Mazzucato is of course not the first economist to criticize neoclassical economics. What she does is not just benefitting from the critical analysis of Heilbroner's 'worldly philosophers', Keynes, Polanyi, and Schumpeter, she expands their ideas.

[50] Ibid., 9.
[51] *Mission Economy*, 200.

Keynes

Central Elements of Keynes's Work

Keynes proved that economies are inherently unstable. Worse, during a recession they may remain in a chronic condition of sub-normal activity in which unemployment continues to be politically problematic, and tragic for the unemployed. In these circumstances, Keynes argued that government had to act as spender of last resort. Doing so, would not only result in additional consumers' spending but would also trigger optimistic expectations of future consumption, prompting the private sector to invest again. As a result, government would create value as the economy would produce more goods and services. Keynes did not intend government to do much more.

He observed how financial markets and public attitudes to financial trading were changing; gradually, they became ends in themselves rather than facilitators of economic growth. In *The General Theory*, he wrote that Wall Street was acting not to contribute to production, but to 'betting'; speculation, in other words. Growth depends on productive investment, which is crucial for a healthy economy. This was only possible without speculation (extracting value). If 'the capital development of a country becomes a by-product of the activities of a casino, the job is likely to be ill-done.'[52]

Mazzucato and Keynes

Mazzucato *broadened* Keynes's government as spender of last resort during an economic downturn. She argues that Keynes went only part of the way. She observes that to rely strictly on Keynes, is to accept that only in a depressed economy the state might as well fund a useless search for banknotes in an abandoned coal mine, as the master himself suggested in *The General Theory*. What about the state's role in good times?

Keynes had indeed not much to say about the value creating role of the state in good times. Mazzucato quotes, with appreciation, what the late Steve Jobs argued in this realm. He said that the state should 'stay foolish' in its pursuit of technological development and social problem solving.[53] *The Entrepreneurial State* and *Mission Economy* contain, as we saw, many examples of value creating government investments. Mazzucato's idea of

[52] *The Value of Everything*, 119.

[53] *The Entrepreneurial State*, 209–210.

an entrepreneurial state includes government investing in areas that the private sector would not invest in, even if it had the resources. Indeed, another visionary risk-taking role of the state.

Polanyi

Relevant Elements of His Work

Polanyi argued that it was wrong to treat nature and human beings as objects whose price is determined by market forces. Such a concept, he said, violates the principles that have governed societies for centuries; nature and human life have almost always been recognized as having a sacred dimension. Polanyi presented a dark perspective: Once the natural environment is turned into economic commodities, one can be sure of its destruction.

When in 1944 *The Great Transformation* came out, Polanyi hoped that after the end of the war, a situation might emerge in which both national economies and the global economy would be subordinated to democratic politics. He proposed that human beings use the instruments of democratic governance to control and direct the economy to meet their needs.[54]

Polanyi's central theme is that instead of the historically normal pattern of subordinating the economy to society, the system of self-regulating markets required subordinating society to the market. This meant running of society as an adjunct to the market, instead of the economy embedded in social relations, as in antique societies. Polanyi called this latter notion: embeddedness. Before the nineteenth century, when, as he called it, market liberalism took off, the human economy was always embedded in society. He observed that price-making markets never completely dominated economic decision-making. Even during the nineteenth century, a large percentage of allocative decisions did not occur in price-making markets; elements of reciprocity and redistribution also played a significant part.

The tumultuous developments of the late nineteenth and first half of the twentieth century, demonstrated that unfettered market liberalism triggered an inevitable response: A concerted effort to protect society from the market. Polanyi called this continuing tension and conflict the

[54] 'As regards national economies, perhaps the Nordic countries, applying a Middle Way, come closest to functioning as proposed by Polanyi in maintaining a delicate balance between the exigencies of the market and societal considerations.'. Source: De Haan, P. (2016) *From Keynes to Piketty, The Century that Shook Up Economics*. London: Palgrave Macmillan, 163.

double movement. This consisted of efforts to establish, maintain, and spread the self-regulating market on the one hand, and efforts to protect people and society from the market's consequences on the other. Hence, the self-regulating market was impaired in its movements through the correcting influence of the other movement.

Towards the end of *The Great Transformation*, Polanyi concluded: 'Economic history reveals that the emergence of a national market was in no way the result of the gradual and spontaneous emancipation of the economic sphere from government control. On the contrary, the market has been the outcome of a conscious and often violent intervention on the part of government which imposed the market organization on society for non-economic ends. In short, the self-regulating market was simply a myth! The author observed that the road to the free market was opened by an enormous increase in centrally organized and controlled State interventions.

> To make Adam Smith's simple and natural liberty compatible with the needs of a human society was a most complicated affair....Just as, contrary to expectations, the invention of labor-saving machinery had not diminished but actually increased the use of human labor, the introduction of the free market, far from doing away with the need for control, regulation and intervention, enormously increased their range. Administrators had to be constantly on the watch to ensure the free working of the system.[55]

Mazzucato and Polanyi

Mazzucato recognizes and appreciates important functions of the state beyond the 'duties of the sovereign', as Smith had defined them. And she appreciates Polanyi's analysis of the market. Neoclassical economists maintain that the market should best be left alone to optimally run the economy. We saw that Polanyi begged to differ; he argued that government intervenes and co-shapes the market. In *The Value of Everything*, Mazzucato observes that government is totally missing from, what in microeconomics is known as the production function. This implies that only firms create value. Government is left outside the production boundaries.[56]

[55] *The Great Transformation*, 146–147. Even free market champion and Mont Pèlerin Society inspirator, Friedrich Hayek also acknowledged the role of the state in shaping the market. 'Hayek also stressed how the state necessarily shaped what he later called 'the competitive order'.' Source: Burns, J. (2023) *Milton Friedman; the Last Conservative.* New York: Farrar, Straus and Giroux, 165.

[56] *The Value of Everything*, 232.

She elaborates Polanyi's insight of the state's increased role, not just in co-shaping markets but also as a value creator. The state evolved from an inertial bureaucratic 'leviathan' to the very catalyst for new business investment. In other words, from a market fixer and co-shaper to a value creator; from simply 'de-risking' the private sector to welcoming and taking on risk, due to the opportunities it presents for future growth.[57] Rather than analysing the state's active role in only correcting market failures, Mazzucato argues that it is necessary to build a theory of the state's role in not just co-shaping markets but also creating entirely new ones. She thus expands Polanyi's ideas about the relationship between state and market. This also applies to innovation: The state should not just 'crowd in' business investment but also dynamize it in creating the vision, the mission and the plan.

Mazzucato concludes that, again in line with Polanyi, the market economy will always be subordinate to the state and subject to its changes. But she has a warning: Policymakers must better learn how to efficiently use the tools and means to shape and create markets, i.e., making things happen, as Keynes said, that otherwise would not. She combines this warning with hope: 'The very fact that the market is co-shaped by different actors—including policymakers—offers hope that a better future *can* be constructed.'[58]

Schumpeter

Life and Work

Unlike the typical economist, Joseph Alois Schumpeter did not lead a dull life; far from it. In his younger years he was an *enfant terrible*. He was alleged to have said that he had three wishes in life: To become a great lover, a great horseman, and a great economist. He quipped that two of the three had already been granted to him and added that there were already too many fine horsemen in Austria.

Schumpeter was born in February 1883 in Triesch (now Trest, Czech Republic), then part of the Austro-Hungarian Empire. His father died when Joseph was only 4 years old. His mother decided to move to Graz in

[57] *The Entrepreneurial State*, 15–16.
[58] *The Value of Everything*, 275.

Austria, as she wanted the best possible education for her son. When Joseph was eleven years old, his mother married a retired general. She convinced her new husband to move to Vienna. Thanks to his stepfather's aristocratic connections, Joseph could attend the *Theresianum*, one of the best secondary schools of the empire. At the *Theresianum* he developed his aristocratic manners, promiscuous habits, and elegant tastes. But he was also a curious scholar, who, besides law, read philosophy, economics, and sociology. He studied law, in which he earned a PhD, at the University of Vienna. He lived for some time in England, where in 1907, he married an English lady. The couple left for Egypt where he managed the capital of a wealthy person and where he wrote his first scholarly work. After Schumpeter fell ill, the couple returned to England in 1909.

He was appointed associate professor at the University of Czernowitz, Ukraine, where he wrote *The Theory of Economic Development* (1911). After three years in Czernowitz, Schumpeter was appointed professor in political economy at the University of Graz. During the academic year 1913–1914, Schumpeter was invited to teach at Columbia University, New York. During the Great War, Schumpeter stayed in Austria. After the war, he was invited to become Minister of Finance in Chancellor Karl Renner's Cabinet. But Austria was broke; the empire had fallen apart, and inflation was running out of control. The war reparations Austria was supposed to pay, sealed the country's fate. Schumpeter could not turn the tide. This ended his brief political career. As farewell present he was given a banking license, and in 1921, he was appointed director of the Biedermann Bank. Also this career did not end well; in 1924 the bank collapsed. Schumpeter lost his savings.

Schumpeter plunged into work; he accepted guest-lectureships at Harvard and, subsequently, Tokyo College. In 1932, he was appointed full professor at Harvard University, and seven years later he became an American citizen. He married Elizabeth Boody who assisted him in preparing his publications, including *History of Economic Analysis*, which came out four years after Schumpeter died on 8 January 1950.

Creative Destruction

Schumpeter contributed much to economics. His best-known invention of creative destruction was an important inspiration for Mazzucato. Creative destruction, observed Schumpeter, is brought about by visionary entrepreneurs. Such an entrepreneur, or group of entrepreneurs, is willing to convert a new idea, or invention, into a successful innovation. Innovation includes not just the introduction of a new product, but can also involve a new process, or a new market for an existing product or process. This type of entrepreneurship replaces in whole or in part, inferior innovations in markets and industries, while at the same time creating new products, including new business models, and in so doing destroying the lead of incumbents. Entrepreneurship involves, in short, taking risks and facing uncertainty. An entrepreneur is willing to put his career and financial security on the line. Creative destruction is responsible for the dynamism of industries and long-term economic growth. 'Each major new technology leads to creative destruction: The steam engine, the railway, electricity, electronics, the car, the computer, the Internet.'[59]

Mazzucato's Inspiration from Schumpeter

Not just entrepreneurs invest in innovation, as Schumpeter suggested, governments do so as well, as Mazzucato demonstrates in *The Entrepreneurial State*. Where the costs are large, and the risks are high, not entrepreneurs but government provides the majority of long-term finance. In other words, in these conditions the state is leading in radical but always risky innovation. In 2008, the US government funded 57% of basic research, while the private sector funded only 18%. The development of Silicon Valley is exemplary. Only after high-risk public funds had been invested, risk-averse venture capital was prepared to step in. In short: Government investment triggered private sector wealth creation. Mazzucato regrets that very little or nothing of government's investment is being paid back by benefitting firms by way of taxes or other means.

A distinction can be made between funding research and development (R&D) in general advancement of knowledge, and mission-oriented projects. The latter target a government agency (such as NASA) or a specific goal that government wants to achieve in e.g., defence, health, energy, or industrial-technology programmes. The former, the general advancement of knowledge type, is typically undertaken in overcoming market failures. It is not so much the quantity of R&D that matters, but how it is distributed throughout an economy, often—and this is important in Mazzucato's thinking—reflective of the crucial role of the state in influencing its distribution.

[59] *The Entrepreneurial State*, 64.

Mazzucato observes that the connection between Keynesian fiscal spending and Schumpeterian investment in innovation is the missing micro-macro connection in modern-day economics.[60] However, in the real economy the connection is there. Not only is it true that productive investments (thanks to innovation) generate growth, but it is also true that when spending was directed at the IT Revolution, as during the past few decades, and the green revolution now, the Keynesian multiplier effect will be even stronger. Nonetheless, Mazzucato warns that in order to understand the dynamics of these investments, it is fundamental to better understand different perspectives on the theory of economic growth first, and then to establish the role of technology and innovation in driving that economic growth.[61]

Conclusion

Mazzucato attacks neoclassical economics not just in having replaced value by utility, but also in its over-appreciation of the role the market plays in an economy and under-appreciation of government's role in redressing market anomalies, and in its value-creating role. She is one of the most prominent economists demonstrating where economic developments have gone wrong since the early 1980s when neoclassical economics was transformed into neoliberalism, moulded by the political leadership in America and Great Britain.

Mazzucato contributes to a re-appreciation of the role of government in the economy, not just as value creator but also as an engine promoting the economy's productivity. A recent proof is Mario Draghi's report *The Future of European Competitiveness*, commissioned by the European Commission, in which a European DARPA is proposed.

[60] Mazzucato may have overlooked that in the 1960s, Economics Nobel Laureate, Edmund Phelps developed the beginnings of a micro-macro theory. 'My work in the 1960s on the formation of expectations on which to build a micro-macro theory and the further contributions at the ensuing microfoundations conference in January 1969 constituted a new body of micro-macro theory that might be called new modern—with Knight, Keynes and Hayek being the *first* modernists.' Phelps further observes: 'The work of Lucas and others built the micro-macro theory often called New Classical Theory.' Subsequently, Phelps makes a critical remark: 'As I saw it, the New Classicals, with their adherence to 'rational expectations', showed they had little or no sense of a modern economy—an economy that, at its core, is driven by the judgement, intuitions, and imagination of a modern people.' Source: Phelps, E. (2023) *My Journeys in Economic Theory*. New York: Columbia University Press, 96–97.

[61] *The Entrepreneurial State*, 39.

References

Arendt, H. (2018). *The Human Condition* (2nd ed.). Chicago University Press.

Burns, J. (2023). *Milton Friedman; The Last Conservative.* Farrar, Straus and Giroux.

De Haan, P. (2016). *From Keynes to Piketty, The Century that Shook Up Economics.* Palgrave Macmillan.

IMF. (2010). *World Economic Outlook.* International Monetary Fund.

Mazzucato, M. (2013). *The Entrepreneurial State; Debunking Public Vs. Private Sector Myths.* Anthem Press.

Mazzucato, M. (2018). *The Value of Everything; Making and Taking in The Global Economy.* Allen Lane.

Mazzucato, M. (2021). *Mission Economy; A Moonshot Guide to Changing Capitalism.* Allen Lane.

Mazzucato, M., & Collington, R. (2023). *The Big Con; How the Consulting Industry, Weakens Our Businesses, Infantilizes Our Government and Warps Our Economies.* Allen Lane.

Norberg, J. (2023). *The Capitalist Manifesto: Why the Global Free Market Will Save the World.* Atlantic Books.

Perez, C. The Double Bubble at the Turn of the Century: Technological Roots and Structural Implications. *Cambridge Journal of Economics.*

Phelps, E. (2023). *My Journeys in Economic Theory.* Columbia University Press.

Polanyi, K. (1944). *The Great Transformation; The Political and Economic Origins Our Time.* Beacon Press.

Robinson, J. (1974). *Economic Philosophy.* Pelican Books.

Sandel, M. (2013). *What Money Can't Buy; The Moral Limits of Markets.* Penguin Books.

Skidelsky, R. (2010). *Keynes, A Very Short Introduction.* Oxford University Press.

CHAPTER 9

Thomas Piketty's Crusade Against Inequality

Prologue

Thomas Piketty, like Mazzucato, is a global celebrity. He drew the world's attention with his blockbuster *Capital in the Twenty-First Century*, which came out when the Great Recession had just been brought under control. There was much which had gone wrong. The neoliberal order had turned economies in, as Piketty calls it, hyper capitalistic economies.

But there was also a long-running undercurrent in the economic system which Piketty exposed: The growing gap between rich and poor. Robert Solow underscored that this insight is one that no one before Piketty had discovered. This gap is not just widening; the wealthy had benefitted disproportionally—they got richer by the day. The system was based on neoliberal notions about freeing up the market and keeping government small, so as to promote growth, of which everybody, it was thought, would benefit. All along, liberalism had promoted equal opportunities, rather than redistribution of income and wealth. This did not work; the gap was widening, observes Piketty, and in drawing the attention to this lethal trend, he is a game-changer, strongly refuting trickling down theory or any other soothing perspectives.

He was not the first one to draw attention to this phenomenon. Long before him, Plato had argued that it was impossible for the wealthy to be just to others. Plato had been inspired by Socrates who had spoken of a

P. de Haan, *Great Economists and the Evolution of Economic Liberalism*, https://doi.org/10.1007/978-3-031-93831-3_9

'city of the rich' and a 'city of the poor', and concluded that two different modes of existence made a single society impossible.[1]

The timing of *Capital*'s launch was perfect. The reason why *Capital* received worldwide attention was that people were still shocked of what had gone wrong in the economy; they saw that the system, resulted in a widening gap between the rich and poor. The second reason why Piketty and *Capital* drew so much attention was his unprecedented thorough historical analysis.

Introduction

Inequality has been around for most of mankind's history. Adam Smith published *The Wealth of Nations* in 1776. His analysis of economic development centred around the creation of wealth through the efficient division of labour. As for labour, Smith presented the subsistence theory of wages, allowing workers to survive. He died before the Industrial Revolution brought about a wide gap between rich industrialists and poor workers. Karl Marx predicted that capitalism, which created wealth *and* poverty, would collapse. His prediction was wrong. Nonetheless, inequality of capital and income remained on the political agenda; however, it did not always get the attention it needs. Piketty brought inequality forcefully back on top of the agenda, thanks to his monumental work *Capital in the Twenty-First Century*.[2]

As regards the economists presented in this book, Keynes discussed inequality in *The General Theory*. In the chapter dealing with observations on the nature of capital, he wrote that in a situation where capital goods would be so abundant that the marginal efficiency of capital would drop to zero, this might be the most sensible way of gradually getting rid of many of the objectionable features of capitalism. One consequence would be, in Keynes's own words 'the *euthanasia of the rentier*, and, consequently, the euthanasia of the oppressive power of the capitalist to exploit the scarcity-value of capital.' Keynes concluded:

[1] Snyder, T. (2024) *On Freedom*. London: The Bodley Head, 154. On p. 256, Snyder quotes what Thomas Jefferson had dreamed about equality: 'Can any condition of society be more desirable than this?'

[2] Piketty, T. (2014) *Capital in the Twenty-First Century*. Cambridge: The Belknap Press of Harvard University Press.

> For a little reflection will show what enormous social changes would result from a gradual disappearance of a rate of return on accumulated wealth. A man would still be free to accumulate his earned income with a view to spending it at a later date. But his accumulation would not grow.[3]

That Keynes was not insensitive about income and wealth distribution also shines clearly through in yet another observation: He argued that the outstanding faults of the economic society in which we live are its failure to provide for full employment and its arbitrary and inequitable distribution of wealth and incomes.[4]

Friedman also analysed the inequality issue, not from a moral, but from a efficiency point of view. However, he was not totally insensitive about the plight of the lowest income earners. In *Capitalism and Freedom*,[5] he presented his *negative income tax* proposal, meaning that income earners below a certain minimum level should receive a subsidy (i.e., a negative income tax) from the government to make both ends meet.

In *The Road to Serfdom*, Hayek argued that governments' income redistribution policies will only put a brake on economic growth, as the rich will have less incentive to invest; the fruits of their efforts will be taken away by high taxes.[6]

Kuznets presented the *Kuznets curve* in his 1954 Presidential Address at the American Economic Association's meeting in Detroit. Kuznets argued that, across time, inequality follows a U-shaped path. Inequality will increase during the initial stages of industrialization and then decrease over the course of the industrialization process. Once this is maturing, the demand for specialized knowledge will increase, resulting in higher wages for those who can offer this special knowledge. So, first there will be a widening gap between the various income groups, which will be followed by sharply decreasing inequality. As we will see, Piketty rejects the economic automatism implied in the Kuznets Curve. The reduction in

[3] Keynes, J.M. (1964) *The General Theory of Employment, Interest and Money*. New York: A Harvest Book; Harcourt Brace & Company, 221.

[4] Ibid., 372.

[5] Friedman, M. (2002) *Capitalism and Freedom*. Fortieth Anniversary Edition. Chicago: Chicago University Press.

[6] Hayek, F. (1944) *The Road to Serfdom*. London: Routledge. Hayek also argued that any political project based on social justice would lead straight to collectivism and totalitarianism.

inequality between 1914 and 1945 was due, not to the evolution of the economy, says Piketty, but to the two world wars and the Great Depression. In addition, inequalities have grown sharply in the US over the last thirty years, returning to their 1930 level. In an article published in 2011, written by him, Anthony Atkinson, and Emmanuel Saez, they explained why inequality first rose, then dropped, but subsequently rose again.[7] This article was a harbinger of what Piketty would present a couple of years later in his best seller *Capital*.

Samuelson had the following to say about the relationship between inequality and the market mechanism. He confessed that in this realm he had a dream: '…I have a dream of a humane economy that is at the same time efficient and respecting of personal (if not business) freedoms. Much of producing and consuming decisions involve use of the market mechanism. But the worst inequalities of condition that result from reliance on market forces—even in the presence of equality of ex ante opportunity—can be mitigated by the transfer of powers of the democratic state.'[8] He called this economics with a heart.

Sen is clearly preoccupied with inequality, poverty, and the *capabilities* people have (or not have) to leave poverty and inequality behind. In Chap. 7, Sen describes his capability approach. Piketty writes about Sen's capability approach:

> '…. Basic rights and material advantages must be extended insofar as possible to everyone, as long as it is in the interest of those who have the fewest rights and opportunities to do so. The 'difference principle' introduced by the US philosopher John Rawls in his *Theory of Justice* is similar in intent. And the 'capabilities approach' favored by the Indian economist Amartya Sen is not very different in its basic logic.'[9]

Mazzucato is a vocal critic of the philosophy of neoclassical philosophy, as extensively described in Chap. 8. Inequality is just one of the phenomena, argues Mazzucato, for which neoclassical economics is to blame and how

[7] Atkinson, A., Piketty, T., Saez, E. Top incomes in the Long Run of History. In: *Journal of Economic Literature*, 49 (March 2011), 3–71.

[8] Szenberg, M.(1992) *Eminent Economists; Their Life Philosophies.* Cambridge: Cambridge University Press, 240.

[9] *Capital in the Twenty-First Century*, 480.

it was moulded by politicians into neoliberal policies. Mazzucato criticizes inequality in various instances in her works. Right at the beginning of *The Value of Everything*, she observes:

> America's GDP roughly tripled from \$5.49 trillion to \$17.29 trillion. During these four decades, productivity grew by about 60%. Yet from 1979 onwards real hourly wages for the great majority of American workers stagnated or even fallen. In other words, for almost four decades a tiny elite has captured nearly all the gains from the expanding economy. Is this because they are particularly productive members of society?[10]

Finally, Ingrid Robeyns wrote *Limitarianism* in which she attacks inequality from the top down: Extreme wealth is to be brought down to acceptable levels.[11] What she has to say is presented in the text below.

Part I Piketty's Life and Work

Piketty argues that capitalism is good for the wealthy, but not for the less well-off. There is no automatism within the capitalist system to keep the gap between rich and the rest within reasonable proportions. This, according to Piketty, can only be achieved through state intervention. Neither did he have warm feelings for centrally planned societies. In 1991, young Thomas visited the Soviet-Union and he saw there that central planning did not work. He became a believer in capitalism, private property, and the market. However, he felt that checks and balances had to be applied by the state, to keep the system stable.

Thomas Piketty was born on 7 May 1971 in the Parisian suburb Clichy. His parents had left-leaning sympathies. Thomas's brilliance came to light at an early age. He entered the prestigious École Normale Supérieure (ENS) when he was 18 years old. He studied economics and mathematics and earned his PhD when he was only 22. He wrote his thesis at the École des Hautes Études en Sciences Sociales (EHESS) and at the London School of Economics (LSE). His thesis dealt with wealth distribution and won the award for the best thesis from the French Economics Association.

[10] Mazzucato, M. (2018) *The Value of Everything; Making and Taking in the Global Economy*. London: Allen Lane, xiii.

[11] Robeyns, I. (2024) *Limitarianism; The Case Against Extreme Wealth*. New York: Astra House.

From 1993 to 1995 Piketty held the position of associate professor in the Economics Department of the Massachusetts Institute of Technology (MIT) at Cambridge, Massachusetts. In 1995, he returned to France to take up a research position at the French National Centre for Scientific Research. In 2000, he became professor at the EHESS.

One important reason for my choice (to return to France; PdH) has a direct bearing on this book: I did not find the work of US economists entirely convincing. To be sure, they were all very intelligent, and I still have many friends from that period of my life. But something strange happened: I was only too aware of the fact that I knew nothing at all about the world's economic problems…I quickly realized that there had been no significant effort to collect historical data on the dynamics of inequality since Kuznets, yet the profession continued to churn out purely theoretical results without even knowing what facts needed to be explained.…When I returned to France, I set out to collect the missing data.'[12]

In 2006, Piketty founded the Paris School of Economics where he is Professor of Economics. As of 2015, he combines this position with that of Centennial Professor of Economics in the International Inequalities Institute at LSE, where he participates in research activities of LSE's International Inequalities Institute.

While at the Paris School of Economics, he worked on his 'chef-d'oeuvre' *Capital au XXIe siècle*, which, surprisingly, did not receive an overwhelming reception when in 2013 the *Seuil* edition came out in France. One year later, it was Arthur Goldhammer's English translation *Capital in the Twenty-First Century* that catapulted Piketty to world fame. Other noteworthy books by Piketty are *Capital and Ideology*, which appeared in 2019, focusing on income inequality in various societies in history. Three years later, Piketty published a much shorter book than its predecessor: *A Brief History of Equality*, which deals with wealth distribution once again.

[12] *Capital in the Twenty-First Century*, 31–32.

In 2012, Piketty supported François Hollande's candidacy for the French Presidency. However, he became disappointed in Hollande's tenure as President; he described the latter as 'hopeless'. During the period 2015–2016, Piketty briefly helped the British Labour Party with the formulation of an economic policy that would tackle Britain's biggest economic challenges. However, having blamed Labour for its weak EU referendum campaign, he resigned.

Honours

In 2002, Piketty won the prize for best young economist in France, comparable to the American John Bates Clark Medal.[13] In 2013, Piketty received the Yrjö Jahnsson Award for the economist under the age of 45 who 'made a contribution in theoretical and applied research that is significant to the study of economics in Europe'. On 2 October 2015, Piketty received an honorary doctorate from the University of Johannesburg. The next day, he delivered the 13th Annual Nelson Mandela Lecture there.

Work

Looking at his publications, Piketty is an economic historian, specialized in public finance and issues of wealth concentration and inequality, with a heavy emphasis on long-term trends supported by statistical data, including tax records. Some of his best work was co-authored by Emmanuel Saez, a French-American economist. Piketty and Saez were both influenced by Sir Anthony Atkinson, the *éminence grise* of inequality and poverty at Nuffield College, Oxford, and LSE. Piketty considers himself primarily to be a social and economic historian. In his work as a social scientist, he looks at the history of equality.[14]

[13] There is a striking similarity between Piketty's career and that of his compatriot Esther Duflo. Both studied at the ENS. Duflo is now Abdul Latif Jameel Professor of Poverty Alleviation and Development Economics at MIT. In 2010, she received the John Bates Clark Medal. And in 2019, she was awarded the Nobel Prize in Economics for her groundbreaking work on Randomized Control Trials, together with her husband Abhijit Banerjee, and Michael Kremer.

[14] Piketty, T., and Sandel, M. (2025) *Equality; What It Means and Why It Matters.* Cambridge: Polity Press, 18. On p. 26 Piketty adds: 'I view my work more as that of doing social and economic history -I mean somewhere at the intersection between socioeconomic history and political economy, in the old sense which recognizes the full moral and political dimension of political economy.'

Capital in the Twenty-First Century offers the reader an impressive historical analysis, spanning 250 years of income and wealth data across the countries that had collected statistical and other economic data, such as tax declarations. Piketty uses them to underscore his concern about the growing inequality in income and wealth. During the *Belle Epoque*, the richest people in Europe controlled 90% of all wealth. Piketty calls this period *patrimonial capitalism*. He argues that, once again, a similar situation is emerging in Europe:

> In the years after World War II many people thought capitalism had been almost eradicated. Yet at the beginning of the twenty-first century, Europe seems to be in the avant-garde of the new patrimonial capitalism, with private fortunes once again surpassing US levels. This is fairly well explained by the low rate of economic and especially demographic growth in Europe compared with the United States.[15]

The essence of *Capital* can be captured by the formula: $r > g$. As long as the return on capital (r) is higher than the percentage of economic growth (g), this will result in an ever-increasing concentration of wealth. This process is not self-correcting. Taking into consideration that the wealth distribution is (very) uneven, it can be projected that inequality will increase.

Inequality is not an accident, argues Piketty, but a feature of capitalism. Once constituted, capital reproduces itself faster than the increase in output. Even a small gap between the return on capital and the rate of growth can—in the long run—have powerful and destabilizing effects on the structure and stability of societies. To address this threat, Piketty proposes, apart from more investment in education, redistribution through a progressive global wealth tax. After *Capital*, Piketty did not stop publishing. He wrote many articles (often together with other economists) and more books saw the light since 2014. *Capital and Ideology*[16] stands out, not just because it is even more bulky than *Capital*, but also it describes the philosophical underpinnings of unequal income and wealth distribution, which will be elaborated in Part II.

[15] *Capital in the Twenty-First Century*, 154.

[16] Piketty, T. (2020) *Capital and Ideology*. Cambridge: The Belknap Press of Harvard University Press.

Capital in the Twenty-First Century

Introduction

Inequality tends to evolve pro-cyclically, i.e., it moves in the same direction as the economic cycle. One of its consequences is that during the Great Recession, the purchasing power of the lower and middle classes stagnated or even diminished, which was not helpful in overcoming the recession. From a political view point, the superrich wield more and more political influence, including over their own remuneration packages. Piketty argues that large and increasing inequality may trigger political instability.

As regards the high remuneration of 'supermanagers', that contributes to widening the gap, Piketty questions the justification for such high levels of compensation. There is none: Empirical studies revealed that there is no relation between very high salaries of these supermanagers and their performance. Now, what can be done about increasing inequality? Piketty suggests investing more in education, as better educated people can get better-paid jobs. However, his central proposal is taxing the (very) wealthy by introducing a global wealth tax. As this is not easy to achieve; he proposes a gradual approach towards this goal.

A 685-page long book, like *Capital in the Twenty-First Century*, can be summarized either in an expanded manner or by way of capturing the essence of *Capital*'s analysis and message. I have chosen the latter option, as this book, given its political implications, should in fact be read in full by politicians, scholars, students and the general readership alike. To underscore my choice, I quote *New Yorker* staff writer John Cassidy: Piketty has written a book that nobody interested in a defining issue of our era can afford to ignore.

Apart from an introduction, the book consists of four parts. Part one is about income and capital. The second part is entitled: *The Dynamics of the Capital/income Ratio.* Part three deals with the structure of inequality, and part four includes proposals regarding the regulation of capital in the twenty-first century.

Inequality: How It Began

A memorable sentence in *Capital*'s Introduction sets the book's tone: '…capitalism automatically generates arbitrary and unsustainable inequalities that radically undermine the meritocratic values on which democratic societies are based.'[17] Piketty describes the thinking of the 'classics', starting with Adam Smith, and how they valued the role of capital in the process of economic development. Until the Industrial Revolution, the possession of land embodied wealth. Since then, capital took the upper hand. More and more capital was concentrated in the hands of a few industrialists. Labourers received very low wages resulting from an oversupply of workers who had left the countryside to look for work in industrial cities.

Once the industrialization process matured, the demand for specialized skills increased, resulting in higher wages for workers. The gap between the owners of capital and those who acquired their income through work diminished. This is what Kuznets observed—the *Kuznets Curve* is a reflection of the same. But was Kuznets right? No, says Piketty. The reason being that Kuznets developed his curve during the middle of the past century, when capital had dramatically diminished as a result of the two world wars (during which a lot of installed capital was destroyed); the decolonization process that started after WW II; some industries were nationalized; and labour improved its bargaining power. So, not only economic factors, but also institutional and political factors played their part. The *capital/income ratio* changed in favour of income, which explains why the role of capital in the analysis of inequality lost the interest of economists at the time.[18]

This lack of interest was unjustified, as the situation changed in the second half of the past century. Private capital regained prominence. Thanks to higher wages, people were able to save and invested their savings in capital (such as real estate); others gained a lot of money in private business, sports, and entertainment. The income from capital also increased substantially.

First Fundamental Law of Capitalism

The capital/income ratio (ß) is simply related to the share of income from capital in the national income, denoted as α, and r is the rate of return on

[17] *Capital in the Twenty-First Century*, 1.

[18] Perhaps illustrative is the title of the book of the late Groningen University professor Jan Pen (1921–2010), published by Penguin Books in 1971: *Income Distribution*. Pen put the emphasis on income, while Piketty emphasized the role of capital. Another striking difference with Piketty's work is that Pen discussed the relationship between the decreasing share of the very rich with the decreasing share of capital.

capital, so: $\alpha = r \times \text{ß}$. Piketty calls $\alpha = r \times \text{ß}$ the first fundamental law of capitalism, which links the stock of capital to the flow of income from capital. The author gives an example: if ß is 600% and $r = 5\%$, then $\alpha = \mathrm{r} \times \text{ß} = 30\%$. In simple terms, if national wealth represents the equivalent of 6 years of national income, and if the rate of return on capital is 5% per year, then capital's share in national income is 30%. It expresses a transparent relationship among the three most important concepts for analysing the capitalist system: (i) The capital/income ratio, (ii) the share of capital in income, and (iii) the rate of return on capital. The capital/income ratio is, as noted, changing again in favour of capital. Piketty observes that in most developed countries capital represents 4 to 6 times national income of these countries.

To summarize: Towards the end of the *Belle Epoque* capital provided the largest contribution to total income. This contribution diminished during the first half of the twentieth century. As of the second half of the twentieth century, the role of capital is increasing again.

Piketty also analyses the development of the return on capital:

> More important, there is a set of forces of divergence associated with the process of accumulation and concentration of wealth when growth is weak and the return of capital is high. This second process is potentially more destabilizing than the first (i.e., top earners who quickly separate themselves from the rest; PdH), and it no doubt represents the principal threat to an equal distribution of wealth over the long run.[19]

In such a situation—*when the return of capital is higher than economic growth*—concentration of wealth will be in the hands of an ever smaller number of individuals. This is contrary to what the standard economic theory tells us. It suggests that the return on capital would be dependent on the level of economic growth; when g (economic growth) would drop, so would r (return on capital).

Piketty analyses the historical trend of r in relation to g, and concludes that r, including return on inherited wealth, grew faster than g. And in a situation where g drops, r diminishes less. So, all told: $r > g$.

He warns us that one should interpret his findings with care. He based his insight partly on estimates and extrapolations. And we know from history that economic extrapolations are not necessarily reliable indicators of

[19] *Capital in the Twenty-First Century*, 23.

what will happen. In addition, he only took the developments in France and Britain as the basis for a global trend.[20]

Piketty estimates the average *r* to be 4–5% per annum, based upon the average rate of return on capital growth in the period 1900–2010. Given the low economic growth prevailing in the developed world, *r* would remain larger than *g* in the foreseeable future.

Forces of convergence also exist, and in certain countries at certain times they may prevail, but the forces of divergence can at any point regain the upper hand. A likely decrease in the rate of growth of both the population and the economy in coming decades makes this trend all the more worrisome.[21]

Average low economic growth percentages should not be confused with those of exceptional periods, such as Europe's reconstruction period after the end of WWII, Japan's phenomenal growth in the same period, or China's during the past four decades. Nonetheless, Piketty estimates that economic growth during this century will be between 1% and 2.5%.

Now, given the trends of (i) the rate of return on capital *r* has historically been higher than *g*, and (ii) wealth as a source of income is growing again, this leads to the conclusion that inequality must be increasing as well. The rich will see their income and wealth grow faster than people who do not possess capital and only receive a salary for the work they perform.

Second Fundamental Law of Capitalism

A country that saves a lot and grows slowly will, over the long run, accumulate a substantial stock of capital relative to its income, which can have a significant impact on its social structure and distribution of wealth. Piketty then introduces the second fundamental law of capitalism: ß = *s/g;* wherein ß is the capital/income ratio, *s* the savings rate and *g* the economic growth rate. Again, Piketty provides an example on page 170: If a country is saving 12% of its income every year, and if its initial stock is equal to 6 years of income, then the capital stock will grow at 2% a year,[22] thus at exactly the

[20] Piketty's main data source is the World Top Income Database (WTID), in the establishment of which he participated. Twenty seven countries are included in this database; it is debatable whether this group of 27 is representative enough for the entire world. For example, no data are included from Russia, neither from most African countries, nor from emerging economies. Apart from WTID, Piketty also used data from tax declarations, data on wage and price developments, capital and household enquiries, as well as wealth rankings from *Forbes Magazine*.

[21] *Capital in the Twenty-First Century*, 27.

[22] 12% of income gives 12 divided by 6, or 2% of capital. More generally, if the savings rate is *s* and the capital/income ratio is ß, then the capital stock grows at a rate equal to s/ß.

same rate as the national income, so that the capital/income ratio will remain stable. In a quasi-stagnant society, wealth that was accumulated in the past will inevitably acquire disproportional importance.

The Structure of Inequality

Part three of *Capital* is devoted to the structure of inequality. The question is what does inequality look like worldwide? How did it evolve across time? In almost every country there has always been a more unequal distribution of capital than income:

> The first regularity we observe when we try to measure income inequality in practice is that inequality with respect to capital is always greater than inequality with respect to labor. The distribution of capital ownership (and of income from capital) is always more concentrated than the distribution of income from labor.[23]

This goes for all parts of the world and for each historical period.

Piketty then analyses, for different periods and for different countries, how much capital or income would go to the top 10% and, subsequently, to the very top 1%. In some instances Piketty analyses the share that goes to the 0.1% of the population. Looking at the distribution of income from labour, the top 10% earns between 25% and 30% of the total labour income. As regards capital, the picture is as follows: Through time, the top 10% owns 50% of total capital.

In short, capital is, generally speaking, more concentrated in the hands of a smaller percentage of the population than income. There were exceptions though. During the *Belle Epoque*, the richest 10% of the French population owned 90% of all capital. Between 1910 and 1970, however, their share dropped to 60%. As noted, the two world wars and France's loss of its colonies explain to a large extent this fall in capital.

As regards the poorest 50% of the population, they owned on average at most 5% of the capital stock, again through time. This even goes for the past century, despite the fact that there was a *convergence* between rich and poor during a considerable period. True, everybody benefited from economic growth; however, the *distribution* of the fruits of this growth did not change much; the 50% poorest section of the population did not see their capital share increase.

[23] *Capital in the Twenty-First Century*, 244.

Looking at France's total income, since 1910 the share of the top 10% fell considerably: dropping from close to 50% to 35%. Given the fact that the share of income from labour of the top 10% remained more or less stable, this implies that their share of income from capital must have decreased considerably. The trend in America was quite different: The share of the richest 10% measured in income terms—while it had dropped during the middle part of the twentieth century—increased sharply since the 1980s. To date, the richest 10% owns 45% of America's total income. This sharp increase can be explained by the sharp increase in top salaries.

The Difference Between Europe and America

The history of the distribution of capital and income in Europe is different from that of the US. Up to the beginning of WWI, the distribution in Europe was very uneven. That was not the case in America; the gap between rich and poor was smaller. Europe had larger inequalities around the turn of the nineteenth century than America today. At that time, the US was still a young society that needed time to catch up with the richest Europeans. Land in America was available in abundance; the population was still relatively small especially in comparison with the enormous landmass available to them.

In the years after WWI, many people felt that capitalism was done for. Yet, at the beginning of this century, Europe is again in the avant-garde of new *patrimonial capitalism*, as Piketty calls it, with private fortunes surpassing US levels. This is explained by Europe's lower economic and demographic growth compared with America's, automatically leading to increased influence of wealth accumulated in the past. The author concludes that European countries have never been so rich. And then Piketty makes a political statement:

> What is true and, shameful on the other hand, is that this vast national wealth is very unequally distributed. Private wealth rests on public poverty. And one particularly unfortunate consequence of this is that we currently spend far more in interest on the debt than we invest in higher education.[24]

[24] Ibid., 567. In fact the book is to some extent also a political treatise. That is not surprising, as the author writes on page 574: 'Everyone is political in his or her own way. The world is not divided between a political elite on one side and, on the other, an army of commentators and spectators whose only responsibility is to drop a ballot in a ballot box once every four or five years...... It is illusory, I believe, to think that the scholar and the citizen live in separate moral universes.'

The Comeback of Private Capital

What happened, not only in Europe, but throughout the developed world? At the beginning of the 1970s, the total value of private wealth (net of debt) stood between 2 and 3.5 years of national income in all the countries studied by Piketty. Since then, there is a strong comeback of private capital in rich countries; this explains how this new patrimonial capitalism came about.

There are three factors at play: The first one is slower growth in the long run, especially demographic growth, which, together with a high savings rate, automatically gives rise to a structural increase in the capital/income ratio, owing to the above-mentioned ß = s/g. Secondly, the gradual privatization of public wealth, and, thirdly, since the 1980s and 1990s, a long-term catch-up phenomenon affecting real estate and stock market prices, in a more conducive political environment than during the postwar decades.

Inequality really took off in America since the 1980s. Capital played its part, but not the most important one. In particular *income* inequality exploded. Piketty introduces the term '*supermanagers*'. They did not exist yet when Honoré de Balzac's novel *Le Père Goriot* came out in the early part of nineteenth century. The novel's main theme is what the best way would be to climb the social ladder: Would it be working hard, or to find a rich marriage partner? At the time, the latter option was preferred, as working hard for a salary would not make one rich, let alone add to one's prestige.

The Gap Widens

Supermanagers have grown rich during their own lifetime; think of Elon Musk, Bill Gates, Mark Zuckerberg, Jeff Bezos, and the like. Sky-high remunerations are a reflection of the social and political changes since the 1980s. The average CEO salary of a firm, whose shares are traded on the stock exchange, was around $2 million at the end of the 1980s. In 2007, it had risen to $16 million. CEO salaries in the financial sector are even higher. However, the salaries of mid- and lower income earners hardly rose; with a few percents per year at best. This explains the rapidly widening gap between the top-earners and the rest. The top earners are in a position to put aside a large part of their income to add to their own capital. Piketty fears that this large, and increasing, gap between the super-rich and the rest may trigger political instability. He observes: 'Inequality is not necessarily bad in itself: the key question is to decide whether it is justified, whether there are reasons for it.'[25]

[25] Ibid., 19.

Our democracies rest on a meritocratic worldview, says Piketty, and a belief in a society that is based more on merit and effort than on kinship and rents. As regards the high remuneration of supermanagers, Piketty wonders what the justification is for such high levels of compensation, which he calls *meritocratic extremism*. Is it a reward for their exceptional contribution to a firm's productivity and profitability? It is neither, he responds, as empirical studies have found that there is no relation between very high salaries of these supermanagers and their performance. Some firms that are managed by managers who earn less than their peers perform better. The author also observes that the reduction of top marginal income tax rates and the rise of top incomes do not seem to have stimulated productivity or did not stimulate productivity enough to be statistically detectable at the macro level.[26]

Apart from the fact that tax percentages for these salaries in the US has fallen from 90% in 1970 to 30% in 1990; more important is the manner in which the salaries are being established. Managers decide the salary levels for their employees, but their own salaries are decided by compensation committees whose members are appointed by the firm's management.

There are additional factors that add to growing inequality. One factor is that a large capital fund grows faster than a small one. Large funds yield higher returns, which can be reinvested, and so on. Moreover, owners of a small capital fund have to manage it themselves and, thus, cannot benefit from professional advice.

> The only way to make sense of these wealth rankings is to examine the evolution of the amount of wealth owned by a fixed percentage of the world's population, say the richest twenty-millionth of the adult population of the planet: roughly 150 people out of 3 billion adults in the late 1980s, and 225 people out of 4.5 billion in the early 2010s. We then find that the average wealth of this group has increased from just over $1.5 billion in 1987 to nearly $15 billion in 2013, an average growth rate of 6.4% above inflation.[27]

[26] Ibid., 150.
[27] Ibid., 434.

It is not easy to do research on capital investments and their returns; after all, people are not eager to share this very personal information. However, Piketty identifies one source that could be researched: University endowments. Based on the investment results of these funds, he was able to confirm that large endowments yielded more returns than small ones. Harvard's endowment, for example, amounts to roughly $30 billion. Princeton's and Yale's follow with $20 billion and $15 billion, respectively. Their average annual return on capital was 10.2%. Endowments of less than $100 million were doing not so well; their annual return was 6.2%.

The Influence of Education

The author wonders whether educational institutions promote social mobility.[28] After all, the better a child is educated the greater the chance that he or she will get a well-paid job. This would contribute to limiting the gap between the rich and not-so-rich. Even with the considerable increase in the average level of education during the twentieth century, earned income inequality did not diminish. Qualification levels have shifted upwards, which partly explains why inequality did not diminish. Tuition fees rose sharply in America in the period 1990–2010 which contributed to reduced social mobility. Only well-off parents could afford to send their children to the best American universities. Research demonstrates that the proportion of college degrees earned by children whose parents belong to the bottom quartiles of the income hierarchy stagnated at 10–20% in the period 1970–2010, while it rose from 40% to 80% for children with parents in the top quartile.

The main forces of convergence are the diffusion of knowledge and investment in training and skills. Piketty understands that achieving real equality of opportunity in higher education is not easy. Nonetheless, it is

[28] Regarding social mobility, I came across Gregory Clark's study in which he uses rare surnames to test whether societies are fluid or static: 'Take the case of Samuel Pepys (1633–1703), the diarist who served as secretary of the English Admiralty. In the past five centuries, people with the surname Pepys have attended Oxford and Cambridge universities at a rate at least twenty times that of the general population. Where we can observe that the value of their estates, Pepyses left wealth at least five times the British average. Only in a society with extremely low levels of social mobility would we expect a name to persist among the elites in this way.' Source: Leigh, A. (2024) *How Economics Explains the World; A Short Story of Humanity*. New York: Mariner Books, 28.

an important policy challenge to overcome this barrier, as it would contribute something positive to counter the threat of more income inequality in the future.

Inheritance

A person inheriting a large sum of money on top of what that person already owns, results in faster growth of the total capital sum. Capital that was generated by past generations is now going to play an important role. If one takes into consideration a lower population growth rate, this leads to more capital for each inheritor, and the inherited capital will constitute an important factor in the total capital sum.

Piketty shows that the capital owned by a person at the time of the person's death is on average 20% larger than the capital owned by a living person. If one would include the spectacular rise in capital transfers of parents to their children (e.g., to help them buying a house) during their life time, then the capital owned at the time of death would be twice as high compared with the average capital of a person still alive. This may suggest that we are moving into a situation that existed during the *Belle Epoque*. This, however, is not the case; income from labour is still the most important source of income, this also goes for the top 10%.

For the very top 1% the situation is different; capital eclipses income as the most important source of income. Supermanagers' salaries make it now possible to reach the exclusive league of the superrich. In the nineteenth century, this was not the case, observes Piketty, as during that time only *rentiers* belonged to the top.

What will the situation be towards the end of this century? Piketty estimates that global output will gradually decline from the current 3% a year to 1.5% in the second half of this century. The long-term savings rate will stabilize at about 10%. With these assumptions, including a slowing-down of demographic growth, ß = *s/g* implies that the global capital/income ratio will continue to rise and could reach 700% before the end of this century, or approximately the level observed in Europe from the eighteenth century to the *Belle Epoque*.

In the Annexe, Piketty provides his opinion about the so-called *Two Cambridges Debate*, about the question of capital accumulation and a possible dynamic equilibrium.[29]

[29] *Capital in the Twenty-First Century*, 230–232.

What Can Be Done to Limit the Gap?

After the wide ranging analysis of capital and income trends through time, Piketty proposes measures to 'regulate capital in the twenty-first century'. His overall conclusion is as follows:

> ...a market economy based on private property, if left to itself, contains powerful forces of convergence, associated in particular with the diffusion of knowledge and skills; but it also contains powerful forces of divergence, which are potentially threatening to democratic societies and to the values of social justice on which they are based.[30]

Piketty's analysis suggests that a new *Belle Epoque* is beckoning, wherein a small section of the population owns almost all capital. Can something be done to prevent such a situation from emerging? Yes, and he argues that the fact that history tells us that r was larger than g does not necessarily imply that it will be like this forever; it may be an historical fact but it is not a logical necessity. Trends like this one can be adjusted through the adoption of economic and fiscal policies.

Piketty notes that the influence of the state is much greater now than it was in the past; indeed, it is larger than it has ever been. Tax income increased through time and so did the state's social expenditures.[31] Education, for example, is now much more important than in the eighteenth century, contributing to social and economic upward mobility.

To prevent a global trend of growing inequality, Piketty proposes the introduction of a global progressive tax on capital (but not on the income generated by this capital). As regards the annual percentages to be applied, Piketty suggests: (i) 0.1–0.5% for capital between €1 and €5 million, (ii) 2% for capital between €5 and €10 million, (iii) 5–10% for capital more than €10 million, applied progressively, i.e., the higher the capital the higher the tax percentage.

The effect of this global capital tax would be a dampening effect on the income from capital. And through the introduction of this *global* tax, tax

[30] Ibid., 571.

[31] Regarding the role of the state in poor and emerging countries, Piketty observes that: 'The development of a fiscal and social state is intimately related to the process of state-building as such. Hence, the history of economic development is also a matter of political and cultural development, and each country must find its own distinctive path and cope with its own internal divisions.' Ibid., 491.

havens will be something of the past, which would promote efficient capital investments. Transparency of where capital is moving to, and who owns it, will be enhanced as well. Tax evasion will also be curbed, and international financial stability will be improved.

The author realizes that his proposed global capital tax is utopian, yet it might initially be introduced regionally, e.g., in the European Union and in America. Piketty concludes:

> But if the idea is utopian, it is nevertheless useful, for several reasons. First, even if nothing resembling this ideal is put into practice in the foreseeable future, it can serve as a worthwhile reference point, a standard against which alternative proposals can be measured.[32]

Limitarianism

Compared to Ingrid Robeyns's limitarianism, Piketty's proposals are relatively modest. Indeed, hers are tougher. Limitarianism is a moral principle that should guide the design of our economic and social institutions, and our own personal decision-making. The author explains in clearcut terms what the limitarian ethos is: '…we should not want to hold on to more money than we need to lead a secure life, and beyond that we should heed the moral call to share what we have with the least fortunate.'[33]

When is a person is simply too rich?—this is the key question. Robeyns attempts to establish what too rich means. She also looks for reasons why having too much money might be a bad thing. Needless to say dealing with these questions has, apart from a political, a high moral content.

Robeyns warns us that limitarianism does not come with a silver bullet. It is best understood as a regulative ideal—an outcome to strive for (i.e., a radical equitable income and wealth distribution), but which is unlikely to be ever completely achieved.

Three kinds of action are required. First, people should be given equal opportunities through affordable childcare, free high-quality education, and an anti-poverty strategy, in order to end up with an equitable distribution of wealth, and a decent standard of living for all, including a guaranteed minimum wage. Second: fiscal action. This is needed to tax away extreme wealth concentration. These two actions are necessary but not sufficient, hence the third action—the ethical action. We all need, argues

[32] Ibid., 515.
[33] *Limitarianism*, 186.

Robeyns, to embrace a limitarian ethos. This would give superrich people reasons to donate their excess wealth that reduce suffering and address collective problems.[34]

All of this sounds rather idealistic. However, during her field research, the author met with a variety of people, including very rich people, who were thinking along the same lines. She refers to the many multimillionaires who warned that inequalities are becoming too great and that governments must increase taxes on the richest. An increasing number of the very rich give away their fortune during their life time.

The time has come to discuss the dangers of wealth concentration and the opportunities that a cap on wealth offers. Regarding this wealth cap, the intriguing question is at which amount should it be established, and, perhaps even more intriguing, on which criteria would such a cap be based? In fact, Robeyns proposes not one but two caps: The top limit is political; it is the limit that our societal structures and fiscal system should enforce. The second, much lower, limit is personal—this is where ethics cone into play. The first limit is €10 million, for countries with a socio-economic profile similar to her home country the Netherlands.[35]

This limit was established after two studies had been undertaken, one in the UK and another in the Netherlands. The study conducted in London attempted, in essence, to find out the dividing line between the rich and superrich. The second study was conducted in the Netherlands by a team led by Robeyns. Almost all respondents had no problem in drawing a 10 million (euros, dollars or pounds) line between rich and super-rich. Beyond the 10 million dividing line, the author concludes that a fortune starts to become wasteful, since it could be better used to rectify climate-related injustice and to meet urgent human needs.[36]

Regarding the second limit, Robeyns argues that there are good reasons to set the limit at much less than the political threshold of ten million. She contends that for people who live in a society with a solid collective pension system, the ethical limit will be around one million pounds, dollars or euros. Obviously, the ethical limit also depends on the context; in some circumstances this limit will be lower, in others higher.

[34] Ibid., xvi.

[35] 'This figure, whether in euros, dollars or pounds, roughly holds for most developed economies, though it is important to note that, more than the specific amount, the method for calculating it is what matters.... this method should allow anyone living in a different socio-economic system to make their own estimate of where the upper limit should be pitched.' Ibid., xix.

[36] Ibid., 16.

Robeyns is not a supporter of a completely egalitarian society. There are good reasons for allowing some degree of inequality. For example, some people work harder and take more financial risks, or assume more responsibility than others. There are also those who do dangerous or extremely stressful work, or work that kills their health. And some work hours jeopardize a normal family life.[37] Robeyns is no fan of USSR-style communism or any other type of regime that requires the abolition of markets or private property. She underscores that markets are a powerful tool for securing material welfare. In addition, private property is a cornerstone of our security, autonomy, and prosperity; they are essential for a functioning society, in conjunction with public goods and collective resources accessible to all. The key question, the author stresses, is rather which constraints on the market and on private property we need if we are to achieve limitarianism.[38]

But let us return to Piketty's *Capital*, and present a few critical reactions.

Critical Reactions to Capital in the Twenty-First Century

Understandably, there were many reactions and reviews on *Capital in the Twenty-First Century*. Self-respecting journalists, bloggers, and columnists felt they had to vent their opinions about the book everybody was talking about. The same applied to the academic community. Most reviews were favourable; all were impressed with *Capital's* wide scope, going back to the time of the French Revolution, supported by an overwhelming wealth of data. Surely, there were also critical observations; yet, all in all, the book was praised.

Given the enormous flood of reactions, I have chosen three types of reactions which, I believe, are fairly representative of the large majority of them. The first type is about Piketty's statistical data. The second represents observations about the book's perceived weak theoretical underpinning, and the lack of a distinction between capital and wealth. The third type of reviews draws attention to the missing institutional dimension of inequality.

Regarding Piketty's supposedly shaky statistical data, *Bloomberg View's* Clive Crook wrote on 20 April 2014 that Piketty's data would be shaky

[37] Robeyns adds that the moral case for allowing inequality is limited to inequalities due to compensation for differences in the burdens of work and differences in the effort and hours people put into their job. *Limitarianism*, 161.

[38] Ibid., xx.

and that, based on the data, he drew far-reaching conclusions that are not justified. However, *The Economist's* Free Exchange column of 31 May 2014, supported Piketty:

> All told, Mr. Piketty is guilty of sloppiness (certainly in his notation), and perhaps of some errors. But there is little evidence, so far, to support the serious charge of cherry-picking statistics. Nor have his findings that wealth concentration is, once again, rising, been fatally undermined.[39]

Piketty reacted to these criticisms by putting all his data on line, and he explains which methodologies he applied. He adds that it would surprise him if improvements, such as suggested by Crook, would alter his main conclusions.

Regarding the weak theoretical underpinning, Harvard professor Dani Rodrik's *Project Syndicate* article of 13 May 2014 had this to say. On the one hand, Rodrik found *Capital* a fantastic read, but on the other he blamed Piketty for not paying more attention to formal theory. Piketty is not, and I quote Rodrik: '…beyond sprinkling an occasional equation or Greek letters throughout the text'. Rodrik also argued that Piketty's extrapolations are dangerous. After all, r could go down in a situation when there is too much capital relative to labour and other inputs, or when the pace of innovation slows down. Moreover, the world economy may be growing faster than Piketty anticipates. Hence, Piketty's formula $r > g$ may not be applicable throughout the remainder of this century.

Australian economist, Joshua Gans, refers to a long article that Solow wrote in the 22 April 2014 issue of *New Republic*, about *Capital*.[40] In this article Solow admitted that in a situation—as presented by Piketty—wherein r > g, income and wealth of the rich will grow faster than the average income from labour, Solow calls this a 'rich get rich dynamic'. Piketty's prediction of where inequality is heading is not based upon a solid theoretical model; it is speculative and based on the rich get rich dynamic. Yet, Solow underscored that this insight is one that no one before Piketty discovered. Solow concluded that the economy apparently has been able to absorb increasing quantities of capital that did not result in a decreasing rate of return on capital.

[39] *The Economist*, 31 May 2014, 66.

[40] *Digitopoly, Capital Creators, Piketty and the Growth Theory;* 23 April 2014.

This absorption ability must have been done by 'capital creators', as Gans calls them. But would not these capital creators also be able to further promote economic growth? If so, this would not justify Piketty's low economic growth projections. Gans is critical of Piketty not having referred to older theories, including Solow's, on the basis of which he proposed the same sort of taxes Piketty proposes, so as to bring about a more equal income and wealth distribution.

Regarding capital and wealth, Piketty does not make a clear distinction between them while the two differ in their respective role in the productive process. Capital encompasses means of production, such as machinery, buildings, equipment, and the like. The term wealth is used to express what someone owns, such as a house, a building, pieces of art, shares, etc. minus his or her debts. Capital wields a far larger socio-economic influence than wealth. The issue is thus how much influence a rich person can exert. That influence is concretized through the productive capital he or she invests. However, Piketty's main objective is to analyse the *distribution* of wealth. He analyses the evolution of wealth and the development of the ratio between wealth—in general terms—and income. The influence that wealth in the form of capital can wield as explained above is—strictly speaking—another subject matter. Piketty analyses the development of the growth of wealth and how this impinges upon the concentration of wealth in fewer hands. In doing so, he evades the need to clearly distinguish between capital and wealth.

Then, inequality's institutional dimension. Economics Nobel Laureates, Daron Acemoglu and James Robinson, wrote *Why Nations Fail* (2013), in which they argue that institutions play a crucial role in the development of economies. In an interview, Robinson criticized Piketty for his disregard of the role of institutions.[41] Robinson said that limiting inequality is not determined by Piketty's formula $r > g$ but by changes in the political domain and through government intervention in the economy.

In *Why Nations Fail* a distinction is made between extractive and inclusive institutions. The more inclusive institutions are, the greater the chance that economic development unfolds. Institutions that provide incentives for people to develop in economic terms play a fundamental part in overcoming inequality, argues Robinson. He gave a few examples to underscore his point. Take Sweden; the social-democratic government there had more influence on the distribution of income and wealth than a

[41] *NRC Handelsblad*, 3–4 September 2014, W8–9.

supposedly autonomous development of *r* and *g*. Another example is South Korea. During General Park's autocratic rule in the 1960s, the country was characterized by extractive economic growth. But growth continued throughout the next two decades because South Korea adopted democratic rule and thus transformed itself into an inclusive political system.

Just before this book went to press, Swedish economist Daniel Waldenström published *Richer and More Equal*, telling his analysis of the gap between rich and poor.[42] Waldenström, Professor of Economics and Program Director of the Research Institute of Industrial Economics in Stockholm, presents a fresh interpretation of wealth accumulation and inequality over the past century in advanced capitalist countries.

He analysed the income and wealth distribution in six countries: France, Germany, Spain, Sweden, The UK the US. His analysis suggests that, compared with a century ago, not just more wealth than ever before has been created, but its distribution—contrary to what Piketty argued—has become *more equal*, resulting from the rising importance of private housing and private pension funds, which Piketty had not included in his analysis.

Waldenström, like Piketty, observes that at the beginning of the twentieth century, wealth-was very unevenly distributed: The richest 1% of the population owned between 45% and 70% of all wealth. But around the 1980s, the picture was completely different: The 1% richest people's wealth had gone down to between 23% and 16%, while the wealth of the lowest section of the population had increased appreciably. Waldenström admits that since the 1980s, the wealth gap widened again, especially in America, but the gap is still much smaller than it was a century ago.

Resulting from sustained economic growth over the past century, which Waldenström finds an important factor in income and wealth distribution, the wealth share of the richest 1% may have gone down, but—thanks to economic growth—their wealth still increased, while the share of the lower and middle classes increased more. So, the increased wealth of the middle and lower classes has not affected the wealth of the rich. How come? The property(houses) and pension wealth (the 'great equalizers') of the working class has grown faster over the past century than the capital holdings of the elite. Hence, Waldenström concludes that the past century

[42] Waldenström, D. (2024) *Richer and More Equal; A New History of Wealth in the West*. New York: Wiley.

has been marked by the democratization of wealth. As Robinson observes, institutions also played a constructive role in this realm. Waldenström agrees; he found that the positive influence of democratic institutions, reforms of the labour market, and much broader access to education, boosted productivity and promoted social upward mobility.

Waldenström's findings will certainly open a fresh debate on the distribution of income and wealth. In May 2024, Piketty and Michael Sandel met in Paris to talk about equality; their dialogue is presented in a booklet entitled *Equality* which came out in early 2025.[43] In the dialogue, Piketty makes comparable observations about income and wealth distribution as Waldenström's over the past century:

> We've been able to reduce inequality enormously—not just access to basic goods and participation, but also monetary inequality in income and wealth. If you look at today, even with the rise of inequality in recent decades, the income gap in Europe between the top 10% or the top 1% and the bottom 50% or bottom 10% is enormously smaller than 100 years ago. This is less true in the US, but even in the US it is true as compared to 100 years ago. So, we've moved toward more equality in the long run, and not only has this not been at the expense of prosperity or any other legitimate goals that we might want to balance with equality, but in fact this has been a key component of the rise of modern prosperity.[44]

Part II Piketty's Ideological and Philosophical Inspiration

Piketty is driven by socialist ideals. This shines clearly through in the pages of *Capital in the Twenty-First Century.* The question is which philosophers inspired him? I hoped to find the answer in *Capital and Ideology;* after all, inequality is not just an economic or political issue; above all, it is a phenomenon studied by philosophers as well.

First, the essence of this impressive book is presented, followed by Piketty's inspirations.

[43] Piketty, T., and Sandel, M. (2025) *Equality; What It Means And Why It Matters.* Cambridge: Polity Press.

[44] Ibid., 6–7. Piketty's quotation suggests that he was aware of Waldenström's findings. At any event, further clarification is called for.

Capital and Ideology

Introduction

After having digested many comments on *Capital in the Twenty-First Century*, Piketty realized that he had taken a too limited view of the history of income and wealth distribution and inegalitarian ideologies. His approach had, in his own words, largely been 'Western'[45]; he had not included developments in non-Western cultures and countries, and that—he admits—was a shortcoming.

In *Capital and Ideology* he broadens the scope by including historic developments in many non-Western countries such as Brazil, India, China, Russia, South Africa, Tunisia, Lebanon, Ivory Coast, Korea, Taiwan, and other countries around the globe. But this was not the only shortcoming. Encounters with other scholars, including discussions and reading, gave Piketty the opportunity to learn more about the politics and ideological dynamics of inequality in subsequent societies in history, ranging from premodern trifunctional and slave societies to modern postcolonial and hyper capitalistic ones.

It was the author's wish to understand what institutional arrangements, and what types of socio-economic organization, had contributed to human and social emancipation. All this resulted in *Capital and Ideology*. Piketty admits that in *Capital in the Twenty-First Century*, he had treated political and ideological changes associated with inequality as a black box.

After completing *Capital and Ideology*, the author concludes that capitalism and private property can be superseded and that a just society can be established on the basis of participatory socialism and social federalism.

The Book's Summary

Capital and Ideology tells the history and evolution of inequality regimes, how inegalitarian ideologies evolved and how they have often been justified by power holders. Regarding inequality, the author relied, apart from documents and other sources (including films and novels[46]), on data collected in the *World Inequality Database* (WID).

[45] Piketty realized that he had to 'de-Westernize our gaze', *Capital and Ideology*, 1037.

[46] Such as Carlos Fuentes's *Destiny and Desire*, Pramoedya Ananta Toer's *This Earth of Mankind*, and Chimamanda Ngozi's *Americanah*. Also the film *Black Panther* is dealt with by Piketty.

The approach taken, explains Piketty, is not 'Marxist', according to which the state of the economic forces and relations of production determines a society's ideological superstructure. By contrast, he insists that the realm of *ideas* is truly autonomous. Marx wrote that all history is the history of class struggle. The plough gave us the feudal manor, and the steam engine gave us the capitalist mill. Instead, Piketty believes that it is the history of the struggle of ideologies and the quest for justice that count. So, if inequality is to be attacked, the prevailing ideology has to change.

A leading theme in the book is that throughout history, and in different cultures, inequality was justified by ideologies.[47] This is very well captured in the book's first few sentences:

> Every human society must justify its inequalities: unless reasons for them are found, the whole political and social edifice stands in danger of collapse. Every epoch therefore develops a range of contradictory discourses and ideologies for the purpose of legitimizing the inequality that already exists or that people believe should exist. From these discourses emerge certain economic, social, and political rules, which people then use to make sense of the ambient social structure. Out of the clash of contradictory discourses—a clash that is at once economic, social, and political—comes a dominant narrative or narratives, which bolster the existing inequality regime.[48]

So choices are made, and these choices are shaped by each society's conception of social justice and economic fairness, and by the relative political and ideological power of contending groups and discourses. Throughout history it was the hypocrisy of elites that shone through in successive ideologies, condoning inequality.

When the book came out in 2020, neoliberalism was still dominant in the majority of societies. This ideology includes themes like private property, entrepreneurship, and the principle of meritocracy, resulting in, as Piketty calls it, hyper capitalistic economies. What about inequality? Well, this exists because it is the result of a freely chosen process in which everyone enjoys equal access to the market and to property, and automatically

[47] Ideologies, in Piketty's words, include 'a set of a priori plausible ideas and discourses describing how society should be structured, in an attempt to respond to a broad set of questions concerning the desirable or ideal organization of society.' *Capital and Ideology*, 3. He also wrote on p. 592 that 'every ideology is the victim of some form of sacralization—of private property in one case, of state property in another; and fear of the void always looms large.'

[48] Ibid., 1.

benefits from the wealth accumulated by the wealthiest individuals, who are the most enterprising and useful for society. And they deserve to be properly remunerated, so the narrative went—even billionaires deserve their wealth.

Piketty shows that during the egalitarian phase 1950—1980, top-income tax rates in America and in the UK moved between 80% and more than 90%. After the 1970s, these rates came down considerably.[49] The rationale behind this dramatic downward move was that in the preceding period not just equality had gone too far, but also that lower taxes (as high rates would sap the entrepreneurial spirit) and higher remunerations for top-income earners would help boost overall economic growth. This would be good for these top-income earners but also for low-income earners; it was thought that 'a rising tide would lift all boats'.[50]

The fact of the matter, observes Piketty, is that growth rates in e.g., Europe and America were higher in the egalitarian period than in the subsequent phase characterized by far less progressive taxation and rising inequality. In addition, productivity growth in the US and the UK was higher in the period 1950—1990 than in 1990—2020, again casting doubt on the argument that reducing top-income tax rates would spur economic growth. Obviously, Piketty is not the only economist praising what was achieved in economic terms during the egalitarian phase. Bradford DeLong, as described in Chap. 3, is also enthusiastic about this period. Word has it that Paul Krugman remembers the period as 'the America we love'.

Fair enough, Piketty acknowledges the positive sides of neoliberalism. For example, hundreds of millions of very poor people's income increased. As a result, the number of the extremely poor dropped worldwide. The gap between low-income and middle-income earners decreased. However, there has been a sharp increase in inequality between middle-income and

[49] A study of the *National Bureau for Economic Research* shows that business people moved towards corporate structures such as partnerships, where what was earlier shown as wage income was now misleadingly shown as profits or income to capital. Correcting for this, the authors of the study found that most top earners in the US today are the self-made 'working rich', such as lawyers, doctors, and car dealers, deriving their income from their skills rather than their physical or financial capital. In addition, in the glorious high-tax years that Piketty favours, the personal income tax collected in the US averaged 7.6% of GDP, while in the supposedly lower-tax 1980–2018 period he disfavours, it averaged a higher 7.9%. Source: Raghuram Rajan's review of *Capital and Ideology* in the *Financial Times*, 25 February, 2020.

[50] Inequality has risen in most countries in recent decades but it remains much lower than it was a century ago. So, there is some merit in this oft-quoted metaphor.

top-income earners. Piketty concludes that the 27% of global income growth captured by the world's 1% top-income earners was twice as large as that (12%) of the 3.5 billion individuals at the bottom end of the income scale.

Referring to the insights gained of the egalitarian period, Piketty wonders whether the share going to the top-income earners could not be reduced to, say, 10% or 20%, while still allowing significant improvement in the living standards of the bottom 50%. He concludes that what the global growth figures reveal is that the *distribution* of gains is just as important as overall growth. So there is room for a debate about the political and institutional choices that affect distribution.

We saw that *Capital in the Twenty-First Century* pays much attention to the role of education. This subject is, not surprisingly, brought up again in *Capital and Ideology*. The author argues that the most striking aspect about the increase of inequality in the US is the collapse of the share of total national income going to the bottom 50%. This resulted, among other things, in inequality of access to education. In addition, the concentration of educational investment in elitist institutions is particularly extreme in the US, where admission procedures are opaque and public regulation is lacking. So, goodbye equality of opportunity in America. Inequality of access to and financing of education is somewhat less extreme in Europe and Japan. Nonetheless, educational inequality and absence of democratic transparency in this area are issues to reckon with. True, admits Piketty, social democracy also failed in this realm.

As for ideology, Piketty observes that the broadly social-democratic redistributive coalitions were not just party coalitions, they were also intellectual and ideological—ideas mattered, as Keynes also had said. Central themes were redistribution and an enhanced role of the state in society. True, the existence of a communist countermodel in the Soviet Union at the time also played a crucial role in this realm.

However, the traditional social-democratic electorate in Europe and the US changed horses. They bade farewell to their parties and joined conservative, and increasingly, populist parties, while social-democratic and liberal parties attracted the better educated. In short, they forfeited the support of the least well-off voters; they began to focus more and more on the better educated.

People without a degree, a fortune, or a high income felt being left out. This partly explains the rise of populism. The traditional class-based political system broke down. Ultimately, these divisions led to the breakup of the 1950–1980 egalitarian coalition. The egalitarian social-democratic coalition of the postwar era was incapable of renewing its ideology.

Piketty also observes that a key failure was the inability to conceptualize or organize progressive taxation and redistribution at the *transnational* level. The context of social justice is no longer national; now it is global and transnational. The failure of ensuring equal access to (higher) education is already mentioned. Just ownership was neither reconsidered by social-democrats. Ethnic diversity was also an issue overlooked by them. All this prompts the question: What defines the boundaries of the human community when it comes to reducing inequality and establishing norms of equality acceptable to a majority?

In the quest for solutions, Piketty choses a historical approach (the *longue durée*), not just because issues of redistribution had already been debated during e.g., the French Revolution, but also because the various regions of the world have only gradually come into contact with one another.[51] Again, in line with *Capital in the Twenty First Century*'s approach, Piketty uses mathematics and statistics to underscore what historical insights reveal.

> Piketty presents India as an example of an inequality regime: 'The Indian Union is an example of very large-scale democratic federalism. It shows how the state can use legal tools to overcome the heavy inegalitarian legacy of an ancient society of castes made more rigid by the encounter with British colonial power. The institutional tools that India developed to deal with this legacy took the form of quotas and 'reservations' of places in universities, public employment, and elective office: places were reserved for individuals born into disadvantaged social classes that had suffered from discrimination. This system has not resolved all of India's problems—far from it. But such experiences are highly instructive for the rest of the world…'.[52]

[51] Just one example. During the time of the French Revolution, the Marquis de Condorcet proposed a form of progressive taxation in 1792, but it was a relatively modest measure (with a maximum rate of less than 5 percent on the highest incomes). *Capital and Ideology*, 118. In 1794, the Marquis observed that 'fortunes tend naturally toward equality' once one eliminates 'artificial means of perpetuating them' and establishes 'freedom of commerce and industry.' Ibid., 139.

[52] Ibid., 1037.

Modern inequality exhibits discriminatory practices as well as social and political tensions. At the end of the book, Piketty formulates the key challenge: How to reorganize the global economy along social federalist lines so as to allow the emergence of new forms of fiscal, social, and environmental solidarity, with the ultimate goal of substituting true global governance for the treaties that today mandate free movement of goods and capital. Making use of the lessons of history, we might, argues Piketty, achieve greater justice in ownership, education and immigration. This implies huge transformations in, indeed, ideology, politics, and people's perceptions and attitudes.

What more does Piketty propose? 'Participatory socialism' is the term he introduces, in which capitalism is gradually abolished via a progressive income tax and a tax on inherited wealth.[53] Their proceeds are used to finance a basic income (i.e., 60% of the average income after tax) and a capital endowment for every citizen. Ownership of capital will be made temporary. In addition, power is to be shared between a company's workers and shareholders. Piketty proposes temporary ownership by which successful businesspeople will not accumulate wealth but will see it taxed away, giving others the chance to succeed. Carbon emissions require a collective regulation. The proceeds will go to finance social insurance and a basic income, and to the ecological transition and true educational equality.

There is still more: The global economy needs to be reorganized by means of co-development treaties incorporating quantified objectives of social, fiscal, and environmental justice. Liberalization of trade and financial flows must be conditioned on progress toward meeting the above goals. Existing treaties need to be replaced by new rules based on the principle of financial transparency, fiscal cooperation, and transnational democracy.

Are these proposals; and his remark 'tax capitalism out of existence', not be way beyond what is realistic and possible, as one reviewer wondered?[54] No, says Piketty: Some proposals belong to a historical

[53] Piketty elaborates the term participatory socialism: 'Specifically one can imagine a society that allows privately owned firms of reasonable size while preventing excessive concentration of wealth by means of a progressive wealth tax, a universal capital endowment, and power sharing between stock-holders and employees.' Ibid., 592.

[54] Paul Mason made this observation in his review of the book in *The Observer* of 1 March 2020.

movement toward democratic socialism, which, since the late nineteenth century has been working toward profound transformations of legal, social, and fiscal systems. The author reminds us of the significant reduction of inequality that took place in the middle of the past century. This was made possible by the construction of a social state based upon relative educational equality and a number of radical innovations, such as co-management in the Germanic and Nordic countries,[55] as well as progressive taxation in the US and the UK.

However, the development of a more egalitarian society was interrupted by the neoliberal revolution of the 1980s and the fall of communism. The limits of deregulation were clearly exposed during the financial crisis of 2007. People have once again begun thinking about a new, more equitable and more sustainable, economic model. Piketty may have foreseen the contemporary geopolitical protectionist sentiment when he wrote, in the Hobbesian tradition, of the danger of 'intensifying the competition of all against all.'[56]

Summing up, Piketty's proposals are radical. Although there is no disagreement between Left and Right thinkers about inequality being too high, yet most of them resist the idea of a thorough socialist overhaul. The reason is that they fear that, in the end, it would leave everyone, including the poorest, worse off.

Piketty's Ideological and Philosophical Inspiration

I was curious to learn more about Piketty's own inspiration. We saw that he understands ideology to refer to a set of a priori plausible ideas and discourses describing how society should be structured. An ideology has social, economic, and political dimensions. It is an attempt to respond to a broad set of questions concerning the desirable or ideal organization of society.

Piketty has interesting things to say about who and what inspired him, which he does on the final pages of *Capital and Ideology*:

> 'No doubt my gaze has also been shaped by my personal history, perhaps even more than I imagine. I could describe the diversity of the social milieus

[55] 'We know from experience with Germanic and Nordic versions of co-management that the employee and the shareholder representatives can each control half the voting rights in a firm and that such power sharing can improve overall economic performance.' *Capital and Ideology*, 592.

[56] Ibid., 1037.

> and political ideas to which I was exposed by my family background. My two grandmothers suffered from the patriarchal model imposed by their generation. One was unhappy in her bourgeois life and died prematurely in Paris in 1987. The other became a servant on a farm at age 13 during World War II and died in 2018.... Born in 1971, I obtained from my parents the freedom I needed to become an adult. As a student in 1989, I listened to the collapse of the communist dictatorship on the radio. In 1991, I listened to reports of the Gulf War. When I look at how my vision of history and economics has evolved since I was 18, I think that it was the study of history—the sources I discovered and the books I read—that led me to change my views significantly (I was initially more liberal and less socialist than I am now). In particular, writing *Top Incomes in France in the Twentieth Century: Inequality and Redistribution, 1901–1998*, made me realize in 2001 how much violence accompanied the reduction of inequality in the twentieth century. The crisis of 2008 led me to take a greater interest in the fragilities of global capitalism and the history of capital and its accumulation, subjects at the heart of *Capital in the Twenty-First Century*.[57]

Regarding Piketty's ideological inspirators, German-American political philosopher Hannah Arendt influenced him quite clearly, principally regarding the political and economic destruction that took place in Europe during the first half of the twentieth century, i.e., two World Wars, the Great Depression, resulting in millions of people killed, wounded, maimed, or impoverished.[58] Piketty explains the 1950–1980 egalitarian phase as a strong reaction to this economic and political disaster. Apart from Arendt, Polanyi, Rawls and Sen influenced him as well.

Arendt

In *Origins of Totalitarianism*,[59] Arendt analysed the reasons why various European societies destroyed themselves. She argued that the collapse of 1914–1945 could be seen as a consequence of the contradictions of unbridled and unregulated European capitalism in the preceding period 1815–1914. She observed that European nation-states had been transcended by globalized industrial and financial capitalism they themselves had helped to create. They were no longer able to control and regulate economic forces or their social consequences.

[57] Ibid., 1038–1039.

[58] A brief biography of Hannah Arendt is included in Chap. 8.

[59] Arendt, H. (1951) *The Origins of Totalitarianism.* Boston: Harcourt.

We saw that Piketty blames social-democratic parties for having shut their eyes to global processes and thus failed to forge transnational bonds with like-minded parties. Arendt made similar observations. She argued that, during the Interbellum, the principal weakness of social-democrats was that they had not understood the need to *transcend* the nation-state. They failed to conceive of new federal forms. In order to regulate the unbridled forces of global capitalism, new forms of transnational politics needed to be developed. Piketty underscores that what Arendt had to say is quite pertinent for understanding the limitations of post-WWI social-democratic societies. Arendt concluded that social democrats settled for a façade of internationalism when their actual political project was to build a welfare state within the limits of the nation-state.

Piketty agrees that these parties were alone in this realm. By contrast, the colonial ideologies on which the British and French empires rested, transcended the nation-state during the phase of accelerated expansion (1880–1914). Indeed, empires were a manner of organizing global capitalism through large-scale imperial communities and strongly hierarchical civilizational ideology, with the superior metropole at the centre and the subordinate colonies on the periphery. However, in the course of the first half of the twentieth century, they would be undermined by centrifugal forces of independence.[60]

Polanyi

Polanyi's analysis of the consequences of the self-regulating market ideology, which he called market liberalism, met with Piketty's appreciation[61] Polanyi, like Arendt, argued that this ideology led to the destruction of European societies in the period 1914–1945. He added that it would also lead to the demise of economic liberalism. As for this latter opinion, he was, as it turned out, too straightforward.

Piketty nuances Polanyi's conclusion by stating that this demise was only temporary. Piketty reminds us, as mentioned in Chap. 3, that in 1938 liberal economists and intellectuals met in Paris to reflect on the attacks on the liberal doctrine by the success of economic planning, as applied in the Soviet Union, and by the rise of totalitarianism. They came up with the

[60] *Capital and Ideology*, 479—480.

[61] Polanyi's biography is summarized in Chap. 4.

idea to reinvigorate the liberal ideology through 'neoliberalism'. Hayek was one of the participants in Paris. He would carry the neoliberal torch forward to the Mont Pèlerin Society, briefly described in Chap. 5.

Another aspect which inspired Piketty was Polanyi's thesis about the collapse of the ownership society, elaborated in *The Great Transformation*.[62] Polanyi's point of departure was that nineteenth-century civilization rested on four pillars: the balance of power, the gold standard, the liberal state, and the self-regulated market. Polanyi believed, like Piketty, in the possibility of democratic socialism, as an alternative to the liberal order. But to achieve this, the market economy had to be socially embedded.

Regarding the labour market, this meant that all matters pertaining to wage setting and the like, were matters to be settled by social and political negotiation and not by the market. Second, self-regulation, in combination with the broadening of the market and the generalized monetization of economic relations, resulted in modern society ending in a very fragile condition.

The collapse of the gold standard and related disruption of the global financial system had serious economic consequences which came to light after the end of the Great War. Hyperinflation in Germany and Austria ruined many people, while speculators amassed fortunes. The demand was for authoritarian governments which were established in Germany, Italy, and Spain.

After the end of the Great War, five empires collapsed: The Austrian-Hungarian, the German, the British, the Ottoman and the Tsarist empire either disappeared or started their unstoppable decline. The thinking used to be that the existence of European nation-states of more or less equal size and power, all committed to the liberal doctrine, would suffice to guarantee the continuation of the process of capital accumulation and the prosperity of the continent, and the world at large. However, their hunger for power had desensitized them to the social inequalities that were undermining them from within.

Polanyi died before he could have observed that after WWII, a Golden Age emerged that would last three decades. Piketty agrees with Polanyi's sombre analysis of the period after 1914. At the same time Piketty is very appreciative of the egalitarian period 1950–1980, but laments, yet

[62] Polanyi, K (2001) *The Great Transformation; The Political and Economic Origins of Our Time*. Boston: Beacon Press.

understands, that this would not last. In *Slouching Towards Utopia*, Bradford DeLong summarizes:

> Piketty's central point was that we shouldn't have been surprised. In a capitalist economy, it is normal for a large proportion of the wealth to be inherited. It is normal for its distribution to be highly unequal. It is normal for a plutocratic elite……to use its political power to shape the economy to its own advantage. And it is normal for this to put a drag on economic growth.[63]

Rawls

In the chapter entitled *Elements for a Participatory Socialism for the Twenty-First Century*,[64] Piketty writes that he was inspired by John Rawls's *Theory of Justice*.[65] As the contents of Rawls's theory of justice are summarized in Chap. 7, only Piketty's interpretation of Rawls's theory is presented. He admits that Rawls's philosophy is similar to his own. He observes, however, that the Rawlsian approach has limitations, in that it remains fairly abstract and says nothing precise about the levels of inequality and fiscal progressivity that these principles imply.

Piketty defines a just society as follows; 'A just society is one that allows all of its members access to the widest possible range of fundamental goods. Fundamental goods include education, health, the right to vote and, more generally, to patriciate as fully as possible in the various forms of social, cultural, economic, civic, and political life.'[66] The author underscores that a just society is in no way a society characterized by uniformity and equality. Inequalities are the result of different aspirations and distinct life choices. The society can also permit improvement of the standard of living and expansion of the opportunities available to the disadvantaged. But, adds Piketty, this must be demonstrated, not assumed, and this argument cannot be invoked to justify any degree of inequality.

Piketty's definition is useful, he says, because it allows us to lay down certain principles. In particular, equality of access to fundamental goods must be absolute. After all, one cannot offer greater political participation

[63] Bradford DeLong, J. (2022) *Slouching Towards Utopia; An Economic History of the Twentieth Century* London: Basic Books, 453.

[64] *Capital and Ideology*, 966–1034. Piketty says that especially Rawls's difference principle is similar to his own: This is what Rawls formulated: Social and economic inequalities are to be to the greatest benefit of the least advantaged members of society.

[65] Rawls, J. (1971) *A Theory of Justice*. Cambridge: Cambridge University Press.

[66] *Capital and Ideology*, 968.

or a higher income to certain groups while at the same time depriving others of e.g., the right to vote. Like Rawls, Piketty refers to Western societies and to the more developed non-Western ones. He added: 'But I have tried to think about them in a universal perspective, and they may gradually become applicable to poor and emerging countries as well.'[67] He did this because he had argued in the *Introduction* that the context of social justice must be explicitly global and transnational.[68]

As regards Piketty's thinking about justice, Paul Mason observes in his review of *Capital and Ideology* in *The Observer*, that Piketty's implicit method is that of the Enlightenment philosopher Hegel: Human progress exists, the state is nearly always its main actor, and history is driven by supra-historical ideas—above all the idea of justice.

Although *Capital and Ideology* is to some extent sociological in its analysis, Piketty is mainly focused on taxation in redressing what went wrong and how to put it right.[69] Tax, however, is not the only cause of inequality. Nor can greater government spending be the solution to the problem. As Sen argues in Chap. 7, inequality is not just a matter of income. It is also inequality of opportunity, i.e., the lack of *capabilities* that explain the gap between the haves and have-nots.

Conclusion

Piketty reminds me of Keynes: Both bestseller authors and global stars. Both also very active in the political and economic debate. Both erudite and enormously productive in their scientific work. Keynes was a new liberal, although later in his life he proposed the euthanasia of the rentier and also socialization of investment. Former liberal Piketty, is now a radical socialist, practicing one of Keynes's famous remarks: When the facts

[67] Ibid., 969.

[68] Ibid., 41.

[69] On this matter Piketty's analysis is quite different from Hayek's. Hayek wrote in *The Road to Serfdom* that any political project based on social justice leads straight to collectivism and totalitarianism. In *Law, Legislation and Liberty,* Hayek argued that if anyone begins to question existing property rights or gets caught up in the works of progressive taxation, it will be impossible to know where to stop… collectivization would be near. In an earlier work, Hayek had argued that the very idea of progressive taxation should be constitutionally prohibited. The tax rate on the highest incomes in any given country should not exceed the average overall rate but certainly not be progressive.

change, I change I mind. What do you do, Sir?[70] Both also had opinions about the long run, which they did not share. Keynes's most famous bon mot is: In the long run we're all dead. What he meant to say was that economists cannot make long-term projections simply because the future is not exclusively influenced by predictable economic factors. Piketty's historical approach is analysing the long run, supported by an impressive wealth of statistical data.

While Keynes revolutionized economics, Piketty is yet to witness whether his participatory socialism may see the light. Keynes did not stray much from the Middle Way, while Piketty, rejecting liberalism's downsides, presents himself more and more as a political ideologue of the socialist variety, which shines so clearly through in *Capital and Ideology*.

Annexe

Piketty pays attention to the so-called *Two Cambridges Debate*, which is about the question of capital accumulation and a possible dynamic equilibrium.[71] The first observation he makes is that national accounts and other statistical data available in the late nineteenth and early twentieth century were inadequate for a correct understanding of the dynamics of the capital/income ratio. By the middle of the twentieth century, following the shocks of 1914–1945, the reverse was true. This explains why the question of capital accumulation and a possible dynamic equilibrium continued to feed controversy. Hence the Cambridge capital theory controversy, or the 'Two Cambridges Debate', between Cambridge, England and Cambridge, Massachusetts. The former was represented by, among others, Joan Robinson, Nicholas Kaldor, and Luigi Pasinetti; the latter by Paul Samuelson and Robert Solow.

(*continued*)

[70] Keynes was a notorious mind changer. Legend says that while conferring with Roosevelt at Quebec, Churchill sent Lord Keynes a cable reading, "Am coming around to your point of view." His Lordship replied, "Sorry to hear it. Have started to change my mind."

[71] *Capital in the Twenty-First Century*, 230–232.

(continued)

First, a bit of history: Roy Harrod and Evsey Domar had introduced the formula ß = s/g, in which ß is the capital/income ratio, s is the savings rate and g the growth rate. It was common to be inverted as g = s/ß. Harrod argued that ß was *fixed* by the available technology, so that g was entirely determined by the savings rate. Suppose that the savings rate is 10% and a capital/income ratio of 5, then the growth rate g of the economy's productive capacity is 2% per year. However, since the growth rate must be equal to the population's growth rate (and of productivity, which—as Piketty adds—was still ill-defined at the time), it follows that g is an intrinsically unstable process. There is either too much or too little capital, which gives rise to excess capacity and speculative bubbles, or else to unemployment, or perhaps both at once. Remember, Harrod was writing during the time of the Great Depression, a period of significant macroeconomic instability.

The conclusion then was that growth was a highly volatile process. To bring saving into line with investment decisions is difficult, as decisions about saving and investment are made by different people, especially since it is difficult in the short run to alter the capital intensity and organization of production. Piketty observes that in the long run the capital/income ratio is relatively flexible, together with the fact that the elasticity of substitution of capital for labour has been greater than one (1) over a long period of time.

In 1956, Robert Solow introduced a production function with substitutable factors, which made it possible to *invert* the formula and thus write ß = s/g. In the long run the capital/income ratio adjusts to the savings rate and the structural growth rate of the economy, rather than the other way round. So, the two Cambridge schools differed about the equation, in that—as the Americans suggested—growth would always be balanced, contrary to the British emphasis on the Keynesian importance of short-term fluctuations.

As of the 1970s, Solow's neoclassical growth model, with substitutional factors, called the shots, when Keynesianism was in retreat. The British suspicion of the Americans not being sensitive of short-term fluctuations, was unfounded, says Piketty, as Samuelson and Solow understood that short-term growth was unstable and that, consequently, the economy would require Keynesian policies; they viewed their ß = s/g solely as a *long-term* law!

(*continued*)

(continued)

Long-term growth does not guarantee a harmonious distribution of wealth, and in no way implies the disappearance (or even reduction) of inequality in capital ownership. Furthermore, ß= *s/g* does not preclude very large variations in the capital/income ratio over time and between countries. Piketty argues that: '...the virulence of the Cambridge capital controversy was due in part to the fact that the participants in the debate on both sides lacked the historical data needed to clarify the terms of the debate. It is striking to see how little use either side made of national capital estimates prior to World War I.... The two world wars created such a deep discontinuity in both conceptual and statistical analysis that for a while it seemed impossible to study the issue in a long-term perspective, especially from a European point of view.'[72]

References

Arendt, H. (1951). *The Origins of Totalitarianism*. Harcourt.

Atkinson, A., Piketty, T., & Saez, E. (2011). Top incomes in the Long Run of History. *Journal of Economic Literature, 49*, 3–71.

DeLong, B. J. (2022). *Slouching Towards Utopia; An Economic History of the Twentieth Century*. Basic Books.

Friedman, M. (2002). *Capitalism and Freedom. Fortieth Anniversary Edition*. Chicago University Press.

Hayek, F. (1944). *The Road to Serfdom*. Routledge.

Keynes, J. M. (1964). *The General Theory of Employment, Interest and Money*. A Harvest Book; Harcourt Brace & Company.

Leigh, A. (2024). *How Economics Explains the World; A Short Story of Humanity*. Mariner Books.

Mazzucato, M. (2018). *The Value of Everything; Making and Taking in the Global Economy*. Allen Lane.

Pen, J. (1971). *Income Distribution*. Penguin Books.

Piketty, T. (2014). *Capital in the Twenty-First Century*. The Belknap Press of Harvard University Press.

Piketty, T. (2020). *Capital and Ideology*. The Belknap Press of Harvard University Press.

[72] Ibid., 232.

Piketty, T., & Sandel, M. (2025). *Equality; What It Means and Why It Matters.* Polity Press.

Polanyi, K. (2001). *The Great Transformation; The Political and Economic Origins of Our Time.* Beacon Press.

Rawls, J. (1971). *A Theory of Justice.* Cambridge University Press.

Robeyns, I. (2024). *Limitarianism; The Case Against Extreme Wealth.* Astra House.

Snyder, T. (2024). *On Freedom.* The Bodley Head.

Szenberg, M. (1992). *Eminent Economists; Their Life Philosophies.* Cambridge University Press.

Waldenström, D. (2024). *Richer and More Equal; A New History of Wealth in the West.* Wiley.

CHAPTER 10

Epilogue

What is the liberal order's political and economic outlook? There are various reasons to be pessimistic. Anne Applebaum, for example, observes that this order no longer exists. Before drawing final conclusions, let us first have a look at the economic dimension of the liberal order and how it fared.

The Economic Dimension

In general terms, isolationism and deglobalization are on the rise. In Chap. 2, a few trends are described which are undermining the post-1945 liberal order.

A first undermining trend is the erosion of global institutions such as the IMF, WTO, and the UN. It did not start recently; no, it began quite some time ago. In 1971, President Nixon suspended convertibility of dollars into gold, after which the Bretton Woods system of fixed-exchange rates collapsed. The IMF, after having received criticisms of its harsh policy prescriptions, now devotes growing attention to climate change and inequality, at the detriment of its principal mission: Financial stability through sound macroeconomic management. With the rise of new international creditors, such as China and India following their own course, it is more difficult for the IMF to broker deals on behalf of all creditors with highly indebted countries. The WTO, hoping to celebrate its 30th

P. de Haan, *Great Economists and the Evolution of Economic Liberalism*, https://doi.org/10.1007/978-3-031-93831-3_10

birthday in 2025, is rapidly losing relevance. WTO is paralyzed for more than five years due to America's vetoes of appointing new members of WTO's Appellate Body, which is freezing up appeals by member countries. The start of President Trump's second term does not bode well neither for free trade, nor for the WTO. The UN's Security Council is paralyzed by the lack of unity and incessant use of vetoes.

The proliferation of punitive economic measures, such as economic sanctions and trade wars, further undermine the liberal notion of free markets. Sanctions are imposed four times as often as they did in the 1990s. Also, protectionist national industrial policies undermine the liberal economic order, which first reigned during the *Belle Epoque*. It made a comeback after WWII, and, again—in its neoliberal variety—during the last two decades of the past century and the first decade of this century, when it reached 'the high point of liberal capitalism', as *The Economist* characterized it at the time. Neoliberal pundits claim that poverty was largely wiped out in erstwhile poor countries; infant mortality rate worldwide is now less than half what it was in 1990. And the oft-criticized 'Washington Consensus', was one in which poor countries began to enjoy catch-up growth, narrowing the gap with high-income countries.

But the tide turned. As a result of protectionist policies and trade wars, production processes are getting more expensive, and—above all—consumer prices are going up, hitting the poorer sections of society hardest. Inflation may also return. The number of the world's poor may increase again. Rapidly growing developing countries may see the gap with higher-income countries growing again.

Economic uncertainty is rising. Foreign direct investment is going down. Manufacturing businesses are pulling out of emerging economies and are 'reshoring' their activities at home. In addition, countries are increasingly competing in the build-up of domestic supply chains and local industries in e.g., clean energy, electric vehicles, and battery production. The IMF found that a subsidy given in a big economy has a 74% probability that it is met with a subsidy for the same product from another big economy within a year.

In short, the world economy is *atomizing* rather than integrating. The trends, if continued, will throw the world back in a situation comparable to that of the end of the 1920s and beginning of the 1930s, when countries adopted protectionist policies which resulted not just in political instability, but also in a collapse of world trade, economic stagnation and mass unemployment.

We have seen different economic orders emerging since the *Belle Epoque*. The New Deal order demonstrated that a strong central government was able to manage a dynamic capitalist economy for the common good. Later, the neoliberal order convinced voters that free markets would free capitalism from state controls, spreading prosperity and personal freedom the world over. Neither the philosophy of the New Deal order nor the neoliberal one enjoys the popular support they used to have.

The Political Dimension

In liberalism, the individual occupies a central position. Each individual is blessed with a unique personality. This can create tensions. However, John Stuart Mill argued that this would only enrich social life. John Gray argues that liberalism is universalist, affirming the ***moral unity*** of the human species, according a secondary importance to specific historic associations and cultural differences.

Since the beginning of this century, identity politics gained popularity. Add to his the growing influx in Europa and the US of migrants, each with different religions and values. Self-determination of ethnic, geographic, religious or gender-based groups claim a prominent place in the liberal discourse. This identity countercurrent undermines liberalism's universalistic pretensions. All along, liberals' assumption has been that the pursuit of the good would encourage interaction between different groups. However, once self-determination claims are recognized, it is harder to imagine that Gray's 'moral unity' of humans would prevail.

Political tensions resulting from migrants with different religious and cultural backgrounds are being used by populists to turn migrants into scapegoats of what has gone wrong in the society. Liberal-minded societies have difficulties presenting politically appealing alternatives. Liberal philosophers also struggle to come up with convincing solutions. Fukuyama, for example, suggests that it is much better to deal with citizens as ***individuals*** rather than as members of identity groups. A sensible suggestion, but would it take away these tensions?

Liberal triumphalism of the late 1980s is being eclipsed by concern and pessimism. Some say that liberalism is suffering from a crisis of confidence; a crisis made deeper by erosion of the esteem of institutions that keep societies together. Add to this the rise of illiberal democracies and the growing undermining actions of autocracies, as described by Applebaum. The Freedom House Report of 2024, concludes that global freedom declined for the 19th consecutive year. Democratic decline has become increasingly global. Nearly 75% of the worlds' population lives in a country that faced deterioration of democratic standards. This ongoing decline has given rise to claims of democracy's inherent inferiority. Proponents of this idea include official Chinese and Russian commentators. Political philosophies, praising authoritarian rule have gained popularity.

A stand-off between liberal democracies and BRICS+ is unfolding. The acronym BRICS (Brazil, Russia, India, China, and a bit later South Africa) was invented in 2001 by Jim O'Neill, chief economist at Goldman Sachs. He reckoned that fast-growing large emerging economies would offer attractive investment opportunities. From the start, economically and politically, BRICS was a mixed bag: Democracies, Brazil, India and South Africa, were grouped together with autocracies China and Russia.

Not so long ago, BRICS did not make much impression on the global stage. But not any longer—BRICS is transforming itself into an alternative international institution. It invited other countries to join: Iran, Egypt, Ethiopia, Saudi Arabia, and the United Arab Emirates. Thirteen additional countries expressed interest to join BRICS, among them NATO-member Turkey, and four important ASEAN members, including Indonesia. Poor countries belonging to the Global South may find this expanded BRICS+ an attractive alternative for their traditional, former colonizing, partners.

BRICS+ is developing its members' common stance in international fora, such as the G-20 and WTO, to enhance BRICS+ interests. This also goes for the BRICS+ plea to adjust the governance structure of the IMF, World Bank, and UN's Security Council, reflective of BRICS+'s growing economic, political, and demographic clout. Alternative institutions are being established by BRICS+, such as its Interbank Cooperation Mechanism, promoting innovative financial practices to undermine the position of the US dollar as the leading international currency.

BRICS+ is becoming an autocratic Moscow-Beijing oriented international political and economic institution. The BRICS+ group, says Applebaum, may want to use the institutions they create to help spread the same autocratic power they enjoy at home around the world.

In sum, a multipolar world is beckoning, in which the US is no longer the undisputed leader.

Conclusion

Liberal economic policies are being eclipsed by protectionist and national industrial policies. As for reshoring, a manufacturing paradigm shift from global to local is taking place. Sanctions further undermine the liberal order. Institutions, such as the IMF, World Bank, no longer enjoy universal recognition. Alternative institutions, among them the one established under China's initiative, the Asian Infrastructure Investment Bank, and the Interbank Cooperation Mechanism, are challenging the liberal order that we have known since 1945 under America's leadership.

Illiberal democracy is no longer an uncommon phenomenon and autocracies are joining hands and make their undermining influence felt.

In the past, despite its ups and downs, liberalism, in its different guises, displayed considerable resilience and continuity. But has the liberal order come to an end? According to Applebaum and others this is the case, but other analysts may say: Not entirely. It depends whether political systems inspired by alternative philosophies would be better than liberal democracies in 'delivering the goods' people expect from their leaders.

Liberal democracies, in spite of their weaknesses, have demonstrated, time and again, that they are more flexible and better in serving the population than any other system. After all, liberalism has many appealing notions to offer, such as freedom, tolerance, enabling individuals to develop their intellectual or artistic talents, equality before the law, independent judiciary, protection of property rights, promotion of economic growth, and the recognition that a fair society cannot do without adequate provision of social services. Time will tell whether or not liberal democracy, including liberal economic policies, will overcome the threats and, once again, prevail.

Index[1]

[1] Note: Page numbers followed by 'n' refer to notes.

P. de Haan, *Great Economists and the Evolution of Economic Liberalism*, https://doi.org/10.1007/978-3-031-93831-3

L

N

GPSR Compliance
The European Union's (EU) General Product Safety Regulation (GPSR) is a set of rules that requires consumer products to be safe and our obligations to ensure this.

If you have any concerns about our products, you can contact us on

ProductSafety@springernature.com

In case Publisher is established outside the EU, the EU authorized representative is:

Springer Nature Customer Service Center GmbH
Europaplatz 3
69115 Heidelberg, Germany

www.ingramcontent.com/pod-product-compliance
Lightning Source LLC
Chambersburg PA
CBHW061550220925
32987CB00005B/471
9783031938306